P9-DGC-413

BEYOND HELL AND BACK

BEYOND HELL AND BACK

How America's Special Operations Forces Became the World's Greatest Fighting Unit

Dwight Jon Zimmerman
and John D. Gresham

ST. MARTIN'S PRESS
NEW YORK

To my mother, Darlene, my brother Chris and his wife, Mary,
and my sister, Mary. The journey continues.
—Dwight Jon Zimmerman

For the special women in my family: my mom, Pansy Colleen
Gresham, my sister, Diana Lee Gresham-Corpus, and
my "Aunt Bev," Beverly J. Gresham. All I am, you have made me.
—John D. Gresham

Edited by Howard Zimmerman
Interior design by Gilda Hannah
Cover design by Erin Fiscus
Maps by Laura Newman

A **Z FILE, INC.** BOOK

www.stmartins.com

Library of Congress Cataloging-in-Publications Data
is available upon request.

ISBN-13: 978-0-312-36387-1
ISBN-10: 0-312-36387-7

First Edition: October 2007

10 9 8 7 6 5 4 3 2 1

CONTENTS

ACKNOWLEDGMENTS

The authors are in debt to many individuals and to institutions that contributed their time and knowledge to the creation of this book. Foremost among them are St. Martin's Press senior editor Marc Resnick and editor and project manager Howard Zimmerman (no relation to the coauthor). To borrow from former secretary of state Dean Acheson, they were "present at the creation." Their support, guidance, advice, and patience helped make this project a true pleasure to write and place them squarely in the category of good people.

This book would have been impossible without the assistance of a number of people from the military, either still serving or retired. First we must thank Major General John K. Singlaub, USA (Ret.), who kindly provided the foreword. Other personnel include Senior Chief Petty Officer David Nagle, USN, public affairs officer of the USS *Kearsarge,* who escorted one of us on a personal guided tour of that proud vessel. His patience in answering a landlubber's many questions during a period when he had to attend to the whims and needs of fleet officers and diplomats, as well as those of local politicians during Fleet Week in New York City, is deeply appreciated.

We also had the rare honor and privilege of being able to talk with many of those who were there when these missions were taking place. General Chuck Horner, USAF (Ret.), who graciously set aside time for a lengthy telephone interview and later reviewed the chapter on Task Force Normandy. General Bryan "Doug" Brown, who has always been a source of support and wisdom, and whose contributions to this book were numerous and always worthwhile. So, too, were the inputs from Major General Geoff Lambert, USA (Ret.), who saw U.S. Army Special Forces Command through its toughest trials and greatest triumphs following the attacks on 9/11/01. Colonel Chris Conner, USA, gave freely of his time in the midst of getting ready for one of many overseas deployments to give us a macro view of Operation Iraqi Freedom in 2003.

These included interviews with members of Charlie Company/3rd Battalion/3rd Special Forces Group (the Roughnecks), Bravo Company/2nd Battalion/5th Special Forces Group, the 24th MEU(SOC) of 1995, the 160th Special Operations Aviation Regiment (the Night Stalkers), the Son Tay Raiders Association, and others, for whom security concerns must keep their contributions anonymous. All of you made these stories come alive for us and provided valuable guidance along the way.

Behind them is a host of military public affairs officers who have the difficult job of getting stories out while protecting those who make us all safer. Colonel Tim Nye, lieutenant colonels Hans Bush and Gary Kolb, majors Jim Gregory, Rob Gowan, and Jim Whatley all made time for our inquiries. Backing these officers up is a corps of fine civil-service professionals who provide the structure and guidance to make our work possible. Ken McGraw, Carol Darby, Kimberly Laudano, and Judy Myrick all helped us along the way and continue to do their vital jobs well as this book goes to press.

The Internet enabled the authors to pay numerous virtual visits to a wide variety of institutions scattered across the nation. The result was access to archives, a number of which were only recently declassified, that added immeasurably to our project. In alphabetical order, they are the Air Force Historical Research Agency at Maxwell Air Force Base, Montgomery, Alabama; Air Force Link Web site; Command and General Staff College Combined Arms Research Library Digital Library, Fort Leavenworth, Kansas; Defense Visual Information Center, Riverside, California; Federation of American Scientists, Washington, D.C.; GlobalSecurity.org, Alexandria, Virginia; Joint Chiefs of Staff Joint Electronic Library, Washington, D.C.; National Museum of the U.S. Air Force, Dayton, Ohio; and the U.S. Army Military History Institute at Carlisle, Pennsylvania.

The authors also must thank the people who were in the postwriting trenches on the editorial side: Anne Greenberg, Gilda Hannah, and Laura Newsom.

To all of these people and organizations, the authors are profoundly grateful.

LIST OF MAPS

SOURCES FOR SIDEBAR INFORMATION

Technical specifications for the sidebars in this book were acquired from the following sources:

MC-130 Talon: U.S. Air Force
HH-5 Super Jolly Green Giant: U.S. Air Force
EB-66 Destroyer: Wikipedia
A-1 Skyraider: Wikipedia
O-2 Super Skymaster: March Field Air Museum and Wikipedia
B-52 Stratofortress: Wikipedia
RH-53D Sea Stallion: U.S. Marine Corps
MH-53 Pave Low III: Wikipedia
AH-64 Apache: Wikipedia
AGM-114 Hellfire: Federation of American Scientists; Wikipedia
UH-60 Black Hawk: Wikipedia
F-15 Strike Eagle: Wikipedia
F-117A Nighthawk: Wikipedia
F-16 Fighting Falcon: U.S. Air Force, Wikipedia
E3 Sentry (AWACS): Federation of American Scientists; Wikipedia
AV-8B Harrier II: U.S. Marine Corps; Wikipedia
AH-1 Cobra: U.S. Marine Corps; Wikipedia
Ground Mobility Vehicle (GMV): AM General; U.S. Army; Wikipedia
MRE: Meal, Ready to Eat: Wikipedia
GFM-148 Javelin: army-technology.com; Wikipedia

FOREWORD

Major General John K. Singlaub, USA (Ret.)

As a lifelong special-operations professional, I cannot view the events of America's war on terrorism these past few years without thinking back to my own youth and the World War that defined my generation. As a young paratrooper officer, I had volunteered in 1943 to join the new science of clandestine warfare with the Office of Strategic Services (OSS). As America's first chartered agency for intelligence collection and special operations, the OSS provided a number of critical services as the United States and her allies fought the forces of fascism across the planet. Just a year later, I found myself in charge of a three-man Jedburgh team, preparing to leap out of a British bomber to join a French Resistance group. As I looked down into the darkness, there was little but uncertainty before we dropped into the night skies.

It is with those memories that I think today of the men of America's Special Operations Forces (SOFs), as they fight the global war in this new century. No less consequential than the wars in which I fought, it is with no small pride that we shared a common set of training and experiences that is unlikely to change. For what I learned as a young OSS officer in World War II is that while the unique qualities of what we call "unconventional warfare" (UW) were new to my generation, they are in fact as old as history itself.

Alexander the Great and Hannibal both regularly practiced UW as a part of their war-winning campaigns; and the story of the Trojan horse is a classic example of a small SOF team "opening the gate" for conventional military forces. America's own revolution had its roots based solidly in UW tactics, beginning with the Minutemen militia who fought at Lexington and Concord. Later, in the Civil War, mounted insurgency teams like those of the legendary Confederate colonel John Singleton Mosby raised panic in the rear areas of the Union forces. Despite this, it seems that each succeeding generation of American warriors has had to "discover" UW and SOF anew. Each one but the present.

The weeks following the attacks of 9/11 were a time of great uncertainty for the American public, which saw few options for countering the worldwide forces of terrorism. Formed around a base of heavy conventional armed forces, the American military looked to many like a sumo wrestler trying to counter a nimble ninja. There were, however, ready U.S. units skilled in exactly the kinds of combat al-Qaeda and the Taliban were fighting from their Afghan lair: SOF units.

Within weeks of the September 11 attacks, American SOF units were inserted into Afghanistan to strike back, into exactly the same kind of dark skies and uncertainties I knew back in 1944. And like the OSS teams of my generation, they swept to victory in a matter of just weeks. And as the years have passed since 2001, American SOF warriors and units have continued to be at the tip of the spear for the U.S. global war on terrorism. But why were such forces ready at all in the fall of 2001? The story is little known and seldom told, even among military professionals.

America's SOF community exists today for a few basic reasons. First, they are extremely flexible, able to adapt to virtually any kind and level of conflict the world can offer. Most conflicts since the fall of the Berlin Wall have been small and insurgency-based, making SOF units a good "fit" in the last two decades. Second, they are far more discreet and unobtrusive than conventional military forces with their large equipment, personnel "footprints," and long logistical "tails." Finally, SOF units, though expensive in start-up time, eventually prove to also have the virtue of being quite economical to deploy and sustain.

Ironically, none of these virtues are what helped create and sustain the American SOF community we know today. On the contrary, the six decades since I jumped into France have been a tale of adversity and opposition for American SOF warriors. Completely disestablished following World War II, it took most of a decade to rebuild the rudimentary capabilities of the 10th Special Forces Group and early CIA operations groups. And despite enormous contributions during the Vietnam War, the SOF community found itself downgraded and defunded for most of another decade, until the Congress created the U.S. Special Operations Command in 1987. Through it all, enormous sacrifices in personnel, treasure, and careers had to be made to keep the seed corn of today's SOF community ready for their time in the twenty-first century.

Much of the adversity that SOF warriors have faced arises from one of our greatest virtues: discretion. The SOF ethos says that men specially selected, trained, and with years of field experience can accomplish feats that stealth bombers and armored divisions cannot. This ability comes with an extreme sense of duty, loyalty, patriotism, and, most of all, discretion. The nature of SOF missions requires that they are normally highly classified—and remain so for long periods of time to protect sources, methods, and personnel. Therefore, SOF personnel, achievements, and capabilities have generally remained unpublished and unknown to leaders in the conventional forces and to the public in general.

In fact, while our various SOF service components and specialty warfare communities all have their individual titles and mottos, we all share one common nickname: "The Quiet Professionals." This means that most of what we do never makes it into print or even gets told to friends and family. I recall, from my own military service, being unable to discuss my five years of overseas clandestine activities between 1943 and 1948 with peers because of its highly classified nature. It was not the only difficulty I faced as a career SOF officer.

I was just one of the many young SOF warriors who had to bounce back and forth between the SOF and conventional military worlds so that I could have a "balanced" career and keep up with my contemporaries. General Hugh Shelton, one of my Studies and Analysis Group soldiers in Vietnam, had the same experience on his path to becoming chairman of the Joint Chiefs of Staff. Others today are all but forgotten, like my old friend, General Bob Kingston, who remains unknown to most despite the fact that he was the originator of numerous U.S. SOF innovations. Lieutenant General Bill Yarbrough, perhaps America's greatest special operation professional and considered the father of the modern Green Berets, is virtually unknown outside of a small circle of SOF professionals, friends, and veterans.

The failure of national leadership to sustain our SOF capabilities in the late 1970s cost the lives of eight U.S. American servicemen and left Iran a festering problem that continues today. Similar negligence in 1993 left eighteen more American SOF professionals dead and Somalia another hive of Islamic insurgency. The reality is that the inability of America's elected leaders, policy makers, and citizens to understand the capabilities of the SOF community has exacted a high price. And the price will go up unless the nation begins to understand and use its military, especially the American SOF community, with real effectiveness.

One of the best ways to raise public and governmental awareness is through books dedicated to telling the saga of how the American SOF community has developed. *Beyond Hell and Back* is the story of seven milestone American SOF missions, all of which were critical in the building of today's special warfare community. Author Dwight Jon Zimmerman is known for his work on a fine series of young-adult military history books and an intriguing study of the early careers of general officers, *First Command*. His coauthor, John D. Gresham, is one of the handful of writers who has taken the time to make special operations his specialty, and he has written extensively on SOF-related topics for most of the last decade. Together, they have assembled a book that goes a long way toward showing how American SOF got to where they are today.

That story however, is not always a happy one. Unlike the movies, where the "good guys" always win, real life in the SOF world is hardly as certain. Several of the missions described here, such as the raid on Son Tay Prison and Operation Eagle Claw (the failed Iranian hostage rescue mission), ended with the objective not achieved, or outright failure and death. Others, like the rescue of Captain Scott O'Grady and the Karbala Gap reconnaissance by ODA 551 in Iraq, were nearly perfect in their execution. Nevertheless, all of these missions are critical milestones that led to the operational primacy and respect enjoyed by today's American SOF professionals.

As you read these stories, always remember that they are not so much tales of technology and machines as they are of men and ideas. So please enjoy these rare looks at what we have done, and perhaps remember them the next time we have to make a hard choice as citizens of a country at war.

INTRODUCTION

Photo: U.S. Department of Defense

Twenty-first-century warfare is often described in high-tech terms: GPS navigation systems, computer-guided smart bombs, laser range finders, Blue Force trackers—even the uniforms worn into combat have computer-designed digital camouflage patterns. This perception made it all the more startling to see photographs in 2001 and 2002 of U.S. Army Special Forces (SF) soldiers and U.S. Air Force combat controllers astride horses in Afghan tribal mufti, looking more like the insurgent army of T. E. Lawrence than those engaged in the first great global conflict of the twenty-first century. It is a simple image, but one that relates a complex story, for in it we see a continuation of the unconventional warfare legacy of American special operations, the origins of which reach back to 1755 and Rogers' Rangers.

The early stages of Operation Enduring Freedom—Afghanistan, the campaign against the Taliban, was largely a Special Operations effort, and a stunningly successful one. Yet just a decade earlier, Special Operations would never have been given such a sweeping mission. How Special Operations came to achieve its current position in the U.S. military establishment is the core exploration of this book.

This is not a history of American Special Operations per se. The subject is vast, and a good share of that history is still classified. Rather, *Beyond Hell and*

Back presents seven benchmark missions that were integral in the building of modern U.S. Special Operations. Rescue, reconnaissance, and raiding form the basis of almost all special operations, and here you will find accounts of four watershed rescue missions, one extraordinary recon mission, one landmark raid, and one mission (the Roughnecks at Debecka Pass) that became a doctrine-changing demonstration of another quality of SOF soldiers: their intelligence and adaptability. We have tried to provide a greater understanding of just how extraordinary these men are, the complex nature of their missions, how Special Operations is different from the conventional-force military, and why Special Operations is so important, particularly now.

As this book was being written in 2006, the top of the home page of the United States Special Operations Command (SOCOM) (www.socom.mil) contained the following command vision statement:

> To be the premier team of special warriors, thoroughly prepared, properly equipped, and highly motivated: at the right place, at the right time, facing the right adversary, leading the Global War on Terrorism, accomplishing the strategic objectives of the United States.

This statement, this Web site, and SOCOM itself are proof of how far special operations (lowercase) has come in the American military world, and the command vision statement is embodied by four essential "truths" carried into battle by every U.S. SOF warrior. They are:

- Humans are more important than hardware.
- Quality is better than quantity.
- Special Operations Forces cannot be mass-produced.
- Competent Special Operations Forces cannot be created after emergencies occur.

Rarely have wiser words been written or spoken about military affairs, and they became the basis for building a new generation of American special operations warriors.

The history of the American military has as much, if not more, to do with unconventional warfare and special operations as with large conventional warfare armies. Long before there was a United States, American soldiers were notable for their use of unconventional warfare, most famously with Captain Robert Rogers and his Rangers, who fought alongside the British during the French and Indian War. Captain Rogers's "Standing Orders" of nineteen commands and his twenty-eight "Rules of Ranging" continue to resonate with Special Operations, more than 250 years after Rogers wrote them. As a few examples from the Standing Orders reveal, though one can find fault with Rogers's grammar, what cannot be refuted is the common sense in them and why they remain as important to combat operations now as they were in the eighteenth century. Here are some pertinent excerpts:

> Rule #1: Don't forget nothing.
> Rule #4: Tell the truth about what you see and what you do. There is an army depending on us for correct information. You can lie all you please when you tell other folks about the Rangers, but don't never lie to a Ranger or officer.
> Rule #14: Don't sit down to eat without posting sentries.
> Rule #16: Don't cross a river by a regular ford.

World War II saw a high-water mark for American Special Operations Forces, as tens of thousands of men and women served in an amazing variety of SOF units and communities. Ranger battalions led the way everywhere from the Normandy beachheads to rescuing POWs at Cabanatuan in the Philippines. Marine Raiders under legendary commanders like Colonel Evans Carlson and Lieutenant Colonel Merritt A. Edson conducted raids on Japanese bases on Makin and Tulagi, and U.S. Navy underwater demolition teams (UDTs) cleared landing beaches around the globe, often delivered there by navy vessels and submarines piloted by professionals skilled in SF operations.

Air commando units like the "Carpetbaggers" delivered Jedburgh teams—three-man units of Office of Strategic Services (OSS) members, America's first intelligence agency—behind enemy lines from Norway to Yugoslavia. Other air commandos delivered supplies and personnel in remote theaters like Burma, pioneering the emerging mission concept of combat search and rescue.

Yet despite the contributions of these and other unconventional warfare commands during World War II, SOF units were regarded as bastard stepchildren by their parent branches: unwanted, unloved, but tolerated due to the exigency of war. The Allied victory saw most of the SOF units and agencies disestablished or dissolved. Almost none of their wartime capability was retained. And their parent services were unrepentant in their justification for such draconian cuts.

SOF units are expensive on a per-person basis. Today, for instance, the cost for selecting, qualifying, and training one special operations warrior runs well into six figures, more if aviation or medical specialties are involved. Weapons, transport, and equipment, much of it specialized, is also expensive. Historically, when money got tight for a service branch, its special operations community was the first to suffer the budget-cutting ax. This is a trend that on some levels continues even today.

There also was the belief that SOF units had no place in the idealized postwar world of the late 1940s, where atomic weapons, strategic bombers, and grand diplomacy seemed to be the order of the day. This misguided assumption did not last long. The emergence of the cold war and showdowns and conflicts in Berlin, Korea, China, and the Middle East showed that our world had become more complex and more dangerous. And a new reality emerged: proxy wars and insurgencies.

What President John F. Kennedy described as "so-called wars of national liberation" became the points of conflict between the postwar superpowers, a substitute for direct confrontation that would have called for the use of strategic nuclear weapons, which was seen by all parties as an unacceptable alternative. These wars were fought with conventional weaponry, often against insurgent or paramilitary forces using guerrilla warfare tactics. At first, the United States had no units capable of responding in kind with counterinsurgency or UW operations.

That changed on June 19, 1952, at Fort Bragg, North Carolina. On that day on Smoke Bomb Hill, on the western side of the base, Colonel Aaron Bank stood up what became known as the 10th Special Forces Group (SFG). The 10th SFG was an SOF unit with a particular focus: to provide a stay-behind capability for NATO in the event of a Soviet invasion of Western Europe. Composed mostly of so-called Lodge Amendment immigrant soldiers displaced by the Communist takeover of Eastern Europe, the 10th SFG was to help establish partisan or guerrilla forces behind the Communist lines. Based on the template of the OSS Jedburgh teams of World War II, it was a humble start, involving only around 1,500 soldiers. But that was the moment that modern U.S. Special Operations warriors point to as their birthday, and the moment they were enlisted to stand up and fight what would be many long battles both in the field and with the Pentagon brass, to reach their present-day structure and capability.

The war emerging in Southeast Asia in the early 1960s could have been a renaissance for America's new SOF units like the Special Forces and U.S. Navy Sea, Air, Land (SEAL) teams. And certainly those units and others did honorable and impressive, often amazing, service during that conflict. But without a real goal to work toward, or a government worth propping up in South Vietnam, they became part of the ugly quagmire that was America's longest war to date. In short, they were warriors unsupported by national policy or will, a state of affairs they shared with a generation of American conventional armed forces.

Though the American SOF community survived, it did so by the barest of margins. Leaders in services like the air force actively tried to eliminate their SOF capabilities, preferring to spend their budgets on technically advanced weapons systems like new fighter jets and guided missiles. The army even went so far as to have SF units do conservation and relief work on Native

American reservations rather than keeping them trained and ready in the event of war.

This fragmentation and erosion of special operations units and capabilities in the different branches, coupled with the chronic shortages of men, equipment, training, and money in the 1970s, carried inevitable consequences. Though the different special operations units and communities managed to survive, it was obvious that only an extraordinary event like a public disaster of some sort would change the status quo. That disaster occurred in 1980 in central Iran, at a location called Desert One. (The story of the failure of Operation Eagle Claw and its watershed impact on U.S. SOF is the subject of chapter 3.)

The failure of American SOF units to rescue the American hostages held by Iran in 1980 came as a huge shock to the nation, which thought itself capable of accomplishing anything. What was seen as the triumph of a second-rate power rolled across the American military and political landscape like a runaway freight train. In its wake, Americans rejected the failed policy of one president and elected a new president who supported the rebuilding and augmenting of the SOF units and capabilities that had been found wanting at Desert One. However, SOF capabilities don't magically come up to speed just by throwing money in their direction. In fact, reestablishing SOF units and buying them new aircraft and weapons is only the first part of the building-up process to create a world-class special operations community.

It took another ten years after Operation Eagle Claw, and several other costly SOF incidents, to convince the country and Congress that what was really needed, in effect, was a fifth military service, one specifically organized for special operations. When that was realized with the passing of the Goldwater-Nichols Department of Defense Reorganization Act and Nunn-Cohen amendment in the late 1980s, SOF warriors finally had a home of their own within the U.S. military, and even their own funding line in the Department of Defense budget. U.S. Special Operations Command was the embodiment of almost four decades of effort by SOF warriors to make themselves relevant in the American military. With the most important aspects of the bureaucratic battle finally behind them, America's SOF units and warriors, perhaps not surprisingly, have enjoyed an almost uninterrupted string of successes on the battlefield and have moved to the forefront of U.S. military capabilities.

But this does not mean that America's political and military leaders are even now fully conversant with the capabilities of such units or how they fit into the vast construct that is the U.S. military. Even more uncertain is the public perception of special operations and the American servicemen and servicewomen who live their lives in the insular world of the SOF community. Hollywood's image of a special operations mission is that of a small group of highly trained (and usually insubordinate) soldiers parachuting to a target site deep behind enemy lines in the dead of night, shooting the place up, and destroying what needs wrecking or rescuing whoever needs rescuing. The cinematic scenarios often involve crippling casualties, and only one or two remain alive to consider the cost of what they have done. This image, both of the men and their missions, is unmitigated garbage.

That said, just what sort of mission qualifies for the designation "special operations," and what kind of individual is a member of the Special Operations community?

The Joint Chiefs of Staff's *Doctrine for Joint Special Operations*[1] describes special operations (SO) as:

> Operations conducted in hostile, denied, or politically sensitive environments to achieve military, diplomatic, informational, and/or economic objectives employing military capabilities **for which there is no broad conventional force requirement** [emphasis in the original]. These operations often require covert, clandestine, or low-visibility capabilities. SO are applicable across the range of military operations. They can be conducted independently or in conjunction with operations of conventional forces or other government agencies and may include operations by, with or through indigenous or surrogate forces. **SO differ from conventional operations** [emphasis in the original] in degree of physical and political risk, operational techniques, mode of employment, independence from friendly support, and dependence on detailed operational intelligence and indigenous assets.

At the risk of oversimplification, this basically means high-risk/high-reward missions that can be conducted only by small, highly trained units. To put it another way, think of a potential assignment that a conventional-size unit such as a division, a carrier battle group, or a bomber squadron would have difficulty executing, and broadly you have the basis for a special operations mission. That said, they are anything but suicide missions, and the men who execute them are certainly not desperate.

A huge misconception about SOF units and warriors is that they are all brawn and combat skills, short on brains and judgment. SOF warriors, whatever their service and community, are the antithesis of the swaggering braggart. These complex men are confident, mentally and physically tough, highly professional warriors. They have the lightning-quick ability to size up situations, make difficult (as in life-and-death) decisions, and do so from a moral and ethical foundation embraced by American society. In this "situational awareness," SOF professionals represent the most highly skilled and evolved warriors today. They rarely discuss their missions, even among themselves. Their families and friends are kept close, and outsiders are usually avoided. In this they truly are "the quiet professionals"—a phrase that originally referred to a few SOF units in World War II and now includes the entire Special Operations community.

And because they are tasked with high-risk operations, too often it's assumed (even sometimes within the military) that they willingly accept "suicidal missions." Every time a Special Operations unit is given a mission, it conducts a thorough analysis. If the team thinks the mission will end in failure (as shown in chapter 7), they will turn it down. Often it takes more intelligence and guts to say no than to salute and march into harm's way. And usually, it is the right thing to do as well.

Herein are seven stories of hard men and their missions on distant soil who went beyond hell and back. Some are still in uniform; some have retired and grown old; some never returned; others are now gone. These stories represent key milestones on the path that led to today's American Special Operations community, which has the distinction in the early twenty-first century of being the best in the world. We offer these stories and these men to you for consideration with respect for those described and humility for being able to tell their adventures.

> Thus far, with rough and all-unable pen,
> Our bending author hath pursu'd the story,
> In little room confining mighty men,
> Mangling by starts the full course of their glory.
>
> —William Shakespeare, *Henry the Fifth*

Dwight Jon Zimmerman
Brooklyn, New York

John D. Gresham
Fairfax, Virginia

1. Department of Defense, Joint Publication 3-05, December 17, 2003, www.dtic.mil/doctrine/jel/new_pubs/jp3_05.pdf.

1

Operation Kingpin: The Son Tay Raid

> You are to let nothing, nothing interfere with the operation. Our mission is to rescue prisoners, not take prisoners. And if we walk into a trap, if it turns out that they know we're coming, don't dream about walking out of North Vietnam—unless you've got wings on your feet.
>
> —Colonel Arthur D. "Bull" Simons,
> Operation Kingpin final briefing[1]

By 1970, the Vietnam War had brutally demonstrated that it was a limited war with unlimited consequences. The president identified with the war, Lyndon B. Johnson, had been out of office for two years, his reputation and legacy, along with that of his administration, shredded. The war had deeply divided the United States; antiwar demonstrations were not only frequent occurrences, but some, most notably one in May 1970 at Kent State University in Ohio, had ended in bloodshed. But by far, the individuals who were suffering the worst of the war were the American prisoners of war (POWs) held in North Vietnam. Because the United States had not declared war against North Vietnam, Hanoi claimed that the American men in uniform it held in captivity, most of them aviators, were not protected under the Geneva Conventions that regulate the treatment of captured combatants. Instead, Hanoi insisted that these men were criminals, often referring to them as "Yankee air pirates," who had committed atrocities against North Vietnam and its people.

The result was that the Communist government callously exploited them for political purposes while at the same time refusing to provide any accounting of the ɔ3 POWs and MIAs (missing in action) in Southeast Asia in 1970. Most tragi-ılly, the prisoners were subject to horrendous physical and psychological abuse ncluding isolation, starvation, and torture.

Numerous efforts in the United States, both private and government sponsored, were made in an attempt to improve the prisoners' conditions. POW wives tried to deliver a petition to the North Vietnamese delegation in Paris, where peace talks were being conducted. They were rebuffed. Four hundred and seven members of the U.S. House of Representatives signed an appeal for humane treatment of the prisoners, which they tried to get delivered to the North Vietnamese delegation in Paris. That effort also failed. President Richard Nixon sent astronaut Colonel Frank Borman of Apollo 8*, the first spacecraft to circumnavigate the moon, on a fourteen-nation tour to rally support for the use of the International Red Cross to provide better treatment for the prisoners. When he returned after a month, Borman reported in a speech to a joint session of Congress that every head of state he talked to believed that North Vietnam would refuse to change its position regarding POWs. Separately, the peace talks in Paris between North Vietnam and the United States were at a deadlock with no resolution in sight.*

In effect, Hanoi was telling the United States and the world to shove it.

President Richard Nixon was determined to break this deadlock one way or another. Since Hanoi was not responding to diplomacy, he would get its attention the hard way, through military action. Simultaneously with his diplomatic attempts, President Nixon had authorized a top-secret military option. According to intelligence sources, at least sixty American POWs were being held at a prison compound at Son Tay, approximately twenty-three miles west of Hanoi. It was a tantalizing target. The rescue of these prisoners in the "backyard" of the North Vietnamese capital city would send a powerful signal regarding America's resolution. And the potential political capital for a president already under siege for what had happened at Kent State earlier in the year was too substantial not to contemplate.

On August 8, 1970, a top-secret task force was organized to develop Operation Ivory Coast, a plan for the rescue of the American prisoners at Son Tay. The operation was so secret and sensitive that for the first time ever, the office of the chairman of the Joint Chiefs of Staff, America's highest-ranking military leader, was placed directly in command of the mission.

For four months, plans were created and revised, and men were selected and trained. U.S. Army Colonel Arthur D. "Bull" Simons, an experienced and respected special operations commander, would be the field commander of the rescue team. Finalized under the code name Operation Kingpin, the mission would be the largest, most complex special operation in the Vietnam War. It was a joint operation involving the army, air force, and navy, with fifty-nine men in the rescue team itself, with at least 116 aircraft ranging from helicopters to fighters and fighter-bombers, and three aircraft carriers.

From the moment the first helicopter deliberately crash-landed in the Son Tay prison courtyard to the departure of the rescue helicopters, the mission was planned to last no more than twenty-six minutes because the estimated response time of a nearby North Vietnamese garrison was thirty minutes.

On the night of November 20, 1970, Colonel Simons's men took off in their helicopters from a staging area at the royal Thai air force base in Udorn, Thailand, and headed east into "Indian country," as North Vietnam was sometimes called, on the most important mission of their lives. What lay ahead was North Vietnam at its most powerful and deadly. What they would do that night would become the legend of Son Tay.

The Night of November 20–21, 1970: En Route to Son Tay, North Vietnam

Major Irl L. Franklin was the pilot of Cherry 1, the Lockheed C-130 Hercules Combat Talon leading a flight of six Sikorsky helicopters: five HH-53 Super Jolly Green Giants and one HH-3 Jolly Green Giant. Franklin had throttled back until his aircraft was flying at 105 knots, just above the speed at which his huge airborne tanker-transport would stall. To help keep the Hercules airborne, Major Franklin was flying with the Fowler wing flaps 70 percent extended as he prepared to let the helicopters come in to refuel. Designed for low-speed flights, the Fowler flaps increased the overall wing surface and provided extra lift in the humid tropical air of Southeast Asia without creating additional drag. Major Franklin needed the extra control and lift that the flaps provided because the helicopters behind him were having the opposite problem he was.

The five Super Jolly Greens (code-named Apple 1 through 5) were flying at almost full throttle, and the HH-3 Jolly Green Giant (Banana 1), the oldest helicopter in the force, was redlining at maximum speed in order to keep pace. The formation was so tight that Cherry 1, even though it was in the lead, was buffeted by the air beats from the rotor blades of the nearest helicopters.

Cherry 1's role in the mission was to rendezvous with the helicopters on the Laotian side of the Laos–North Vietnam border and with its pinpoint, low-level navigation system, guide the helicopters to Son Tay and back. Then, while over the prison, Cherry 1 was to drop a series of flares that would turn night into day, and then drop pyrotechnics called firefight simulators to further distract and demoralize the North Vietnamese garrisons at and near Son Tay.

Based at Takhli Royal Thai Air Force Base just north of Bangkok, Cherry 1 almost didn't make the rendezvous. As the aircraft was preparing for takeoff, the number three engine, the right inboard engine, refused to start. Though the Combat Talon could still fly the mission, everyone wanted that fourth engine running if it were possible. Maintenance crews racing against the clock

MC-130 COMBAT TALON

The MC-130 Combat Talon is a variant of the C-130 Hercules transport designed to provide infiltration, exfiltration, and resupply of special operations forces and equipment in hostile or denied territory. Additionally, they can conduct psychological operations and helicopter air refueling. There are two models, the MC-130E Combat Talon I and MC-130H Combat Talon II. The primary difference between them involves the degree of integration of the mission computers and avionics suite. The Combat Talon I was conceived and developed during the 1960s, and though extensively upgraded in the 1980–1990s, it still features analog instrumentation and does not fully integrate the sensors and communications suites. The Combat Talon II, designed in the 1980s, features an integrated glass flight deck that improves crew coordination and reduces the crew complement by two.

SPECIFICATIONS

Manufacturer: Lockheed Martin
Crew: MC-130E: nine; MC-130H: seven
Power plant: Four Allison T56-A-15 turboprop engines; 4,910 shaft horsepower each engine
Length: MC-130E: 100 feet 10 inches (30.7 meters); MC-130H: 99 feet 9 inches (30.4 meters)
Height: 38 feet 6 inches (11.7 meters)
Wingspan: 132 feet 7 inches (40.4 meters)
Load: MC-130E: 53 troops, 26 paratroopers; MC-130H: 77 troops, 52 paratroopers, or 57 litter patients
Ceiling: 33,000 feet (10,000 meters)
Maximum takeoff weight: 155,000 pounds (69,750 kilograms)
Range: 3,107 miles (2,700 nautical miles; 4,344 kilometers)
Speed: 300 mph

Photo: U.S. Department of Defense

did a series of checks. Perhaps the problem was a stuck bleed-air valve or an electrical short of some sort (common in the humid tropical climate). Cherry 1 was cleared for a three-engine takeoff when, as Captain William A. Guenon Jr., a Cherry 1 copilot later recalled, one last attempt was made, "using a subtle combination of ball peen maintenance and convenient recall of an almost forgotten, simultaneous, double-starter-button trick."[2]

It worked.

With all four engines running at full power, Major Franklin took off, twenty-three minutes late. By eliminating some doglegs in the flight plan, Cherry 1 reached the rendezvous site to link up with the helicopters on schedule. At 12:04 A.M., the combat air patrol (CAP) flight composed of another MC-130 Combat Talon (Cherry 2) leading four Douglas A-1 Skyraiders (Peach 1 through 4) rendezvoused with the group. A moment later, the two flights took a bearing to the northeast that would lead them across the Laos–North Vietnam border and to Son Tay.

* * *

Captain Richard J. "Dick" Meadows was the leader of the fourteen-man rescue team aboard Banana 1. Already well-known inside the Special Forces community for his exploits in Southeast Asia, Meadows's participation in this particular facet of the coming raid would take his reputation to another level. Banana 1 was not returning home from the mission.

The plan was that the helicopters of Apple flight, led by Colonel Frederic M. "Marty" Donohue, would take positions allowing them to train their 7.62 mm miniguns on Son Tay's guard towers and shred them with fire. Once the assault helicopters of Apple flight had destroyed the towers, Banana 1's pilot, Major Herbert D. Kalen, would deliberately crash-land the Jolly Green Giant in Son Tay's small courtyard. The plan called for it to be a "gentle" crash landing.

Some early-stage concerns had surrounded this part of the mission. Overhead photographs of the prison compound showed a line of trees, estimated at a height of forty feet, along the north side of the courtyard. There were a few other trees along buildings to the east and south as well. After taking measurements, the debate was between using a Bell UH-1 Iroquois, better known under its nickname, "Huey," or an HH-3 Jolly Green Giant.

Though the Huey could easily fit into the space, it could not carry the minimum of fourteen heavily armed men needed for the rescue. The Jolly Green Giant could carry the requisite amount of men, but there was a question as to whether it would fit. Eventually, the decision was made to go with the HH-3 Jolly Green Giant and sacrifice it. It would be deliberately crash-landed in the cramped courtyard—about the size of a volleyball court—and at the conclusion of the rescue, destroyed with special explosive charges.

Not long after that decision was made, U.S. Army Brigadier General Donald Blackburn, who as the Special Assistant for Counterinsurgency and Special Activities reported directly to the chairman of the Joint Chiefs of Staff and was responsible for coordinating everything to do with the rescue attempt, heard that a general officer not connected with the mission but with influence in the Pentagon bureaucracy was concerned about "losing" a Jolly Green Giant. Blackburn arranged a meeting with the officer to forestall any change.

During the meeting, the officer expressed his concern that if they destroyed an HH-3 in the mission, they'd lose an aircraft costing almost a million dollars. The officer suggested that Blackburn switch to a Huey, as it cost only about $350,000. Outraged, Blackburn refused, and because he had the authority of the office of the chairman of the Joint Chiefs of Staff behind him made the decision stick.

The interior of the HH-3 was cramped. In anticipation of the crash landing, the sides and floor of the helicopter's interior were heavily padded, and mat-

Photo: U.S. Department of Defense

Captain Dick Meadows (second from right) and three raiders in Banana 1 en route to the Son Tay prison.

tresses covered the floor. Captain Meadows and his team were lying flat on them so that their whole bodies would absorb the impact of the landing. On paper, their portion of the Son Tay mission, code-named Blueboy, looked to some like a one-way ticket into the very prison they were trying to take down. But Meadows had designed Blueboy to be anything but a suicide mission.

Blueboy's arrival had been timed around the prison guards' schedule. The guards rotated on the hour or half hour. The rescuers wanted to land as close as possible to the quarter hour so that the guards off duty would be falling asleep and the ones on duty would have settled down to another boring shift. Even just one less guard being sharp and alert might well be the difference between success and death.

About three and a half nautical miles from Son Tay, the aircraft separated to assume their positions prior to the beginning of the raid. In the distance to the east, Colonel Donohue in Apple 3 could see the lights of Hanoi. Farther east, flares illuminated the sky over Haiphong Harbor—the U.S. Navy's diversionary contribution to the mission.

At 2:18 A.M., Cherry 1 began dropping its flares above Son Tay prison and the firefight simulators over the garrison two miles east and south of Son Tay city. Then, just as Colonel Donohue was bringing his Super Jolly Green Giant around to attack the guard towers at the prison, a yellow warning light on his instrument panel began flashing: "Transmission." His copilot, Captain Tom Waldron, pointed at it in agitation. According to the warning, the helicopter's transmission was moments away from catastrophic disintegration. But Colonel Donohue was already committed, and the most critical moment of the raid was almost upon them.

"Ignore the sonovabitch," Colonel Donohue told his copilot. Having taken a gamble with one problem, he suddenly found himself having to solve another. His helicopter, code-named Apple 3, had drifted four hundred yards south of the prison. He corrected his flight and spoke into the intercom to alert his gunners manning the Gatling guns on each side of the Super Jolly Green Giant, stating, "Okay, ten seconds and open fire." Then, with his helicopter hovering in position above the prison he ordered, "Ready—fire!"

Within seconds, the northwest and southwest guard towers were annihilated by an almost solid stream of 7.62 mm machine-gun bullets. Additional bursts tore into a nearby guard barracks. As soon as his gunners confirmed the destruction of their targets, Colonel Donohue accelerated and flew to the prearranged holding area nearby to wait out the rest of the mission, all the while watching the yellow transmission light with a mixture of concern and relief.

Then Major Herb Kalen bore in with Banana 1 and, as soon as he was over the courtyard, began his controlled crash descent. The helicopter unexpectedly lurched when, just before touchdown, its landing skids snared a clothesline that had been strung across the courtyard. Major Kalen almost lost control of Banana 1. The rotors of the HH-3 slashed into tree branches bordering the courtyard like a giant weed whacker. Abruptly, Banana 1 landed hard on the courtyard ground—harder than anyone expected.

A fire extinguisher tore loose from its mounting bracket and hit flight engineer Technical Sergeant Leroy Wright hard enough to break his ankle. Although First Lieutenant George L. Petrie wasn't supposed to be the first man out of the helicopter, that's what happened. Having been improperly braced, he later explained that "the crash landing *threw* me out." The men picked themselves up and dashed out the rear of the helicopter.

Once he had cleared Banana 1, Captain Meadows knelt, and as the thirteen men in his team fanned out and dashed toward the cell bocks, he lifted a white bullhorn to his mouth, pressed the trigger, and calmly spoke into the mouthpiece, "We're Americans. Keep your heads down. We're Americans. This is a rescue. We're here to get you out. Keep your heads down. Get on the floor. We'll be in your cells in a minute."[3]

As small arms fire crackled around him, he repeated his announcement. Meanwhile, his radio operator was on the command network to Colonel Simons, stating, "Wildroot [Simons's call sign], this is Blueboy. We're in."

Captain Dick Meadows on the night of the raid. The white bullhorn he used to announce the raiders' presence in the Son Tay prison courtyard is hanging on his left side.

Photo: U.S. Department of Defense

Three minutes later, there was an explosion at the south wall of the prison. The concussion knocked Meadows to the ground. When he looked up, he saw a group of men rush through the opening made by satchel charges. Captain Meadows was relieved, thinking that Bull Simons and his men had arrived.

But Meadows was wrong. Colonel Simons and his men weren't in the area at all. They had mistakenly landed in the wrong location, well away from the prison. *That* was the lucky part of the Son Tay raid.

When Hell Was in Session: POW Life in the Vietnam War

It goes without saying that there really were no winners in the Vietnam War, only survivors. For the Vietnamese people, there were more than one million dead to count and bury as the war proceeded. For Americans, more than 58,000 would die, their names eventually inscribed on a black granite monument wall in Washington, D.C. But perhaps the most tragic group were a few hundred men who lived in a strange limbo, some for almost eight years: American POWs.

It is a matter of record that one of the earliest such POWs, U.S. Navy Lieutenant Everett Alverez, was captured following his shootdown on the very first American air strike after the Gulf of Tonkin incident in August 1964. His captivity was followed by those of a string of other aviators, along with a smattering of captured ground troops, a single CIA officer, and even a sailor who had the singularly bad luck to just fall overboard. Unfortunately, they were not treated with anything like the respect or dignity that their fathers had known at the hands of the Germans or Italians in World War II.

Responsibility for this fell, ironically, on the governments of both the United States and North Vietnam. In using Congress to give him authority to conduct military operations against the North Vietnamese under the Gulf of Tonkin resolution passed in August 1964, President Johnson avoided the need to ask for a resolution of war. However, since no official declaration of war existed, the North Vietnamese chose to ignore the combatant status of the captured Americans. And despite being a signatory of the Geneva Convention of 1957, the North Vietnamese denied their American captives POW status under the terms of the convention. The result was that the POWs lived in a brutal netherworld, where their captors refused to treat them as what they were and their own government acted as if they did not exist.

For most POWs, their transition from warrior to prisoner began with the horrible realization that their aircraft had been hit and that they were not going to make it home that day. If they were lucky and had a moment or two, they might have time to assume the proper position prior to pulling the handles of the ejection seat of the aircraft they had flown into battle. More likely though, they would be kicked out of a burning aircraft with the force of a 40 mm cannon shell, arms flailing in a tornado-force slipstream while moving at several hundred knots and in the process usually sustaining compressed or cracked vertebrae.

After they had parachuted to the ground, their options would depend upon how badly injured they were by the ejection and if they had landed anywhere near Hanoi or Haiphong. Thick antiaircraft defense nets composed of MiG interceptors, SA-2 surface-to-air missiles (SAMs), and thousands of antiaircraft artillery (AAA) guns protected both cities. Rescue helicopters dared not go near there, so capture was essentially certain. After that, the aviators' options depended upon whether any North Vietnamese troops or civilians were in the immediate area and if the aviators still had friendly air cover. If no hostile forces were nearby and air support was overhead, the aviators more often than not soon found themselves dangling in the business end of a rescue device called a jungle penetrater connected to the hoist of an HH-3 Jolly Green Giant rescue helicopter.

Those who were not rescued, however, began an odyssey that would take them to the blackest depths of human suffering. Often, if North Vietnamese civilians found the aviator, they would attack and sometimes kill him. Assuming he survived that encounter, the aviator would likely be turned over to the local militia or military forces and then be taken to Hanoi for in-processing to the North Vietnamese POW system. Normally, this was done at the notorious facility originally constructed by the French, onetime colonial masters of Indochina, called Hoa Lo Prison, better known as the Hanoi Hilton.

Hoa Lo was just one of four such facilities in Hanoi proper, with another seven within an hour's drive and two others located farther out. All received nicknames by their captives. "Portholes" was near Bao Cao in southern North Vietnam. "Dogpatch" was near Loung Lang, next to the Chinese border in the north. The others bore names ranging from "the Plantation" and "Dirty Bird" in Hanoi, to a pair west of Hanoi, known as "Briarpatch," at Ap Lo, and "Camp Hope," near Son Tay.

The reason for all these camps was simple: Operation Rolling Thunder, the American bombing campaign conducted during the Johnson administration, which was designed to force North Vietnam to the peace table. As a result of shootdowns of American military aircraft, new POWs were arriving at an impressive rate. Particularly during 1966 and 1967, when American fighter-bombers were flying into increasingly stronger North Vietnamese air defenses, several dozen new POWs arrived every month. That is why Camp Hope near Son Tay was opened in 1968. Not only did it provide room for another sixty or so American POWs, but its rural location allowed it to grow much of its own food in the fields around the camp.

Whichever camp an American POW wound up in, the experience was remarkably similar and can be summed up in one word: torture. According to the Geneva Convention, a captured combatant was required to provide only his name, rank, and serial number. But this proved impractical with the North Vietnamese, and many of the POWs broke at one time or another. The North Vietnamese captors seemed to take an almost perverse joy in physically punishing their American captives, the abuse usually delivered during so-called interrogations. These interrogations were designed to psychologically break the will of the POWs and cause them to sign a contrived "confession" that supported North Vietnamese propaganda efforts. For the POWs themselves, life was summed up by the title of Admiral Jeremiah Denton's book about his imprisonment, *When Hell Was in Session*.

The worst of the beatings came toward the end of the 1960s, usually at a Hanoi complex named Cu Loc, which the prisoners called "the Zoo." There some of the most brutal assaults were dealt to the POWs, some of which turned deadly. According to several POWs, as many as fifteen of their fellows were killed during torture sessions, many of which were conducted by interrogators other than the North Vietnamese. One group of Cubans proved particularly savage, killing several American POWs who were bound to their chairs.

Another technique used to break the American POWs was the simple expedient of total isolation—any attempt by a prisoner to communicate with a fellow inmate, even in a nearby cell, resulted in severe physical punishment. A number of POWs went years without any direct contact with other Americans, often reduced to using a covert communication system known as the tap code to pass messages and news of the world between cells. Based on a five-by-five alphabetical keypad with the letter *k* deleted, the tap code provided a relatively secure way of keeping in touch between the POWs.

The POWs did what they could to organize, resist, and support one another. New POWs were queried for news of the world, letting older prisoners know everything from the election of Richard Nixon as president in 1968 to the lunar landing in 1969. And sometimes, they just fought back. A portion of the Medal of Honor citation for Rear Admiral James Stockdale, shot down in 1965, gives some indication of how desperate things could get on the inside:

> Recognized by his captors as the leader in the Prisoners' of War resistance to interrogation and in their refusal to participate in propaganda exploitation, Rear Adm. Stockdale was singled out for interrogation and attendant torture after he was detected in a covert communications attempt. Sensing the start of another purge, and aware that his earlier efforts at self-disfiguration to dissuade his captors from exploiting him for propaganda purposes had resulted in cruel and agonizing punishment, Rear Adm. Stockdale resolved to make himself a symbol of resistance regardless of personal sacrifice. He deliberately inflicted a near-mortal wound to his person in order to convince his captors of his willingness to give up his life rather than capitulate. He was subsequently discovered and revived by the North Vietnamese who, convinced of his indomitable spirit, abated in their employment of excessive harassment and torture toward all of the Prisoners of War.[4]

Sadly, news of such bravery was suppressed by the Johnson administration, which, because it was embarrassed that it was helpless to stop the abuse, refused to even comment on the status of the POWs. It was not until May 1969 that Richard Nixon's new secretary of defense, Melvin Laird, made a public statement that U.S. POWs were not being treated humanely. It would fall to President Nixon and his administration not only to end the Vietnam War through "peace with honor," but to also find a road home for the hundreds of American POWs held in North Vietnam.

Breaks and Buffalo Hunters

For American leaders concerned about the status of POWs, the late 1960s were frustrating. Occasional North Vietnamese propaganda films or leftist French newsreels showing a handful of POWs told them little or nothing about conditions on the inside. Occasional messages hidden in photos and letters did make it into the camps, but the POWs had few ways to convey information about their situation. In fact, the United States did not even have a roster of the POWs held by North Vietnam for most of the war, much less a sense of where most of the camps were and how they were being operated. That changed, however, thanks to an unlikely hero with a remarkable memory.

Seaman Douglas B. Hegdahl was unique among American POWs for a number of reasons. For one thing, he was not an officer or even a flyer. An enlisted seaman aboard the cruiser USS *Canberra,* Hegdahl had been on the fantail of the ship when he was washed overboard while the ship was maneuvering off the coast of North Vietnam. After swimming for hours, he was picked up by North Vietnamese fishermen in international waters, who then delivered him into the hands of the North Vietnamese government.

Hegdahl quickly adopted the resistance culture of the American POWs, doing his best to be a constant pain in the butt to his captors. He was constantly disruptive when he was being filmed by the occasional French news crew that accompanied American antiwar activists who visited North Vietnam as guests—a paradox made possible by the lack of an American war declaration. Hegdahl always gave everyone with a camera the "finger," so that anyone back home seeing his picture would know what his true feelings were. Also, if food were present, he would stuff his mouth full and fill his pockets like a beggar. Though he took beatings for his actions, Hegdahl always took pride in them. Ironically, his North Vietnamese captors thought he was slow or retarded, though he was soon to prove anything but.

Between February 1968 and August 1969, nine American POWs were released by the North Vietnamese for propaganda reasons. One of them was Seaman Hegdahl. But unlike the other eight, all of whom had accepted release in violation of the POW code of conduct, Hegdahl was *ordered* by his fellow POW commanding officer to accept release. The reason was unknown to his captors: Hegdahl had a nearly photographic memory. When he left North Vietnam, he carried in his head the most precious commodity of all: information about more than 250 American POWs.

Months before his release, his fellow POWs had told him every fact they possibly could, from camp locations to interrogation procedures. But most important was a long mnemonic poem incorporating the names of more than 250 POWs. It was an incredible compilation of information, as it gave U.S. intelligence analysts their first real roster of American POWs in North Vietnamese custody since the start of the war in 1964. It also told the United States where to look for their people.

Then, as now, the United States had an amazing array of intelligence collection systems that were the envy of the few intelligence professionals allowed to know of their existence. Among these were photographic satellite systems such as the KH-4B Corona, KH-6 Lanyard, and KH-8 Gambit; aircraft such as the famous Mach 3 SR-71 Blackbird; and a lesser-known aerial reconnaissance program known as Buffalo Hunter that used drones.

Buffalo Hunter was a program making use of Teledyne Ryan 147 series target drone airframes converted into reconnaissance drones, now called unmanned aerial vehicles, or UAVs. Launched from modified C-130 Hercules transports, the 147s could take photos, collect electronic intelligence, and even act as decoys for U.S. airstrikes when needed. Created in the early 1960s in response to the shootdown of the CIA U-2 spy plane flown by Francis Gary Powers on May 1, 1960, the 147 series drones had proven invaluable as an alternative to manned aircraft reconnaissance systems like the RF-4C Phantom, RF-8 Crusader, or RA-5C Vigilante. The lack of a human operator meant the Buffalo Hunters could be used over denied areas like the People's Republic of China, where a shootdown would leave just a pile of wreckage and no smoking gun in the form of a captured pilot or body. With all these tools at hand, the U.S. intelligence community began their first concerted effort to find their people held hostage in North Vietnam.

Along with interviews with other released POWs, the sudden influx of information began to pay off in early 1970. The 1127th Field Activities Group at Fort Belvoir, Virginia, was the intelligence unit tasked with collecting information on POWs, and it began to piece together a solid picture of the North Vietnamese POW system, who was in it, and where the camps were. It was during this period that both the camps at Ap Lo and Son Tay began to draw the attention of the 1127th's analysts. They began to suspect that both locations were active. Then, on May 9, 1970, a bombshell exploded on the light tables of the 1127th.

A sergeant looking over a group of intelligence photos from a recent Buffalo Hunter mission found what he thought was a message from POWs announcing a planned escape attempt. The letters "SAR," "K," and a short message indicated that six POWs were going to try to escape. Laid out in a modified version of the tap code, the message was designed to be visible only

A low-angle aerial photograph, possibly taken by a Buffalo Hunter drone, of the Son Tay prison.

from the air and clearly was a request for help. Quickly assembling a profile of the camp and the fifty-five POWs it was believed to hold, the sergeant began to brief his superiors about the discovery. By May 25, the information had made its way a few miles north to the Pentagon. There it came to the attention of Brigadier General Donald Blackburn, the Special Assistant for Counterinsurgency and Special Activities (SACSA), working directly for the chairman of the Joint Chiefs of Staff, General Earle Wheeler.

Blackburn was well qualified to evaluate the material from the 1127th, as he had been involved in clandestine field operations since he had taken to the hills with Filipino insurgents following the Japanese invasion in 1941. Since that time, Blackburn had headed the famous Studies and Observations Group (SOG) in Vietnam and had been assistant division commander of the 82nd Airborne.

By the time the information reached Blackburn, the 1127th staff had added some details on how a potential rescue mission to Son Tay might be run, including having an army Special Forces A-Team inserted into the area to recon the camp and evaluate whether or not it was still active. But there is a vast gap between a sergeant briefing some ideas at the Pentagon and actually turning such a mission into an operational reality. Fortunately, Blackburn and SACSA were exactly the right folks to make that happen, and they quickly saw greater possibilities than just rescuing six POWs on the run. As he questioned the briefer, Blackburn began to wonder if it would not be possible to raid the camp and grab all fifty-five POWs suspected of being there.

While Blackburn did not have the authority to run such a mission, his boss, General Wheeler, did. After Blackburn told him about Son Tay, Wheeler saw the possibilities. He ordered Blackburn to brief the JCS during their next meeting in the secure briefing room in the Pentagon known as the Tank on June 5, where he got a go-ahead to continue his research on the rescue mission idea. Over the next six weeks, Blackburn, his assistant Colonel Edwin E. "Ed" Mayer, and a team at SACSA put together a plan for raiding Son Tay with a picked force of men flown in by helicopter. By July 10, Blackburn and Mayer were back in the Tank, briefing the JCS on the results of their study. By this time, they had additional information that made a raid even more tantalizing. Ap Lo had gone quiet, but Son Tay now appeared to hold sixty-one POWs. There also was suspicious activity at a secondary school nearby, indicating possible POWs there as well.

A rescue of prisoners at Son Tay represented a unique opportunity. The prison was outside the worst of the North Vietnamese air defenses, and far enough west of Hanoi that a raid appeared feasible. The JCS immediately ordered Blackburn and Mayer to recruit and train a force to conduct the raid and report back when they were ready.

Recruitment

With the authorization of the Joint Chiefs of Staff in hand, Blackburn and Mayer headed south to Fort Bragg, North Carolina. The facility was well-known to Blackburn; he had been assistant division commander for the "All Americans" of the 82nd Airborne Division, which was stationed there. At Fort Bragg, they visited the headquarters of the XVIII Airborne Corps and made their recruitment pitch for the Son Tay operations ground commander: Colonel Arthur D. "Bull" Simons, USA. Bull Simons was already a legend in the Special Forces, long before Blackburn and Mayer walked though his office door that Monday morning, having lived a soldier's life in the Special Operations world.

A founding member of the 6th Ranger Battalion, famous for its massive POW rescue at Cabanatuan in the Philippines, Simons had a talent for raids and reconnaissance. Simons was a winner who never considered the possibility of failure and always knew a way home. He had led into Laos one of the famous White Star teams created by Blackburn at SOG to help build effective combat units from the mountain tribesmen there. Months later, when he returned from Laos, Simons had with him every SF soldier he had gone in with. A man with a face only his mother might have loved, Bull Simons inspired unwavering devotion in his men. Regardless of the type of mission or what happened during its execution, he always brought them back, and for that they loved him.

While in Simons's office, the three men also decided on several other members of the team they needed to recruit. The first two were U.S. Army Lieutenant Colonel Elliott P. Sydnor and Captain Richard J. "Dick" Meadows. Both were assigned to the Ranger department of the U.S. Army Infantry School at Fort Benning, Georgia. Earlier in their careers, Sydnor and Meadows had served with Simons. Like Simons, Dick Meadows was already a living legend in the Special Forces community, gaining his reputation during a tour in Southeast Asia where he served on one of Blackburn's SOG teams in Cambodia. His capture of a North Vietnamese artillery piece caused him to be flown to Saigon and given the first battlefield commission of the Vietnam War—an honor bestowed personally by Military Assistance Command, Vietnam (MACV), commander General William C. Westmoreland. To this day, those who knew him well consider Meadows perhaps the finest SF soldier in the history of the community,

With the ground force leaders selected, next came the matter of where to train. Fort Bragg was an open post at the time and far too public for an operation that was rapidly headed into the "black," securitywise. After some consideration, Blackburn, Mayer, and Simons agreed that the training and live fire ranges around Eglin Air Force Base in the Florida Panhandle would make an excellent choice. Close to Hurlburt Field, the home of the Air Force Special Operations Forces (AFSOF) helicopters and tanker-transports they would use on the raid, the Eglin ranges had the advantage of being secure, discreet, and far from anywhere anyone really cared about. It also had a little bit of appropriate history of its own, for it was the same location where Lieutenant Colonel Jimmy Doolittle had trained his crews prior to their famous air raid on Tokyo in April 1942.

By this point, as the raid moved from feasibility study to operational plan, it was time for a new code name: Operation Ivory Coast. At the same time, the rapidly growing Son Tay team was given the innocuous title of Joint Contingency Task Force, or JCTF. This also meant getting a new commanding officer, one with the appropriate rank to shepherd Ivory Coast through the Pentagon bureaucracy. This was Brigadier General LeRoy J. Manor, USAF, who had flown more than 350 combat missions in World War II and Vietnam. Manor, who was commanding AFSOF at the time, was an intriguing complement to Simons and the youthful-looking Blackburn. Simons was respected by his peers, but they also regarded him as an outspoken renegade. In contrast, Manor, who had extensive special operations experience with

Photo: U.S. Army Signal Corps

A group photo of the 6th Rangers during World War II in the Pacific theater of operations. Bull Simons is in the first row, third from the left.

both fixed-wing aircraft and helicopters, was quiet and a skilled organizer capable of quickly gaining the confidence of his superiors.

Now it was time to recruit the men who would make up the ground contingent of the raider force. This was done by Simons and Lieutenant Colonel Joseph Cataldo, MD, a medical officer from the Surgeon General's office in Washington, D.C. Cataldo, formerly chief surgeon for the Special Forces, had volunteered immediately when Simons had asked for a "combat-type" medical officer. By the time the raid was dispatched, "Doc" Cataldo's contributions would be invaluable.

The two officers discreetly traveled from the Pentagon to Fort Bragg and summoned a number of SF soldiers from the 6th and 7th Special Forces Groups (SFGs) into a room; then they made their request for volunteers. Simons gave no details except to say that the job would be hazardous, with no extra pay for the temporary duty. About half the men left. Those who stayed went on a list of candidates that included a number of others personally recommended by the sergeants major of the 6th and 7th SFGs. This resulted in three days of individual personnel file reviews and interviews. Of that group, fifteen officers and eighty-two NCOs were selected as candidates for the ground team.

The soldiers who passed the screening process were an eclectic group even by SF standards. Though specialized training and experience in Southeast Asia was desirable, it was not required; the area of operations responsibility for both groups was actually elsewhere in the world. The 6th SFG normally handled African contingencies, while the 7th SFG specialized in Latin American operations. There was even a member of the World War II "Alamo Scouts"—the reconnaissance unit made famous for its participation in the liberation of American prisoners of war from the Japanese POW camp at Cabanatuan, the Philippines. But since Ivory Coast was scheduled to be a raid, as opposed to a months-long A-team deployment, strength and stamina, along with combat and technical skills were more important than language or cultural knowledge. In fact, Ivory Coast rapidly became a field test laboratory for the science of raiding, whose lessons would be incorporated into doctrine still used today.

Getting personnel and aircraft from the air force turned out to be easy, thanks to a "To Whom It May Concern" letter Manor got from General John D. Ryan, chief of staff of the U.S. Air Force. The letter, which gave Manor almost unlimited authority over anyone and anything in the USAF "no questions asked," was a powerful statement about how committed the Joint Chiefs were to Ivory Coast and the POWs. Ryan, who had previously commanded the Pacific Air Forces, had ordered a number of the missions on which many of the POWs had flown into captivity. Despite what the country and its political officials might think of the war, Ryan and his fellow JCS members were going to move heaven and earth if necessary to make sure Manor and his force had whatever they needed to do the job.

Getting Ready

With the people picked, the focus of Ivory Coast turned to Duke Field at Eglin Air Force Base in the Florida Panhandle, where the training program kicked off on September 9, 1971. The first window for execution of the raid, based on the moon, weather, and other factors, was from October 20 through October 25, and Manor wanted the team ready by then, if possible. There was much to do and very little time to do it if they wanted to make that date.

As it turned out, Eglin AFB was an almost ideal place to train and practice for Ivory Coast. The weather and topography were surprisingly close to that of the Southeast Asian flatlands where Son Tay was located. In addition, the AFSOF home base was right on the Eglin range, at Hurlburt Field, making scheduling, repairs, and modifications relatively easy. The only negative—and it was a big one—was a few hundred miles to the south: Cuba. More specifically, it was the large Soviet intelligence facility at Lourdes, the biggest such complex operated by the USSR in the Western hemisphere.

A leftover from the 1962 Cuban missile crisis, Lourdes was an intelligence vacuum cleaner for any electronic transmissions coming from Florida. Radio and data communications, missile and spacecraft telemetry, even phone calls relayed by microwave towers, could be swept up by the thousand-plus Soviet technicians at their monitoring stations in the twenty-eight-square-mile facility.

If the Lourdes facility was not enough of a security problem, there was also another batch of Soviet spies to deal with: those in outer space. Cosmos 355 was the last of the Zenit-4 series of Soviet photographic reconnaissance satellites, first launched in 1963. Able to image small details on aircraft, missiles, vehicles, and buildings, Cosmos 355 was perfectly capable of photographing anything out in the open at Eglin's Hurlburt Field or on the ranges. In addition, the Zenit-4 series satellites had an onboard electronic intelligence-gathering capability. Launched on August 7, 1970, Cosmos 355 operated eight days before sending its film and data earthward.

Cosmos 355 was followed by four improved Zenit-4Ms and one Zenit-4MK, which were launched from Pletesk in northern Russia during the workup for Ivory Coast. These had even better photographic resolution, a longer service life, and could be tasked to maneuver after launch to catch fast-breaking developments on the ground. Together with Cosmos 360 on August 29, Cosmos 361 on September 8, Cosmos 364 (the Zenit-4MK) on September 22, Cosmos 370 on October 9, and Cosmos 376 on October 30, they provided near-total coverage of the entire Eglin complex.

This meant that the entire training effort for Ivory Coast would have to be carefully timed to avoid observation from the orbiting satellites during their flyover periods. Nothing visual could be left behind for them to photograph. In addition, a detailed radio emissions plan had to be created so as to not give away anything more than what would appear to be normal peacetime operations at Eglin.

The satellites turned out to be relatively easy to evade, thanks to the help of the North American Aerospace Defense Command (NORAD) at Cheyenne Mountain in Colorado. NORAD analysts were able to create detailed coverage timelines for each of the Soviet satellites and forward them directly to Manor's team in Florida. If one of the satellites did an unexpected orbital maneuver, the information could be relayed from NORAD in minutes to the Ivory Coast team. That way, training and flight schedules could be tailored to avoid the satellites when they were overhead, once each day.

The larger problem was that of training and dress rehearsals, which would require a full-size model of the prison compound. Simons and his men came up with a brilliant solution in the form of a wood and ballistic cloth mockup, which could be assembled and struck in a matter of minutes. To further familiarize the raiders with the Son Tay compound, the CIA model shop created an amazingly detailed diorama of the camp. Called Barbara, the model became a frequent point of study for the raiders, thanks to the exquisite detail and special lighting effects, which simulated the way the camp would appear the night of the raid.

With the security plan and the training aids in place, the entire Ivory Coast force went into an intensive period of training, much of it at night. For the ground force, this began with step-by-step walk-throughs, whose speed was gradually increased and which were performed under increasingly varied and more difficult lighting conditions. Adjustments were made, ideas tried and discarded. Out of these practice sessions came all kinds of useful lessons and ideas, along with some ominous warnings. And through the entire training cycle, intensive physical training and conditioning was emphasized, as it was entirely likely that along with their weapons and gear, the raiders might have to run back to the helicopters with POWs on their backs.

From the beginning, it was clearly understood that the raiding force would have very little time on the ground to accomplish their tasks and get away. Intelligence studies of the ground forces in the area of Son Tay, along with a hard look at the response times of the MiG bases in western North Vietnam, told Manor, Blackburn, Simons, Sydnor, and the other senior leaders that they could spend no more than thirty minutes on the ground. Anything longer risked the ground force being counterattacked by arriving North Vietnamese ground troops, as well as the Americans' supporting helicopters, tanker-transports, and escort aircraft coming under attack by MiG-21 Fishbed fighters flying out of the air base at nearby Phuc Yen.

With that in mind, Simons and his ground teams rehearsed the assault 170 times, until they got the practice times on the ground to just twenty-six minutes. But they needed a lot of help and hardware to meet that schedule. There were scaling ladders, specialized explosive charges for everything from breaching the compound walls to destroying Banana 1 when the raiding force withdrew—the long list of required equipment and weapons proved to be a supply sergeant's nightmare. As it turned out, some of the items had to be obtained outside the regular military supply system. Cutting torches, chain saws, bolt cutters, and special machetes wound up being commercially procured, some equipment bought off the shelf at Sears. In a nod to the future, Ivory Coast was going to have the first large-scale use by assault team leaders of a new technology: the night vision goggle, or NVG. Though NVGs greatly enhanced an individual's ability to function at night, they were far from the perfect answer—particularly the models then available. Normal vision is binocular, which provides depth perception; its field of view is about 190 degrees and is in full color with sharp detail. A view through NVGs, however, is like looking through a tunnel. The field of vision is only 40 degrees,

20 degrees left and 20 degrees right. Depth perception is absent, detail is degraded, and everything that is seen appears in shades of an eerie electric green. In addition, the early models were heavy. Wearing them for long periods of time caused severe neck and shoulder strain.

Training for the air operations part of the raid was conducted in a three-phase plan. The AFSOF flyers flew 268 training sorties, for more than one thousand flight hours. Lieutenant Colonel Herbert Zehnder alone made thirty-one practice descents of the Blueboy landing—though not the crash part of it—with Meadows's team. Despite the bizarre mix of helicopters and fixed-wing aircraft all flying in formation and at low level, not one flight accident occurred in training. Perhaps most amazing, neither the Soviets nor the North Vietnamese got a hint of what was going on at Eglin. But making that twenty-six-minute planned time on the ground depended upon a lot of things working right.

By the time that phase 3 was run between September 28 and October 6, the ground and air elements of Ivory Coast were already integrated and functioning well together. Two decades before joint operations became fashionable, Ivory Coast was bringing together elements from all the services, the intelligence community, and even the politicians in the Nixon administration into one seamless force. The result was that when the final planned dress rehearsal was run successfully on October 6, Manor and Simons were confident enough to assure President Nixon; Henry Kissinger; and Kissinger's deputy, General Alexander Haig, "a ninety-five to ninety-seven percent chance of success."

Then a month's delay occurred. The reasons were political considerations, which were never explained, and a threatened grounding of the HH-53 Super Jolly Green Giants for safety reasons. While these problems were being cleared up, the teams continued to train. Manor and Simons, meanwhile, traveled to Southeast Asia to coordinate a number of necessary and important details before the team deployed. Key among these was a decoy mission by carrier aircraft of the U.S. 7th Fleet designed to confuse the sophisticated North Vietnamese air defense system. Aircraft from three carriers of Task Force 77 were to use flares and photoflash "lightbulbs" to keep the North Vietnamese looking east to the Gulf of Tonkin while the Son Tay task force flew in from the west.

Finally, the political and mechanical problems were resolved. Meteorological and lighting conditions set the new date for the raid on the night of November 21–22. With the assurance of Manor, Simons, and his own genuine desire to bring at least some of the POWs home, President Richard Nixon conditionally authorized the deployment and execution of the raid, now under its third code name, Operation Kingpin, on November 12, with the final execute order to be issued on November 18. The next day, the president was moved to write the following note on White House stationery to Defense Secretary Melvin Laird:

> Mel—
> As I told [Admiral Tom] Moorer [chairman of the Joint Chiefs of Staff] after our meeting yesterday—regardless of results the men on this project have my complete backing and there will be no second guessing if the plan fails.
> It is worth the risk and the planning is superb.
> I will be at Camp David Saturday. I would like for you to call me as soon as you have anything to report.

Yet, troubling signs were coming out of North Vietnam that indicated the raid might not even be feasible anymore. The POWs at Son Tay had gone missing.

Last-Minute Intelligence

Ever since the first indication that POWs might be in Son Tay, the American intelligence community had done its best to keep a close, albeit discreet, eye on the camp. This had included overflights by SR-71 Blackbirds, KH-4B Corona and KH-8 Gambit reconnaissance satellites, and a number of the Model 147SC Buffalo Hunter drones. The problem was that as good as these systems were, they could not see through bad weather or compensate for the technical problems inherent to early remote-sensing systems. These ranged from misprogramming of several of the 147 series drones, to making sure that the North Vietnamese did not notice that Son Tay had become a major target for intelligence collection.

And what was missed was a simple detail: all the POWs had been moved out of Son Tay on August 14.

To this day, the reasons for the move have never been fully explained. The North Vietnamese version was that the river running next to the camp had risen to an unexpectedly high level, due to the fall monsoon rains, and threatened to flood the camp. The irony was that the U.S. Air Force had been conducting cloud-seeding operations upriver in Laos, trying to control the weather in order to flood North Vietnamese rivers, roads, and other facilities. Whatever the reason, the prisoners were trucked to another nearby facility, and Son Tay was empty.

Or so it seemed.

The first indications that Son Tay might be a dry hole came following an SR-71 mission in early October, which showed the camp to be "inactive." This meant that normal patters of erosion and wear from foot traffic, laundry hanging from lines, and other "housekeeping" signs were no longer present at the camp. Immediately, Manor had the intelligence agencies recheck their data to try to get further information. While Manor and Simons were on their coordinating trip to Southeast Asia, analysts studied the latest batch of reconnaissance photos and concluded that they saw a sudden increase in activity at both the prison and a related place nearby referred to as the secondary school. The conclusion was that at least some the prisoners were in fact in the camp and being kept indoors as punishment.

Ideally, Manor would have liked to have some kind of real-time intelligence source giving them data on activity at Son Tay. But the reality of the twelve thousand North Vietnamese troops billeted just a few dozen miles west of Hanoi made that kind of human intelligence operation impossible. U.S. planners had been forced to depend upon remote systems, and they just did not have the ability to see through the roofs of the camp to observe who was in the holding cells at Son Tay.

The question was: go or no go?

On November 20, Blackburn was dealing with all manner of news, none of it good. The director of the Defense Intelligence Agency informed him that their best estimate was that there were no POWs presently at Son Tay, though he could not give a 100 percent guarantee of this. Then there was news that Typhoon Patsy was due to hit North Vietnam on the evening of November 21. There were a number of other points to consider as well, including signs of eleven freshly dug graves near the prison compound. After conferring with the new chairman of the Joint Chiefs of Staff, Admiral Thomas Moorer, and Secretary of Defense Laird, President Nixon made the decision to go, run the mission, and hope that the POWs were at Son Tay. Kingpin was now operational, with an execution date of that very evening: November 20–21.

Deployment

Early in November, the first elements of the Kingpin force had begun to move to Takhli Royal Thai Air Force Base (RTAFB) near Bangkok, which was to be the staging base for the raid. The four E-130Es and HC-130s had flown in from Hurlburt Field, but the rest of the force was using local aircraft, already in theater. This meant that everything from the HH-3 that would be lost in the Blueboy landing to the A-1 Skyraiders of the Peach escort flight would be borrowed from combat units in Thailand. Not everyone was happy with the arrangement, expecially the CIA, which had several field operations interrupted by Kingpin. But General Ryan's "To Whom It May Concern" letter silenced anyone who raised objections, and the Kingpin forces got what they needed without further debate.

By the afternoon of November 18, the entire force was in place, with the various elements getting ready for their parts in the coming action. Up to this point, only a handful of the personnel assigned to Kingpin knew the actual target of the raid, though a number of the ground force had already guessed it would be some kind of a POW rescue in Southeast Asia.

This changed on the afternoon of November 20, when Simons called them all together in one of the hangars to finally explain the mission. He told the men, "We are going to rescue seventy American prisoners of war, maybe more, from a camp called Son Tay. This is something American prisoners have a right to expect from their fellow soldiers. The target is twenty-three miles west of Hanoi."

For a few moments, stunned silence followed Simons's announcement. Then the entire raider force rose to their feet and applauded. When Simons offered any of the fifty-five men in front of him the chance to drop out and be replaced by one of the spare personnel, not one man moved. As the men began to break up to begin their final preparations, he heard one of them say, "I'd hate to have this thing come off and find out tomorrow I hadn't been there."

The next few hours were a mix of feverish last-minute preparations and, for the raiders, rest before they launched. Each man was carrying his personal weapons, along with the specialized tools required of his specific role in the raid. All had specially tinted goggles to preserve their night vision, and some carried special medical kits designed by "Doc" Cataldo, who would also be going along. These contained water, ponchos, shoes, pajamas, and baby food, since the depleted digestive tracts of the POWs would be unlikely to accept normal rations.

The force began loading late on the evening of November 20, and the first helicopters took off at 11:10 P.M. local time.

Insertion

From all points of the compass on the night of November 20–21, aircraft participating in Operation Kingpin began to rise into the night skies over Southeast Asia. As they did, the worldwide resources of the American military, intelligence, and national security apparatus came to life. From the decks of three aircraft carriers in the South China Sea, to the Pentagon on the banks of the Potomac River, men gathered to play their part in what would become the raid on Son Tay.

In the Pentagon, what cynics called "the five-sided funny farm on the Potomac," it was just past noon in the new situation room of the National Military Command Center (NMCC). Colonel Mayer was there, trying to keep his superiors from picking up a phone or microphone and give orders that might disrupt things. The facility was being used for the very first time to control an actual operation, and in fact, all of the JCS members were present—even General William Westmoreland, whose two-year tenure as army

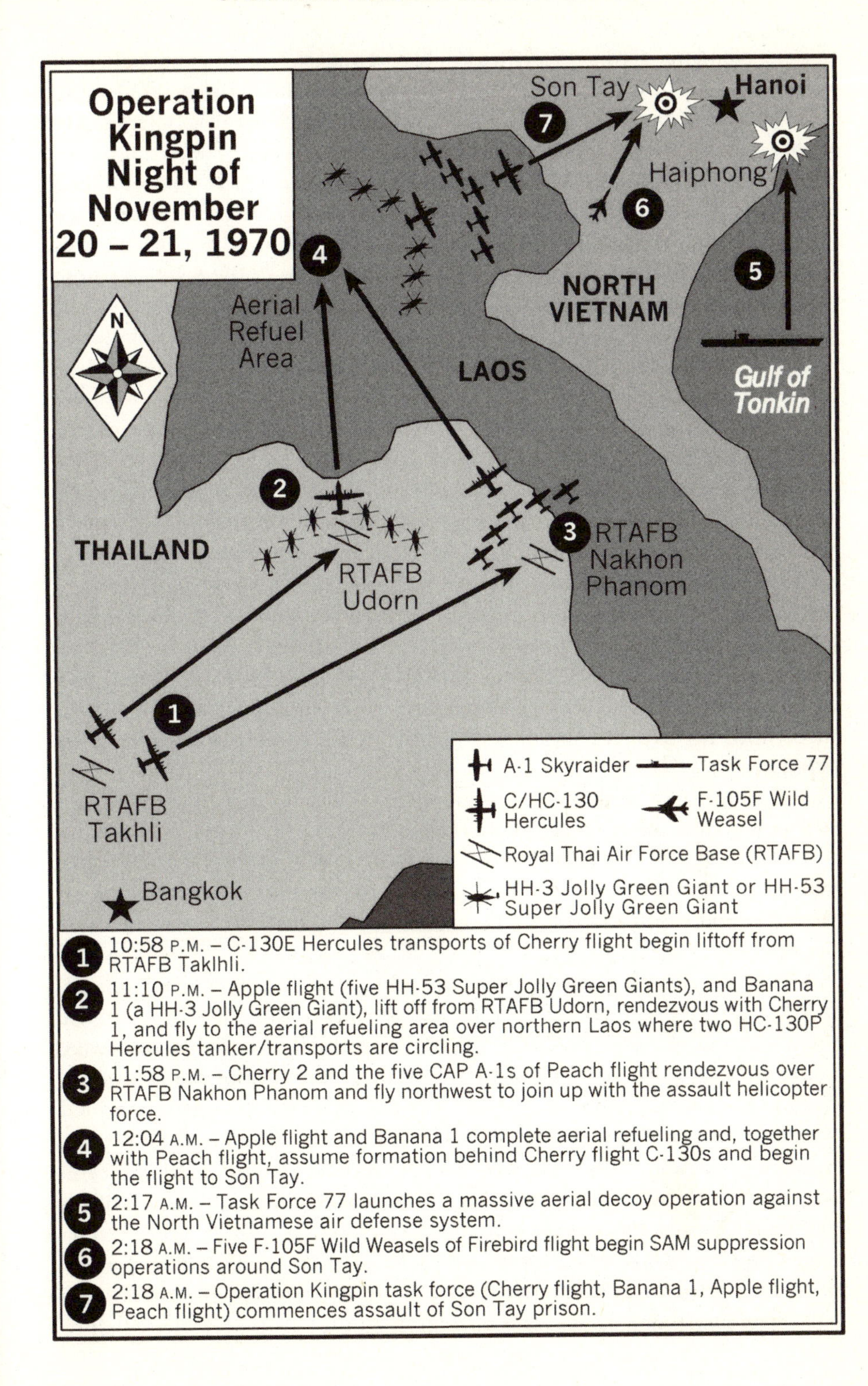
Operation Kingpin Night of November 20 – 21, 1970
N
Son Tay
Hanoi
Haiphong
7
6
5
4
Aerial Refuel Area
NORTH VIETNAM
LAOS
Gulf of Tonkin
2
THAILAND
RTAFB Udorn
3
RTAFB Nakhon Phanom
1
RTAFB Takhli
Bangkok
A-1 Skyraider
Task Force 77
C/HC-130 Hercules
F-105F Wild Weasel
Royal Thai Air Force Base (RTAFB)
HH-3 Jolly Green Giant or HH-53 Super Jolly Green Giant
1 10:58 P.M. – C-130E Hercules transports of Cherry flight begin liftoff from RTAFB Taklhli.
2 11:10 P.M. – Apple flight (five HH-53 Super Jolly Green Giants), and Banana 1 (a HH-3 Jolly Green Giant), lift off from RTAFB Udorn, rendezvous with Cherry 1, and fly to the aerial refueling area over northern Laos where two HC-130P Hercules tanker/transports are circling.
3 11:58 P.M. – Cherry 2 and the five CAP A-1s of Peach flight rendezvous over RTAFB Nakhon Phanom and fly northwest to join up with the assault helicopter force.
4 12:04 A.M. – Apple flight and Banana 1 complete aerial refueling and, together with Peach flight, assume formation behind Cherry flight C-130s and begin the flight to Son Tay.
5 2:17 A.M. – Task Force 77 launches a massive aerial decoy operation against the North Vietnamese air defense system.
6 2:18 A.M. – Five F-105F Wild Weasels of Firebird flight begin SAM suppression operations around Son Tay.
7 2:18 A.M. – Operation Kingpin task force (Cherry flight, Banana 1, Apple flight, Peach flight) commences assault of Son Tay prison.

chief of staff was thus far notable for two things: a near-total avoidance of rooms where all his JCS peers were in attendance, and an obsessive effort to restore a reputation that had been damaged by the Vietnam War.

Mayer and the JCS director of operations, U.S. Air Force Lieutenant General John Vogt, were trying to manage the flow of cleared personnel in and out of the situation room, which was supposed to be limited to just nineteen people. That went totally out the window, however, when Secretary of Defense Melvin Laird arrived with more than a dozen others, all of whom were mesmerized by what was happening on the other side of the world; they hung on reports being relayed by General Blackburn, who had stationed himself at the well-equipped communications facility on Monkey Mountain (Nui Son Tra), near Da Nang in South Vietnam.

At the same time, at Pearl Harbor, the Pacific commander in chief, Admiral John McCain, stood by, wondering if his own son, who had been shot down several years earlier in Hanoi, might be coming home that evening. He knew his son, badly injured in the ejection from his crippled A-4 Skyhawk over Hanoi, had been offered early release at the same time as Seaman Hegdahl. The younger McCain, a third-generation navy officer, had decided to remain with his fellow POWs rather than dishonor himself, his family, and the navy. All over the world, the handful of people who knew of Kingpin prayed that it might be successful. Meanwhile, at Clark Air Base in the Philippines, a C-141A Starlifter was standing by on alert, configured as a flying hospital, ready to medevac any prisoners who were brought back to Takhli by Kingpin.

As the Son Tay task force rose into the night skies, three hours and twenty minutes from Son Tay, it began to form up in a series of tight, complex formations designed to minimize their radar signatures when they appeared on North Vietnamese radar. (For a breakdown of the task force, see the table opposite.)

The MiG combat air patrol (MIGCAP) aircraft were ten McDonnell-Douglas F-4 Phantom IIs from the 13th and 555th Fighter Squadrons of the 432nd Tactical Reconnaissance Wing at Udorn RTAFB. These in turn were being supported by a pair of Lockheed EC-121T Warning Star (also known as College Eye) airborne warning and control system (AWACS) aircraft, which would monitor the airspace over North Vietnam that evening. Finally, there were five two-seat Republic F-105G Thunderchiefs of the 6010th Wild Weasel Squadron from Korat RTAFB, loaded with antiradiation missiles (ARMs) designed to knock out SAM tracking radars.

The F-105Gs, nicknamed Thuds, were a last-minute addition, due to a pair of North Vietnamese SAM battalions near Son Tay. These battalions were self-contained units containing radars, command and control gear, and four

Call Sign	Aircraft Type	Aircraft/Flight Commander	Mission	Carrying
Cherry 1	C-130E	Maj. I. Franklin	Raid force mission lead	Flares and napalm markers
Cherry 2	C-130E	Lt. Col. A. Blosch	A-1 (Peach flight) mission lead	Flares and napalm markers
Lime 1	HC-130P	Maj. W. Kornitz	Tanker	Fuel
Lime 2	HC-130P	Capt. C. Westbrook	Tanker	Fuel
Banana 1	HH-3	Lt. Col. H. Zehnder	Blueboy assault force	Capt. Meadows, 13 personnel, and 7.62 mm miniguns
Apple 1	HH-53	Lt. Col. W. Britton	Greenleaf support element lead	Col. A. Simmons, 21 personnel, and 7.62 mm miniguns
Apple 2	HH-53	Lt. Col. J. Allison	Redwine command element lead	Lt. Col. E. Sydnor, Lt. Col. J. Cataldo, 18 personnel, and 7.62 mm miniguns
Apple 3	HH-53	Maj. F. Donohue	Guard tower neutralization team	7.62 mm miniguns
Apple 4	HH-53	Lt. Col. R. Brown	POW transport and spare flare deployment	Flares and 7.62 mm miniguns
Apple 5	HH-53	Maj. K. Murphy	POW transport and spare flare deployment	Flares and 7.62 mm miniguns
Peach 1 to 5	5 A-1s	Maj. E. Rhein	CAS/strike	Rockets, bombs, and 20 mm cannon
Falcon 1 to 10	10 F-4 Phantom IIs	Maj. K. Gardner	MIGCAP	Air-to-air missiles
Frog 1	EC-121T	Lt. Col. J. Mulherron	AWACS	N/A
Frog 2	EC-121T	Maj. R. Weber	AWACS	N/A
Firebird 1 to 5	5 F-105Gs	Lt. Col. R. Kronebush	Wild Weasel/SEAD	Antiradiation missiles and 20 mm cannon

SA-2 SAM sites, each with six launchers and twelve missiles. The Wild Weasels would conduct suppression of enemy air defense (SEAD) operations to keep the North Vietnamese SAM gunners busy while the raid was in progress.

Behind this muscle in Operation Kingpin were two RC-135M Combat Apple airborne mission coordination aircraft out of Kadena AFB on Okinawa, a Boeing KC-135 radio relay aircraft, and ten KC-135 Stratotankers based at U-Tapao RTAFB. Along with the EC-121Ts, these would fly patterns over Laos and the Gulf of Tonkin, and stand by to support the Kingpin aircraft as they made their run into Son Tay.

Meanwhile, out in the Gulf of Tonkin, the carriers of Task Force 77 were readying planes on their decks to provide the navy's part of the military pageant that was Operation Kingpin. This aspect of the plan had been coordinated with the Task Force 77 commander, Vice Admiral Frederic A. Bardshar, when Manor and Simons had visited the vice admiral's flagship the previous month. What they came up with was an inspired deception plan that took advantage of one simple fact: the U.S. Navy had not conducted an air strike on North Vietnam since October 31, 1968.

The carriers *Oriskany*, *Ranger*, and *Hancock* would launch seven A-6 Intruders, twenty A-7 Corsairs IIs, eight F-4 Phantom IIs, four F-8 Crusaders, along with six electronics countermeasure (ECM) and fourteen assorted support aircraft. These would create a massive set of radar target tracks and visual cues using flares and photoflash bombs, in order to distract the North Vietnamese air defense controllers into looking east, toward the Gulf of Tonkin. That way, it was hoped, the Operation Kingpin force would be able to sneak into North Vietnam airspace "the back way," and, if spotted, would simply appear to be a small combat search and rescue (CSAR) contingency force for the carrier planes. One of the carrier captains quipped after being briefed on the plan, "We've flown three hundred thousand sorties over the north, and we're finally going to make them see the light!"

Bardshar was counting on the fact that navy aircraft had not intruded on North Vietnamese airspace in significant number in more than two years. President Lyndon B. Johnson had declared a bombing halt to help tempt the North Vietnamese to the peace talks in Paris, along with trying to buoy the 1968 presidential campaign of Vice President Hubert H. Humphrey against Republican candidate Richard Nixon. Neither objective had worked out for Johnson, but his moratorium, which President Nixon had continued, was now about to pay dividends for the Son Tay raiders.

The downside for the navy fliers was that they would not be allowed to actually bomb anything in North Vietnam. Other than the radar-seeking AGM-45 Shrike ARMs and air-to-air weapons systems for shooting down any MiGs foolish enough to come their way, all the navy planes would be dropping on North Vietnam would be flares and photoflash bombs. As they were not on the need-to-know list, the pilots were not informed about the reason for the bizarre mission that evening. The Task Force 77 naval aviators would discover only later the decisive part they played in the raiders' success and survival that evening.

* * *

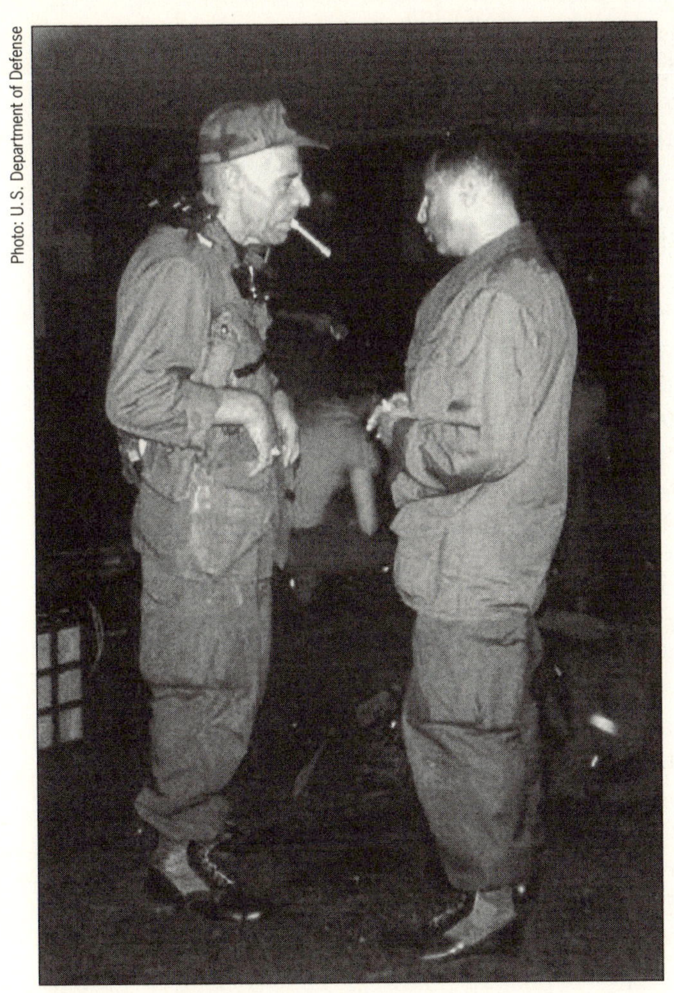
Photo: U.S. Department of Defense

Colonel Bull Simons (left, with cigar) talks with one of the participants of Operation Kingpin on the night of the mission, just before they board their helicopters.

The two C-130Es launched from Takhli and flew to Udorn and a third Thai air base, Nakhon Phanom (called NKP), where they rendezvoused with the helicopters and the A-1 Skyraider escort. From there the aircraft flew almost two hours to an aerial refueling track over central Laos. There the helicopters took on fuel from the tankers of Lime flight. With the refueling done, the helicopters formed up on Cherry 1 and the A-1s on Cherry 2 for the final hour's run to the target area. All of this flying was done in total radio silence, at low altitude (hopefully, below radar detection), and in tight formation. If the North Vietnamese radars did detect them, it was hoped that the radar signature would show only two large blips and not an attention-grabbing thirteen small ones.

That last hour before reaching Son Tay was a continuing battle for the pilots and copilots of each aircraft in the force. The Combat Talons flew on the edge of a stall, while the helicopters ran with their engines firewalled and the transmissions screaming in protest at the strain. For sixty minutes they stayed on a course of 072 degrees, all the way to the planned initial point (IP), just three and a half miles from the Son Tay compound. As they neared the IP, all hell began to break loose over the Tonkin Gulf and eastern North Vietnam.

Sweeping in from the sea at exactly 2:17 A.M. local time, the largest formation of U.S. Navy aircraft ever to intrude into the skies of North Vietnam began to fan out over the port city of Haiphong, dropping flares, ejecting photoflash bombs, firing Shrike ARMs at any SAM or AAA radar that lit up, and otherwise doing their best to rattle the command and control personnel at the top of the North Vietnamese air defense system. That "best" succeeded beyond the wildest dreams of the planners of Operation Kingpin. What the navy pilots created was mass panic.

One North Vietnamese MiG fighter on strip alert—emergency readiness—at Phuc Yen airfield, just twenty-two miles from Son Tay, launched immediately. But the pilot could not get a controller to vector him onto an enemy aircraft. After four minutes, the flummoxed controller told the pilot, "It doesn't make any difference, they're all over! I don't care what you do. Go to China if you want to . . ."

For Vice Admiral Bardshar, it was a moment of personal triumph. Listening to a real-time translation of the radio chatter between the MiG pilot and his controller, he knew that his own fliers had just given the North Vietnamese a scare they would not soon forget. Best of all, he knew that the Son Tay task force had not been picked up on radar. Limited by the bombing halt to essentially sentry duty, Bardshar's tenure as commander of Task Force 77 had been one of frustration. But on this one night, he got to screw with the minds of his enemy and pave the way for some very brave men sweeping in on the prison at Son Tay.

Twenty-nine Minutes: The Raid

Cherry 1 and her charge of helicopters swept down from the final range of mountains at 500 feet above ground level (AGL) and arrived at the IP. At 2:18 A.M., things in the formation began to happen quickly. Apples 4 and 5 peeled off, climbed to 1,500 feet AGL, and flew to a predetermined landing zone on a small island in the middle of a lake seven miles west of Son Tay. There they awaited the radio message that would summon them to pick up the "items," the code word for POWs, if they were present. At the same time, Cherry 1 accelerated, climbed, and began to drop parachute flares and pyrotechnic firefight simulators (like long strings of firecrackers) around the Son Tay area. Cherry 1 also dropped napalm bomb fire markers, over which the A-1 Skyraiders established a pair of protective orbits at 3,000 feet AGL to wait for any calls for support, if needed. Far to the east, the navy diversion continued to light up the skies with flares, photoflash bombs, SAMs, and AAA fire.

Seeing that the flare drop was turning the night into daytime over Son Tay, Major Donohue in Apple 3 took the lead, with Banana 1 (the HH-3 with the Blueboy element), Apple 1, and Apple 2 in trail at forty-five-second intervals. As he did, Donohue suddenly saw that he was headed for the wrong compound, the so-called secondary school four hundred meters south of the prison. Reorienting himself, he made a left turn and headed toward the POW compound to have his gunners take out the guard towers of the prison. Lieutenant Colonels Zehnder in Banana 1 and John Allison in Apple 2 followed as planned, but Lieutenant Colonel Warner Britton in Apple 1 did not. Britton had made the same recognition error as Donohue, but he had not realized his mistake and, because radio silence was still in force, was unaware of Donohue's correction.

Britton's mistake proved to be the biggest break of the entire raid.

As the other three helicopters continued on to the prison compound, Lieutenant Colonel Britton landed Apple 1 in a field just south of the secondary school.

HH-53 SUPER JOLLY GREEN GIANT

The HH-53 was the first helicopter specifically designed for combat search and rescue operations. The Super Jolly was the successor to the HH-3 Jolly Green Giant. It was faster and had nearly triple the takeoff weight of the HH-3. For its combat rescue and recovery role, the HH-53B was equipped with armor plating, self-sealing fuel tanks, three 7.62 mm miniguns, and an external rescue hoist with 250 feet of cable. It could transport 38 combat-equipped troops on side-facing troop seats, or 22 litter patients and 4 medical attendants, or 18,500 pounds of freight. The external hook had a 20,000-pound capacity. The heavy-lift helicopter was used extensively during the Vietnam War for special operations, rescue of combat personnel, and later as a primary recovery aircraft for spacecraft in space operations.

SPECIFICATIONS

Manufacturer: Sikorsky
Crew: Three or five
Power plant: Two General Electric T64-GE-7 turboshaft engines producing 3,925 shaft horsepower each
Length: 67 feet 2 inches
Height: 25 feet
Rotor diameter: 72 feet 2.7 inches (22.01 meters)
Maximum speed: 195 mph
Range: 540 miles
Ceiling: 18,400 feet
Armament: Three 7.62 mm miniguns

Photo: U.S. Department of Defense

From top to bottom: HH-53 Super Jolly Green Giant, H-3 Jolly Green Giant, and a UH-1 Iroquois, or "Huey."

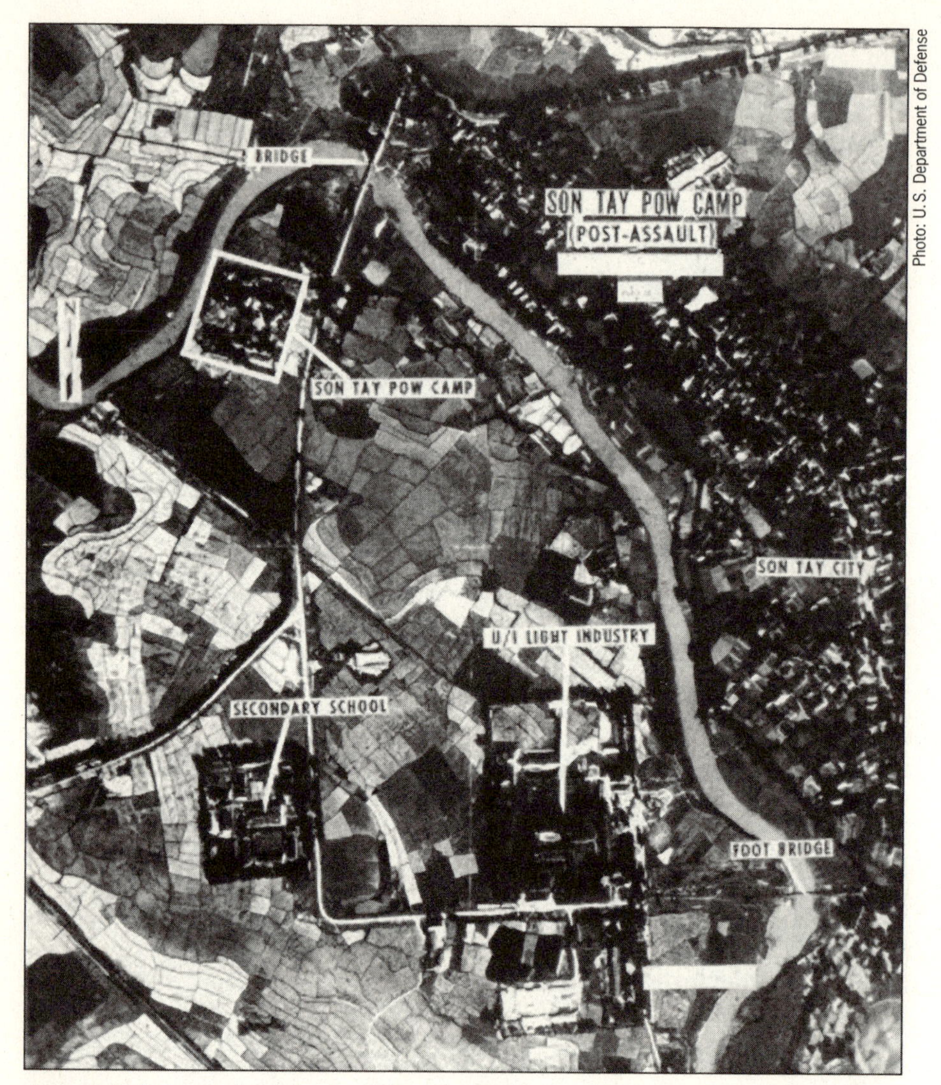

Photo: U.S. Department of Defense

An aerial photograph of the Son Tay prison and the surrounding area showing the prison, the secondary school, and other locations.

As Britton later recalled: "I saw the flares dropped by the C-130 ignite and was impressed by the surrealistic appearance of the illuminated landscape. This light enabled me to see Donohue [piloting Apple 3] hover across the building complex toward which we were heading. I noticed that he didn't fire [on the guard towers with the miniguns] as scheduled and commented on this to Montrem [Major Alfred C. Montrem, his copilot]. Then Kalen [Major Herb Kalen, pilot of Banana 1] followed the first aircraft and he did fire. That was the last Montrem and I saw, as just after Kalen crossed the buildings, we were landing on a heading slightly away from the buildings, so that our troops could proceed out the rear ramp and have their objective in sight. We had no idea we had landed in the wrong place until we had taken off and turned toward the holding area."

Simons and the rest of Greenleaf element piled out of Apple 1, which departed in a matter of seconds. Not realizing that he had inserted Greenleaf into the wrong landing zone until after he had taken off, it took several minutes for Britton to reorient himself, make a circuit of the area to come back in to pick up Simons and his troops, and take them the four hundred meters to the prison complex. By the time he got Apple 1 back on the ground, Simons and the rest of Greenleaf had done something that is still not completely understood to this day.

As soon as he was out of the helicopter, Simons realized from his weeks of study back at Eglin of the Barbara model and reconnaissance photos that he was in the wrong place and reacted immediately. He had his radio operator call Apple 1 back to pick them up and ordered Sydnor in Apple 2 to execute Plan Green, the option that allowed for the nonsimultaneous arrival of helicopters at the prison complex. That done, Simons turned to confront the problem immediately before him.

Almost as soon as the Greenleaf team had landed, armed troops began to pile out of the secondary school and fire upon the Americans. Simons and the headquarters element of Greenleaf responded by shooting the enemy troops and assaulting the building. As they did, Simons heard a loud whoosh and saw what was obviously an SA-2 SAM being fired at one of the Firebird flight F-105Gs that was performing its Wild Weasel duties. Turning back to the fight at hand, Simons and his headquarters troops entered the building though a hole, one he was never quite sure how it got there. As they did, the other troopers of Greenleaf flanked the building on the east side; then the slaughter began.

Over the next few minutes, at least seventeen of the enemy troops were killed, without one of Simons's men getting a scratch. Nobody was really counting, though. More than a few of the enemy were killed by Simons himself, who began to withdraw the Greenleaf team when he heard Britton's radio call that he was inbound in Apple 1 to pick them up. During the debriefing, the Greenleaf team recalled one unusual thing about the enemy troops: very few of them appeared to be Vietnamese. Most were taller than the North Vietnamese troops. And they didn't appear Asian; rather, they looked Eurasian or Caucasian.

By the time Britton returned in Apple 1, only eight minutes had elapsed since his mistaken landing at the secondary school. As they withdrew to the helicopter, everyone in Greenleaf continued to fire into the secondary school, which was a hornet's nest of fire and activity. In just a minute the team was all loaded, and within another minute was on the ground at the Son Tay prison compound with the rest of the raiding force. During the short flight, Simons called in the A-1s to strike in and around the secondary school, and he informed Sydnor that they would revert to the basic Kingpin plan. Behind them, they left an estimated one hundred to two hundred enemy troops dead—nationality unknown.

Meanwhile, overhead, the F-105Gs of Firebird flight were doing their own deadly dance with the SA-2s from the two antiaircraft battalions stationed in the Son Tay area. A total of eighteen of the telephone pole–size missiles would be fired at the Wild Weasels during the raid, with only two aimed at any of the helicopters, A-1s, or C–130s. The only contact came when two of the SA-2s managed to score shrapnel hits on Firebird 5, flown by Major Don Kilgus and his electronic warfare officer, or "bear," Captain Clarence Lowery. Banking their damaged Thud to the west, they worked to fly over the mountains into the somewhat more permissive environs of Laos. There they could take stock and possibly nurse the wounded F-105G to one of the air bases in northern Thailand.

The fliers of Firebird flight and Simons were not the only ones who saw the fight between the Wild Weasels and the SAMs. Twelve miles east of Son Tay was Camp Faith, another North Vietnamese POW prison, and it was located next to one of the SA-2 sites that was engaging Firebird flight. The POWs at Camp Faith were awakened by the sounds of the SAM launches and all raced to their barred windows to try and see what was happening. They could see very little as the walls were too high. Those along the west wall had a slightly better view. Suddenly they shouted as they saw flares and exploding SAMS. Very quickly the word was spread: "Damn, they're raiding Son Tay!"[4]

When Apple 1 arrived at Son Tay, ten minutes into the raid, a disturbing reality was beginning to dawn on the raiders: no POWs were in the prison compound. In the minutes immediately after Banana 1 had crash-landed and Sydnor's Redwine force had breached the walls, Dick Meadows's Blueboy force had been checking the compound room by room and finding nothing but guards, who were quickly killed. Doc Cataldo had set up a small aid and processing station but had only the crew chief from Banana 1 to take care of. Teams Blueboy, Redwine, and eventually, Greenleaf, killed an estimated total of more than fifty of the Son Tay camp guard force, and an unknown additional amount of North Vietnamese troops around the perimeter of the raid site.

When the reality of the situation took hold, Sydnor called "Negative items" over the main radio circuit and ordered the HH-53s to come in and

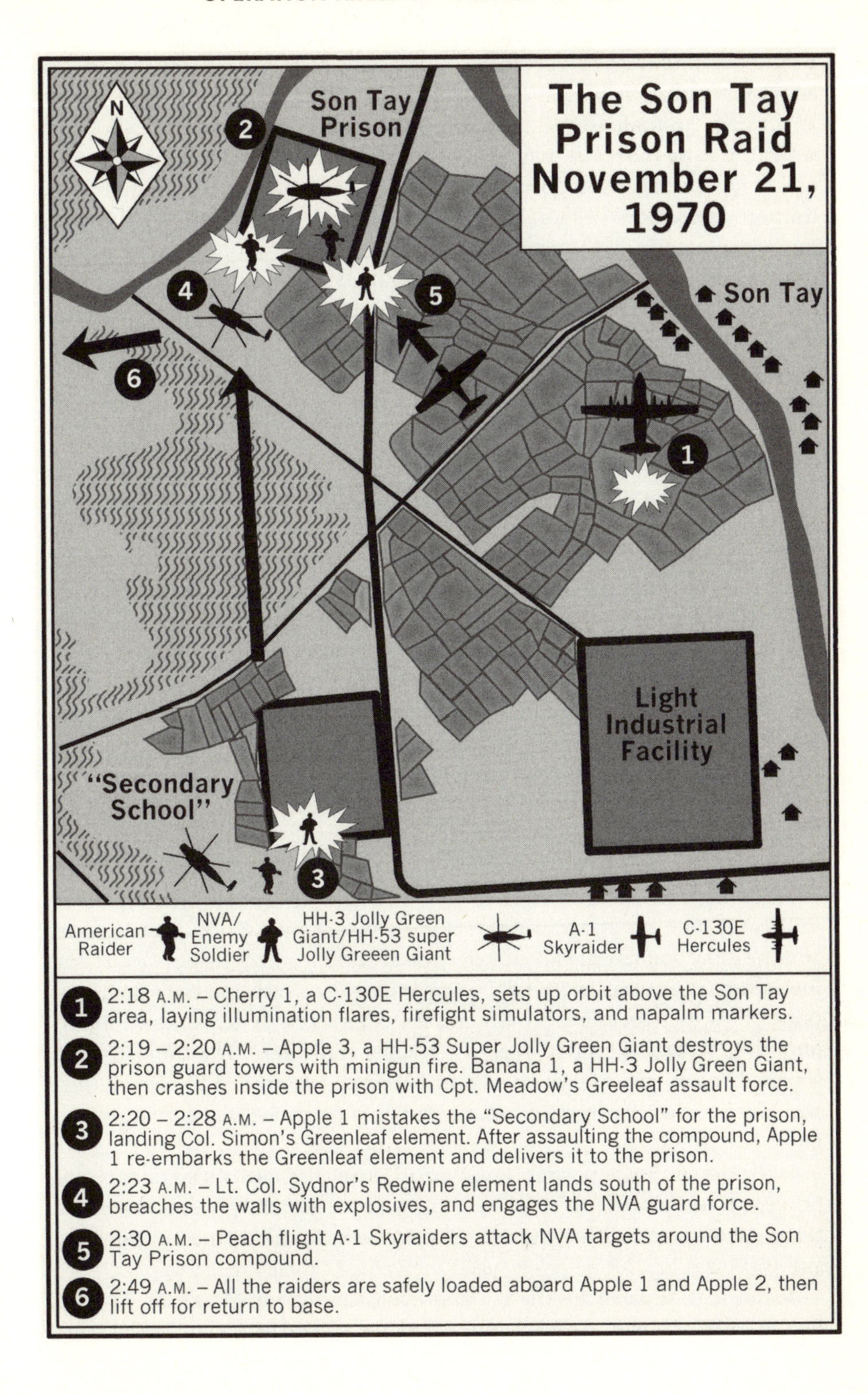
The Son Tay Prison Raid November 21, 1970
N
Son Tay Prison
Son Tay
Light Industrial Facility
"Secondary School"
1
2
3
4
5
6
American Raider
NVA/ Enemy Soldier
HH-3 Jolly Green Giant/HH-53 super Jolly Green Giant
A-1 Skyraider
C-130E Hercules
1 2:18 A.M. – Cherry 1, a C-130E Hercules, sets up orbit above the Son Tay area, laying illumination flares, firefight simulators, and napalm markers.
2 2:19 – 2:20 A.M. – Apple 3, a HH-53 Super Jolly Green Giant destroys the prison guard towers with minigun fire. Banana 1, a HH-3 Jolly Green Giant, then crashes inside the prison with Cpt. Meadow's Greeleaf assault force.
3 2:20 – 2:28 A.M. – Apple 1 mistakes the "Secondary School" for the prison, landing Col. Simon's Greenleaf element. After assaulting the compound, Apple 1 re-embarks the Greenleaf element and delivers it to the prison.
4 2:23 A.M. – Lt. Col. Sydnor's Redwine element lands south of the prison, breaches the walls with explosives, and engages the NVA guard force.
5 2:30 A.M. – Peach flight A-1 Skyraiders attack NVA targets around the Son Tay Prison compound.
6 2:49 A.M. – All the raiders are safely loaded aboard Apple 1 and Apple 2, then lift off for return to base.

pick them up. As the helicopters landed, the A-1s were called in to make additional strikes around the prison compound, to keep down the heads of any North Vietnamese soldiers still alive. While the Skyraiders did their work, the teams boarded their assigned helicopters and a positive head count was done to make sure nobody had been left behind. With all accounted for, the Super Jolly Green Giants took off and headed back to Udorn. During the flight, the men began to take stock; in twenty-nine minutes on the ground the raiders had suffered only two wounded. One was the crew chief of Banana 1, and the other was a raider who suffered a minor bullet wound. In return, the Kingpin force had killed an estimated two to three hundred enemy troops and, though they didn't know it, *really* scared the government of North Vietnam.

Going Home

Meanwhile, up on Monkey Mountain, General Manor never got the picture of the raid that he had hoped. The raiding force's automated display equipment failed early on, and he had only intermittent reports over the radio circuits. But the "Negative items" radio call was apparently heard by everyone who was monitoring the frequency, and that phrase became the beginning of the reckoning that would become part of the legend of the Son Tay raid.

At the same time, back in Washington in the NMCC situation room, there was bitter disappointment. Calls were made to President Nixon, General Haig, and other officials. Congressional leaders, diplomats at the State Department, and many others would get calls later that afternoon, as the consequences of the "failed" raid on Son Tay became public knowledge.

Despite Don Kilgus's considerable flying talents, Firebird 5 was too badly damaged to make it back to Udorn or NKP. Fuel lost due to the many holes in the fuel tanks meant they could not use one of the KC-135 aerial tankers, and the crew had to eject a few miles south of the Plain of Jars in Laos. Landing in the mountains south of the flatlands, they began radioing their position via rescue radio. As it turned out, the closest rescue helicopters were the returning Apples 4 and 5. After a midair refueling with the HC-130Ps assigned to the raid, the two helicopters made a side trip and grabbed Kilgus and Lowery, making the two officers the only personnel rescued during the raid.

With the return of Apples 4 and 5 to Udorn, the last of the raiders were home, proud of their mission execution but dejected. All had wanted to bring Americans out that night and send them home to the United States and their families. None yet realized the value of their incursion.

As soon as he knew all the raiders were safely home, Manor fired a "Red Rocket" priority message to Admiral Moorer in the Pentagon, providing a preliminary report on the raid. Meanwhile, with the North Vietnamese announcing publicly that the United States had bombed a POW camp, it was clear to the JCS and the administration that a public statement would be needed from the American military—and soon. Both Manor and Simons were promptly flown back to Washington, where they briefed the JCS. Then they were became part of a press conference conducted by Secretary Laird and Admiral Moorer that recounted the rough details of the raid.

Meanwhile, back at Udorn RTAFB, the raiders turned in their ammunition, cleaned up, and prepared to return the United States. As they were doing so, a wily sergeant in the group managed to slip off base, and just before the men departed from Thailand, the sergeant presented each participant in the raid with a locally made mission patch. Eventually, even Manor and Simons received theirs. Against a simple background was an embroidered mushroom with the letters KITD/FOHS, which stood for "Kept in the Dark/Fed Only Horse Shit," in reference to the security surrounding the mission. The force returned to Eglin AFB and waited for the repercussions to follow. They did not have long to wait.

In the wake of the first public announcement of the raid, political opponents of the war voiced their outrage. Congressmen and senators who had not said a word about the POW issue suddenly presented themselves as diplomats and Special Operations experts, and the raid was denounced on television and in the halls of Congress. There would be investigations and hearings into the "failure" of the mission, focusing on the intelligence of where the POWs were and weren't, making life for all who testified unpleasant for a while. Nevertheless, not everyone in government regarded the Son Tay raid as a failure.

On November 25, in a While House ceremony, President Nixon decorated Colonel Simons and Sergeant First Class Tyrone Adderly with the Distinguished Service Cross, Brigadier General Leroy Manor with the Distinguished Service Medal, and Technical Sergeant Leroy Wright with the Air Force Cross, and thanked them for their efforts. Later, Secretary Laird would decorate every man who went on the raid, the awards including the Distinguished Service Cross, Air Force Cross, the Silver Star, and the Distinguished Flying Cross, thus making sure that the world knew that the Nixon administration did not consider the raid a failure. Secretary Laird was right, though there was no way to know it at the time.

The critics of the intelligence effort behind Kingpin were quick and loud in their criticism. As soon as the "Negative items" call came into the NMCC, General Westmoreland lividly announced, "*Another* intelligence failure!" But in fact there was no intelligence failure. The limitations of 1970 remote sensing technology, combined with the difficulty of North Vietnam as an intelligence target, made Operation Kingpin a hit-or-miss situation at best when it launched on November 20, 1970. The fact that the CIA director had proclaimed that Son Tay was probably a dry hole on the very day of the raid shows that American intelligence had a sense of what was happening there.

Not that it made any difference to the politicians in Washington, D.C. In one of the more shameful examples of bureaucratic duck and cover, Director of Central Intelligence Richard Helms authorized a leak to the press saying that the CIA had nothing to do with the Son Tay raid—notwithstanding the Barbara model and all the other support given to the Kingpin planners and raiders.

But the contretemps in Washington was in one sense irrelevant. The benefits of the raid began to be felt within just two days, and by the group who most needed it—the POWs.

In the immediate aftermath of the raid, the entire military and government hierarchy of North Vietnam was thrown into a panic. Initially, they thought the war was about to reach a new level of escalation, one that might even include an invasion. Always concerned that the ponderous giant that they saw in the United States might awaken and use its full power against them, the North Vietnamese politburo viewed the Son Tay raid as a potential threat to them directly. Then, as emotions settled, they began to finally realize the true value of the POWs in future dealings with the United States. Their first move was to gather all the POWs from the outlying camps and put them into the complex of camps in downtown Hanoi. Only there, under the full strength of the air defense "bubble" over the capital city, did the government feel safe from SOF raiders like those who had attacked Son Tay.

For the POWs, the raid proved to be a godsend. They were shoved into already overcrowded camps in Hanoi, which effectively eliminated the Vietnamese tactics of torture and isolation. POW morale skyrocketed as news of what had happened at Son Tay spread among the prisoners. Overall treatment of the prisoners improved as well, though diet remained poor up until a few weeks before their release in 1973.

More than two years would pass before the United States and North Vietnam were able to negotiate an end to the Vietnamese conflict—and only after President Nixon ordered a massive eleven-day bombing campaign with B-52 strategic bombers on targets all over North Vietnam. The agreement ensured the release of the POWs, which was accomplished in early 1973. After their release, the former POWs referred to their stay in North Vietnam in terms of two kinds of time: before Son Tay, and after.

It would be nice to report that the Son Tay raiders were given all the rewards and honor they were due, but that did not happen. Like the rest of their generation of American warriors, the raiders who went into Son Tay that night were pushed aside following the war by a public that wanted to forget about Vietnam and anything connected to it. It is one thing for the

American public to fail to honor the men and women who wear the country's uniform. It's something else when senior leadership in the military fail to do so. Not long after the raid, Secretary of Defense Melvin Laird was presented with a list of eighty colonels selected for promotion in the spring of 1971. Simons's name was not on the list. Secretary Laird contacted Army Chief of Staff General William Westmoreland and requested that Simons's name be added to the list. Westmoreland said that such a request was "impossible." After acknowledging Simons's qualities as a combat leader and commander, the general proceeded to elaborate on the rigid selection system the army had in place, pointing out that Simons had never attended any of the war colleges and raising other "issues." Colonel Arthur Simons retired from the army on July 7, 1971.

But not everyone treated the raiders shabbily.

Several years later, H. Ross Perot, the billionaire computer mogul and a longtime supporter of the POWs, underwrote a huge party that he hosted for the raiders and the POWs they had tried to free. It was held in San Francisco, and Perot earned the everlasting gratitude of the raiders, former POWs, and their families for his gesture. Gradually, those who understood the SOF business began to pass the word through their elite community: to be a Son Tay raider was a badge of honor for anyone who had one of the little patches with the mushroom on it.

In fact, the only issue about Operation Kingpin that remains completely unresolved is who were the men in the secondary school that Simons and the Greenleaf force massacred. Only one souvenir of the raid was taken, a belt with a buckle taken from one of the Eurasian bodies and used to replace a raider's broken belt. It was given to Ross Perot as a memento. But the belt and its buckle did nothing to resolve the question of the identity of the foreign solders, though most of the raiders today believe they may have been foreign instructors for air defense troops or some other technical specialty. To this day, however, nobody in the United States knows for sure, and nobody from Vietnam, or its allies China and Russia, is telling.

Son Tay became a model of how to run a large-scale SOF operation, and was referenced a number of times in the after-action report of Operation Eagle Claw, the failed Iranian hostage rescue mission, a decade later (see chapter 3). Today, there are few physical signs that the raid ever took place, though if you know where to look there are some intriguing tidbits. Just off the All American Freeway, which runs through Fort Bragg, there is a small museum just across the street from the John F. Kennedy Special Warfare Center and School, where you can still see Barbara, the CIA model that was such a useful training aid. And in the courtyard is a massive bronze statue of Bull Simons, posed leading the way into battle for his soldiers, just as he did so many times during the turbulent years of the 1960s and 1970s.

Simons died in 1979, following one last rescue of American hostages—this time for Ross Perot, whose employees were being held for ransom by the government of Iran, following the departure of the shah. Dick Meadows would have his own role in the American hostage rescue attempt in 1980, and other raiders continued on in successful careers in the military and business. They formed their own association, complete with a scholarship fund for the children of raiders who have passed on. But their most lasting achievement is something else. Even if the raid did not succeed in its assigned mission, it cannot be considered a failure. Though Operation Kingpin did not gain freedom for the small group it sought to rescue, it gave *all* the American POWs in North Vietnam a priceless commodity—hope.

That was the real value of the raid on Son Tay.

1. Schemmer, *The Raid,* 159.
2. Guenon, *Secret and Dangerous,* 30.
3. Schemmer, *The Raid,* 168.
4. U.S. Army Center of Military History Web site, Medal of Honor Recipients: Vietnam War (M–Z), www.army.mil/cmh-pg/mohviet2.htm.

2
The Rescue of Bat 21

It is my duty, as a member of the Air Rescue Service, to save life and to aid the injured. I will be prepared at all times to perform my assigned duties quickly and efficiently, placing these duties before personal desires and comforts. These things I do, that others may live.

—Code of the U.S. Air Force Air Rescue Service

In attacking aircraft of this type, we must aim right at the cockpit compartment where the pilot sits in the nose of the helicopter—and open fire. It contains the controls for the mechanical systems and a fuel tank.

—Excerpt from instructions for downing helicopters printed in a 1970 edition of *Quan Doi Nhan Dan,* the official newspaper of the People's Army of Vietnam

The war in Vietnam in 1972 was a far cry from the one that had seared the conscience of the American nation in the 1960s. Gone were the guerrilla Viet Cong, immolated by American military might during the Tet offensive of 1968. Gone, too, were the hundreds of thousands of uniformed Americans stationed in the region. The watchword now was "Vietnamization"—President Richard Nixon's policy of handing over primary responsibility for fighting the war to the South Vietnamese. Fewer than 150,000 American servicemen and servicewomen remained in the region, and only 65,000 were stationed in South Vietnam. Of the latter amount, approximately 6,000 were combat troops, and their responsibility was to guard the few remaining active American bases. On March 30, 1972, Easter weekend, the North Vietnamese army launched what Americans called the Easter offensive, an all-out bid by the Communists to conquer South Vietnam. Unlike the Tet offensive in 1968, when the Americans and South Vietnamese received some advance warning, the Easter offensive took them by surprise. On April 1, U.S. Air Force Lieutenant Colonel Iceal Hambleton was the navigator in an EB-66 electronic warfare aircraft, call sign Bat 21, assisting in a bomber strike against an unknown number of North Vietnamese troops that had crossed the Demilitarized Zone and were attacking South Vietnamese troop positions. During the mission, the EB-66 that Hambleton was in was shot down by a North Vietnamese supersonic surface-to-air SA-2 missile. Hambleton was the only survivor. The effort to rescue Hambleton became the largest, longest, and most complex search-and-rescue attempt by American forces in the Vietnam War.

April 6, 1972

Lieutenant Colonel Iceal "Gene" Hambleton, call sign Bat 21 Bravo, was in the fifth day of escape and evasion following his ejection from an EB-66 jamming aircraft that had been hit by an SA-2 surface-to-air missile (SAM). His refuge, a shallow hole covered with jungle leaves, was near the Cam Lo Bridge, about fifteen "klicks"—kilometers—south of the Demilitarized Zone (DMZ). The monsoon season had started a few days earlier, but on this day he saw that the sky was clearing. Hambleton could hear the sounds of aircraft and the explosions of ordnance, the opening round of preparatory air strikes designed to neutralize enemy forces around him and make a pickup possible. At 3:15 in the afternoon, a search-and-rescue (SAR) task force of four Douglas A-1 Skyraider attack aircraft and two Sikorsky HH-53 Super Jolly Green Giant helicopters took off from the U.S. military base in Da Nang to retrieve him.

The SAR task force mission leader, Captain Fred Boli, flew an A-1 Skyraider, his call sign Sandy 01. The other A-1s were Sandys 02, 05, and 06. Following them in the standard high-low SAR formation were the two Sikorskys—Jolly Green 60, the high helicopter, behind and above Jolly Green 67, which was piloted by Captain Peter Hayden Chapman II and copilot First Lieutenant John Henry Call III.

Jolly Green 67 was responsible for going in and getting Hambleton. Two additional Jolly Greens were following as backups. The HH-53s usually carried a crew of three or five. For this mission, Jolly Green 67 had a crew of six. Technical Sergeant Roy Prater was crew chief. Technical Sergeant Allen Jones Avery and Sergeant William Roy Pearson were pararescuemen. Many times a combat photographer would accompany search-and-rescue missions, and for this one Sergeant James Harold Alley was on board.

All of the SAR teams had conducted rescues in landing zones under attack by enemy troops in what were euphemistically called hot LZs. But they were shocked by the amount, intensity, and variety of North Vietnamese Army ground fire they had encountered over the past few days. This included masses of fire from handheld AK-47 assault rifles and radar-directed antiaircraft (AAA) guns, to massive telephone-pole-size SA-2 SAMs. The real surprise, however, was the SA-7 "Grail," a handheld SAM deployed for the first time in Southeast Asia. It was an infrared-guided "tail chase" missile that locked onto the heat signature of airplane engine exhaust, which made life hell for forward air controllers (FACs) and gunship crews flying missions against enemy troop and vehicle concentrations. Already, these enemy weapons had made the effort to rescue Bat 21 a bloody and tragic enterprise.

A "quick snatch" attempt made within minutes of Hambleton's forced landing on April 2 ended in disaster. Several aircraft were damaged and one, a UH-1 Huey helicopter, call sign Blueghost 39, was shot down. Its pilots, First Lieutenant Byron Kulland and Warrant Officer John Frink, and crew chief Specialist Fifth Class Ronald Paschall were killed and the wounded gunner, Specialist Fifth Class Jose Astorga, captured. Additional rescue attempts conducted on April 3 were also driven back by a deadly mixture of SAMs and AAA fire.

EB-66 DESTROYER

The Destroyer was originally designed as a Strategic Air Command light bomber. The first variant, the RB-66, used for photoreconnaissance, went into production at about the same time as the B-66 bomber version. Electronic reconnaissance and electronic warfare variants (designated EB-66) followed in 1966. The first of the electronic warfare models were deployed in Southeast Asia in 1967.

SPECIFICATIONS

Photo: U.S. Air Force

Manufacturer: McDonnell Douglas
Crew: B-66: three; EB-66: six
Power plant: Two Allison J71-A-11 or -13 turbojets producing 10,200 pounds of thrust each
Length: 75 feet 2 inches (22.9 meters)
Height: 23 feet 7 inches (7.2 meters)
Wingspan: 72 feet 6 inches (22.1 meters)
Maximum speed: 631 mph (548 knots; 1,020 kmh)
Service ceiling: 39,400 feet (12,000 meters)
Maximum takeoff weight: 83,000 pounds (38,000 kilograms)
Combat radius: 900 miles (780 nautical miles; 1,500 kilometers)
Armament (bomber): Two 20 mm cannon, 15,000 pounds (6,800 kilograms) bomb load

Photo: U.S. Air Force

A formation of four Douglas A-1 Skyraiders flying a mission over South Vietnam. As a result of President Richard Nixon's Vietnamization program, designed to transfer prosecution of the war to the South Vietnamese, there were only twenty Skyraiders in the entire Southeast Asia theater at the time Bat 21 was shot down.

Boli's mission was further complicated because he had not one, but two Americans trapped in the hot area below. Bat 21 Bravo (Hambleton) on the north bank of the Cam Lo River and First Lieutenant Mark Clark, call sign Nail 38 Bravo, about six klicks east of Hambleton on the south bank. Thanks to intelligence reports, Boli knew that he had to run a gauntlet of at least five North Vietnamese army battalions and their support AAA and SAM batteries before he could reach the two Americans. The plan presented that morning called for the rescue task force to go first to Bat 21, who was farther away, and at a minimum, deliver a Madden resupply kit containing emergency food, water, ammunition, and extra radios with batteries, which was mounted on the fuselage weapons pylon of Boli's Skyraider. As the SAR mission commander, Boli had the on-the-spot responsibility to decide whether or not to conduct any rescue attempt. If he felt rescue was possible—and given what had happened on the previous attempts it was a very big if—the Super Jolly Greens would dash in and perform the pickups.

One thing in the task force's favor was a break in the weather. The spring monsoon season had started, and the weather had been miserable for days. Now the sky was clearing, and the full range of American airpower could be brought out in force to support the rescue effort. This ranged from tiny FAC "bird dog" spotter planes to three-plane cells of Boeing B-52 Stratofortress heavy bombers flying in from air bases in Guam and Thailand.

The task force reached its predetermined holding point just southeast of Quang Tri. While Jolly Greens 67 and 60 and Sandys 05 and 06 waited, Captain Boli and Sandy 02 flew ahead to reconnoiter. As this was being done, the two backup Super Jolly Greens took position off the South Vietnamese coast, east of Hue. The next half hour was a busy one for the air force captain. Forty aircraft from other squadrons were in the area, available for targets of opportunity, and Boli used them to help attack and destroy real and suspected enemy positions. At the same time, he selected and checked out promising entrance and exit routes for his task force, kept Hambleton and Clark updated, and tried to flush out any enemy defenses. His low-level flying over the area was dangerous but necessary. And there was no airplane in Vietnam better built for the mission at hand than this throwback in the age of jet-powered war birds, the A-1 Skyraider.

The propeller-driven, single-seat Douglas A-1 Skyraider became operational in 1946. Though it just missed action in World War II, the Skyraider made up for it in Korea, where it saw extensive service and earned a reputation as the best close-support aircraft of the Korean War. Standard armament and ordnance specs called for four 20 mm cannons and a two-thousand-pound bomb load. Before production ceased in 1957, twenty-eight variants and 3,180 aircraft were built, making the Skyraider one of the more successful U.S. warplanes ever designed. One variant was capable of carrying a bomb load of eight thousand pounds, almost half the dry weight of the airplane itself. Heavily armored and armed, the Skyraider was built not only to take it and dish it out, the A-1 could also stay airborne for ten hours, which made it particularly valuable in air-ground support or complex and risky combat search-and-rescue missions.

Unlike during the missions flown earlier in the week, this time Boli noticed his airplane and the other aircraft supporting the mission received little or no return fire. Some of the assisting aircraft radioed warnings about SAMs, but initially the missiles were few, and no one was hit. Either the enemy was playing possum, or this was finally going to be Bat 21's lucky day.

At approximately 4:15 P.M., Boli called off the air strikes. He then flew in over Hambleton's position, hit the release for the Madden resupply kit, and made a final feasibility check for the rescue. Jolly Green 67 and Sandys 05 and 06 flew to the final holding point above an Army of the Republic of Vietnam (ARVN) tank unit approximately six kilometers from the pickup points.

A-1 SKYRAIDER

The Douglas A-1 Skyraider was a single-seat attack bomber of the 1950s, 1960s, and early 1970s. A propeller-driven anachronism in the jet age, the Skyraider had a remarkably long and successful career. At the time of the first prototype's flight, on March 18, 1945, it was the largest production single-seater aircraft in the world. The low-wing monoplane design started with a Wright R-3350 radial engine, which was later upgraded multiple times. Its distinctive feature was the presence of seven hardpoints on each wing, enabling it to carry a tremendous amount of ordnance for its size. Although the Skyraider entered production too late for active service in World War II, it turned out to be of great value in both the Korean and Vietnam wars, as its weapon load and ten-hour flying time far surpassed the jets that were then available.

SPECIFICATIONS

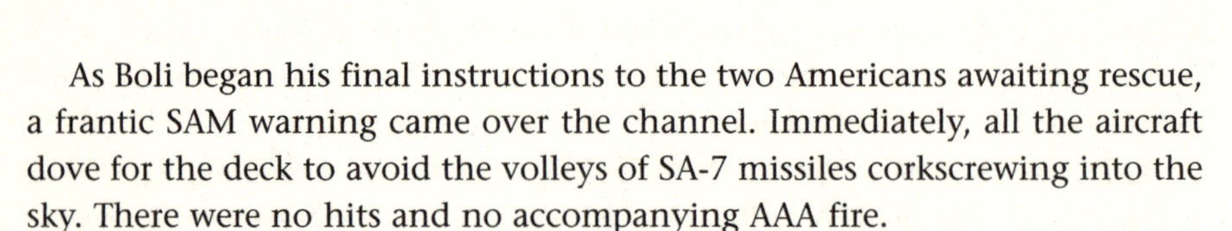
Photo: U.S. Air Force

Manufacturer: McDonnell Douglas
Crew: One
Power plant: One Wright R-3350-26WA radial engine; 2,700 horsepower
Length: 38 feet 10 inches (11.84 meters)
Height: 15 feet 8 inches (4.78 meters)
Wingspan 50 feet (15.25 meters)
Cruising speed: 295 mph (256 knots; 475 kmh)
Maximum speed: 320 mph (280 knots; 520 kmh)
Range: 1,315 miles (1,142 nautical miles; 2,115 kilometers)
Ceiling: 28,500 feet (8,660 meters)
Maximum takeoff weight: 25,000 pounds (11,340 kilograms)
Armament: Four 20 mm cannon, up to 8,000 pounds (3,600 kilograms) of ordnance on a total of 15 external hardpoints

As Boli began his final instructions to the two Americans awaiting rescue, a frantic SAM warning came over the channel. Immediately, all the aircraft dove for the deck to avoid the volleys of SA-7 missiles corkscrewing into the sky. There were no hits and no accompanying AAA fire.

At 5:10 P.M., a fifth Skyraider, Sandy 03, arrived. Its primary role in the mission was to provide cover in the form of white phosphorous smoke bombs that would be dropped just before pickup. Boli was confident he had seen and taken out every major threat to the rescue. But if anything had survived, he had his Sandys and roughly forty other air force aircraft still in the area for support. Sunset was now just over an hour away. It was time to move in and pick up the downed pilots.

Just then Boli saw some South Vietnamese Air Force A-37 Dragonflies making attack runs on the Cam Lo Bridge. These turbojet aircraft, also known as the Tweety Bird because of their small size, were used in both attack and reconnaissance missions. The last thing Boli needed was for one of the aircraft in his command or Hambleton to be hit by friendly fire during the rescue. Several minutes were spent trying to find who was controlling the Dragonflies. Finally, the South Vietnamese forward air controller controlling the air strike was reached and the mission was aborted.

With the Dragonflies gone, it was time to get in, get Hambleton and Clark, and get out. Sandy 02 took the lead and marked the pickup sites with smoke rockets. Sandy 03 immediately followed and laid the protective white phosphorous smoke screens. That done, Sandy 03 formed up with Sandys 02, 05, and 06 into a mutually supportive Lufbery circle with Jolly Green 67 in the middle. If things went well, after Hambleton was aboard, Chapman would lift off and immediately head down the Cam Lo River and pick up Clark.

As Jolly Green 67 approached Hambleton's location, heavy ground fire suddenly erupted from camouflaged positions on both sides of the river. The big HH-53 started taking hits, but Chapman continued toward Hambleton's location. When Jolly Green 67 was about a hundred meters away, Boli radioed Hambleton to pop a red smoke flare to mark his position.

Hambleton had his flare ready when suddenly over the radio they heard Jolly Green 67 yelling, "I'm hit!" and, "They got a fuel line." NVA antiaircraft artillery fire continued to pour into the wounded helicopter as, at the last moment, Jolly Green 67 broke away from Hambleton's position.

Captain Boli, flying overhead, immediately called the other Sandys to cover the helicopter's flanks while he flew on to strafe positions ahead of the wounded helicopter. But instead of flying southeast and away from enemy positions as discussed in the morning briefing, Jolly Green 67 took a bearing due east, straight over enemy positions on the north bank of the river.

Frantically, Boli and the other pilots called on their radios, "Turn south, Jolly! Turn right!" But their messages weren't getting through. One of the helicopter crew's transmit buttons was pressed "on," and the hot microphone was jamming out other transmissions.

As Jolly Green 67 took more and more hits, Boli managed to get through on the radio. But in the confusion the helicopter flew over a village, where the ground AAA fire was heavy. Boli ordered the stricken helicopter to bank to the left as he flew in for a strafing run on the village. But someone else came on the frequency and called for the HH-53 to turn right.

Jolly Green 67 hovered for a moment.

"No! Turn left, Jolly, turn south!" Boli ordered.

Ignoring the fierce antiaircraft fire directed at him, Boli began another strafing run as the badly wounded Jolly Green 67 slowly began turning for safety. But before it could get out of range, something later believed to be an SA-2 exploded near the helicopter and sprayed it with fragments. When Boli could spare a glance at Jolly Green 67, he saw that a fire had broken out between the middle of the left engine and the main rotor. Pieces started flying off the tail rotor, and the fragments slammed into the main rotor hub, shattering it. The fatally wounded helicopter continued rolling to the left, crashed to the ground, and burst into flames approximately a kilometer and a half south of Clark's position. Quickly, explosions and flames erupted from the helicopter as ammunition began cooking off. Immediately, Boli checked the rescue frequency used by the survival beepers carried by all pilots and air crew. He heard nothing. The fire in Jolly Green 67 had become a funeral pyre that would burn for days. Six men were dead, having given their lives trying to save two of their own.

It was 5:40 P.M. Sunset was in about a half hour. There would be no rescue that day. With ground fire continuing unabated, Boli realized the whole area was just too hot for the SAR package to continue working. Bitterly, the survivors of the SAR task force and the other aircraft headed for their bases. After Captain Boli landed, he discovered that he was carrying more weight than he expected. The Madden resupply kit was still tucked under his Skyraider. The release mechanism had failed, and Hambleton was going to stay cold, hungry, thirsty, and alone. It was the low-water mark of the Bat 21 SAR effort.

Meanwhile, on the bank of the Cam Lo River, Lieutenant Colonel Iceal Hambleton was crying. Six more men had died trying to rescue him. He was tired and hungry, and his morale was plummeting. But as darkness came, Hambleton vowed to himself, "I'm going to get out of this, regardless."

At his headquarters in Saigon, General Creighton Abrams, commander of U.S. Military Assistance Command Vietnam, grimly reviewed the cost to date of the attempts to rescue Bat 21 Bravo. Not long after assuming command in 1968, General Abrams had stated that the recapture of American prisoners and the rescue of downed airmen had an absolute priority in operations, and that no expense would be spared in accomplishing that goal. But what had been lost trying to rescue Gene Hambleton was beyond even the strongest interpretation of that command intent. In just five days, twenty-four aircraft had been damaged or destroyed, and at least fourteen men were missing, with eleven of them presumably killed in action. Worse, if the air rescue attempts continued as they had, the casualty count could go even higher. Reluctantly, General Abrams ordered the SAR crews to stand down. There would be no more helicopter rescue operations for Bat 21 Bravo.

It was not, however, the end of the effort to rescue Bat 21 and the others who were trying to escape and evade the enemy in his area. On the contrary, if the Special Operations Forces professionals of the air force's Aerospace Rescue and Recovery Service who had done their best could not fight their way through, then perhaps another set of Special Operations warriors might get in under the North Vietnamese AAA and SAM defenses to snatch the Americans from waiting death or capture: the U.S. Navy SEALs.

> The War of Liberation is a protracted war and a hard war in which we must rely upon ourselves—for we are strong politically but weak materially while the enemy is weak politically but stronger materially.
>
> —General Vo Nguyen Giap[1]

Vo Nguyen Giap, the former high school history teacher turned general, had written that statement in the 1950s at a time when French colonialism ended in Southeast Asia and American suzerainty began. Less than twenty years later, in 1972, the ground truth, or reality, he had previously described was different. The Communists' political strength had not changed, but its military strength had. The commanding general of the People's Army of the Republic of Vietnam (PAVN), minister of defense, and hero of Dien Bien Phu, stood at the head of the third largest army in the world,[2] behind only the Red Army of the Soviet Union and the People's Liberation Army of the People's Republic of China. Not only did General Giap have the men (and women), but thanks to Communist China and the Soviet Union he also had the matériel and heavy weapons necessary to invade South Vietnam. This included T-34 medium battle tanks carrying 85 mm main guns, T-54 main battle tanks with 100 mm main guns, and PT-76 light amphibious tanks that mounted a 76 mm main gun. His artillery battalions bristled with 130 mm cannons and 160 mm mortars. Antitank defense was augmented with new AT-3 Sagger wire-guided antitank missiles.

If Giap was deficient militarily it was in airpower. Even though President Nixon's Vietnamization program had reduced the United States air forces in Southeast Asia to a shadow of their peak strength, there were still almost 650 navy and air force fixed-wing aircraft assigned to theater operations, including just over 400 strike aircraft. Still, North Vietnam was not helpless against an aerial onslaught. Premier Pham Van Dong's petition to Moscow in 1964 for aid to build a modern air defense system around Hanoi and Haiphong had over the years resulted in arguably the world's best. And for the first time, that system had been made mobile and brought south as part of the offensive.

Over the previous few months, Giap's forces in South Vietnam and in bases in Laos and Cambodia near the South Vietnamese border had been reinforced with a Soviet-style mobile air defense "bubble" composed of every antiaircraft weapon in the North Vietnamese inventory. This integrated air defense system (IADS) included everything from heavy machine guns to several battalions of Soviet-made SA-2 SAMs. These had been laboriously dragged down the Ho Chi Minh Trail, completely hidden from the prying eyes and cameras of American aircrews and reconnaissance systems. Every American intelligence-gathering resource from army Green Berets to earth-orbiting satellites had missed the movement of the deadly missiles and guns, and their unexpected appearance had been as big a surprise as the just-launched invasion itself.

Thanks to years of combat experience defending Hanoi and Haiphong from American air attacks, the antiaircraft batteries had become first-rate in their use of the supersonic SA-2 SAMs and AAA guns. These antiaircraft pieces ranged from small caliber 14.5 mm, 23 mm, and 37 mm guns, to the larger twin-mounted 57 mm tracked artillery, and 85 mm and 100 mm cannons equipped with tracking radar. Giap now had an even more dangerous ace to play from his air defense deck: the new shoulder-launched SA-7 Gainful, or Strela (Russian for "arrow"), heat-seeking SAM. The general had them in quantity, and they would be put to their first operational test in the largest military operation launched by the North Vietnamese Army, the Nguyen Hue campaign. With these assets, Giap would employ an air denial strategy similar to the one he had used in 1954 against the French at Dien Bien Phu. And the upshot for American airmen was that for the first time south of the DMZ, they were flying into an integrated air defense bubble as tough as any seen over North Vietnam. The Americans would discover that no longer was the sky in the region theirs to command and control.

The North Vietnamese Easter offensive was officially called the Nguyen Hue campaign. Giap named it after the birth name of the eighteenth-century Vietnamese general Emperor Quang Trung. The emperor's victory during the Tet holiday in January 1789 against a Chinese army twice the size of his own had made Quang Trung a national hero and a legend. Because it was launched on Good Friday, the Americans named the North Vietnamese campaign the Easter offensive. The purpose of Giap's plan was to once and for all knock South Vietnam out of the war. It called for a rolling three-prong thrust designed to overextend the South Vietnamese army's resources. Logistics came from supply depots situated along the DMZ and Ho Chi Minh Trail that had been built up in the preceding weeks, and two fuel pipelines stretching from Haiphong to the DMZ, a distance of just over three hundred miles. The attack would begin in the north with a multidivisional spearhead across the DMZ. It would be followed by a second spearhead attacking from bases in Cambodia toward the South Vietnamese capital of Saigon. The third spearhead, based in Laos, would attack east through the Central Highlands and attempt to cut the nation in two.

Ironically, the North Vietnamese were going to wage war in the conventional way desired by General William Westmoreland, Abrams's predecessor, but denied him. Just four years earlier, General Giap's force would have been going on a death ride into the real strength of the American army. Now, in 1972, with just a token American force remaining, the North Vietnamese were going to make the most of their opportunity.

It was a bold, ambitious plan, and not without risk. Even after the drawdown caused by Vietnamization, the American air forces were still a dangerous resource to be reckoned with. The army of South Vietnam (ARVN) inherited large quantities of American equipment that had been left behind, which greatly increased the combat strength of their units. Also, ARVN morale was generally good, and training had improved. However, the total American ground troop strength in South Vietnam was only 65,000 men, almost all being advisers. The Easter offensive was timed to kick off right after the spring monsoon season began, thus limiting the effectiveness of America's airpower. And 1972 was a presidential election year in the United States. General Giap and the PAVN had scored big in the American political arena in 1968 with the Tet offensive. Though the Viet Cong guerrilla forces were essentially destroyed in the offensive and never again were a significant factor in the war, the Tet offensive proved to be a crucial psychological turning point for the American home front. It gave a boost to the antiwar movement, caused politicians to refuse further troop increases in Southeast Asia, and was a big factor in President Lyndon Johnson's decision not to run for reelection. The Easter offensive might produce similar results, this time causing Americans to vote the troublesome and firm-willed president, Richard M. Nixon, out of office.

So it was that in 1972, when the first monsoon rains came, Giap gave the order, and more than one hundred thousand North Vietnamese army troops began the march south. It was into the middle of this massive enemy invasion that Gene Hambleton would be forced to parachute and have to conduct his escape and evasion.

April 2, 1972, Easter Sunday

The South Vietnamese high command and their American advisers knew that it was only a matter of time before North Vietnam attempted an invasion in 1972. Through various intelligence sources—strategic surprise is almost impossible to maintain in the era of electronic warfare—they were aware that something big was up.

On March 30, more than six North Vietnamese divisions, forty thousand men, crossed the DMZ and slammed into a defense force composed of fewer than nine thousand men from the South Vietnamese 3rd Division and ARVN marine forces. They were stretched over a three-hundred-square-mile area and had been anticipating an attack from Laos.[3] Thus, ARVN positions were facing west, not north. Worse, they were caught in the middle of repositioning many units when the attack came.

The result was chaos. Some exposed positions were overrun so quickly that the North Vietnamese captured abandoned artillery batteries intact, stocked with ammunition and ready to fire. Other South Vietnamese units reacted courageously, fighting and dying where they stood. Still others managed to regroup and stage delaying actions. Gradually, the North Vietnamese attack was slowed. But unless the South Vietnamese troops got help—specifically, from the United States Air Force, Navy, Marine Corps, and Army—and quickly, the Communists would conquer all of Quang Tri province and capture the old imperial capital of Hue

During the Vietnam War, help routinely came in the form of American airpower, supplied in vast quantities. Usually, all it took was a code word over the radio ("Broken Arrow" had been used early in the Vietnam War), indicating a ground unit was being overrun, and everything from A-1 Skyraiders to B-52 Stratofortresses would be overhead, raining death on enemy forces. The early days of the 1972 Easter offensive were different. In the midst of a major redeployment of air units back to the United States, the 7th Air Force was thin in a number of critical areas. One of these was the hunting-and-suppression aircraft and aircrews used to find and destroy sophisticated enemy air defenses. One of the remaining aircrew members was Gene Hambleton.

Lt. Colonel Iceal "Gene" Hambleton was a fifty-three-year-old senior navigator for the 42nd Tactical Electronic Warfare Squadron (TEWS) stationed at Korat RTAFB, Thailand. Hambleton was one of the few people still in the Southeast Asia theater who knew everything there was to know about the gathering of electronic intelligence, waging electronic warfare, and interdicting its weapons systems. Normally, he would be the one handing out mission assignments to the navigators and electronic warfare officers, conducting the briefings, and then watching them fly off in their EB-66 Destroyers, Korean War–era bombers reconfigured as electronic warfare aircraft and affectionately nicknamed Souiees by their six-man crews.

But this Easter Sunday, Hambleton himself was in the air. There were a number of factors that caused him to be in the navigator's seat in the cramped EB-66C, and they all stemmed from Vietnamization. In 1968, the 7th Air Force had two TEW squadrons, the 41st and 42nd, and thirty-eight EB-66s in Southeast Asia. In 1969, following the conclusion of the Rolling Thunder bombing campaign, there was one squadron and twenty aircraft. In 1970, the remaining TEW squadron consisted of eight EB-66Es and five EB-66Cs. The number of aircraft had risen somewhat after that, but the Easter offensive caught the 42nd TEWS stretched dangerously thin, particularly in skilled electronic warfare personnel. President Nixon, at General Abrams's request, would soon authorize Operation Constant Guard, a series of deploy-

B-52 STRATOFORTRESS

The B-52 Stratofortress is a long-range jet strategic bomber flown by the United States Air Force that has been on active duty since 1954. Originally built to carry nuclear bombs, its primary role is now conventional aerial warfare. The B-52 has the longest range of any bomber and carries a heavy strategic or tactical weapons load. Its economy in operation and high subsonic performance compared to the rest of the USAF strategic bomber fleet has enabled it to remain in active service. The B-52 is capable of dropping or launching a wide array of conventional weapons including "dumb" free-fall gravity bombs, cluster bombs, and precision-guided ordnance.

Photo: U.S. Department of Defense

SPECIFICATIONS

Manufacturer: Boeing
Crew: Five
Power plant: Eight Pratt & Whitney TF33-P-3/103 turbofans; 17,000 pounds of thrust each
Length: 159 feet 4 inches (48.5 meters)
Height: 40 feet 8 inches (12.4 meters)
Wingspan: 185 feet (56.4 meters)
Maximum speed: 650 mph (560 knots; 1,000 kmh)
Combat radius: 4,480 miles (3,890 nautical miles; 7,210 kilometers)
Ceiling: 55,773 feet (17,000 meters)
Maximum takeoff weight: 488,000 pounds (220,000 kilograms)
Armament: All models up to the H had a pod of four .50-caliber guns. The H model had one Vulcan 20 mm Gatling cannon. Presently, all operating B-52s have had their tail guns removed. Maximum bomb load is 60,000 pounds (27,200 kilograms).

ments designed to restore depleted air assets in order to counter the North Vietnamese campaign. But the first aircraft to be sent, eight EB-66s, would not arrive until April 7. Until then, there were simply too many missions for too few men.

During the Vietnam War, Arc Light was the code name used for bombing missions involving only B-52 bombers. When reports arrived at General Abrams's headquarters in Saigon indicating large-unit enemy activity south of the DMZ, a series of bombing missions, including Arc Lights, were scheduled; their purpose was to disrupt and/or destroy the enemy troop concentrations. Originally, the mission Hambleton was on had been scheduled to make its run without electronic warfare escort. But earlier strike missions over the weekend had encountered dramatically increased SAM activity from Giap's forces below. As a result, a late request was made to the 42nd TEWS for help.

Two Destroyers were assigned the mission, Bat 22, an EB-66E, and Bat 21, an EB-66C. The older C model was both slower and more vulnerable to antiaircraft defenses, particularly SAMs, than the later E model. But both versions were needed because each had a different electronic warfare specialty. The purpose of the EB-66E was to jam radars. The EB-66C was the only version "capable of gathering ELINT [electronic intelligence] data."[4] Because Hambleton was shorthanded, particularly in officers skilled in gathering and interpreting electronic intelligence data, he slotted himself in as the navigator on Bat 21. Major Ed Anderson, piloting Bat 22, would run electronic interference for the Arc Light strike near the DMZ. Accompanying the group were two F-105G Wild Weasels. Their task was to take out any Fan Song SA-2 SAM tracking radar making its presence known in the mission area. And just in case the North Vietnamese air force wanted to join the party, two jet fighters were added to ride shotgun against any MiG threat. At the time of the briefing, no one knew that a full-scale offensive from the north had been launched, only that there was an increased threat of SAMs.

It was a late-day mission. Weather over the target area contained layers of scattered cloud cover reaching to an elevation of fifteen thousand feet. As the aircraft neared the target area, they started getting "hits" from Fan Song missile-guidance radars. This was ominous. Fan Song radars were exclusively linked to the SA-2 missile system. These particular Fan Song signals were coming from new locations, including sites *south* of the DMZ. The enemy was up to something bigger than Hambleton and the others had been told. But what?

At about 4:50 P.M., two Fan Song radars locked onto Hambleton's group flying at approximately thirty thousand feet. Suddenly, four SA-2s rocketed through the cloud cover at the unseen aircraft above. Major Ed Anderson, piloting Bat 22, immediately called out a warning. The pilots had a maximum of ten seconds to react. Decoy chaff was deployed from all the aircraft, defensive jammers were activated, and Bat 22 pilot Anderson initiated a diving "SAM break" maneuver. The first volley of SA-2s missed.

Then came a second attack—a one-two combination of six SA-2s along with a barrage of 100 mm radar-guided antiaircraft artillery shells aimed at a cell of three B-52 bombers. The lead B-52 was forced to evade and abort. The other two B-52s in the cell managed a blind drop into the clouds before initiating countermeasures. Again, the aircraft escaped untouched. As they left, the Wild Weasels headed down to take out the radar sites.

But before they could do so, a third volley of three SA-2s streaked into the sky. Two got a solid lock on Bat 21 flying at twenty-nine thousand feet. The first detonated beneath the fuselage, just below Hambleton's position in the navigator's seat, tearing the guts out of the aircraft. As the dying EB-66 began to fall out of control, and with the intercom destroyed, the pilot turned to Hambleton and hand-signaled for him to eject. Hambleton pulled the ejection seat handles and was immediately shot out of the stricken airplane. Moments later, the second SA-2 scored a direct hit, turning the EB-66 into a flaming funeral pyre for five American airmen.

Gene Hambleton, call sign Bat 21 Bravo, was the only survivor.

> When the history of the war in Vietnam is finally written, the story of Air Rescue may well become one of the most outstanding human dramas in the entire history of the Air Force.
>
> —Harold Brown,
> former secretary of the air force
> and secretary of defense[5]

One of the few bright spots for the United States military in Vietnam was its combat search-and-rescue service, which came into its own during this conflict. Many experts have called it the "golden age of combat search and rescue."[6] It certainly was a busy time for the men who performed this dangerous and vital mission.

In 1964, the air force assigned to the Air Rescue Service (ARS) the duty to conduct combat aircrew recovery missions (as they were then known) in Southeast Asia. In 1966, the ARS was redesignated the Aerospace Rescue and Recovery Service (ARRS), but its mission in Southeast Asia remained the same. When the war ended, the ARRS had successfully rescued 3,883 aircrew members in Southeast Asia, and the 3rd Aerospace Rescue and Recovery Group was the most highly decorated unit in U.S. Air Force history.[7]

Like so much else to do with the Vietnam War, the reasons for this success were both simple and complex. More than twenty-five years after the end of the Vietnam War, Major General Lance L. Smith, USAF, summarized the multifold value of rescuing downed air crews: "Combat search and rescue (CSAR) preserves critical combat resources while denying the enemy a potential source. It is a key element in sustaining the morale, cohesion, and, ultimately, the operational performance of friendly forces."[8]

There were consequences to this doctrine, though. On the plus side was the obvious positive morale factor. An F-105 Thud pilot call sign Marlin 01 expressed a common sentiment by downed airmen when he said of his rescue, "Absolutely the most beautiful thing I've ever seen was that big helicopter hovering over me."[9] On the negative side was the awareness by the North Vietnamese and the Viet Cong of American policy and efforts to go all out to recover downed aircrews. They were not above using these men as "'bait' in an effort to shoot down more aircraft."[10]

Successful search-and-rescue missions under combat conditions are among the most time-sensitive of operations. Air force studies begun during the Korean War and continued throughout the Vietnam War revealed that "an airman's chances of being rescued were very good if recovery forces could reach him within fifteen minutes, but the probability of recovery decreased significantly if the ACR force took longer than thirty minutes to reach the area."[11] Ominously, that recovery dropped to less than 20 percent if the aircrew member was on the ground more than four hours.[12]

To reduce that time to the minimum, in 1966, Colonel Bestow Rudolph of the ARRS planning staff stated, "Rather than stand by and wait for a call, we want to be as close as possible to the strike area, loitering on the periphery of the action and then going right in when a man needs us. We want to pick him up in seconds, not in minutes or hours."[13] The ARRS coordinated with mission planners so that rescue assets would be in place in the event of a shootdown. Prior to each mission, a Hercules HC-130P (the "H" being the code letter for rescue and recovery) would orbit in a preestablished location. On board the HC-130P was a mission coordinator whose task was to manage any rescue effort. Additionally, the Hercules would provide refueling assistance to rescue helicopters that might need it.

So it was that on Easter Sunday, 1972, even in the hostile afternoon sky near the DMZ, Lieutenant Colonel Hambleton, floating alone in his parachute, was not without many friends on hand and ready to assist. People were already aware of what had happened to Bat 21 and that Hambleton was in need of help.

The first was Major Jimmy Kempton of the 390th Tactical Fighter Squadron. He was leading four F-4 Phantoms in a Skyspot mission. Skyspot missions were bombing operations designed for poor or zero visibility low-level weather conditions that prevent visual fixes on a target. Strike aircraft were guided to the drop site by radar controllers in other aircraft, who also oversaw the bomb release. Kempton immediately alerted King 22, a Hercules search-and-rescue command-and-control craft, whose assigned station was over the South China Sea. As it turned out, King 22 was much closer. Earlier, another aircraft had been shot down, and when Bat 21 was hit, King 22 was inland, just south of Quang Tri and already running a SAR mission. Its rescue mission commander, Major Bruce Driscoll, had actually seen Bat 21 explode and promptly began setting up a new search-and-rescue operation. But two complications confronted him. King 22 had been airborne all day and was almost out of fuel. Also, HC-130s did not operate at night, and dusk was a little more than an hour away. King 22 called Korat RTAFB in Thailand and requested the standby HC-130 on alert for such contingencies to fly up in relief.

As this was going on, pilot First Lieutenant Bill Jankowski and Captain Lyle Wilson were in an 0-2 FAC (forward air controller) aircraft code-named Bilk 34, flying between the cloud layers trying to locate and target Communist forces. They had seen the SAMs rocket up through the solid cloud mass below them and observed a large explosion high above. A moment later

Photo: U.S. Air Force

The HC-130 (call sign "King") was the search-and-rescue variant of the versatile C-130 Hercules transport. Prior to each mission, an HC-130 would orbit in a pre-established location. A mission coordinator onboard was responsible for managing any rescue effort. The HC-130 was also equipped to refuel rescue helicopters.

Jankowski heard a beeper from a rescue radio. It was Gene Hambleton, Bat 21 Bravo, in his parachute.

Automatically, Jankowski keyed his mike and said, "Beeper, beeper, come up voice." Hambleton acknowledged, identified himself, and said that he had the 0-2 in sight. Jankowski, thinking that Hambleton was on the ground, commented on the acuity of Bat 21 Bravo's vision since he couldn't see anything through the pea soup cloud cover below. Hambleton replied that he was *above* the 0-2. "I'm the parachute at about twelve thousand. Coming down in the middle of your orbit." Startled, Jankowski banked his 0-2, looked up, and saw Hambleton descending.

Jankowski then flew up to Hambleton and radioed a status report of Hambleton's position and condition to the search-and-rescue command aircraft, King 22. While flying around Bat 21 Bravo, Jankowski and Wilson discussed the possibility of literally plucking the electronics warfare expert out of the sky by slowing the 0-2 to minimum speed, snaring the parachute with a wing, and then hauling Hambleton in. But both decided that such a move, while possible, was too risky.

Jankowski followed Hambleton down as he disappeared into the low cloud bank. When the 0-2 broke through the clouds at nine hundred feet, they saw Hambleton's collapsed parachute in a dry rice paddy roughly two kilometers from the Cam Lo Bridge. Hambleton confirmed that he was okay

0-2 SUPER SKYMASTER

The 0-2 is the military version of Cessna's Model 337 Super Skymaster. It began service in the Vietnam War in 1967, where it was used on forward air control, reconnaissance, and psychological warfare operations. It was easy to fly and easy to maintain, important factors for both pilots and crews stationed in Southeast Asia. Pylon mounts under the wings enabled the Skymaster to carry many types of light weapons and target markers, including smoke and explosive rockets, flares, bombs, and miniguns. Other modifications included additional glass panels to increase air-to-ground visibility and the installation of 600 watt amplified speakers and leaflet pods for psychological warfare operations.

SPECIFICATIONS

Photo: U.S. Air Force

Manufacturer: Cessna
Crew: One
Power plant: Two Continental IO-360C piston engines delivering 210 horsepower each
Length: 29 feet 9 inches (9.07 meters)
Height: 9 feet 4 inches (2.84 meters)
Wingspan: 38 feet 2 inches (11.63 meters)
Maximum speed: 200 mph (170 knots; 320 kmh)
Range: 764 miles (664 nautical miles; 1,220 kilometers)
Ceiling: 19,500 feet (5,940 meters)
Maximum takeoff weight: 4,400 pounds (1,204 kilograms)

and that he had moved to a position of relative safety on a rise near a small grove of trees. "Relative" was stretching it, because Hambleton had landed near TL 88, a secondary highway that was one of the major road arteries being used by the North Vietnamese Army. The otherwise minor bridge at Cam Lo was now a strategically important choke point meriting extra antiaircraft protection by the Communists. Within seconds of emerging from the clouds, Jankowski's 0-2 came under heavy antiaircraft fire. Jankowski and Wilson were astonished; they had never seen so many NVA troops, heavy weapons, and equipment in one place. As yet, the North Vietnamese didn't know that Hambleton had almost literally landed in their lap.

Ducking in and out of the clouds, Jankowski got on the radio again, this time sending out a request for any aircraft in the vicinity that could assist in a quick-snatch SAR. Two Skyraider pilots, Captain Don Morse, flying Sandy 07, and his wingman in Sandy 08, were the first to respond. As they flew to link up with Jankowski, Hambleton moved from his exposed position into the grove of trees.

Blueghost 39, an army UH-1H Huey flying near Hue, had also heard Jankowski's call. It quickly landed at Hue/Phu Bai Airfield, where it dropped off its passengers, including Captain Thomas White, the operations officer for F Troop of the 8th Cavalry, and refueled. Captain White immediately organized a rescue mission composed of two Cobra gunships; Blueghost 28, piloted by Captain Mike Rosebeary, and Blueghost 24, piloted by Warrant Officer George Ezell; along with Blueghost 39, piloted by First Lieutenant Byron Kulland. The Cobras would provide close escort and suppressive ground fire for the rescue Huey. Five minutes after the three helicopters lifted off, Captain White sent another Huey, Blueghost 30, to assist.

Unaware of the exact strength of the ground threat ahead, Captain Rosebeary ordered one of the gunships, Blueghost 24, to drop back and escort Blueghost 30. As soon as Rosebeary reached the pickup area, Jankowski gave him a quick update, adding that A-1s and F-4s had been pounding enemy positions nearby. The strike aircraft were receiving an assist by Hambleton himself, who coolly acted as a ground FAC, accurately targeting directions and correcting attacks against the enemy formations on and around TL 88. (Afterward, Captain Morse of Sandy 07 would marvel at how Hambleton was able to stay calm in such a stressful environment.) After getting final instructions from Jankowski, Blueghost 28 and Blueghost 39 accelerated toward Hambleton's location.

Procedure called for the helicopters to fly in low and at or near top speed. Blueghost 39 was in the lead, hugging the ground at treetop level. Rosebeary's Cobra rode shotgun at three hundred feet up and about three thousand feet behind. In normal combat circumstances, if the Huey came under fire, Rosebeary would be in perfect position to return fire with rockets or machine guns and knock out the enemy positions. The problem was that along both banks of the Cam Lo River, the enemy was everywhere, ready and loaded for bear.

The moment the helicopters reached the river, the countryside seemed to erupt in a firestorm of hot lead. Rosebeary returned fire with his rockets and 40 mm automatic grenade launcher, but it was no contest. Outmatched and outgunned, enemy rounds perforated both helicopters, shattering canopies and controls. Operating systems in Rosebeary's Cobra began failing en masse. The cockpit panel was ablaze with sparks and illumination from the warning and failure lights that hadn't been destroyed. Fighting to control his heavily damaged helicopter, Rosebeary called for Blueghost 39 to break off and clear the area. Though Blueghost 39 didn't reply, Rosebeary saw that his message had apparently gotten through, for the Huey was beginning to turn away. But partway into the turn, smoke began to billow out of the engine compartment of Kulland's Huey. Blueghost 39 was losing altitude, but Kulland somehow managed to maintain control long enough to land it in an open area about fifteen hundred meters on the wrong side of the Dong Ha River—the north side, where the enemy was in force.

Specialist Fifth Class Astorga, the gunner on Blueghost 39, had been firing his machine gun since the action had started. But his gun jammed, and he was wounded in the leg and chest and knocked out before he could clear his weapon. He awoke to find the helicopter on the ground and on fire, with thick smoke from the engine swirling all around. Astorga quickly unstrapped himself and began checking his crewmates. A survival vest was pushed into his hands by one of them, and he then slipped out of the helicopter and started putting distance between himself and the burning Huey. He suddenly heard someone still in the Huey cry out a warning about approaching enemy troops. Looking up, he saw North Vietnamese soldiers advancing, firing their weapons. Just then the Huey exploded. Astorga was captured and led away. The rest of the crew, First Lieutenant Byron Kulland, copilot John Frink, and crew chief Specialist Fifth Class Ronald Paschall never got out. The first of the fourteen Americans who would die trying to save Gene Hambleton had just perished.

Meanwhile Captain Rosebeary was making a Mayday call. His Cobra was too heavily damaged to return to base. In fact, he was lucky it was in shape to clear the area. Jolly Green 67 answered his call, and the Cobra crew was safely rescued soon after it made an emergency landing.

When Captain Morse learned that the quick-snatch attempt had failed, he broke off action, and he and his wingman returned to base. It was getting dark, and the weather conditions were deteriorating. Also, their A-1s had not gone unscathed in the action. After landing they discovered that their aircraft were so badly damaged that they would be in the repair shop for several days. With only twenty A-1s in the entire theater, the North Vietnamese had just knocked out of commission 10 percent of one of the most powerful air-ground weapons that could be used against them and in rescue support.

During debriefing that evening it became obvious that getting Bat 21 Bravo out was going to be a bigger challenge than expected. But search and rescue was the Aerospace Rescue and Recovery Service's job. They were proud of their track record and not about to admit failure. The enemy had surprised them with the size and strength of its force, and the next time they went in, they'd go prepared. The crews went to bed, still unaware that they were up against the northernmost prong of the North's Easter offensive.

Earlier in the day, when word of Bat 21's shootdown reached the joint search and rescue center (JSRC) at 7th Air Force headquarters at Tan Son Nhut Air Base outside Saigon, the news initiated a sequence of decisions and events that would add controversy to the efforts to rescue Hambleton. The decision that was arguably the most troubling and problematic was the one to establish a no-fire zone fifty-four kilometers in diameter around Hambleton's position.

No-fire zones were commonly used throughout the war. Their purpose was to prevent friendly fire incidents arising from multiple operations being conducted in the same area. In this case, any request for an air strike, artillery, or naval gunfire support had to be sent to JSRC for approval. The problem was that when the order went out, 7th Air Force was unaware of the full extent of the ground situation and particularly of the crisis confronting the ARVN 3rd Division. The size of the no-fly zone was particularly dangerous. It covered almost entirely the 3rd Division's zone of operations and, crucially, the Cam Lo Bridge. In effect, 7th Air Force was denying its allies the most potent means to stop the Communist offensive in the north so that it could rescue one of its own. This problem was compounded by 7th Air Force's ignorance of the situation immediately south of the DMZ. The South Vietnamese had not told them, General Abrams, or any of the senior leaders on his staff in Saigon what was happening.

According to one postwar analysis, "They had been deceived by the enemy, besieged under the heaviest artillery attack of the Vietnam War, and were further surprised by the employment of massive quantities of Soviet armor. Their inability to regroup and contain the attackers was the ultimate embarrassment for South Vietnam's political and military leaders. They had lost face."[14] And because of Vietnamization, there weren't enough American advisers in the ARVN battalions and virtually none in the smaller units. As a result, reports from the front lines to Saigon during the opening days of the offensive, particularly to General Abrams and his staff, were either false or nonexistent.

The result was that support for the 3rd ARVN Division would be compromised by the search-and-rescue effort for Gene Hambleton, making the division's stand to hold its ground that much tougher.

Captain Morse's departure from the Cam Lo area did not mean Hambleton was left alone. So long as he was alive and free, he would be under an around-the-clock watch until either his rescue or capture. The watch planes not only maintained contact with him, they also served as SAR on-scene commanders and helped coordinate any necessary protective air strikes. That first night would prove to be anything but quiet.

Among the watch aircraft was Nail 59, an OV-10 Bronco piloted by Captain Gary Ferentchak. "Nail" meant that the Bronco was modified with special navigational systems and laser designators particularly useful on night missions or missions conducted under adverse weather conditions, meaning, among other things, that Hambleton could receive survival supplies at any hour of the day or night, regardless of weather. The other airplane in the sky that evening was King 27, an HC-130 commanded by Major Dennis Constant. King 27 had been monitoring the radio traffic from Bat 21, and Hambleton's continuing stream of reports of large-scale enemy movement were Constant's first clues that something very big and very bad was going on south of the DMZ. At one point, Constant ordered that the area around

Hambleton be carpeted with CDU-14 "gravel"—miniature antipersonnel mines first used along the Ho Chi Minh Trail. The North Vietnamese had to be aware that Hambleton was in the area, and the aerial laying of a minefield between the enemy and Hambleton was employed to keep him out of enemy hands long enough for a rescue to be effected.

It was a rescue that came close to including the crews of Nail 59 and King 27. They suddenly found themselves painted by Fan Song radar and dodging salvos of SA-2s. Fortunately, the SAMs' exhaust plumes stood out starkly in the night sky, and both airplanes were able to successfully evade a shoot-down. Even so, King 27 was damaged by a near miss and had to retire. Thereafter, the HC-130s would make sure they stayed well south and east of the DMZ.

Meanwhile, plans were being drawn up to get Hambleton out the next day, April 3. The SAR task force consisted of two A-1s and two HH-53s (Jolly Greens 65 and 67). Captain Don Morse in Sandy 07 would be the mission commander, and his wingman was Sandy 08. Jolly Green 65, tasked with extracting Hambleton, was piloted by Coast Guard Lieutenant Commander Jay Crowe, who was on an interservice exchange tour and well experienced in rescue operations. Additional assets to lay down suppression fire were in place, including four more A-1s, bringing the total on this mission to six Skyraiders—one third of all the operational air force A-1s in Southeast Asia.

The North Vietnamese probably knew exactly who had ejected from Bat 21 and were making a concerted effort to capture him. One of the consequences of the Vietnamization effort was that particularly skilled or valuable American personnel were regularly tracked and identified by NVA agents, even in Thailand and other bases outside South Vietnam. In addition, the Russians were probably supporting North Vietnamese army operations with regular decryptions of American message traffic, thanks to information provided by the Walker family spy ring led by navy communications specialist Chief Warrant Officer John Anthony Walker, which was providing the USSR with the ability to read transmissions in real time. Undoubtedly, Hambleton's loss was reported stateside as soon as it occurred, and the Vietnamese quickly knew of his vast knowledge and skills. This can only have made him a more desirable and valuable capture to the North Vietnamese.

Though rarely spoken of even today, electronic warfare specialists, particularly those with intimate knowledge of strategic bomber systems and procedures, almost never returned if shot down over Vietnam. And Hambleton was arguably the most senior and knowledgeable "Raven" (as these specialists were code-named) of the war shot down inside enemy territory. His loss would be a disaster for American airpower worldwide. For the Communists, his capture would be a godsend from Hanoi to Moscow. Both sides were now racing to pluck him from the battlefield around the Cam Lo River.

It was raining the morning of April 3 when the Skyraiders began air strikes around Hambleton's position. Captain Morse's instructions were clear. As the whole area was hot, all flights to the strike zone should originate south or southeast of the Cam Lo River; the region that had the largest concentration of enemy troops was north and west of the river. The rain impeded the Skyraiders' efforts, but eventually Morse felt that it was sufficiently safe to make the rescue attempt. If the Americans were lucky, the rain would also impede the enemy's attempts to stop them or move in on Hambleton.

The weather began to lift a bit as the escort and rescue aircraft got into position. As soon as everyone was ready, First Lieutenant Glen Prieb, flying Sandy 05, dove through the cloud cover, immediately followed by Jolly Green 65.

All had been briefed about the heavy enemy activity on the ground. Even so, the sight below them when they broke through the clouds came as a shock. Like Jankowski and Wilson, they had never seen anything like it in Vietnam. The enemy was *everywhere*. Trucks, tracked vehicles, antiaircraft and towed artillery guns, along with thousands of soldiers. It seemed that anything that could shoot was doing so, and the primary target was Jolly Green 65.

One of the deadliest antiaircraft artillery pieces in the PAVN inventory, and the one helicopter pilots feared most, was the Soviet ZU-23, a twin-mount 23 mm cannon capable of firing two thousand rounds a minute. A skilled gunner could keep a large helicopter, even a Super Jolly Green Giant transiting across its field of fire at high speed, within the ZU-23's threat envelope for almost sixty seconds. With enemy all around, and terrain largely flat and treeless, the low-flying HH-53 was a big, green target in an open-air shooting gallery. Aboard Jolly Green 65, everything bad seemed to happen at once: the instrument panel exploded in a shower of metal, plastic, and glass; the gyro system, navigational and flight instruments, intercom, electrical, hydraulics, and flight-control systems were wrecked or so badly damaged their failure was imminent. Miraculously, the crew was unharmed, as were the main radio, engines, and transmission. Lieutenant Commander Crowe radioed that he had to abort. It took the full strength of both Crowe and his copilot wrestling with the leaden controls to get Jolly Green 65 on a bearing south and fly it to safety. They were able to fly the crippled HH-53 to the Hue/Phu Bai Airfield and landed it safely—in the middle of a Communist rocket attack.

The departure of Jolly Green 65 did not end the rescue effort for the day. Other SAR aircraft, including another FAC, Nail 22, and Jolly Greens 66 and 60, arrived. Piloting Jolly Green 66 was Lieutenant Colonel Bill Harris, com-

Photo: U.S. Air Force

The Sikorsky HH-53 Super Jolly Green Giant seen from a gunner's position in an accompanying HH-53. This heavy-lift helicopter was used extensively during the Vietnam War for special operations and rescue of combat personnel. For combat rescue and recovery, it was equipped with armor plating, self-sealing fuel tanks, three 7.62 mm miniguns, and an external rescue hoist with 250 feet of cable.

manding officer of the 37th ARRS, based at Da Nang. This time, with Nail 22 in the lead and Jolly Green 66 right behind, the flight bored in. When they broke through the clouds, they discovered that they were over the north bank of the Cam Lo River, right over the heaviest troop concentrations. As before, the Jolly Green became the target of every weapon that could be brought to bear on it. Like Jolly Green 65, Harris's helicopter began taking hits within seconds of emerging from the clouds. Grimly, Harris pressed on. As he neared Hambleton's position, the Skyraiders flew in to lay down suppressant fire. But again the enemy was too strong. Harris was ordered to abort. The heavily damaged Jolly Green 66 managed to reach the Hue/Phu Bai Airfield, where it made an emergency landing, finally coming to a stop beside Jolly Green 65. Fortunately for Jolly Green 66, by this time the attack on the airfield had ended. Jolly Green 66 was lucky to land: the main spar on one of the rotor blades had received such severe battle damage that it almost fell off in the crew's hands. That they had managed to land safely was nothing short of a miracle.

The A-1 Skyhawk and F-4 Phantom air strikes continued, but there would be no third rescue attempt that day. There were too many enemy troops with too many AAA guns and SAMs for a rescue to be possible.

Shortly after he landed, Lieutenant Commander Crowe did some intelligence work of his own. He was concerned about why the briefing he had received about the ground situation had not prepared him for what he had actually encountered. The Coast Guard has a long tradition of interservice liaison and cooperation, and Crowe used his contacts to get the full story. A briefing from ARVN intelligence hit him like a thunderbolt. Five days after the enemy offensive had been launched, Crowe was first hearing details, including the fact that the rescue flight path was taking them over a six-division assault that had crossed the DMZ.

Meanwhile, near Cam Lo, things took another bad turn. Nail 38, an OV-10 Bronco carrying pilot Captain Bill Henderson and copilot Lieutenant Mark Clark, was shot down by an SA-2. Like the earlier attempt to rescue Hambleton, the quick-snatch rescue effort for Henderson and Clark had to abort. The three helicopters involved were so badly damaged that they had to be written off. Henderson was caught later that evening by the North Vietnamese and taken north to Hanoi. Clark managed to successfully evade capture and was in hiding along the south bank of the river, not that far from Hambleton.

Things were no better on April 4. Another SAR aerial task force was assembled, this time with ten A-1s as escort. It, too, failed, and was again mauled by AAA and SAMs for its trouble. When the battered task force returned to base, eight of the ten A-1s had been damaged by enemy ground fire, two quite severely, and of those two, the A-1 piloted by Captain Don Morse was totally wrecked. Incredibly, no one was wounded, but the A-1 Skyraider inventory was now down to an operational level of less than 50 percent.

April 5 was a day of bad weather and planning for the next attempt.

April 6 was a day bordered in black.

Dawn on April 6, 1972, found Hambleton wet, hungry, tired, and hurt. He had four compressed vertebrae as a result of his ejection and parachute landing; a gash in his leg from an incident with a villager, whom he'd had to kill; and assorted minor shrapnel wounds from the SA-2 warhead detonation. Two things had helped Hambleton keep his sanity and his spirits up. One was the belief that somehow, soon, and despite everything, he'd be rescued. The other was a fuzzy, multicolored caterpillar that he had found and named Chester. It had become a pet of sorts.

Hambleton had reflected with some amusement that when he returned he'd be eligible to become a member of the Caterpillar Club, an organization composed of fliers who had been saved by parachutes and so named because the first parachutes had been constructed of silk. But Hambleton was now going into his second week of hiding behind enemy lines. And Chester was dead. He had become a victim of collateral damage when a bomb, dropped during an Arc Light mission, shattered a tree and flung a limb onto the "home" Hambleton had built for Chester. Hambleton was alone and had been told he was no longer going to have a babysitter constantly flying above him, because FAC missions into the area—a full-fledged battle zone—were being reduced. He was starting to feel abandoned.

Morale on the SAR teams was little better than Hambleton's. The rescue effort had turned into its own war of attrition and an even greater test of wills. As many as ninety air strikes a day had been flown to suppress the enemy, including a B-52 Arc Light mission that destroyed thirty-five tanks and an NVA division command bunker.[15]

The SAR teams were accomplished men who were justifiably proud of their record. Yet despite all that had been done, they couldn't get Clark and Hambleton out. Worse, there was now a third American needing rescue, First Lieutenant Bruce Walker, call sign Covey 282 Alpha. He was an OV-10 pilot shot down by a SAM on April 7. Somehow Walker was able to find refuge in some woods. His copilot, Marine First Lieutenant Larry Potts, Covey 282 Bravo, had also safely ejected from the airplane. But after an initial Mayday call, SAR aircraft were not able to establish contact. Listed as missing in action, Potts was never heard from again.

None of the Americans wanted to give up. But as General Abrams's orders made clear, things couldn't continue as they had. An unconventional approach was needed and a marine lieutenant colonel named Andy Anderson believed he had the answer: Bright Light.

Bright Light was the unclassified code word for a variety of POW-related missions, including rescue operations run by the Joint Personnel Recovery Center (JPRC), headquartered in Saigon. The JPRC had become operational in 1966, and in its six years of existence it had compiled a perfect record. Unfortunately, it was the type of perfection no commander desired: zero American POWs rescued. But if Bright Light had been unable to rescue Americans already held captive by the North Vietnamese (it had successfully rescued a number of ARVN POWs), perhaps it could prevent the two Americans hiding near Cam Lo from becoming prisoners of war. That, at least, was the thought of its commanding officer, Lieutenant Colonel Anderson.

Time was of the essence for Anderson. His unit was slated for deactivation in three weeks, on April 30. The Bat 21 rescue mission was his one and, in all likelihood, only chance to end the operation on a high note—provided, of course, that he got approval from his superiors. But Anderson knew if he went through the proper channels, he'd be turned down. To have any sort of chance to launch a rescue, he had to petition someone outside his chain of command. Military hierarchy rarely looks kindly on such moves. Careers have been broken and officers have been disciplined for lesser affronts to military rules and regulations. But Anderson felt that putting his career on the line was a small price to pay if it meant saving fellow Americans. He put in a call to Major General Winton W. Marshall, vice commander of the 7th Air Force and a longtime friend of General Abrams. A meeting was scheduled for the morning of the next day, April 8.

When Anderson walked into Marshall's office, he also met the director of aerospace rescue, Colonel Cecil Muirhead, who had been overseeing all the helicopter rescue attempts of Bat 21. The meeting began with an update of the overall battle situation in the north. This was followed by a rundown of the essential points of previous rescue attempts. No matter which way one looked at it, the scenario was bleak. The enemy had upward of a division in the area immediately around Hambleton and Clark, with more men and vehicles coming through each day. Thanks to liberal use of American airpower, the offensive had slowed. But the situation was fluid. Finally, the update was concluded and Anderson was given the floor.

Anderson came into the meeting with more than a bright idea. From the moment he had heard of Bat 21's shootdown, he and his small staff had monitored the events. He had ordered Captain Bob Covalucci, his operations and intelligence officer, to prepare a preliminary rescue plan, just in case. Anderson detailed what he had in mind. Major General Marshall liked what he heard. He told Anderson that he had Marshall's complete support, including the use of Marshall's private jet as an air taxi. With Anderson's plan in hand, Marshall then went to sell the idea to General Abrams. Abrams listened, asked a few questions, and when his concerns were satisfied, gave the mission the green light. He even agreed to allow B-52s to be used in a diversionary role.

Anderson then flew in Marshall's jet up to Da Nang, where he was ushered into an afternoon meeting attended by all the key leaders involved in the rescue. Anderson informed everyone that the rescue mission was now his responsibility, and he succinctly laid out his plan. The key was the dominant terrain feature in the area: the Cam Lo River.

The Cam Lo River begins in the highlands along the Vietnam-Laos border and flows east, where its name changes to the Mieu Giang River. At the junction city of Dong Ha, the Mieu Giang becomes the Bo Dieu River, which forms the north fork of the Cua Viet River, which empties into the South China Sea. The two main highways in the area are the QL9 and the QL1. The QL9 runs east-west along the southern banks of the Cam Lo and Mieu Giang. At Dong Ha the QL9 intersects with the QL1, which runs north–south. Dong Ha is on the southern side of the river. When ARVN engineers and a U.S.

Marine adviser, Colonel John Ripley, had blown the two bridges at Dong Ha shortly after the offensive was launched, the main axis of the NVA drive shifted inland along TL 88, the road that roughly parallels the north bank of the river to the Cam Lo Bridge and other points farther west.

Anderson's plan in its original form called for a mixed U.S. Navy SEAL and South Vietnamese commando team to covertly rendezvous with the three men at pickup sites along the Mieu Giang riverbank and return with them. A coordinated series of air strikes would provide both cover and diversion for the rescue force. Anderson himself would command the mission from a forward base just off QL9. After briefing the SAR crews, Anderson left to assemble his SEAL team. The critical tasks in the rescue effort, however, fell on Hambleton, Clark, and Walker. They had to get to the riverbank pickup spots on their own. Because the North Vietnamese were monitoring the frequencies used by the rescue radios, instructions to the trio could not be sent in the clear. Ad hoc codes based on their individual experience had to be created for each man so that even though the enemy would hear the messages they would not understand their meaning. The men's parent units were contacted, informed of the situation, and the respective commanders came back with messages that were remarkable examples of personal and cultural cryptology.

Meanwhile, Lieutenant Colonel Anderson encountered manpower problems in assembling his team. He succeeded in obtaining for the mission six South Vietnamese sea commandos led by Lieutenant Tho. Unfortunately, the Naval Advisory Detachment based in Da Nang, which had worked with the joint personnel recovery center (JPRC), was all but shut down and was staffed by only one man. Everyone else had been sent home. Anderson quickly put in a call to Lieutenant Commander Craig Dorman in Saigon and asked for help. Fortunately for Anderson, sitting in Dorman's office, waiting for new orders, was U.S. Navy SEAL Lieutenant Tom Norris. Within minutes, orders were cut and Norris found himself on an airplane flying north.

Tommy Norris was special, even among the elite men of the U.S. Navy Sea, Air, Land (SEAL) teams. A 1967 graduate of the University of Maryland and an ACC wrestling champion, Norris had originally joined the service hoping to fly jets. Unfortunately, vision problems grounded him, and he went into the SEALs instead. It was a professional move that would ultimately make him a legend in an organization almost unknown in 1972.

Just ten years old, the U.S. Navy SEAL teams were an outgrowth of the famous underwater demolition teams (UDTs) of World War II. At the personal direction of President John F. Kennedy, who had a keen interest in counterinsurgency operations and unconventional warfare, the first teams were chartered on January 1, 1962. A hybrid of the UDTs and army raiding units like the Rangers, the SEALs have always been known for their extraordinary physical endurance and strength, along with fearsome combat skills.

Vietnam gave the SEALs an arena to hone their skills and develop a reputation for bravery and combat competence. Their reputation in littoral areas—rivers, deltas, and offshore—was paid for in blood, and earned by completing combat missions others would not undertake. Already, one SEAL, a future U.S. senator named Bob Kerrey, had won a Medal of Honor for his actions. Now Tommy Norris would have his own chance to earn the SEALs more acknowledgment for their skills and growing reputation.

As Norris was flying to Da Nang, Lieutenant Mark Clark was puzzling over the new instructions he had just received. Because he was already by the Cam Lo River, he would be rescued first. The message from the forward air controller flying overhead was, "When the moon goes over the mountains, become Esther Williams and go from Boise to Twin Falls." Clark didn't get it. He requested that the message be repeated. Again he drew a blank, and again he requested the message be transmitted. Finally, Clark understood what he needed to do. When night fell, he was to become like the movie star famous for her aquatics and swim to the designated rendezvous point. But he wasn't sure in which direction he had to swim. Pilots have been called many things, but one fault not normally attributed to them is being geographically challenged. Yet, Clark had to confess that even though he was a native of Idaho, he could not remember if Twin Falls was west or east of Boise. The FAC relayed the news to base. In a few minutes new instructions were transmitted that ordered him to go from Boise to Eglin, that is, Eglin Air Force Base near Valparaiso, Florida. Clark knew Eglin was east of Idaho and began to move that direction. An even more unusual set of instructions would be used for Gene Hambleton.

When Hambleton got his directions, he was so taken aback he asked Harold Icke (call sign Bilk 11) what he was smoking. Hambleton later said it was the "damnedest thing that I had ever heard!" The instructions were similar to those given to the others. They began with him making like Esther Williams and Charlie the Tuna. When Hambleton asked why Charlie the Tuna, Icke replied, "Because nobody ever catches Charlie the Tuna!"[16] Like Clark, Hambleton initially did not understand. Then he began to make sense of it. Charlie the Tuna was the animated "spokesfish" in the StarKist tuna television commercials back home. He never was caught by the StarKist boats because he was never "good enough." Hambleton radioed Icke and said that he thought he understood. Icke then broke into an off-key rendition of the song made famous by Al Jolson, "Swanee." This time it didn't take Hambleton as long to understand. Suwannee was a river in Florida. Hambleton had to admire whoever had come up with the demented code. If *he* had a hard time figuring out what it meant, any NVA radio operator monitoring the frequency would either find it incomprehensible, or think that the Americans were playing word games designed to mess with the enemy's minds.

But as Hambleton was well inland, he needed additional help. Between him and the river were fields, a village, assorted peasant huts, and numerous enemy fighting positions. Icke told him to get some rest. He'd give him his marching orders after the sun set. Icke signed off and returned to base. Hambleton took stock of his possessions. He discarded anything bulky, heavy, or unnecessary for his trek. Into the hole that had been his refuge went his helmet, oxygen mask, and most everything else. He kept his knife and pistol, the first aid kit, and his radio. He also kept his reading glasses. He had been wearing them the day he had been shot down, and amazingly they had not fallen off when he ejected from the EB-66. They were now his lucky charm. So long as he kept them, he felt, he wouldn't be captured. Charlie the Tuna, after all, Hambleton mused, also wore glasses. Hambleton then covered the hole with dirt and ferns. Then he found a new place nearby to hide, made himself comfortable, and waited for the sun to set.

It had been dark for several hours when Hambleton heard the familiar call from Bilk 11 on his radio. After acknowledging, Icke asked Hambleton if he understood where he was supposed to go and if he was ready to move. Hambleton replied affirmative to both questions. Icke then started talking to Hambleton about golf. Hambleton was an avid golfer with a three handicap, but he couldn't understand why that was important now. It was as if Icke decided to engage him in what amounted to an officer's club conversation over a couple of beers. Then Icke told Hambleton that he was going to play eighteen holes of golf: "The first hole is number one at Tucson National." It took Hambleton a half hour before he finally cracked the code.

Hambleton had a near-photographic memory, and golf holes on courses around the globe were his passion. His commanding officer, also a golfer, had briefed the SAR team about Hambleton's hobby and the courses he had played. The team then worked out a meandering route around the assorted dangers to the river based on various holes from a variety of golf courses. Instructions to Hambleton would be in golf terminology, something that the PAVN radio intercept teams had absolutely no knowledge of. Again, Hambleton had to admire whoever had come up with the code. Though it was not the sport of kings, golf was elite and foreign enough to put it outside the typical NVA soldier's cultural experience.

As the first hole at Tucson National was 408 yards long and ran southeast, they needed him to travel that distance to the southeast. Once he reached that "hole" he'd get instructions for his next hole. Hambleton's "course" included holes from courses at Shaw Air Force Base in South Carolina,

Hickam Air Force Base on Oahu, Davis-Monthan Air Force Base in Arizona, and the fourteenth hole from Augusta National Golf Club. With his compass in hand, Hambleton faced southeast and proceeded to "tee off." He had to avoid "sand traps" and "roughs" and keep ahead of assorted "duffers." He lost balls and had to take mulligans. It would take two nights for Hambleton to "play" through the most important golf game of his life.

While Hambleton was beginning his trek to the desired "nineteenth hole," Lieutenant Colonel Anderson was briefing his planned chief rescuer, Lt. Tommy Norris. Norris liked the plan's basic concept. By now, everyone was fully aware of the Easter offensive, and Norris believed that a small team stood a reasonably good chance of successfully completing the mission, since the enemy had bigger fish to fry. As Norris saw it, his biggest problem was not the North Vietnamese, but Lieutenant Colonel Anderson. SEALs are trained for independent operations, and once they know the objective, want to do things their own way. Anderson's plan went too far in its control of the movements of the ground team, and Norris was justifiably concerned. However, Tommy Norris decided early on to keep his counsel. Once he was on the move, what Anderson didn't know wouldn't hurt Norris. And if Anderson got too nosy on the radio, it would "malfunction." For the time being, however, Norris knew Anderson was a necessary part of the planned rescue effort and followed orders.

Anderson needed transport assistance from the 3rd ARVN Division once he and his men arrived in Dong Ha. Anderson explained his needs to the Da Nang base commander, Brigadier General Vu Van Giai. Giai reluctantly agreed to support the mission, something that was no surprise to those who knew his record. Later, Giai's competence as a combat leader during the Easter offensive was questioned, and South Vietnamese premier Nguyen Van Thieu ultimately relieved him of command. As it was, Giai was only partially reassured that he would not be responsible for the Americans' welfare if they got into trouble. He identified for Anderson the forward outpost position they could use: a bunker fortification dating back to French colonial times located on high ground a short distance south of QL9 that had a clear view of the Cam Lo River and bridge. It was an exposed position, well within range of North Vietnamese artillery. Even though he had been expressly ordered not to get too close to the front lines, Anderson decided to station himself there. With this information and permission in hand, Anderson and his team left for Dong Ha. Along the way he picked up additional help.

Lieutenant Colonel Louis Wagner was the American adviser for the ARVN 1st Armor Brigade at Dong Ha, and he agreed to assist as needed. The following morning, Anderson loaded up on rations for the troops at the bunker and headed west. Norris and his men would take up position along the riverbank and await the go signal from Anderson. Anderson had ordered Norris not to go upriver more than a kilometer behind enemy lines, but Norris decided to ignore Anderson's restriction.

Anderson had been told that the bunker was defended by a platoon of infantry reinforced with three tanks. When he arrived, he discovered that the truth was something less than advertised. The platoon turned out to be twenty tired and hungry men commanded by a nervous second lieutenant. The three tanks, though in good defensive positions, shared a total of nine rounds for their main guns. But the outpost site had a good view of the river and bridge. Lieutenant Colonel Anderson, who spoke Vietnamese, distributed his rations, told the platoon about his mission, and promised he would protect them if they were attacked by calling in defensive air strikes. There were, however, other problems developing for the three downed American airmen.

That evening, the American fliers discovered their means of escape and rescue was almost as dangerous as the North Vietnamese Army. The swift-flowing Cam Lo River was swollen by runoff from the spring monsoon rains. Though many stretches of its banks were overgrown with thick vegetation that could provide cover for the Americans, the increased level of the river also submerged branches, trunks, and other obstacles. Checking the river himself, Tommy Norris discovered that the current was so fast that even a strong man would have difficulty swimming long distances upriver. He and his team had to alternate between swimming and walking in order to reach the planned rendezvous point deep behind enemy lines. Now was the time to try to actually link up with the downed Americans and get them to safety. First would be Mark Clark.

Clark's troubles started shortly after he entered the river. A branch snagged on his life vest, causing it to partially inflate. Farther downriver, he almost drowned in a stretch of rapids when his feet got entangled in some submerged obstacles. Then, at the planned rendezvous site, Norris and his men, hiding in the thick riverbank foliage, were forced to watch helplessly as Clark floated by an approaching North Vietnamese patrol walking along the bank. Fortunately, the patrol did not see either Clark or Norris and his men and soon left. Clark, who still had his rescue radio, was told to find a secure location along the south bank and hole up there to await rescue. Dawn was approaching when Norris finally caught up with Clark, who was using a sunken sampan as shelter. Around 10:00 A.M., the group finally arrived back at the bunker, and Anderson happily sent out a message that Clark had been rescued. One down, two more to go.

Not long after Clark had been put in an armored personnel carrier and transported back to Dong Ha, the North Vietnamese launched an attack against the ARVN outpost and Lieutenant Colonel Anderson's bunker.

Artillery and rocket fire pounded the position, wounding Anderson, Lieutenant Tho, and most of the South Vietnamese commandos. While dealing with his wounds, Anderson requested immediate air strikes, which successfully turned back the North Vietnamese attack. When the attack concluded, Lieutenant Norris called for medevacs of the wounded. Lieutenant Colonel Anderson was flown to Saigon. Norris, with only three commandos left to assist him, was on his own, just as he had hoped he might be.

However, things didn't get any better for Norris that evening when he left with his much smaller group to rescue Hambleton. At one point upriver, two of the commandos threatened to stop and return to the outpost. They said they didn't want to risk their lives to rescue an American. Norris, who spoke only a little Vietnamese, managed to convince them that their chances of survival were better if they remained together. Norris and his team eventually reached a site that he judged suitable for a rendezvous and awaited Hambleton's arrival. But Hambleton wasn't coming because he couldn't.

Since the day of his shootdown, Hambleton had lost about forty pounds and was suffering from hunger, malnutrition, and emaciation. Just the effort to reach the river had exhausted him to the point of collapse. Realizing that he had reached the end of his rope, Hambleton radioed his position to Norris and said he couldn't go any farther. Norris began searching upriver, but Hambleton's instructions were so garbled, Norris was unable to find him. With the sun rising soon, Norris and his men were forced to return to the bunker. Gene Hambleton had to wait through another long day alone.

Norris had already stretched the limits of his orders. Now, free of oversight from Lieutenant Colonel Anderson, he threw them out entirely. His monitoring of the radio traffic between Bat 21 and Icke as he waited for the day to pass convinced him that Hambleton's poor condition made it imperative that he go to Hambleton, even though the flyer was well beyond the one-kilometer limit that had been placed on Norris. Thanks to grid coordinates and other information from Bilk 11 and other aircraft providing combat air patrol support over Hambleton, he had a good description of where Hambleton was. Armed with this information, Norris decided that when night fell, he would paddle a sampan upriver to retrieve Hambleton. And he'd take with him the only South Vietnamese commando who hadn't threatened mutiny, Petty Officer Nguyen Van Kiet.

The night was dark as the two men, disguised as local fishermen, quietly paddled upriver. Time and again enemy patrols forced them to seek refuge in the riverbank's foliage. A handy fog bank gave them the cover they needed to paddle swiftly up the Cam Lo, but when they emerged from the mist, they discovered that they had significantly overshot their objective, emerging directly under the Cam Lo Bridge. Fortunately, Norris and Kiet were able to reverse course without being detected by the troops crossing it.

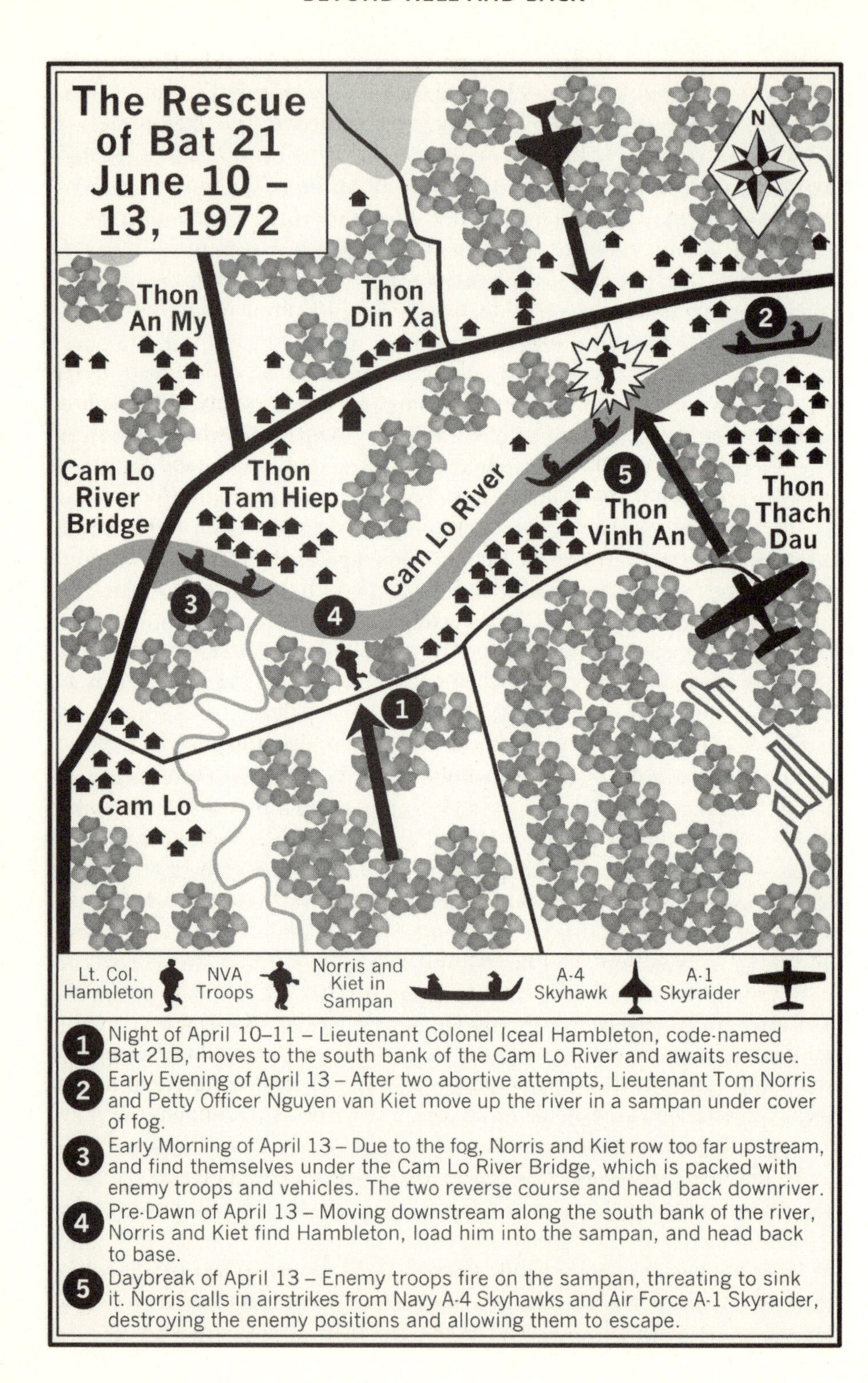
The Rescue of Bat 21 June 10 – 13, 1972
N
Thon An My
Thon Din Xa
Cam Lo River Bridge
Thon Tam Hiep
Cam Lo River
Thon Vinh An
Thon Thach Dau
Cam Lo
1
2
3
4
5
Lt. Col. Hambleton
NVA Troops
Norris and Kiet in Sampan
A-4 Skyhawk
A-1 Skyraider
1 Night of April 10–11 – Lieutenant Colonel Iceal Hambleton, code-named Bat 21B, moves to the south bank of the Cam Lo River and awaits rescue.
2 Early Evening of April 13 – After two abortive attempts, Lieutenant Tom Norris and Petty Officer Nguyen van Kiet move up the river in a sampan under cover of fog.
3 Early Morning of April 13 – Due to the fog, Norris and Kiet row too far upstream, and find themselves under the Cam Lo River Bridge, which is packed with enemy troops and vehicles. The two reverse course and head back downriver.
4 Pre-Dawn of April 13 – Moving downstream along the south bank of the river, Norris and Kiet find Hambleton, load him into the sampan, and head back to base.
5 Daybreak of April 13 – Enemy troops fire on the sampan, threating to sink it. Norris calls in airstrikes from Navy A-4 Skyhawks and Air Force A-1 Skyraider, destroying the enemy positions and allowing them to escape.

Slowly, they made their way downriver along its south side. Finally, they saw what appeared to be a body lying in the mud of the riverbank. It was Hambleton. He was weak and delirious but still alive. Hambleton himself remembered his first sight of Tommy Norris as "the most beautiful thing I had ever seen."[17] Time was now a critical factor because the sun would come up soon. Originally, Norris thought they should hide in the riverbank's heavy vegetation and wait for the following evening, but Hambleton's poor condition nixed that idea. Still, Norris knew he'd never reach friendly lines before daylight unless he got some help. He got on the radio to Bilk 11 flying overhead and laid out his plan.

With Hambleton lying in the middle of the sampan and hidden under some bamboo, Norris and Kiet made their dash toward safety in the fading darkness. They had paddled only a couple hundred yards when a group of North Vietnamese soldiers saw them and called out. Norris and Kiet kept paddling, making it around a bend in the river before an alarm was raised.

Their luck turned sour when they came opposite a village on the north bank. A heavy machine gun position in it opened fire on them. Quickly Norris and Kiet paddled to the south bank and found a hiding spot in the foliage. They were trapped and called in their one remaining trump card: American airpower. Norris radioed Bilk 11 for an air strike, telling Icke that unless he could get that gun position knocked out, their capture was all but certain. Icke put in a call for assistance ASAP and struck pay dirt.

Five A-4 Skyhawks from the USS *Hancock* responded and began a series of sweeps against enemy positions in and around the village. Two air force A-1s carrying napalm, rockets, and white phosphorus smoke bombs joined them. With instructions coming from Icke in the air and Norris from the south bank, the seven airplanes wiped out every enemy position they could find on the river's north bank. Finally, the A-1s dropped their smoke bombs. With the smoke as cover, Norris and Kiet got back into the sampan where they had hidden Hambleton and began paddling downriver as fast as they could.

Finally they reached the shore opposite the bunker, though even there they were still not safe. As the trio clambered up the muddy bank, enemy troops on the north side of the river shot at them with small arms, mortar, and rocket fire. But this time South Vietnamese troops were there to return fire, augmented by another air strike. The enemy threat was eliminated without any further friendly casualties.

An armored personnel carrier soon arrived and took Hambleton, Norris, and Kiet to Dong Ha. After eleven days, Gene Hambleton's ordeal was finally over.

Two men had been successfully rescued. Sadly, there would not be a third. Lt. Bruce Walker was discovered by North Vietnamese troops as he was making his way to the Cam Lo River. Despite air strikes, which immediately took the enemy troops under fire, Walker was killed by the North Vietnamese before he could escape. The final act of the rescue of Bat 21 had been played out. But the story was hardly over.

Two men had been successfully rescued when many people had given up hope. Gene Hambleton and his precious cache of electronic warfare knowledge were denied to the North Vietnamese and their Communist allies, itself a major military victory in the cold war. In gratitude, Petty Officer Nguyen Van Kiet was awarded the Navy Cross, the only Vietnamese to receive the honor. There would be other decorations and awards handed out from the mission as well.

Word of the Bat 21 rescue got out quickly and soon made newspapers around the world. A reporter stationed in Dong Ha, upon hearing the high points of the story, said to Norris, "It must have been tough out there. I bet you wouldn't do that again." Norris looked at him and replied, "An American was down in enemy territory. Of course I'd do it again." It was vintage Tommy Norris, who found himself nominated for the Medal of Honor for his rescue of Hambleton and Clark. Before he could be awarded the decoration however, there would be six more months of combat for the young SEAL, and then the greatest test of his life.

On October 31, 1972, Tommy Norris sustained a near-mortal head wound during combat, and would have died but for an extraordinary rescue by fellow SEAL Michael Thornton. Going to where Norris had fallen, Thornton personally killed two enemy soldiers, then spent over two hours towing the unconscious Norris until they could be picked up by friendly support vessels. Amazingly, Thornton himself was nominated for the Medal of Honor, the only known instance when one recipient of the decoration earned his award saving the life of another recipient.

However, it would take two years in the hospital, six operations, and another year of therapy before Tommy Norris could collect his decoration for the Bat 21 rescue. Finally, on April 3, 1976, President Gerald Ford presented Lieutenant Tom Norris the Medal of Honor. Mustered out of the navy due to his wounds, Norris continued his rehabilitation and eventually joined the FBI as an agent in 1979, beginning a twenty-year career in law enforcement. Today, quietly retired, he stands as an icon in the special operations community for his bravery and service. To the young men today who want to be SEALs, he is the yardstick they measure themselves by, as well as Gene Hambleton, who died in 2004.

The most complex search-and-rescue effort in the Vietnam War was now history, but the lessons from and analysis of what happened in Quang Tri Province that April still go on today. The air force teaches the lessons of the failed rescue attempts to their new combat SAR recruits, making the point that sometimes you need a few good men on the ground to make an extraction possible. For this they now have the pararescue jumpers, or PJs as they are known, who have brought home numerous downed fliers in war and peace. For the SEALs, the actions of Tommy Norris and Petty Officer Kiet are the examples they seek from all their recruits. And down at U.S. Special Operations Command headquarters in Tampa, there is the hope that never again will they need to conduct a rescue operation like the one that saved Bat 21 Bravo.

1. Douglas Pike, "Viet Cong," www.vietpage.com/archive_news/politics/2003/Aug/4/0126.html

2. Davidson, *Vietnam at War,* 3.

3. Lavalle, *Airpower and the 1972 Spring Invasion,* 4.

4. Van Nederveen, *Sparks over Vietnam,* 64.

5. Colburn, *Running on Empty,* 11.

6. Blumentritt, *Playing Defense and Offense,* 1.

7. Colburn, *Running on Empty,* 13.

8. U.S. Air Force, Air Force Doctrine Document 2-1.6, *Combat Search and Rescue,* July 15, 2000, ii.

9. Ibid., 20.

10. Blumentritt, *Playing Defense and Offense,* 33.

11. Colburn, *Running on Empty,* 7.

12. Air Force Doctrine Document 2-1.6. *Combat Search and Rescue,* 23.

13. Colburn, *Running on Empty,* 9.

14. Turley, *The Easter Offensive,* 86.

15. Lavalle, *Airpower and the 1972 Spring Invasion,* 41.

16. Whitcomb, *The Rescue of Bat 21,* 126.

17. Interview Lt. Col. Iceal Hambleton, *American Commandos III: Nightriders,* for Discovery Communications, 2001.

3

For Want of a Nail . . . Operation Eagle Claw

For want of a nail, the shoe was lost;
For want of the shoe, the horse was lost;
For want of the horse, the rider was lost;
For want of the rider, the battle was lost;
For want of the battle, the kingdom was lost;
And all for the want of a horseshoe nail.

—Children's nursery rhyme

On November 4, 1979, a group of Iranian students stormed the U.S. embassy in Tehran and took hostage all the Americans in the compound. Their proclaimed intent was twofold. They wished to force the United States to return the exiled shah of Iran, who was in America for medical treatment. They were also seeking evidence of a CIA plot to overthrow the new Islamic republic that had formed under the cleric Ayatollah Ruholla Khomeini. While publicly pursuing diplomatic efforts to free the captive Americans, President Jimmy Carter covertly authorized a top-secret rescue mission, Operation Eagle Claw. It would be conducted by America's new and equally secret counterterrorist unit, the 1st Special Forces Operational Detachment Delta—Delta Force, commanded by its founder, Colonel Charles Beckwith. The hostage crisis dominated world news, the rescue attempt failed disastrously, the crisis ultimately lasted 444 days, and Eagle Claw's failure in large part contributed to President Carter's defeat in the 1980 presidential election. The mission became a textbook example that has been studied by special operations personnel ever since. More importantly, Operation Eagle Claw became the touchstone for the creation of Special Operations Command (SOCOM).

April 1, 1980: Dasht-e Kavir, Iran

The Dasht-e Kavir, or Great Salt Desert, of Iran is a five-hundred-mile-long and two-hundred-mile-wide expanse of sand and salt (*kavir* is Farsi for "salt marsh") located in the high plateau region of north central Iran. It is both desolate and unpopulated. Large tracts of it are broad, flat, and hard packed. Its western edge is roughly a hundred miles southeast of Tehran.

The desolate nature of the terrain made it a preferred location for mounting a covert rescue operation. On this cold, early spring night, a De Havilland Twin Otter aircraft, favored by the CIA for deep penetration clandestine missions, was parked not far from a forlorn stretch of graded dirt road almost sixty miles from the closest thing that might be called a town. While the two pilots remained in the airplane, a motorcyclist assembled his collapsible off-road vehicle for a specialized midnight cruise on a night he would later say was "so black you couldn't have found warts on a toad."[1] The biker, dressed in black Levi's, black shirt, black cap, and wearing night vision goggles, began driving his dirt bike over the compacted ground in a seemingly random yet purposeful geometric pattern. The three men were supposed to be on the ground for less than an hour; the man on the dirt bike had much to accomplish before they left.

The motorcyclist was U.S. Air Force combat controller Major John Carney, nicknamed Coach as the result of an eight-year stint as an assistant football coach at the Air Force Academy. Described as a natural leader and a person worth a hundred planes or ships, Carney had been "volunteered" for this mission by Colonel Charles Beckwith, who wanted someone he knew and trusted to personally eyeball the site.

Shortly after he began driving his dirt bike, Carney found himself bouncing across the vehicle tracks of the dirt road. Something was wrong—either he was completely disoriented or the plane had landed in a different location from the one it was supposed to. Carney rode back to the Twin Otter, where he found the pilot and copilot, both old CIA hands who had flown Air America missions during the Vietnam War, asleep. He woke the pilot and asked him where he had landed the plane. The pilot opened one eye, glanced around, and said, "We landed north of the road. Look to the south."[2] Then he closed his eye and went back to sleep. During the briefing, the plan called for the Twin Otter to touch down south of the road. Now correctly oriented, Carney returned to his motorcycle and got to work.

Carney's mission was to mark boundaries and install landing lights—turn a barren stretch of salt flat into a clandestine airstrip. Calling it an airstrip was being charitable, as the place was really just a flat spot bisected by a dirt road that ran between "nowhere" and "no place."

But for the American aircraft that would arrive later that month, this remote location would be the most important piece of territory in Iran—

Desert One, the refueling site for Operation Eagle Claw, the planned rescue of the fifty-two Americans being held hostage in Tehran.

The airstrip Major Carney was charged with laying out had to be large enough for a C-130 Hercules transport to make a combat landing and roll out—just over 3,100 feet long. At various points on the perimeter of the intended landing area, Carney used a marine K-bar knife to dig into the hard ground and bury special ground lights, which could be remotely activated by radio. These would provide a landing aim point for six Hercules transports loaded with fuel and special operations commandos and six to eight RH-53D Sea Stallion helicopters.

Carney also took soil samples so that experts back in the States could evaluate the suitability of the ground for C-130 landings and takeoffs. At one point during the night, a pair of approaching headlights appeared in the distance. Carney immediately stopped work and laid his dirt bike and himself flat on the ground, praying that the vehicle and its passengers would just drive by and not notice him or his motorcycle, and especially the Twin Otter. When the vehicle continued down the road, Carney returned to work. Before he was through, three more Iranian vehicles would drive by. None would stop. Whether they saw anything and reported it, Carney had no way of knowing. But within the prescribed hour, Carney, together with his soil samples and collapsed dirt bike and other gear, had wedged himself back into the aircraft.

Their mission accomplished, the pilots, now awake, started the Twin Otter's engines, taxied down the hard-packed desert floor, and took off into the starless sky.

It was Tuesday, April 1, in Iran, Islamic Republic Day—the anniversary of the founding of the new revolutionary theocracy led by the Ayatollah Ruholla Khomeini. Elsewhere, it was April Fool's Day. As the Twin Otter flew back to its base in Oman, Major Carney shifted in the cramped space between the large auxiliary fuel bladder and equipment from the mission and hoped that wasn't an omen.

November 1979

When the Iranian hostage crisis erupted in November 1979, most Americans were as ignorant of its cause as they were in 1964 of the location of Vietnam. What many subsequently discovered was that the hostage crisis had its roots in the generation-long American involvement inside the government of Ayatollah Khomeini's predecessor, the empire of the Peacock Throne. The reason for America's long-term involvement was simple: oil.

Vast underground reserves of petroleum were discovered shortly after World War I on both sides of the Persian Gulf. Oil, specifically the industrialized West's need for it, changed the face of a region heretofore known for its religious history, rugs, sand, and camels. This became especially true once World War II concluded and the regional colonial powers of France and Great Britain transferred official political authority to local leadership, while continuing their positions of commercial dominance and exploitation. This happy (at least in Western eyes) state of affairs lasted until the early 1950s, when a pan-Islamic socialist movement led by dynamic and charismatic young nationalists swept the region from Egypt to Iran. In Egypt, the foremost nationalist was Gamal Abdel Nasser, who led the overthrow of the corrupt regime of King Farouk. In Iran, the nationalist was Dr. Mohammed Mossadegh, who was instrumental in Reza Shah Pahlavi's abdication in 1944 in favor of his twenty-two-year-old son, Mohammad Reza Pahlavi.

Elected Iran's prime minister in 1951, Mossadegh made a move not uncommon to the socialist leaders of his generation: he unilaterally nationalized major foreign assets, the most important of them belonging to American and British petroleum companies. This behavior might have been tolerated in Washington, D.C., and London, had Mossadegh not made one mistake. He became a bit too accommodating to his neighbor to the north, the Soviet Union, which was locked in an ideological cold war with the West.

The United States and England could not afford to allow Iran, with its strategically important oil reserves, to fall into the Soviet sphere. They agreed that Mossadegh had to go. The question was: how? Though the full story of what happened is beyond the scope of this chapter (and some details are still classified), a few known facts are germane.

The American government's response to the Iranian situation was unconventional in its approach and masterful in its execution. Mossadegh never saw it coming. Instead of sending its army, navy, and air force to restore nationalized oil assets, the United States turned to an asset that had been created less than ten years earlier, the Central Intelligence Agency. The CIA was America's first civilian intelligence organization. Though theoretically chartered only to gather information, CIA operatives, many drawn from its World War II military predecessor, the Office of Strategic Services (OSS), had exploited the cold war tensions of the time to expand its mandate to include clandestine field operations, all in the name of national security. CIA field operatives had already conducted black (covert) propaganda operations and helped rig elections in France, Greece, and Italy to ensure the defeat of Communist Party candidates. Now the CIA was told to arrange the downfall of an entire sovereign government. It would accomplish it using just one primary agent—Kermit Roosevelt, the grandson of President Theodore Roosevelt.

Within just a few weeks of his arrival in Tehran in 1953, Roosevelt established himself as a one-man counterrevolution, subverting Iranian military leaders, arranging for the return of the shah from exile in Switzerland, and carefully spreading around CIA-supplied cash to grease the wheels of the plot. Code-named Operation Ajax, it was a masterpiece of simplicity, economy, and boldness. (Ironically, one of Roosevelt's key supporters and subordinates was H. Norman Schwarzkopf, former head of the New Jersey State Police, commander of the shah's imperial guard during World War II, and father of the future general who would command the coalition forces during Operation Desert Shield/Desert Storm.)

In July 1953, Operation Ajax was launched. The shah ordered Prime Minister Mossadegh deposed and a proxy installed. When Mossadegh resisted ousting, he was driven from office by a military coup sponsored by Roosevelt. General Fazlollah Zahedi was installed as Mossadegh's replacement, and a new government acceptable to the West was installed. The Western oil companies then negotiated the return of their facilities and restoration of their oil contracts under very favorable royalty terms. "Normalcy" had been restored to the Peacock Throne, though there would later be consequences, what intelligence professionals call blowback—the unintended consequences of U.S. government international activities that are kept secret from the American people.[3]

However, the serene Western view of Iran between 1953 and 1979 was hardly the whole story of life under the shah. Following Operation Ajax, the shah established a secret police force known as SAVAK, whose repressive policies and interrogation techniques became infamous around the world. In addition, other factors, including the lack of an emerging Iranian middle class, repression of antigovernment Shiite clerics and other religious leaders, and the shah's autocratic "let them eat cake" attitude toward the general populace, ensured that by the end of the 1970s Iran was ripe for revolution.

The upheaval began in 1978 with a series of antigovernment student riots throughout Iran, coupled with news that the shah was terminally ill with non-Hodgkin's lymphoma. When the shah left at the behest of his government to seek treatment, the revolutionaries smelled opportunity, and what today is called the Islamic revolution was under way. The demise of the Peacock Throne was sealed when Ayatollah Ruholla Khomeini returned from his exile in Paris, rejected power-sharing proposals from the existing government, appointed a new Islamic government of his own, and dissolved the monarchy. The shah's exile had begun. With the shah absent and the political situation becoming fluid, if not chaotic, resentment against decades of Western interference in Iran burst to the surface among the populace, causing expatriates, especially Americans, to leave the country.

By the time of the shah's departure, most foreign contractor and military personnel had already left Iran. Only small diplomatic staffs at embassies remained to look after the interests of their respective countries. Already there had been some ugly incidents between the new Iranian government and foreigners, including the detention of a number of American contract workers from the Electronic Data Systems (EDS) Corporation. These detainees were forcibly rescued in a covert civilian operation privately funded by EDS founder H. Ross Perot in February 1970. Code-named Operation Hotfoot, it was led by retired army colonel Arthur "Bull" Simons, who had commanded the Son Tay rescue ground force (see chapter 1). Demonstrations against America—which Khomeini had branded "the Great Satan"— and other Western nations seen as friendly to the shah's regime now became a daily occurrence, and rioting was not unusual.

Twice in February, small groups of Iranians armed with rifles attacked the U.S. embassy compound. In one incident, an Iranian who worked for the embassy was killed and four Americans were wounded before marine guards drove off the attackers. Later that year, a mob clambered over the fence into the U.S. embassy compound and for a time occupied several buildings before withdrawing peacefully.

It seemed that the situation, though tense, couldn't get worse. Then, on November 4, 1979, it did.

Encouraged by Ayatollah Khomeini, the acknowledged supreme leader of the country, fanatic student demonstrators protesting the shah's medical treatment in the United States overran the U.S. embassy complex, occupied the installation, and took hostage sixty-six of the embassy's personnel. Several days later, Khomeini tacitly endorsed the occupation. What came to be known as the Iranian hostage crisis was under way.

Almost from the moment Khomeini's Islamic government took power, it had embarked on a wide-ranging campaign of brinksmanship, asserting its radical Shiite fundamentalism to its Sunni Muslim neighbors and an obdurate nationalism that appeared to have an arbitrary respect for international law. Since the violation of a foreign embassy was technically an act of war, by condoning the students' action Khomeini and his followers were taking a grave risk. However, it proved to be a calculation that worked.

President Jimmy Carter was a man of deep religious convictions whose moral character appealed to an America with still-fresh memories of the recently concluded Vietnam War and the Watergate scandal that had forced President Richard Nixon to resign in disgrace. The former governor of Georgia had successfully exploited his lack of experience in national politics and foreign affairs to win the election. With the hostage situation in Iran, followed by the Soviet invasion of Afghanistan in December, President Carter faced crises of the first order that, coming back-to-back as they did, would have taxed the abilities of many of his more experienced and foreign affairs–savvy predecessors.

A believer in the value and moral superiority of diplomacy, Carter decided initially to try to resolve the hostage crisis peacefully. His secretary of state, Cyrus Vance, was an avowed pacifist—it was widely known in the administration that he planned to resign should the military card ever be played. In a decision that proved strategically disastrous because it ultimately made a captive of Carter's administration as well, both agreed that they would make the lives of the hostages in Tehran the administration's paramount concern. Secretary Vance then initiated a back-channel diplomatic dialogue with the Iranians to seek the hostages' release.

What the president and his secretary of state failed to take into account was the chaotic political power struggle that was wracking the new regime. There was never a question that Khomeini was the leader of the country. Beyond that, the internecine power struggles among the secular and religious leaders in the government turned the Iranian political climate into a literal death trap. Today's high-level official who could broker a release might be tomorrow's executed apostate, with images of his corpse broadcast on television and printed in newspapers across Iran and, in some cases, the world.

If President Carter and Secretary Vance found it difficult to understand and deal with their counterparts in Iran, Ayatollah Khomeini and the radical students showed themselves to be naïfs as well, where American politics were concerned. Khomeini ordered the African American and female hostages to be freed. This release occurred on Thanksgiving Day. Khomeini did so as a "gesture to oppressed African-Americans and as a demonstration of the 'special status' accorded to women under Islamic rule."[4] Another hostage, suffering from multiple sclerosis, was also released. The students believed that this action would inspire African Americans to rally to the Iranians' cause and stage demonstrations throughout the United States in their support. The students were shocked when the imagined demonstrations failed to materialize.

The original intent had been to occupy the embassy for three days. But as sometimes happens, the event, and outsiders, took control of the people who inspired it. The students-cum-jailers ensconced in the embassy soon found that they, too, were pawns in a high-stakes game of international poker. And no one, not even the president of the United States, could predict how long the standoff would last.

Within hours of the embassy's seizure, the Pentagon began to make contingency plans for a rescue of the hostages. However, senior leaders at the White House and the Pentagon quickly realized that American options for action in the crisis were few and thin. Almost everything about a potential rescue mission was either impossible in the short term or outside the experience base of the U.S. military. In addition, there was the state of the U.S. military itself in the late 1970s, which was, in brief, not good.

More interested in enlarging the Great Society programs initiated by President Lyndon Johnson in the 1960s and trying to dictate human rights policy worldwide, President Carter focused his primary interest in the U.S.

military on how its budget could be trimmed so his preferred programs could be funded—a somewhat ironic stand for a former naval officer with a background in nuclear physics and agriculture. When he attended to overseas military commitments, Carter's defense policy was devoted almost exclusively to Europe and NATO's response to a Soviet attack. This was logical but offered no planning or resources for the unanticipated hostage crisis.

Already well into transition to an all-volunteer force, the American military of 1979 was undermanned and poorly trained and disciplined, and lacking the weapons and equipment to accomplish its assigned roles and missions. Now it was being asked to consider the kind of operation it had not undertaken since the Boxer Rebellion in China in 1900, when a multinational force led by the United States rescued its legation and other foreign nationals besieged in Peking (now Beijing). And the tools to do the job were also lacking.

The rescue of the hostages at the American embassy in Tehran called for resources similar to those used in Operation Kingpin, the attempted POW rescue at Son Tay prison in North Vietnam in 1970 (see chapter 1). While the ingress and egress distances in the Tehran crisis were greater, the basic force structure and capabilities required were similar. Unfortunately, the American Special Operations Forces (SOFs) of 1979 were a shadow of their Vietnam-era strength and capabilities. The helicopter situation was just one of many examples of how bare its cupboard had become. The HH-3 Jolly Green Giant and HH-53 Super Jolly Green Giant SOF helicopters had either been retired or were in the process of being upgraded, without backup or replacement available. The gap between the retirement of the Jolly Green Giants and arrival of the Super Stallions (in inventory in other branches) had been extended as a result of the Carter administration's military budget cutbacks, which would ultimately impact every level of Operation Eagle Claw.

If there was a bright spot in the potential rescue capability of the U.S. military, it was in counterterrorism units. The 1970s had seen the rise of international terrorism around the world. A number of countries had been galvanized into creating specialized counterterrorism units as a response to the tragic and sometimes bloody outcomes of encounters with groups such as Black September, the Red Brigades, and the Baader-Meinhof Gang. The British Special Air Service (SAS) and West German GSG-9, among others, had already notched memorable success. Examples include the Israeli rescue of Air France flight 139 at Entebbe Airport in Uganda in 1976, and the GSG-9 rescue of Lufthansa flight 181 at Mogadishu, Somalia, in 1977.

Though the American SOF community had been gutted after Vietnam, there were still visionary leaders who saw the need for their specialized talents, and one of these was then Army Vice Chief of Staff General Edward Charles "Shy" Meyer. General Meyer, who had a terrorist bomb blow up outside his headquarters building in Germany several years earlier, was an early supporter of a specialized counterterrorism unit for the U.S. military. His efforts gained traction in 1977 when the success of the West German counterterrorist unit, GSG-9, at Mogadishu sparked the interest of President Carter. Perhaps seeing this as an alternative to larger military operations in the event of a terrorist strike, Carter supported the idea, and Meyer got permission to raise his unit. The new unit, the 1st Special Forces Operational Detachment–Delta (SFOD-D), or simply Delta Force as it became known, was authorized on November 19, 1977, and Colonel Charlie Beckwith was its first commander.

Charles Alvin "Chargin' Charlie" Beckwith was a career army officer who had made almost as many enemies within the military as he had made friends. Opinionated, tough (he survived a .51-caliber bullet to the abdomen during the Vietnam War), and an inspiring leader, Beckwith had commanded the Special Forces unit code-named Project Delta in Vietnam. He had been awarded the Distinguished Service Cross, the Silver Star with Oak Leaf Cluster, the Legion of Merit, the Bronze Star, and the Purple Heart. He had served as an exchange officer with the elite British SAS special operations unit. This, combined with his experience in Vietnam, made him a passionate advocate for special operations. Beckwith had been pushing for a special counterterrorist team with such determination that more than once his career was at risk. When he was given the go-ahead to form Delta, his sense of vindication was balanced by the sobering reality of what he knew had to be done to make the unit operational.

The recruitment, training, equipping, certification, and documentation so that the unit could be sustained over time took two years. Ironically, SFOD-D finished its final validation the same day that the embassy in Tehran was seized. The good news for Delta was that hostage rescue and embassy takeovers were contingencies that they had worked on during training. The bad news was that the unit lacked transportation to the target area, a command structure to work under, and on-site intelligence and ground support in Iran. It also lacked its own budget. To get most of what it wanted and needed for Eagle Claw, Delta would have to beg, borrow, and steal from the other branches, who were themselves suffering from recent government cutbacks.

Of all the elements lacking for a successful hostage rescue mission in Iran, on-site intelligence and covert ground support were most critical. Here one of President Carter's "corrective" policy decisions came home to roost with unfortunate consequences, this time concerning the CIA.

The CIA had just emerged from the most damaging period in its history, when much of its classified field operations around the world had been exposed during Senate hearings led by Senator Frank Church of Idaho. The

Church committee hearings revealed much of the agency's clandestine field operations, including Operation Ajax in Iran, the Bay of Pigs, Operation Mongoose against Fidel Castro, and the ouster of Salvador Allende in Chile, among others. The result was a massive overhaul and tightening of congressional oversight policy and the near emasculation of CIA field operations.

Carter's director of Central Intelligence (DCI), Rear Admiral Stansfield Turner, made the decision to base national intelligence collection on "technical means," such as aircraft, reconnaissance satellites, and ground intercept stations. HUMINT, or human intelligence, was deemphasized, and the old hands from the early days and/or the OSS were either retired or fired. By 1979, the Operations Directorate, which ran field and embassy operations for the CIA, had only a fraction of its previous personnel and capabilities.

In fact, the Tehran embassy had only two CIA station personnel when it was overrun, and their tiny existing networks of contacts were rapidly rolled up and neutralized (in some cases that meant killed) by Khomeini's followers. So at the very moment when America needed field agents on the ground in Iran, there were none to be had. Worse, fear of an ongoing operation being exposed in an open congressional hearing meant that potentially cooperative locals in a hostile foreign country, the key to any HUMINT collection network, wanted nothing to do with the CIA or the U.S.A. There was, however, a small local network of CIA informants in Tehran that might be reactivated if someone credible could get back into the city and run them.

If the United States wanted a military option to go into Iran to rescue the fifty-two remaining hostages, it would have to patch together an operation from bits and pieces and try to guide it with eyes and ears in Iran that did not exist in November 1979. Despite these obstacles, the Pentagon, led by Chairman of the Joint Chiefs of Staff David C. Jones, was going to try. An old Strategic Air Command bomber pilot who had served under bosses that included the legendary general Curtis LeMay, Jones was not about to tell President Carter and the nation that the military couldn't rescue their fellow citizens.

Within hours of the embassy takeover, Colonel Beckwith found himself at the Pentagon, watching members of the Joint Staff essentially falling over themselves trying to plug Delta into all manner of rescue mission ideas, none of which he was being consulted on. Seeing Beckwith's consternation and knowing the outburst sure to come, Shy Meyer took Beckwith aside, informed him that none of what he had just seen was going to determine the final configuration of Operation Rice Bowl, as the planning stage was called, and introduced him to the real commander of that planning effort, Air Force Major General James B. Vaught. Beckwith would be the ground force commander for Rice Bowl and would coordinate transportation, logistics, intelligence, and all the other details needed to make a credible operation out of the chaos he had seen that Monday at the Pentagon.

During one early conversation with General Vaught during the preliminary planning stage, the dialogue reportedly went:

"What's the risk, Colonel Beckwith?"

"Oh, about 99.9 percent."

"What's the probability of success?"

"Zero."

"Well, we can't do it."

"You're right, Boss."

"I've got to buy time from the JCS."[5]

Beckwith and Vaught got their extra time and continued to look for options to give Rice Bowl a real chance of success. For Beckwith, this meant sending a sizable chunk of Delta Force to a remote site in North Carolina into what is called isolation, to begin planning and study of the Tehran embassy for a possible assault-and-rescue operation. He also dispatched a small team of Delta personnel and advisers to the Pentagon, to try to insert reality into the Joint Staff planning process, since none there was even remotely aware of the unit's capabilities and structure. That done, Beckwith then dove into the planning of the operation with Vaught.

The plan that emerged for Rice Bowl was a patchwork quilt of units, personnel, and ideas that immediately struck those involved as being less than ideal.

In its essence, the ground team (Delta) led by Colonel Beckwith would be transported from a secure location to a site near the embassy, where it would split into separate teams. The main ground team would then move to the American embassy, scale the walls, eliminate the student guards, free the hostages, and then move to a nearby soccer field, where support helicopters would pick them up. Another small ground force would rescue several American diplomats from the Iranian foreign ministry building and load onto their own helicopter. The choppers would then fly to a nearby abandoned airfield, which would be seized by a company of Rangers. Then air force C-141 jet transports would pick everyone up, the helicopters would be destroyed, and the entire force would fly to the nearest permissible international airspace. Navy fighters and attack aircraft would provide cover for this part of the operation, along with air force AC-130 gunships lending close air support (CAS).

From the very beginning, the primary planning problem was the delivery of the ground teams and their extraction following the rescue operation. Beckwith nixed one early idea of parachuting the teams into Tehran. He knew from a lifetime of military experience that such operations invariably created casualties and problems. Rice Bowl required a precision approach, and in lieu of a combat landing with a C-130 Hercules, such as the Israelis had done at Entebbe, the only option available was some kind of transport helicopter.

To help deal with the challenge, Vaught was assigned an air force officer, Colonel James Kyle, to lead the air elements and be the on-scene commander in Iran. Given the limitations of the helicopter fleets of the army, navy, air force, and marines, and the lack of rotary-winged aircraft with in-flight refueling capability, Kyle's choice was the RH-53D Sea Stallion. The RH-53Ds for Rice Bowl would be drawn from navy mine-hunting squadrons, with eight helicopters to be predeployed aboard the nuclear supercarrier USS *Nimitz* (CVN 68). Other RH-53Ds would be used in stateside training.

Used in the clearing of naval mines in shallow water, the RH-53D was equipped with larger fuel tanks than the marine version and had at that time the best payload and range available. While the RH-53D could be equipped with an in-flight refueling probe if needed, the decision was made to stage the aircraft from the covert refueling site in Iran code-named Desert One. In-flight refueling over hostile territory was considered too risky. It was a difficult chore, especially at the low altitudes needed to avoid Iranian radar.

However, that decision raised almost as many problems as it solved. For starters, the Sea Stallions were not exactly factory fresh. Years of hard flying,

RH-53D SEA STALLION

The Sikorsky H-53 is arguably one of the most versatile families of helicopters ever manufactured. It includes the Sea Stallion, Super Jolly Green Giant, Pave Low, Super Stallion, and other specialized models. The Sea Stallion, originally developed for use by the U.S. Marine Corps, is also used by the U.S. Navy, as well as other nations. The navy RH-53D Sea Stallion variant was used primarily for airborne minesweeping countermeasures.

SPECIFICATIONS

Photo: U.S. Department of Defense

Manufacturer: Sikorsky
Crew: Three
Power plant: Two General Electric T64-GE-413 turboshaft engines producing 3,925 shaft horsepower each
Length: 88 feet 6 inches (29.96 meters)
Height: 24 feet 11 inches (7.59 meters)
Rotor diameter: 72 feet 2.7 inches (22.01 meters)
Speed: 130 knots (149.5 mph)
Maximum takeoff weight: 42,000 pounds (19,068 kilograms)
Range: 690 miles (600 nautical miles)
Armament: Two XM-218 .50-caliber machine guns

including helping clear North Vietnamese harbors and the Suez Canal of mines, had worn and torn the airframes. And in another legacy of military budget cutbacks, because mine-clearing helicopters were at the end of the line when it came to doling out maintenance dollars, the squadrons suffered from a chronic lack of spare parts and were forced to extend maintenance cycles.

Helicopter crews were also a problem. Marine Lieutenant Colonel Edward Seiffert, a veteran CH-53 pilot who had flown search-and-rescue missions in Vietnam, was selected to lead the helicopter element. He had considerable experience flying with the early night-vision goggles that would be used on the mission. Unfortunately, not many of his flight personnel, especially the navy pilots, shared that skill, nor did they have other key experience necessary for the mission. The navy mine-clearing aircrews were used to a particular kind of flying, normally straight and level in daylight, at low altitude and over water, towing a mine sled. Rice Bowl would require flying hundreds of miles during the night, using night vision goggles, hugging terrain that included mountains and desert, and doing so under quite austere and stressful conditions.

Initially it was thought the problem could be overcome by uniting navy pilots with marine copilots, but the pairing proved unworkable. Early evaluations showed that most of the navy crews were not equipped for the kind of flying required for Rice Bowl, and Seiffert was able to replace most of the naval aviators with marines from more adequately experienced CH-53D transport squadrons. The final mix of sixteen RH-53D flight crewmen would be composed of twelve marines, three naval aviators, and a single air force pilot—a personnel mix that would have unexpected consequences at Desert One.

The challenges continued. Once the helicopters were selected, there came a host of new problems: refueling the helicopters on the way to Tehran and getting them loaded with Beckwith's commandos, support personnel, and gear. Colonel Kyle decided to use EC-130 Hercules turboprop transports equipped with large rubber fuel bladders to refuel the helicopters at Desert One. The EC-130s would also carry the ground force and their equipment, along with a ground security team of Rangers and air force combat controllers, to run operations at Desert One. The Hercules transports would then fly back to their staging base in Oman and await word to fly back into Iran for the next phase of the operation.

The final element General Vaught and his team had to deal with was the problem of on-the-ground intelligence and support in Tehran itself. Because of the limited personnel available in late 1979, the CIA got a retired field operative with experience in Iran, code-named Bob, to return to active service and enter Tehran to start laying the groundwork for Rice Bowl. Bob was able to move easily, slipping in and out of Iran thanks to the ongoing chaos following the ayatollah's takeover. With the assistance of a wealthy expatriate Iranian whom he knew and trusted, he managed to purchase five trucks and several vans that would be used to transport Beckwith's ground teams from Desert Two, the landing zone outside Tehran, to where the rescue would actually be effected. He also rented a warehouse to store the vehicles.

Unfortunately, neither man was having any success finding out where on the twenty-seven-acre embassy campus the hostages were being kept. The real problem was that someone needed to get into Tehran to act as the advance man for Rice Bowl, continue making arrangements for the mission, and provide regular on-scene reconnaissance of the embassy and "ground truth" (military parlance for conditions that actually exist) in Tehran itself. With the CIA's Operations Directorate gutted under Admiral Turner, somebody with exceptional field skills would need to be recruited to fill the job. That man was retired army major Dick Meadows.

Dick Meadows was perhaps the finest Special Forces soldier in the history of the Green Berets, even to the present day. He was the first NCO to be given a battlefield commission in Vietnam. Meadows received his promotion personally from General William Westmoreland. Later, he led the Blueboy element that crashed inside Son Tay Prison. He was retired from the army in 1977, and it was said that had his personnel folder ever been fully declassified, Meadows would have gotten an almost automatic Medal of Honor for his "black" missions in Southeast Asia. However, just because the army had retired Dick Meadows didn't mean that *he* had retired.

Meadows had been a consultant during the development and formation of Delta Force, and had been involved with the planning for Rice Bowl from the earliest days of the crisis. Now he volunteered to go into Iran, where he would reactivate the local network, conduct the needed on-scene reconnaissance, and coordinate needed personnel and services for Beckwith and his raiders. It was an ambitious and dangerous job, especially for a man whose operational experience was centered on the jungles of Southeast Asia.

The choice of Meadows was not popular at the CIA. DCI Stansfield Turner was opposed to the former Green Beret doing a job his agency should have been (and at an earlier time was) capable of handling. Even the handful of CIA old hands questioned Meadows's ability to get the job done. "An amateur with poor cover, poor backup and poor training" was the assessment of one CIA officer. But having rejected several previous candidates, and with none of his choices acceptable to Beckwith, Vaught, and the Pentagon, Turner gave in and accepted Meadows as "our man in Tehran." As Beckwith later said, "I hung up on one big thing: I ain't going into the embassy unless one of my guys goes in early. I'm not going to risk the lives of ninety-seven people on some guy I don't even know." The turf war over, the CIA's in-house bureaucracy went to work to give Meadows the things he would need to function in Iran.

Major Richard J. Meadows, USA (Ret.), became CIA agent Esquire, though the forged passport indicated that he was Richard H. Keith, an Irish citizen and representative of an Irish auto company. He would stay at the Arya-Sheraton Hotel, spend days observing and casing the embassy compound, all while publicly living the life of a nondescript Irish businessman.

When Meadows went to Tehran, he would not go alone.

Realizing that Meadows would need more eyes and ears to do the job, the CIA culled its staff and managed to find four additional agents they could insert into Iran. Two were Berlin-based Green Berets who would scout the Iranian foreign ministry, where three of the American embassy staff had been staying as awkward "guests" since the start of the crisis. The other two were Iranian-born U.S. servicemen; one, with terminal cancer, had relatives in the city, and both knew their way around. Almost immediately, the five-man team began to produce information and quickly picked up where Bob and the Iranian businessman had left off.

So there it was: a complex operational concept that mixed navy and air force aircraft, navy and marine helicopter crews, army and air force commandos, and CIA personnel secreted into Tehran. It was, as one participant later called it, a lash up. Everything depended on getting at least six of the big RH-53D Sea Stallion helicopters from the refueling base at Desert One to the rescue staging area at Desert Two near Tehran so that all the military personnel and hostages could ultimately be lifted out in a single flight.

If it took more than one flight, a disastrous Alamo-style firefight might result, causing a bloodbath in the middle of the city. This was an outcome that President Carter had specifically told the Rice Bowl planners to avoid if at all possible. But it was obvious from the beginning of the planning that such niceties were going to be all but impossible to deliver in the real world of 1980.

There was also another problem—arguably the biggest—that, incredibly, did not become obvious until after Rice Bowl was over: an overbearing level of operations security (OPSEC). Rice Bowl was so secret that the secretary of state and members of the State Department, otherwise on the need-to-know list, were not aware of it. More important, things were so compartmentalized that commanders who received requests for aircraft and equipment—even members of the Rice Bowl team—were unaware of the reasons for certain requests or what was expected of other members.

For example, the commanders of the navy mine-hunting squadrons (who could have been sworn to secrecy and would have understood its necessity) were not told anything about the nature of the mission the helicopters would be used for. So instead of giving their best aircraft to support the mission, when the request for helicopters came to them, the commanders used it as an opportunity to rid themselves of their clunkers. As a result, Rice Bowl got castoffs and "hangar queens"—the term for aircraft that need constant maintenance.

There was not even a full dress rehearsal for the mission, despite Colonel Beckwith's attempts to get such an exercise scheduled at Fort Carson, Colorado. Given the fractured nature of the operation, especially with regard to the command and control structure, the level of OPSEC turned out to be critical in determining its outcome.

Throughout the winter and early spring of 1980, the various component units of Operation Rice Bowl trained. At the same time, the plan was being sold, and resold, to President Carter and his senior advisers at the White House. This became an ongoing task for Chairman of the Joint Chiefs General David Jones, who as President Carter's senior military adviser, had to deal day-to-day with concerns and desires of the White House regarding the mission and possible fallout. Meanwhile, those elements of the plan that had to be in place early were discreetly deployed to the forward bases in Egypt and Oman.

The actual mission helicopters, along with maintenance and support personnel, were drawn from the navy's Helicopter Mine Countermeasures Squadron 16 (HM-16). Much of HM-16 was transferred en masse to the USS *Nimitz*, which would be the launch platform for Rice Bowl if it ever got the green light from President Carter. The *Nimitz*'s role in the rescue mission would be code-named Operation Evening Light. Meanwhile, flight training for the aircrews was being run near Yuma, Arizona, where there was a large Marine Corps air station. Also, the terrain near Yuma was comparable to that in Iran and provided a high level of OPSEC to the training effort.

Formation flying under night vision goggles, called nods by the marine and navy aircrews, proved both challenging and stressful. Primitive compared to present-day NVGs, these first-generation nods were heavy, grainy in their presentation, and because of their total lack of peripheral vision capability, often led to the users becoming visually disoriented if the nods were worn for extended periods. Nevertheless, using them was the only way to guarantee a totally covert lights-out flight from the carrier to Desert One and on the rest of the mission. And there would be lots of flying for the eight aircrews.

Under optimum conditions, the first leg alone was over six hundred miles, and would require up to six hours to fly. That would be followed by another hundred-plus-mile hop, this one fully loaded with the ground force and their gear, to the planned Desert Two hideout—all in just one night. Though nobody was talking about it in early 1980, the stress of flying under even

Photo: U.S. Department of Defense

The USS *Nimitz* (CVN 68), commissioned in 1975, was the first ship in the new Nimitz class of fleet aircraft carriers.

optimum conditions for Rice Bowl was going to push the flyers to the limits of their endurance, courage, and mental capacities. And what they would encounter in Iran were anything but ideal conditions.

The air force portion of the force, in comparison, came together with fewer problems. A total of six air force Hercules transports would be used for Rice Bowl. Three Hercules, model EC-130, would carry fuel bladders, refueling gear, and the ground rescue force. Three others, MC-130 Combat Talons, would carry the Desert One security force of Rangers, Major Carney, and a six-man combat controller team, along with Colonel Kyle and the mission command team.

Their particular challenge was focused on Desert One. Though they would be flying the same route to Desert One, the six transports had to arrive ahead of the helicopters flying in from the *Nimitz*. Once there, Colonel James Kyle, as commander of the landing site, and his men had to set up a forward fueling and rearming point (FFARP) to refuel the RH-53Ds, get the ground force loaded into the Sea Stallions, and get everyone back in the air without being discovered by the Iranians.

Carney and the two CIA pilots on the April 1 reconnaissance also recorded radar signals from Iranian defense radars. This intelligence, as well as data from other electronic "ferret" aircraft and warships lying offshore in the Persian Gulf, revealed significant gaps and weaknesses in Iran's electronic defense system.

The essential problem for all the aircraft was fuel. Standard mission procedures meant once the transports started their engines at the staging base at Masirah, Oman, they would not be turned off until their return (a situation that also applied to the helicopters even though they would not be returning). This meant that all six aircraft would have their engines turning the entire time they were on the ground at Desert One, limiting the time window the Hercules transports could wait to turn around the RH-53Ds at the FFARP before running out of fuel.

The one part of the mission workup that went according to plan was Beck-

Photo: U.S. Department of Defense

The USS *Nimitz*'s commanding officer, Captain John R. Batzler (left) discusses final plans for Operation Evening Light with Air Force Colonel James Keating (right) from Pacific Command Contingency Plans. Behind them in the hangar bay is one of the operation's Sea Stallions.

with's ground rescue force. Fresh from their final certification exercise in November 1979, Delta Force was at the peak of readiness and was in position to rapidly adapt their capabilities to the situation in Tehran. This meant going over satellite photos, maps, embassy blueprints, and eventually, on-scene reports from Bob and Dick Meadows about their target: the American embassy in Tehran. As a result of the variety and depth of information about the embassy compound, Delta was able to develop an overall assault plan very quickly.

The one problem they faced, and it was a big one, was knowing exactly which building or buildings the hostages were being kept in. From debriefings with the hostages released by the Iranians on Thanksgiving, Beckwith and his planners had a fair idea of where in the embassy compound they would find the fifty-two hostages. They reduced the possibilities to six main buildings. The key would be getting inside quickly and quietly, and eliminating the guards.

Though every one of the Delta operators knew "eliminating" was the gentle way of saying "shoot dead at close range," they kept that to themselves as much as they could, for fear that a senior member of the Carter Administration might get squeamish and impose restrictions on the use of force, which would be impossible to implement or, worse, cause the mission to be canceled. The simple truth was that if Rice Bowl did get the green light—diplomatic efforts, though frustrating, were ongoing—a number of Iranians were going to die, and several pieces of real estate around the embassy were going to be badly damaged or destroyed. If the ground force had to call in AC-130s and navy fighter-bombers for combat air support to hold off Iranian mobs and/or troops, then block-size portions of the city around the American embassy might have to be leveled, and thousands killed.

The planners called that contingency the Fort Apache scenario. To try to avoid it, the Delta Force staff created a plan that looked workable if the helicopters could get them to Desert Two, the "dayover" assembly site for the rescue itself. Located in hills about fifty miles southeast of Tehran, this would be where the ground force made final preparations for the rescue, with the helicopters hidden under camouflage netting. The ground force totaled 132 men, including eight Iranian-born drivers for the trucks. It would link up with Dick Meadows and his team, and once darkness fell, the group would approach the embassy. Beckwith and Meadows would do a final reconnaissance from outside the compound, and then the assault would begin.

Using scaling ladders to quietly get over the compound's walls, one group of Delta operators would rapidly move to the six buildings where the hostages were thought to be held, eliminate the guards, then move the hostages outside to a predetermined collection point in the compound. As this was happening, other Delta operators would breech the compound walls with explosives, and then get everyone loaded onto the trucks. From there they would make a short run to a nearby soccer stadium that had been selected as their departure site out of Tehran because of its close proximity and defensibility. There they would rendezvous with Colonel Seiffert's CH-53D Sea Stallions waiting for them and fly to an abandoned air base at Manzariyeh, about fifty miles southwest of Tehran. A Ranger company flown in on Colonel Kyle's C-130s from Oman was assigned to secure the location while the embassy assault was commencing. Finally, the entire group—Delta, former hostages, Rangers, and other personnel attached to the mission—would be flown out of Iran from Manzariyeh on air force C-141 jet transports, and eventually home.

At the end of March, planning, preparation, and training were all but complete. Dick Meadows was dispatched to obtain final intelligence on Desert One. Soil samples confirmed that the ground could handle the loaded C-130s without any problem.

Now came the *real* challenge: getting final approval for Rice Bowl from President Carter. Spring, and the increasing amount of daylight it augured, had arrived. For Rice Bowl to work, the aircraft needed as much darkness as possible. The celestial clock was ticking. Ten days after Carney's visit to Desert One, President Carter held a senior staff meeting at the White House and announced that the latest diplomatic effort had, like the previous ones, yielded no results. He would be giving Rice Bowl the green light.

Carter later wrote in his memoirs, "I told everyone that it was time for us to bring our hostages home; their safety and our national honor were at stake."

Not everyone in the room was supportive of the decision. Secretary of State Cyrus Vance, informed of the mission for the first time at that meeting, told the president that while he would stay until Rice Bowl was completed, he was resigning whether the plan succeeded or failed.

Five days later, on April 16, Generals Jones and Vaught, along with Colonel Beckwith, went to the White House to give a final briefing to the president, Vice President Walter Mondale, and the senior administration staff. Beckwith later wrote that Carter said to the assembled group, "I do not want to undertake this operation, but we have no other recourse. . . . We're going to do this operation."

Carter then turned to General Jones, and said, "This is a military operation and you're going to run it." He added that he didn't want anyone else in the room involved.

With those words, Rice Bowl went from a concept to an operational plan with an execution date of April 24 and 25. The code name changed as well: Operation Rice Bowl was now Operation Eagle Claw. Colonel Beckwith flew

Photo: U.S. Department of Defense

The six Sea Stallions of Operation Evening Light flying in formation off the USS *Nimitz* during a familiarization flight.

home to Delta's base at Fort Bragg and immediately assembled his staff. Discreetly, he told them, "You can't tell the people; you can't tell anybody. Don't talk about this to anyone. But the president has approved the mission, and we're going to go on April 24."

As soon as Eagle Claw was approved, the various component units, like disparate pieces on a planet-size chessboard, began to deploy. All told, forty-four aircraft were assigned to Colonel Kyle's aerial task force. Some were already in place. The eight U.S. Navy RH-53D Sea Stallion helicopters requisitioned for Eagle Claw had been stowed on the hangar deck of the aircraft carrier *Nimitz* to keep them away from the prying eyes of Iranian patrol aircraft as well as Soviet reconnaissance satellites. Whether or not the Soviet Union would pass information to the Iranians about what it saw on the deck of the *Nimitz* was arguable, but all agreed no one wanted the Russians to know what they were up to. Unfortunately, the helicopters had been treated poorly during their time aboard. They had accidentally been sprayed with corrosive flame retardant (which had been quickly washed off), then seawater when a small fire broke out in the hangar, and maintenance had been delayed until the last minute. When Colonel Seiffert's flight crews arrived on the *Nimitz* in

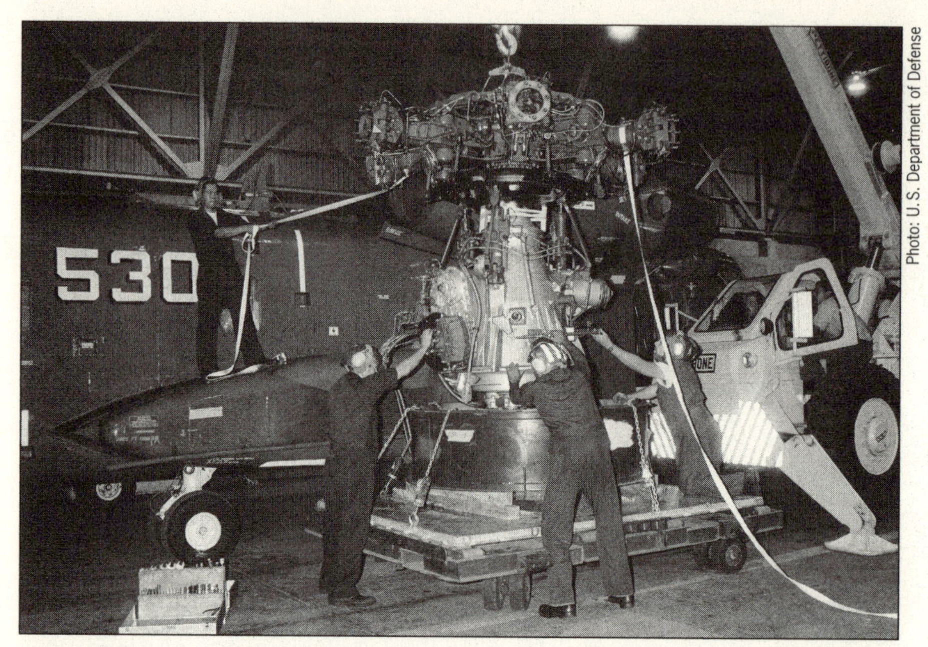

Photo: U.S. Department of Defense

A Sea Stallion transmission is about to be lifted into place on a Sea Stallion helicopter participating in Operation Evening Light. Maintenance of the Sea Stallions assigned to the mission was an ongoing problem because the mission received the castoffs from squadrons that, for security reasons, were not told why the helicopters were needed.

April, they saw for the first time the helicopters they were to fly. After a four-hour shakedown flight to familiarize the crews with their aircraft, the helicopters were taken belowdecks and spray-painted in the brown and tan color scheme of Iranian RH-53s.

The rest of Colonel Kyle's task force assembled at a Russian-built airfield at Wadi Qena, Egypt, which would also serve as General Vaught's headquarters during the mission. Units that had been training all over the world, from Guam to Fort Bragg, North Carolina, assembled at Wadi Qena for the first time. There they met up with Beckwith's ground force, the Rangers and air force combat controllers, and the Iranian drivers. Despite requests by Beckwith and others, it proved impossible to stage a full dress rehearsal for the mission.

On April 23, the CIA delivered a nugget of solid gold information: the exact location of the hostages in the embassy compound. The Iranians had released a Pakistani cook who had been an employee of the embassy prior to the takeover and had helped cook for the hostages during the crisis. In a coincidence that many considered almost too good to be true, the cook was on the same flight out of Tehran as a CIA agent—and they wound up sitting next to each other! The cook was debriefed, and he revealed that all of the hostages at the embassy were being held in the chancery building. When Beckwith at Wadi Qena received the information, the source and its authenticity were not included, and he did not totally trust it.

The next day, the entire force at Wadi Qena was briefed on the complete mission profile for the first time. There was enthusiasm from the entire force, who realized that they would be given a chance to recapture their national honor and free fifty-two Americans from a rogue regime operating outside the norms of international law. Colonel Kyle later recalled that it was an emotional high for everyone, with cheering and fists raised in the air with thumbs up.

What followed was a voyage of the damned for the participants.

Early on the evening of April 24, 1980, Colonel Seiffert's eight RH-53D Sea Stallion helicopters, code name Bluebird, lifted off the deck of the *Nimitz*. The previous day, the rest of the Eagle Claw force had moved from Wadi Qena to the secure air base at Masirah, Oman. There they loaded and fueled the six Hercules transports, and took off shortly after the helicopters from the *Nimitz*. It would take the transports four hours to get to Desert One, where they would set up the FFARP and get ready to receive the helicopters.

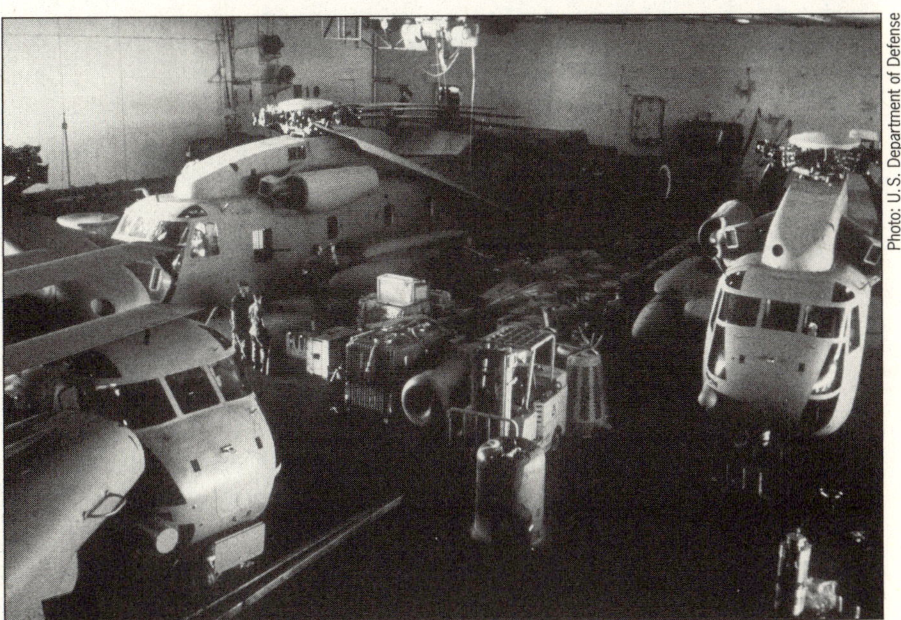

Photo: U.S. Department of Defense

Some of the Sea Stallions used in Operation Evening Light parked in the hangar bay of the USS *Nimitz*. The helicopters have been stripped of their U.S. military paint prior to receiving their Iranian military paint colors.

The first Sea Stallion lifts off as Operation Evening Light gets under way.

At 7:25 P.M. local time, the helicopter and transport formations made landfall on the Iranian coast. The helicopter pilots, flying at a lower altitude, spotted the faster-flying C-130s above them. About an hour later, the transports flew through an unexpected patch of atmospheric haze. About fifteen minutes after that, the transports cleared it. Then, thirty minutes later, and about 230 nautical miles inland, the transports encountered a second bank of haze—this one larger.

Colonel James Kyle, riding in the lead C-130 Combat Talon, asked Major John Carney, one of his subordinates, "What do you make of that stuff out there, John?"

"We're flying through suspended dust. The Iranians call it a haboob," Carney replied after looking out the copilot's window.[6]

Composed of sand the consistency of talcum powder that was suspended in an inversion layer, the haboob, in addition to reducing visibility, was also capable of fouling the turbine engines of aircraft. The real danger that night for the helicopters was that the haboob created a "brownout" condition, which forced aircrews to fly on instruments. The C-130s were able to climb out of the layer. Kyle tried to radio Seiffert to alert him to the haboob and

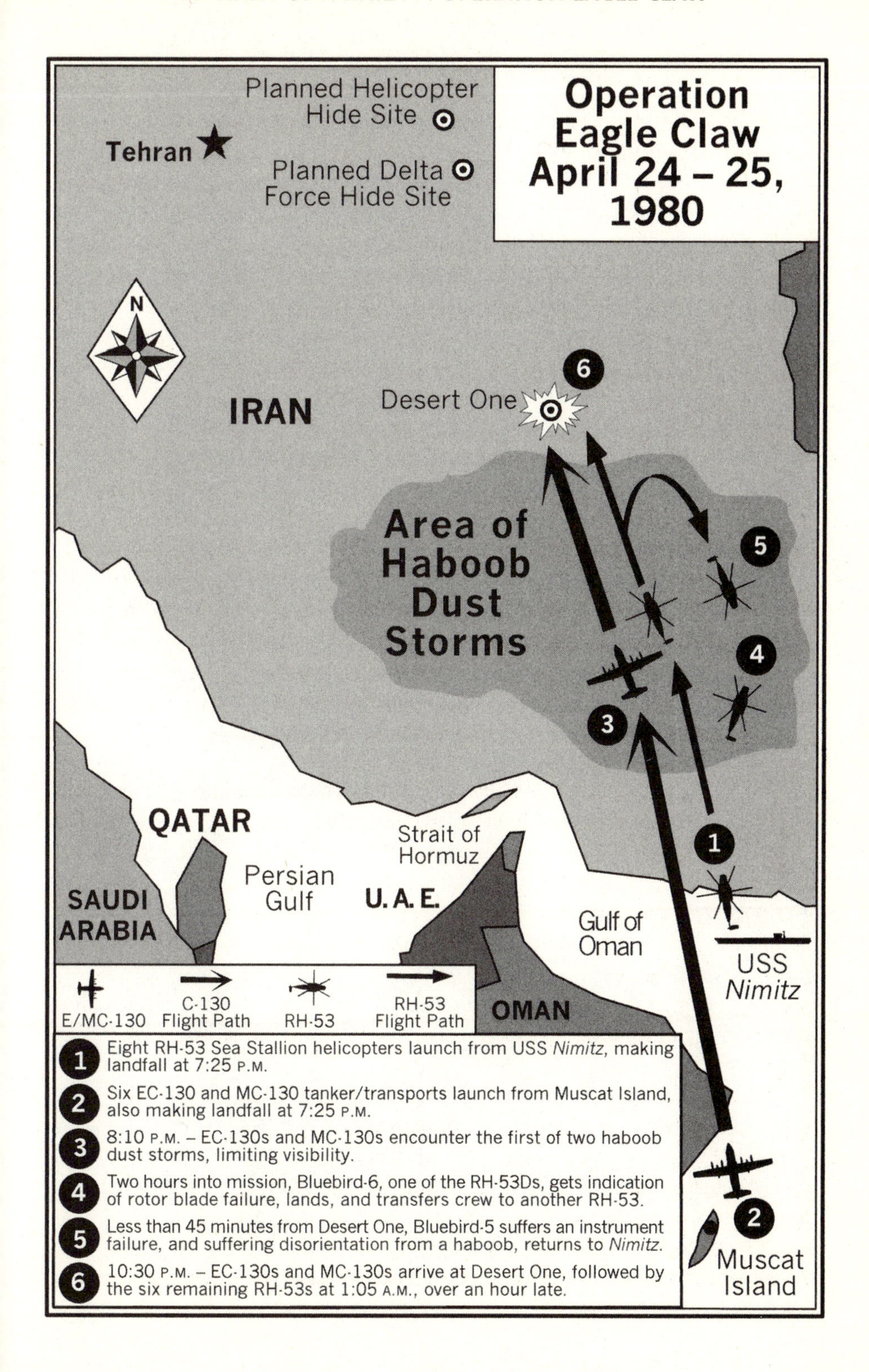
Operation Eagle Claw April 24 – 25, 1980
Planned Helicopter Hide Site
Tehran
Planned Delta Force Hide Site
IRAN
Desert One
6
Area of Haboob Dust Storms
5
4
3
1
2
QATAR
SAUDI ARABIA
Persian Gulf
U. A. E.
Strait of Hormuz
Gulf of Oman
USS Nimitz
OMAN
Muscat Island
E/MC-130
C-130 Flight Path
RH-53
RH-53 Flight Path
1 Eight RH-53 Sea Stallion helicopters launch from USS Nimitz, making landfall at 7:25 P.M.
2 Six EC-130 and MC-130 tanker/transports launch from Muscat Island, also making landfall at 7:25 P.M.
3 8:10 P.M. – EC-130s and MC-130s encounter the first of two haboob dust storms, limiting visibility.
4 Two hours into mission, Bluebird-6, one of the RH-53Ds, gets indication of rotor blade failure, lands, and transfers crew to another RH-53.
5 Less than 45 minutes from Desert One, Bluebird-5 suffers an instrument failure, and suffering disorientation from a haboob, returns to Nimitz.
6 10:30 P.M. – EC-130s and MC-130s arrive at Desert One, followed by the six remaining RH-53s at 1:05 A.M., over an hour late.

how to deal with it. But the radio call did not get through. When the RH-53Ds ran into the dust cloud, they continued to fly through it at low altitude as per the flight plan. By the time the helicopters reached the haboob, Eagle Claw was beginning to unravel.

Two hours into the flight, Bluebird 6's pilots got a warning indicator light for the blade inspection method, or BIM. It warned of a possible leak of the pressurized nitrogen that filled the Sea Stallion's hollow rotors, and usually meant a crack in one of the massive blades; similar damage had previously resulted in a number of rotor failures and fatal crashes. As a result, marine CH-53 pilots were trained to land quickly after a BIM warning. However, this time the marine pilots were not flying marine CH-53Ds, but navy RH-53s that had newer BIM systems that were more sensitive and gave earlier warnings to the crews. Sikorsky, the manufacturer of the Sea Stallion, had determined that the helicopter could fly safely for up to seventy-nine hours after a BIM alert. But this information was never conveyed to the marine aircrews.

Quickly, Bluebird 6 set down in the desert, with another RH-53D of the flight coming in to pick up the crew and continue on to Desert One. Though they did not know it, the crew of Bluebird 6 had just abandoned a perfectly good aircraft that could have flown the rest of the Eagle Claw mission. Worse

Photo: U.S. Department of Defense

A view of the cockpit of an RH-53D Sea Stallion helicopter. The marine pilots, unused to low-level flying for extended periods at night using night vision goggles, experienced extreme cases of stress and vertigo when they encountered the large haboob dust clouds.

was to come. The rest of Bluebird flight was now in the depths of the second haboob, and the aircrews were suffering terribly from the strees of adverse flying conditions. Bluebird 5 experienced a cockpit instrument electrical failure and turned back to the *Nimitz,* despite being less than forty-five minutes from Desert One. Now only six Sea Stallions, the minimum needed for the mission, were in the air—and out of formation and running between fifty and eighty-five minutes late.

Meanwhile, at Desert One, all six of the Hercules transports landed safely. The remote-controlled landing lights set up three weeks earlier by Major Carney were working like a charm. However, the landing conditions proved much different from what Carney had encountered at that time. Instead of the barren, flat salt lake bed, they found the ground now covered with a thin layer of dust with the consistency of baby powder, the residue of one, or more likely several, haboobs. Kicked up by the turboprops of the C-130s, the dust limited visibility, choked the ground personnel, and caused a great deal of confusion.

Then, within ten minutes of touchdown, the supposedly remote road bisecting Desert One seemed to become what one member of the team called the Hollywood Freeway, as first a fuel truck (later assumed to be driven by smugglers) and then a bus loaded with Iranian tourists blundered onto the scene.

One of the Rangers destroyed the truck with a shoulder-fired M72 LAW (light antitank weapon) rocket. The unexpected fuel explosion dramatically lit up the desert landscape, much to the Americans' consternation. The busload of Iranians was another problem entirely. An incident involving the capture of Iranians at Desert One had been anticipated. That was one of the scenarios practiced by Army Major Jesse Johnson and his team, who were assigned security duty. But no one expected to encounter a bus full of Iranian tourists. After consulting via satellite radio with the Pentagon and White House, the decision was made to put them on one of the transports and take them back to Oman with the C-130s returning later that morning. They would be repatriated after the mission was complete. Tensions, already high, began to rise further when the helicopters failed to arrive at the planned time. Only later was it realized that a planning mistake had introduced a fifty-five-minute error in the flight plan for the helicopters.

Finally, Colonel Seiffert's Sea Stallions began to arrive. The flight crews were all exhausted, and some were disoriented by the experience of flying through the haboobs on instruments and while using night vision goggles. One Sea Stallion pilot exited the helicopter upon landing and, in a state of near emotional collapse, staggered aimlessly two hundred yards into the desert. When Beckwith and his men ran him down, the pilot is reported to have said, "You have no idea what I've just been through!" Beckwith, believ-

Photo: U.S. Department of Defense

The hollow, nitrogen-gas-filled rotor blades of the new-model Sea Stallion helicopters had greater structural integrity than the rotor blades on earlier models that the Marine Corps pilots were used to flying.

ing that the helicopter pilots had turned into cowards, became extremely agitated and needed to be calmed down by Kyle. Like the other commanders at Desert One, Colonel James Kyle saw that the fragile emotional state of the helicopter pilots threatened to derail the mission. The severity of their experience was underscored by Major Jim Schaefer, one of the senior helicopter pilots, who emotionally suggested they abort. Fortunately, Kyle, a fellow pilot who had extensive experience in combat special operations in Vietnam, was able to calm the pilots and get them refocused.

With that crisis solved, Kyle did a quick assessment. The transports were in position, the helicopters were refueling, teams were lining up to board their assigned aircraft. There was constant noise from the helicopter and transport engines, and blowing sand was everywhere, drying everyone's eyes and throats. But it appeared that at long last things would finally go smoothly.

Then the Sea Stallion code-named Bluebird 2 shut down its engines. The RH-53D had just suffered a primary hydraulic system failure, which could not be repaired on site. Five helicopters now remained—one short of the designated minimum for success.

Colonel Kyle tried to get Seiffert to have Bluebird 2's crew fly the Sea Stallion to Desert Two using its backup hydraulic system, but the marine aviator made it clear that was a prescription for disaster. Kyle then tried to convince Beckwith to reduce the size of the 132-man ground force so it could fit aboard the five remaining helicopters. This suggestion was refused. Beckwith, not knowing that the April 23 report of all the hostages being in a single building was absolutely accurate and fully credible, was unwilling to leave anyone behind for the move to Desert Two.

That was it. Eagle Claw would have to be aborted.

Colonel Kyle got on the satellite radio and informed General Vaught back at Wadi Qena of the situation. The general relayed the bad news to General Jones and Secretary of Defense Harold Brown at the Pentagon. They called the White House. President Carter asked Brown to get Beckwith's opinion on whether to abort or not. Told that Colonel Beckwith felt he had to abort, Carter said, "Let's go with his recommendation."

Eagle Claw had failed, and now Kyle's responsibility was to get everyone out of Iran, a contingency none of them had rehearsed. Because of the delay in the helicopters' arrival, one of the EC-130s was getting critically low on fuel. It would have to fly immediately back to base. Kyle would also have to get the remaining five flyable helicopters refueled and head them back to the *Nimitz*. Finally, he'd have to get his five remaining C-130s loaded with the rescue teams and support personnel and into the air back to Oman.

It was an excellent ad hoc plan created in an instant under adverse conditions. And then fate stepped in to add to the challenge.

The nose gear of Marine Major James Schaefer's helicopter had suffered a

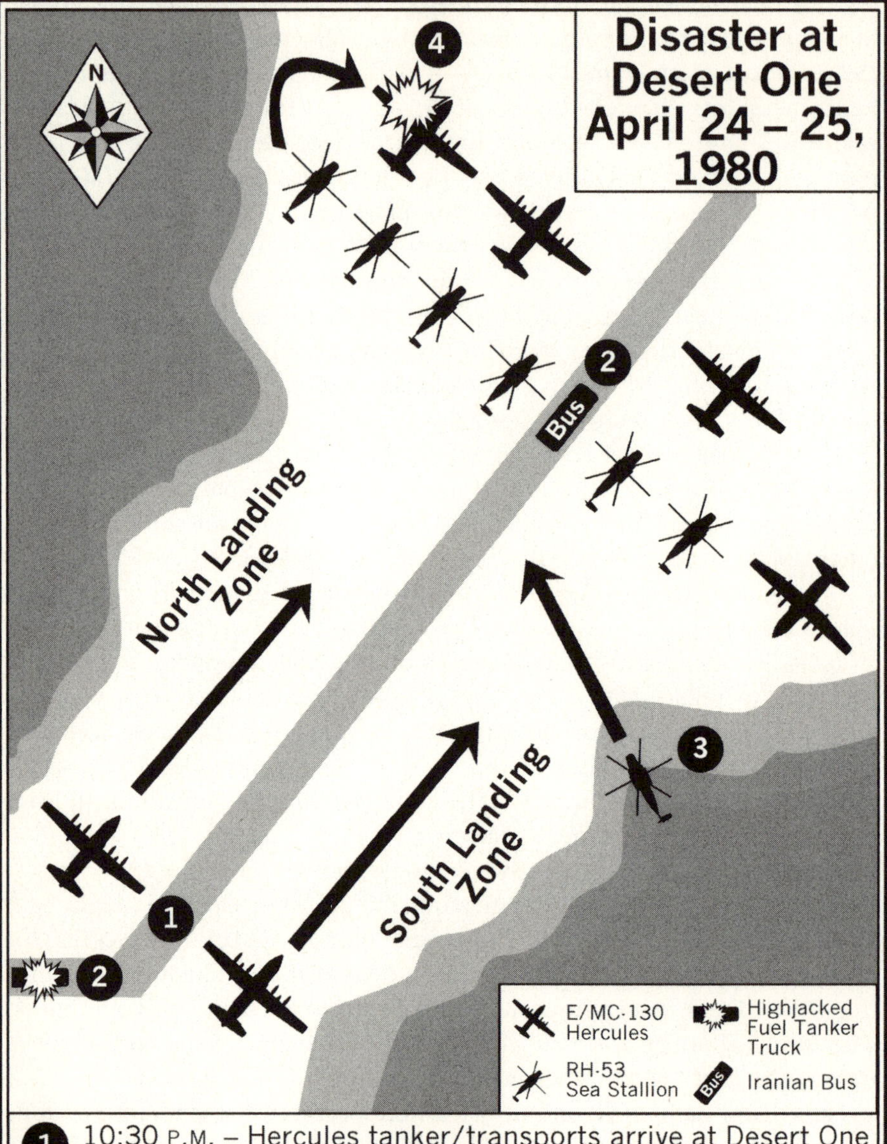

1. 10:30 P.M. – Hercules tanker/transports arrive at Desert One and set up for loading and refueling of RH-53s.
2. 10:45 – 11:30 P.M. – Ranger security force captures busload of Iranian civilians, then destroys a fuel tanker truck with an antitank rocket.
3. 1:05 A.M. – Six remaining RH-53 Sea Stallions arrive an hour behind schedule.
4. 3:00 A.M. – Following mission abort, one Sea Stallion collides with Hercules tanker/transport, destroying both.

flat tire in landing. As the helicopter was blocking the EC-130 low on fuel, it was necessary to reposition the Sea Stallion by "crabbing" it in a series of small up-and-down movements across the desert floor so that the EC-130 would be clear to take off. As he powered up his helicopter and began his maneuver, Major Schaefer suffered a brownout from the blowing dust and lost his bearings. Before he could correct his aircraft's motion, the rotors of the Sea Stallion plowed into the side of one of the Hercules tankers, and both aircraft exploded.

Eight men died in the collision and fire. Four others were badly burned, including Major Schaefer. Three helicopters were hit by flying debris and ammunition that was cooking off. For a short time, there was pandemonium at Desert One, which, incredibly, did not erupt into panic. Colonel Kyle began to sort out the disaster. He immediately decided to abandon the helicopters. They were too near the burning and exploding wreckage, and enough casualties had been taken. He then got the survivors on the remaining transports. The Iranian hostages were released just as the transports began cruising down the airstrip. Within minutes, everyone was in the air and heading back to Oman on what was for the dispirited passengers the longest air voyage they would ever take.

Colonel Kyle contacted General Vaught and requested an air strike from the *Nimitz* to destroy the Sea Stallions stranded at Desert One. He was so certain that President Carter would authorize the air strike, he did not worry about what might have been left behind. Later, he discovered that the helicopters contained classified documents, photographs, maps, and other mission data. Paramount in his mind, and the minds of the others in the transports, was the knowledge that the mission had failed, and that they had been forced to leave behind the bodies of the eight dead Americans.

It was just as well that at that moment they could not imagine that Operation Eagle Claw had gone from missed opportunity to complete failure.

Within hours of the disaster at Desert One, President Carter spoke to the nation, taking full responsibility for the failure. But before that speech, and soon after it, President Carter made several decisions. One was to *not* authorize the strike of A-7 Corsair II attack aircraft on the helicopters at Desert One. Fearing possible civilian casualties, Carter left the helicopters abandoned. When Iranian forces arrived at Desert One, they discovered the classified documents and quickly scooped them up for display on television and the front pages of newspapers around the world. In retrospect, this decision only added to the existing disaster.

Meanwhile, the Eagle Claw forces returned to their home stations, and began to regroup and consider other plans to rescue the hostages. Two plans were drawn up, Credible Sport and Honey Badger. They would have used specially modified C-130s with retrorockets to land in the soccer stadium near the embassy, and then take off assisted by special booster rockets. Unfortunately, the prototype YMC-130 was lost in a test flight crash, and two production aircraft were not finished in time to be used. The plans would have been impossible anyway because the Iranians quickly separated the hostages into small groups and relocated them throughout Iran. The humiliation of having the Tehran embassy overrun and captured by a student mob had now turned into a major military defeat, and the Iranians were quick to claim a victory over the Great Satan.

The toughest road home, however, fell to Dick Meadows and his four-man team of operatives, who were left high and dry in Iran. Forgotten in the confusion following the debacle at Desert One, Meadows had been waiting at Desert Two. Due to an atmospheric anomaly, his satellite communications link did not work properly. Only when the helicopters failed to appear did he know for certain that something had gone wrong. Returning to the warehouse where the trucks and vans were stored, Meadows learned about the failed raid from the Iranian media and realized that the classified documents in the helicopters likely contained information on him and his team members. It was a covert operative's worst nightmare come true, and Dick Meadows was in perhaps the worst situation of his career.

Despite fears that his cover and those of his operatives had been blown, Meadows and his entire team managed an exfiltration from Iran without a scratch. In his case, he just walked into the Tehran airport, boarded a Turkish airliner to Ankara, and flew out without incident. The three other team members managed similar escapes. Once they returned home, Eagle Claw officially came to an end.

Eagle Claw was dead. Now it was time to pick at its bones to discover what had gone wrong, do damage control, or make political hay. In addition to ordering the Pentagon to undertake planning and preparation for another rescue attempt, President Carter ordered the Pentagon to conduct an investigation of why the initial attempt had failed. He also successfully arranged for the bodies of the eight American servicemen killed at Desert One to be returned to the United States.

But the nation was angry over the mission's failure, and it being an election year, President Carter would discover the depth of that anger soon enough. Also outraged by the failure, Congress undertook its own investigation. And again, because it was an election year, much of it occurred in open session and was televised live to the nation. Meanwhile, the hostages continued to wait in Iran for some positive change in their situation. By the end of 1980, they got three breaks.

The first came on July 27 when Shah Mohammad Reza Pahlavi died of

Photo: U.S. Department of Defense

As Vice President Walter Mondale listens, President Jimmy Carter addresses the released hostages upon their arrival in the United States.

complications from his cancer in Egypt. With the shah dead, the basic rationale for the student takeover of the embassy was gone, and the possibility of new diplomatic offerings opened up to Deputy Secretary of State Warren Christopher. Still, it would take more than the shah's death to get Ayatollah Khomeini to let the hostages go home.

That motivation came on September 22 when Iraqi forces under Saddam Hussein invaded Iran. Eventually, the conflict became a bloody eight-year war of attrition between the two nations. The Arab nations in the region are largely Sunni Muslim. The sectarian differences between the Sunnis and the Shiites have been sufficient to inspire wars between these two sects of Islam. Threatened by the possibility of Shiite hegemony from non-Arab Iran, Saddam Hussein, with support from his Arab League neighbors, chose to attack before the new Islamic government dedicated to fundamentalist Islamic revolution had consolidated its power.

Suddenly, the fifty-two hostages became valuable bargaining chips in trying to get billions of dollars in frozen Iranian financial assets held by the United States—money Iran needed to pay for weapons and equipment to fight the Iraqis. The final part of the solution to get the hostages released

Photo: U.S. Department of Defense

The reason for the mission: The newly freed American hostages pose for a group photograph in the hospital in Germany where they were delivered for examination upon their release from captivity in Iran.

came in November when Ronald Reagan defeated Jimmy Carter for the presidency in a landslide.

The Iranians then began to negotiate in good faith with the Carter Administration. The deal took time, and the agreement to release the hostages was completed just hours before President Carter handed over power to Ronald Reagan on January 21, 1981. After 444 days in captivity, the fifty-two American hostages were free, and the crisis ended.

Postmortem: The Holloway Report and the Desert One Legacy

While the hostage crisis and the failed Operation Eagle Claw likely cost President Carter his job, the cost to the prestige of the American military was far worse. The Desert One debacle illustrated in a way nobody could deny the hollow nature of the American military in 1980. Even before Ronald Reagan was elected president, the Carter administration had begun reversing years of cuts to the defense budget and finally began to fund the military in a more appropriate fashion. For the Special Operations Forces community, however, this was hardly the solution to their problems and shortcomings in the post-Vietnam era.

Fortunately, the Joint Chiefs of Staff investigation commissioned by President Carter created a comprehensive report that became a road map for the

American Special Operations Force community. The commission, led by former chief of naval operations Admiral James Holloway, fully examined and evaluated the failures and shortcomings of Operation Eagle Claw. It published what came to be called the Holloway Commission Report, a lengthy document that concluded with twenty-three recommendations. The results of the examination were not pleasant reading, especially for those who had starved or tried to shut down SOF units after the end of the Vietnam War.

Virtually every aspect of the Iran rescue mission came under scrutiny, from the lack of dedicated SOF aviation units and aircraft, to the need for a command structure, as well as particulars in the planning, support, and execution of Operations Kingpin and Rice Bowl/Eagle Claw. In particular, the Holloway Commission Report recommended that Special Operations Forces units from all the services be consolidated into one joint and unified command structure.

There would be more agreement on the recommendations of the Holloway Commission when Congress held its own hearings. While the congressional committees heard much of the same testimony as the Holloway Commission had, it was the open testimony of Colonel Beckwith that laid bare the failings of Operation Eagle Claw. Having gotten control of his anger toward Colonel Seiffert and his helicopter pilots, he praised the men who

Photo: U.S. Department of Defense

Part of the price that was paid: The gravestone of Air Force Major Richard L. Bakke, Major Harold L. Lewis Jr., and Technical Sergeant Joel C. Mayo at Arlington National Cemetery. Shortly before he left office, President Carter succeeded in obtaining from the Iranian government the remains of all the men who died at Desert One.

had tried to make Eagle Claw work and backed the basic recommendations of the commission. His views about what had happened with Eagle Claw and his recommendations for the future were aired at one of the hearings.

In response to a question from Senator Sam Nunn, a supporter of the military, Colonel Beckwith said, "What do we need to do in the future? Sir, let me answer you this way. . . . If Coach Bear Bryant at the University of Alabama put his quarterback in Virginia, his backfield in North Carolina, his offensive line in Georgia, and his defense in Texas, and then got Delta Airlines to pick them up and fly them to Birmingham on game day, he wouldn't have his winning record. Coach Bryant's teams, the best he can recruit, practice together, live together, eat together, and play together. He has a team.

"My recommendation is to put together an organization which contains everything it will ever need. . . . Make this organization a permanent military unit. Give it a place to call home. Allocate sufficient funds to run it. And give it sufficient time to recruit, assess, and train its people. Otherwise, we are not serious about combating terrorism."[7]

It would take more than a quarter century to fully implement the Holloway Commission recommendations, but the road map it laid out in 1980 is today almost complete. U.S. Special Operations Command was created as a result of the Goldwater-Nichols Department of Defense Reorganization Act and Nunn-Cohen Amendment passed by Congress in the 1980s. Also formed was the Joint Special Operations Command, which today provides the needed command and support structure for SFOD-D and other specialized SOF units.

The biggest shortcoming of the Rice Bowl/Eagle Claw plan, the lack of dedicated SOF aviation aircraft, personnel, and units, has been fully overcome. Each of the various service SOF component commands have specialized aviation assets to support their particular types of operations. Perhaps most impressive has been the formation of the army's 160th Special Operations Aviation Regiment, known as the Night Stalkers, at Fort Campbell, Kentucky. Flying specially designed SOF helicopters, they have become some of the finest aviators in the world.

In fact, the Rice Bowl/Eagle Claw plan has been used as a benchmark for everything from training, requirements, and certifications of SOF units, to specifications of new aircraft such as the V-22 Osprey. Every time a marine expeditionary unit goes on deployment overseas, part of their certification is proving their capability of executing the entire Rice Bowl/Eagle Claw plan within six hours of an alert order.

Even the situation that occurred at Desert One airfield has become a valuable lessons-learned standard, as shown in March 2003 when fewer than two dozen Green Berets and air force combat controllers seized an abandoned

Iraqi airfield south of Baghdad. Within twenty-four hours, they made the airfield suitable for MC-130 Combat Talon tanker-transports to fly in a number of Special Forces A-Teams to join the fighting near Baghdad.

But it is perhaps the SOF warriors themselves who represent the ultimate legacy of the disaster at Desert One. For some, like Peter Schoomaker and William "Jerry" Boykin, both young Delta operators, as they are called, at Desert One, there was the personal commitment to make sure that if they rose to higher command, never to allow another Desert One fiasco to happen. And it is a promise both have kept. Jerry Boykin rose eventually to the rank of lieutenant general, having commanded SFOD-D, the army Special Forces, and the JFK Special Warfare Center and School at Fort Bragg. Pete Schoomaker went on to become a four-star general and commanding general of U.S. Special Operations Command, and later the chief of staff of the Army.

For others however, Desert One was the moment that the American SOF community hit rock bottom and began the long climb back to the primacy they know today.

1. Kyle, *The Guts to Try*, 195.
2. Ibid.
3. Chalmers Johnson, "Blowback," *The Nation*, October 15, 2001.
4. Bowden, *Guests of the Ayatollah*, 198–199.
5. Beckwith, *Delta Force*, 221.
6. Kyle, *The Guts to Try*, 281.
7. Beckwith, *Delta Force*, 326.

4

The 100 Percent Solution: Task Force Normandy

On August 2, 1990, Iraq invaded Kuwait, and three days later annexed it as Iraq's "nineteenth province" and appeared poised to invade Saudi Arabia. If that had happened, Iraq's dictator, Saddam Hussein, would have controlled roughly half the world's known oil reserves. President George H. W. Bush responded with his "line in the sand" speech, calling for Iraq to leave Kuwait or be forced out militarily. To back up his words, President Bush, after receiving permission from King Fahd, ordered American troops to Saudi Arabia. Within a week of Iraq's invasion of Kuwait, Operation Desert Shield, the defense of Saudi Arabia, had begun. Six months later, in the early morning hours of January 17, 1991, Operation Desert Shield became Operation Desert Storm, which led to the liberation of Kuwait. The first shots in that war would come from an operation that almost didn't happen. This is the story of Task Force Normandy.

November 29, 1990, New York City

> The Security Council . . . authorizes Member States co-operating with the Government of Kuwait . . . to use all necessary means to uphold and implement resolution 660 (1990) and all subsequent relevant resolutions and to restore international peace and security in the area.
>
> —Excerpt from U.N. Security Council Resolution 678 calling for Iraq to leave Kuwait before January 15, 1991

Early December 1990: Somewhere in a Remote Section of Northeast Saudi Arabia Called Area of Operations Carentan

When troops from the United States and other member nations of the coalition began to arrive in Saudi Arabia, the Saudi government set aside sections in the northeast of the country for use by individual units. These sections, known as areas of operation (AO), served a variety of purposes ranging from training and billeting to sentry duty. AO Carentan was a long rectangular tract containing 6,200 square kilometers set aside for training for the 101st Airborne.

The night was unusually cold. To the four low-flying MH-53J Pave Low III and nine AH-64A Apache attack helicopter crews training that evening in AO Carentan, the conditions were in sharp contrast to the brutal heat they had experienced just three months earlier. Later, the Saudis would tell the coalition troops that the region was suffering the worst winter in fourteen years.

The crews were formed into two teams, code-named Red and White, each composed of two Pave Lows and four Apaches. There was an additional backup Apache in the event that any of the attack helicopters had to abort. Originally there had been three teams, Red, White, and Blue, and three targets—all Iraqi radar sites—in the mission plan. But when Blue team's target was taken off the mission list earlier that month, the team was split up and incorporated into the Red and White teams, giving each of them more firepower.

This was good news to all, because since the mission called for attacking sites deep behind Iraqi lines, the short-range Apache's main battery of Hellfire missiles had been reduced from a standard load of sixteen missiles to eight to accommodate a 230-gallon external fuel tank that was mounted on the right inboard wing store. A pod of nineteen 2.75-inch Hydra 70 unguided rockets and a 30 mm Bushmaster chain gun with 1,100 rounds of high-explosive dual-purpose ammunition rounded out the weapons inventory.

All the helicopters were equipped with a pair of forward-looking infrared (FLIR) sensors, one of which the pilot used for maneuvering, while the other was for the gunner's use. Where the two types of helicopters differed, and why they were flying together, was in their navigation systems. The Apaches possessed a Doppler navigation attitude-heading reference system, or AHRS (pronounced "ay-hars"). All the crewmen wore AN/VIS-6 high-resolution, ultralightweight night vision goggles that were specifically designed for low-level flying. The goggles virtually turned the night into day, albeit a glowing, lime green–tinted one. What the pilots saw below them was a featureless desert that was visually boring and, of more importance, a navigational nightmare.

Two factors about the desert made all but useless the Apaches' AHRS radar navigation system. There were no significant terrain features off of which to

MH-53 PAVE LOW III

The MH-53 Pave Low III is the U.S. Air Force version of the navy's CH-53 Sea Stallion helicopter. The Pave Low's mission is low-level, long-range, undetected penetration into denied areas, day or night, in adverse weather, for infiltration, exfiltration, and resupply of special operations forces. It is a heavy-lift helicopter that is the largest, most powerful, and technologically advanced rotor-wing aircraft in the air force inventory. Features include terrain-following and terrain-avoidance radar, forward-looking infrared (FLIR) sensor, inertial navigation system with Global Positioning System (GPS), and other sophisticated avionics. The Pave Low is also equipped with armor plating. It can transport 37 troops at a time and carry on its external hook a maximum of 20,000 pounds of cargo.

SPECIFICATIONS—MH-53J

Manufacturer: Sikorsky
Crew: Six
Power plant: Two General Electric T64-GE-100 turboshafts producing 4,330 shaft horsepower each
Length: 88 feet (28 meters)
Height: 25 feet (7.6 meters)
Rotor diameter: 72 feet (21.9 meters)
Maximum speed: 165 mph (265 kmh) at sea level
Range: 690 miles (600 nautical miles; 1,100 kilometers)
Maximum takeoff weight: 46,000 pounds (Emergency War Plan allows for 50,000 pounds)
Armament: Any combination of three 7.62 mm miniguns or .50-caliber machine guns mounted on the sides and rear ramp.

Photo: U.S. Department of Defense

bounce the Doppler radar waves. And the Doppler waves themselves penetrated sand. Even if the Apaches encountered landmarks such as significant dunes or wadis, instead of bouncing off the surface of those features, the beams would continue down through them until they (eventually) reached bedrock. But the Pave Lows, from Air Force Special Operations Command's 20th Special Operations Squadron, carried brand-new Global Positioning System (GPS) receivers that used orbiting navigation satellites to fix a ground location. That was why they were the pathfinders for the "hunters" following them, the army Apaches from the 1st Battalion, 101st Airborne Division (Air Assault).

All of the crews assigned to the Iraqi radar sites mission did their training literally and figuratively in the dark. Not only were the exercises conducted at night, but only their commanding officers, Lieutenant Colonel Dick Cody for the army Apache crews and Lieutenant Colonel Richard Comer for the air force Pave Lows, knew the actual details of their mission and targets. The mission was code-named Operation Eager Anvil, and its goal was the total destruction of two important radar outposts, part of the Iraqi integrated air defense system, located in the remote western desert.

The teams had trained intensively under a cloak of secrecy for almost three full months. They had spent hours going over flight profiles, studying sandbox mock-ups of their targets as well as intelligence photos, and keeping their helicopters in combat-ready condition. They had flown at night for hundreds of miles in formation, with only a three-rotor disk radius of separation between the helicopters, no more than a hundred feet above the ground, no navigation or formation lights, and no communications to and from their target area in AO Carentan.

Tonight, however, they were cleared to use live munitions instead of practice rounds when they reached their targets. This night, as in earlier runs, the targets were groups of empty buses obtained from the Saudis. This time there were two groups stationed twenty-nine miles from each other and arranged in a typical Soviet-style field emplacement deployment. However, this live-

AH-64 APACHE

The AH-64 Apache is the U.S. Army's principal attack helicopter. The Apache can operate during the day or night and in adverse weather conditions using the integrated helmet and display sight system. The Apache is equipped with the latest avionics and electronics systems, including target acquisition and designation system, pilot night vision system (TADS/PNVS), black hole passive infrared countermeasures, surface-of-the-earth navigation, and GPS. The AH-64D model is equipped with the AN/APG-78 Longbow Fire Control Radar (FCR) target acquisition system, installed over the main rotor. In addition, a radio modem integrated with the sensor suite allows the D-model Apache to share targeting data with other AH-64Ds that may not have a line of sight to the target. This allows a group of Apaches at different locations to engage multiple targets, with only one Apache revealing its radome.

SPECIFICATIONS

Photo: U.S. Department of Defense

Manufacturer: Boeing
Crew: Two
Power plant: Two General Electric T700 turboshafts producing 1,690 shaft horsepower each
Length: 58 feet 4 inches (17.8 meters)
Rotor diameter: 48 feet (14.63 meters)
Maximum speed: 182 mph (158 knots; 293 kmh)
Ceiling: 21,000 feet (6,400 meters)
Maximum takeoff weight: 21,000 pounds (A model), 23,000 pounds (D model)
Combat radius: 300 miles (260 nautical miles; 480 kilometers)
Armament: One M230 30 mm chain gun, Hellfire and Stinger missiles, Sidewinder and Hydra rockets

AGM-114 HELLFIRE

The AGM-114 Hellfire is an air-to-ground missile system designed to defeat tanks and other individual targets while minimizing the exposure of the launcher to enemy fire. The Hellfire was developed in 1972 and went into production in 1982. It uses laser guidance and is the principal weapon used by U.S. Army helicopters against heavily armored vehicles and reinforced fortifications. The guidance system in the Hellfire models AGM-114A through AGM-114M requires the launcher to illuminate or "paint" the target from launch to impact. The exception is the recent AGM-114L model, which is a true "fire-and-forget" missile.

SPECIFICATIONS

Photo: U.S. Department of Defense

Manufacturer: Rockwell International, Lockheed Martin, Northrop Grumman
Length: 64 inches (163 centimeters)
Diameter: 7 inches (17.8 centimeters)
Weight: 99 pounds (45 kilograms)
Warhead: 18 pounds (8 kilograms) shaped charge high explosive antitank (HEAT)
Speed: 1,529 kph (425 meters per second)
Range: 8,750 yards (8,000 meters)
Guidance system: Semiactive laser homing (SALH)

fire exercise was a departure from normal training exercise procedures, and no small matter. The Apaches' Hellfire missiles cost, depending on the warhead type, anywhere from $40,000 to $65,000 each. The firing of a live missile prompted Apache pilot Warrant Officer Timothy Roderick to joke that triggering one was "like shooting a BMW downrange."[1] The orders called for all of the targets to be attacked at the same time. When the Apaches were in place, and at the right moment, a volley of Hellfires was launched, with cameras recording the action. Then, because orders called for a total neutralization of the targets, the Apaches bore in to employ their secondary batteries of rockets and cannon shells.

At point-blank range, the arpeggio of destruction commenced. It began with the launching of volleys of 2.75-inch Hydra 70 rockets—some with high-explosive warheads, others with flechette warheads that released 2,200 steel darts on impact. Then it was time for the deadly baton protruding from beneath the chin of the Apache, the M230 Bushmaster chain gun. Smoothly weaving back and forth under the power of a 6.5 horsepower electric motor, the Bushmaster fired 625 rounds per minute of 30 mm cannon shells that were armor piercing, incendiary, and fragmenting.

When the shooting stopped, the once recognizable Saudi buses were nothing but twisted, perforated wrecks in the middle of a patch of sand serrated with countless impact furrows. Had the buses been occupied, there would have been no survivors. An after-action review of the tape would confirm yet again that the Apaches had annihilated the practice targets. The mission plan was for the Apaches to destroy their targets at exactly zero hour on the first night of air operations against Iraq. This would open a wide hole in Iraq's southern radar "fence." Once this was accomplished, more than one hundred nonstealthy coalition strike craft such as F-15Es, F-111Fs, and Tornados would fly through the "hole," spread out, and hit tactical and strategic targets throughout Iraq and Kuwait. Including the two sites assigned to Task Force Normandy, the U.S. Central Command's (CENTCOM) target list had grown from a low of 84, back in August, to 238 targets in eleven categories. As commanding officer for the army's side of Eager Anvil, Cody shouldered many responsibilities. One of the easiest decisions he had to make was choosing a name for the attack group. In a nod to the 101st Airborne's combat history in World War II, he christened it Task Force Normandy. The attack group would have the honor of scoring the first hits in Operation Desert Storm.

Photo: U.S. Department of Defense

A helicopter crewman from the 101st Airborne Division (Air Assault) stands beside an AH-64A Apache helicopter as it is prepared for takeoff during Operation Desert Shield. Clearly visible is the 30 mm M230 chain gun. Hellfire missiles are mounted on the Apache's wing pylon (left).

The men were as sharp as a well-honed razor's edge. Outside news reports and their own intelligence indicated that war was no longer a question of if, it was a question of when. Task Force Normandy was good to go. The unspoken question in the minds of senior commanders who knew about Eager Anvil was, would the force be allowed to? After all, this *was* a special operations mission. As Lieutenant General Charles A. "Chuck" Horner, commander of the Central Command Air Forces later observed, his boss, General H. Norman Schwarzkopf, "hates Special Operations."[2]

But whether the mission would get a green light was only the latest in a series of questions beginning in August 1990 that had bedeviled the planners of the air campaign. It was something of a miracle they had even reached this still-precarious point.

In 1990, Iraqi dictator Saddam Hussein was confronting financial ruin. His eight-year war against revolutionary, fundamentalist Iran had ended in a strategic stalemate and left Iraq with an $80 billion debt and a reconstruction bill estimated at a staggering $320 billion.[3] That spring, Hussein demanded generous reparations from his neighbors, particularly Kuwait. His rationale was that since he had saved the Sunni-dominated nations from Iran's Shiite hegemony, they should pay Iraq more than they had for his protection. When his petition did not produce the hoped-for largesse, he raised the ante in July by submitting a written protest to his fellow Arab League members, claiming that Kuwait and the United Arab Emirates were cheating on their oil production quotas and committing "direct aggression"[4] against Iraq by driving down oil prices, thus depriving Iraq of billions of dollars.

On July 21, at MacDill AFB near Tampa, Florida, a response analysis in the event of the outbreak of hostilities by Iraq was conducted by CENTCOM. It was one of the new regional commands formed as a result of the landmark 1986 Goldwater-Nichols Department of Defense Reorganization Act. That legislation, and the subsequent Nunn-Cohen Amendment, also established U.S. Special Operations Command (SOCOM) as a military organization on a par with the other services, with a four-star general as its commander. Though potential Iraqi targets were identified by the response analysis team, and types of forces were tagged for possible deployment, the agenda presented only a patchwork of options. There was no real plan on file that could serve as a basis for an integrated offensive operational plan. The meeting lasted ninety minutes, ending, as Schwarzkopf later recalled, "with no sense of urgency."[5]

Then on August 2, at 1:00 A.M. local time, two Iraqi Republican Guard divisions launched a surprise attack on Kuwait. That evening, President George H. W. Bush issued a statement condemning the invasion and called for Iraq to unilaterally withdraw from Kuwait. Soon after, General Schwarzkopf received an order to prepare to deploy to Saudi Arabia a rapid response force composed of air force fighters, tankers, and AWACS aircraft, along with advance elements of the 82nd Airborne Division. Though the code name would come later, Operation Desert Shield had begun.

Officially, Desert Shield was a defensive action, designed only to protect Saudi Arabia from possible invasion of its northern oil fields. The reality, however, was somewhat different. From the first moments of Desert Shield, Lieutenant General Chuck Horner had been ordered by General Schwarzkopf to begin preparing an offensive air campaign, something that had very specific meaning to the U.S. Central Command Air Forces (CENTAF) commander. A generation earlier, Horner had been a young fighter pilot flying over North Vietnam, where he had been one of the early Wild Weasels, jet fighter-bomber pilots who had dueled with radar-guided surface-to-air missiles and antiaircraft guns. Horner had been lucky. Unlike most of the other Wild Weasel crewmen he'd flown with, he had survived his tour against the North Vietnamese integrated air defense system.

Horner had also learned some hard lessons, things he kept in the back of his mind for the day he might be asked to lead young airmen into battle in a faraway land. One was to be suspicious of plans and orders that came from the lofty heights of the Pentagon and other Washington, D.C., centers of power. Another was, before anything else in an air campaign, to take down the enemy air defense system so that you can operate over the battlefield with total air supremacy. In the case of Saddam Hussein's Iraq in 1990, this was a daunting task.

The Iraqi national IADS included almost twenty types of European and Soviet search-and-acquisition radars linked to an equally wide range of SAM and AAA gun systems. Added to this was the world's fourth-largest army and air force, the latter armed with state-of-the-art Soviet MiG and French Mirage fighter jets. Iraq's IADS was run by a French-built command, control, and communications network known as KARI (the French word for *Iraq* spelled backward). Obtaining intelligence on KARI, sometimes also called the KARI C3 system, quickly became a top priority for CENTCOM. Significant data initially was provided by the U.S. Navy's SPEAR organization. SPEAR (Strike Protection Evaluation and Antiair Research) was a "black" group created to gather intelligence about Soviet Union transportation systems and electrical grids in support of U.S. nuclear response in the event of a Soviet first-launch nuclear attack. They also had amassed much information about the Iraqi KARI system, and they conducted a series of briefings with senior members of the CENTCOM leadership. Later, when France joined the coalition, the contractor that had developed the system was able to provide important information about KARI's facility locations, along with system strengths and vulnerabilities.

However, given that initially all Horner had for staff in Saudi Arabia was a single logistics officer, Schwarzkopf felt his air chief was going to need some help. To do that, Schwarzkopf decided to reach back to Washington, D.C., and the Pentagon, despite Horner's reservations. It was the beginning of the odyssey for what would become Task Force Normandy.

Late August 1990, Saudi Arabia

Operation Eager Anvil was part of the four-phase air campaign, originally conceived and developed by Air Force Brigadier General Buster C. Glosson and his special planning group in Riyadh. That plan was itself the direct result of a disastrous briefing delivered to General Chuck Horner by Colonel John A. Warden III of his own Iraq air campaign plan, code-named Instant Thunder.

A 1965 graduate of the Air Force Academy, Warden was the head of the Deputy Directorate for Warfighting Concepts Development in the Pentagon, known as Checkmate. He had a brilliant mind and was an inspiring leader who freely shared his thoughts with his staff and encouraged them to seek imaginative solutions to problems. When the Pentagon ordered Warden to prepare a plan for an air campaign against Iraq, his team was already at work on it. Though many hands assisted in the creation of Instant Thunder, it truly was Warden's baby. He saw it "as a stand-alone, war-winning strategic air campaign that would force the Iraqi army to leave Kuwait."[6]

After Warden briefed the Joint Chiefs of Staff and General Schwarzkopf (then still in the States), he was ordered to present the plan to General Horner in Riyadh. It was a bad idea, especially given what the CENTAF chief was doing at the time. Horner initially wore two hats. In addition to his responsibility as CENTAF commander until Schwarzkopf arrived in Saudi Arabia to assume overall command, he was also CENTCOM-Forward, the temporary theater commander. Overworked, understaffed, suffering from sleep deprivation, and facing a possible Iraqi invasion with only a handful of American troops and planes, Horner was in no mood to be lectured by some hotshot Pentagon colonel about how to fight an air war. Nevertheless, he took the briefing—one that would become historic because of its role in the air attack plan ultimately developed.

Colonel Warden, along with select members of his staff (Lieutenant Colonel David A. Deptula, Lieutenant Colonel Bernard E. Harvey, and Lieutenant Colonel Ronnie A. Stanfill), arrived at Riyadh on August 19. On the afternoon of August 20, as a handful of aides watched, Colonel Warden began his brief to General Horner. There was tension in the room from the beginning, and Warden's decision to brief the plan himself was a huge mistake. To Horner, Warden's emphasis on striking Baghdad, particularly the bunkers from which Saddam Hussein would be directing operations—

referred to as "severing the head from the body"[7]—ignored, among other things, the possibility of a retaliatory advance into Saudi Arabia by the armored divisions of the Republican Guard lined up along the Kuwaiti-Saudi border. When the briefing concluded a short time later, General Horner thanked Warden and left the room. Everyone remaining in the room realized that Warden's attempt to sell Instant Thunder had failed disastrously.

Though it was true that Horner had rejected Instant Thunder, Horner later commented, "There was a lot of brilliance to the plan. I liked some of the factors. But just as there was genius, there was also no common sense. The thing was not executable. . . . Warden's conclusion was that [the Iraqi army] would all surrender when the first bomb dropped on Baghdad."[8] A dejected Warden departed that evening on a flight back to Washington. But Deptula, Harvey, and Stanfill were ordered to remain and join the CENTAF special planning group. By August 21, they had a new boss, Brigadier General Buster C. Glosson.

Glosson was actually in the region when General Horner called him to become the head of the special planning group. He was stationed on the USS *La Salle,* near Bahrain, working for Rear Admiral William M. Fogarty, the forward naval commander of CENTCOM. A transfer was promptly arranged, and Glosson arrived at Riyadh on August 21. He was told to bring himself up to speed on existing plans, including Instant Thunder, and to use Deptula, Harvey, and Stanfill (who because of what had happened called themselves the Exiles) and other available in-theater planners to produce a two- or three-day air tasking order (ATO). This would provide the basis for the opening moves of an executable air campaign. He was to present it to General Horner in five days. Over time, more people would be added to the planning staff (ultimately it became a multinational group containing fifty-five personnel), causing the office in the basement of the Royal Saudi Air Force building where the special planning group worked to be known as the Black Hole, because it seemed as though anyone who entered the room never came out.

On August 26, General Horner recalled, "Buster came in and said, 'Here's a great idea. . . .' " Horner listened to Glosson's briefing, which laid out the basics of the proposed air campaign. When he finished, General Horner said, "It looks good. Run with it."[9] Glosson returned to the Black Hole, where he and his staff could now work on the details of what would become the opening moves of Operation Desert Storm, as well as a formal presentation to General Schwarzkopf to be made on September 3. Though the name Eager Anvil had yet to be given to the operation, this new plan included an opening attack against those three radar sites in the western Iraqi desert.

But the plan called for the use of Special Operations *ground* forces to destroy the sites. Anyone who knew General Schwarzkopf knew this part of the plan was going to be hated by the CENTCOM chief.

* * *

The air campaign plan created by the Black Hole team borrowed heavily from Instant Thunder's target list, especially the KARI IADS. Working around the clock, the close-knit team managed to draft the basics by September 2. The campaign was broken down into four phases, and the group decided that a different staff member would brief each phase. General Glosson delivered the presentation for phase one, which included a special operations mission targeting the radar sites in western Iraq.

Prior to the meeting, Glosson had rehearsed points with Lieutenant Colonel Deptula, who had fired questions likely to be asked by General Schwarzkopf. The rehearsal was a prescient move as many of the practice questions were actually asked by Schwarzkopf. Even though he had not heard the rest of the plan, Schwarzkopf came away from the briefing impressed, calling it, "the best air campaign I'd ever seen." The Black Hole team felt that they had accomplished "a milestone" of planning, and they were right. And though the operation to take out the Iraqi IADS sites was a small event in the overall air campaign plan, it was enormously important to one man who in almost all other respects had been relegated to the sidelines, Colonel Jesse Johnson.

Colonel Jesse Johnson, the wiry, tough commander of CENTCOM Special Operations Forces, had been fighting an uphill battle ever since he had arrived in Saudi Arabia in August. A colonel in a desert rapidly filling with generals, he was outranked, sometimes outflanked, and frequently overpowered in his efforts to establish special operations as a useful capability within CENTCOM headquarters. Because everyone was aware of General Schwarzkopf's dislike of Special Operations, Colonel Johnson knew there was essentially nothing he could do about it; effectively, he was an outcast.

General Schwarzkopf's attitude about Special Operations troops had its origin in a series of bad experiences during the Vietnam War. As Major General James Guest of Special Operations Command (SOCOM) later observed, "Schwarzkopf's mentality was, 'I have a coiled cobra in a cage and if I open that cage, that cobra is going to get out and possibly embarrass me.'"[10] Schwarzkopf knew he could not legally keep Special Operations Forces (SOF) out of the theater when he began organizing Desert Shield/Desert Storm; Goldwater-Nichols and Nunn-Cohen required him to have an SOF component. But he was determined to keep the number of Special Operations troops as low as possible (ultimately only about nine thousand were deployed), and they'd only be given tasks that kept them on a short leash.

A Special Operations special tactics team handled the air traffic duties at Saudi Arabia's King Fahd International Airport, which was still under construction at the time. Because of their language skills, many of Johnson's

Photo: U.S. Department of Defense

An aerial view of a coalition military encampment located somewhere in the Saudi desert during Operation Desert Shield/Desert Storm. The ring around the encampment is a high sand berm constructed by bulldozers.

men were formed into combat support teams and assigned to various international units, where they acted as liaisons to the coalition. SOF personnel also occupied forward observation posts along the border. In these capacities, Schwarzkopf later acknowledged that Special Operations troops were his "eyes and ears" and "the glue that held the Coalition together during Desert Storm."[11]

But as important as these duties were, they were sideline roles. Johnson knew his men could do more, should do more, and he wanted them to have an active role in the eventual liberation of Kuwait. General Carl Stiner, the four-star commanding general of U.S. Special Operations Command, wanted this as well. Stiner even went to the extraordinary step of scheduling a meeting with General Schwarzkopf in Riyadh on September 16. With Johnson in attendance, Stiner tried to carve out a bigger role for Special Operations. Stiner made a number of suggestions to Schwarzkopf, including increasing the number of SOF troops, replacing Johnson with a major general (a move Stiner discussed with Johnson prior to the meeting) so that the CENTCOM component commander's playing field would be leveled. Stiner even suggested that he establish a small terrorist threat tactical command post in Saudi Arabia that Stiner would command. General Schwarzkopf listened politely and replied noncommittally. When the meeting concluded,

Schwarzkopf said he'd get back to Stiner on his requests. Within a week of his return to the States, Stiner received a message that essentially said, "Thanks, but no thanks."[12]

September 25, 1990, Riyadh

When Colonel Johnson was notified that the ground attack plan on the two Iraqi IADS sites had been approved, he put in a request for the specialized equipment and weapons he'd need, including GPS-equipped ground vehicles. This requisition went up the chain of command to Glosson, who signed off and passed it on as a matter of routine. But when it reached General Schwarzkopf's desk for final approval, Chuck Horner recalled that Schwarzkopf "blew a gasket." When Brigadier General Glosson received an abrupt, angry phone call from Schwarzkopf ordering Glosson to get into his office ASAP, the brigadier general knew he was in trouble.

General H. Norman Schwarzkopf was highly intelligent—some even called him brilliant—and dedicated. During the Vietnam War he had proved himself a brave and resourceful commander who took care of and was loyal to his troops. He had earned the Combat Infantryman Badge, the Silver Star with two Oak Leaf Clusters, the Distinguished Flying Cross, the Bronze Star with a combat "V" Device and two Oak Leaf Clusters, and the Purple Heart with one Oak Leaf Cluster, among other decorations. But he was also insecure, vain, and prone to extremes of histrionics and tirades, earning him the nickname "Stormin' Norman."[13] His taste for theatrics once led his deputy commander in Saudi Arabia, Lieutenant General Calvin A. H. Waller, to state in exasperation, "He's the CINC [commander in chief]. He's not Your CINC-ness."[14]

Schwarzkopf's volatile temper and affection for the displays of the trappings of power at one point caused Secretary of Defense Richard Cheney to consider relieving Schwarzkopf, but he was dissuaded from doing so by Joint Chiefs of Staff Chairman General Colin Powell.[15] Whenever Schwarzkopf had an outburst of temper, which was frequent, his staff would assume a mask known as the stunned mullet look until the moment of rage, real or for show, passed. The staff came to refer to these tantrums as "CINC-abuse." Lieutenant General Horner observed, "You can't let him bully you. Once he bullies you, he loses respect for you."[16]

Brigadier General Buster Glosson was a latter-day Daniel about to enter the lion's den.

When Glosson arrived at the CINCCENT's office, a furious General Schwarzkopf showed him Johnson's requisition and shouted, "I never approved this!"

Glosson replied, "Sir, let me tell you, remember when we walked up to the map?"

"Yes!"

"Well, remember I told you we would take that radar out with Special Ops?" asked Glosson.

"But you didn't say you'll put forces over there!" Schwarzkopf replied. "I can't send forces across the border until the president gives me permission to!"[17]

That statement was not just disingenuous; it made no sense. Phase one was an *offensive* plan, not a defensive one, and the "border" applied to *all* coalition forces whether they traveled in the air, on the ground, over the sea, or beneath its surface. The offensive would commence only after a string of United Nations, congressional, and presidential approvals, giving Schwarzkopf the power to act. As head of a coalition that would ultimately contain troops from thirty-four countries, and was based in a conservative nation whose religion and customs placed many restrictions of the troops' behavior, Schwarzkopf was under a tremendous amount of pressure and had a lot on his mind. Though he had asked many questions regarding other points in the phase one plan, it might have been that he simply hadn't been paying close enough attention when the Special Operations part of the campaign was presented. Whatever the reason, Glosson knew when to open his mouth and when to keep it shut.

What followed was a "gruelingly detailed" recapitulation by Glosson of the entire SOF strike plan in order to convince the suspicious Schwarzkopf that the Black Hole team was not attempting to hide from him aspects of the air campaign they knew he wouldn't like. When Glosson finished, General Schwarzkopf was mollified, and the use of Special Operations ground forces to destroy the radar sites was nixed. Separately, intelligence sources discovered that the Iraqis had moved the sites farther into Iraq, placing them beyond the reach of the ground teams, which would have likely cancelled the raid in any case.

So it was back to square one on how to spike the three Iraqi radar sites. The sites were still a threat that needed to be taken out, and the Black Hole staff now had to find another way to do it. It looked as if Special Operations' small role in the opening moves of Operation Desert Storm was finished before it could start.

Returning to the Black Hole, Glosson immediately went to work with his group and quickly devised a new solution for taking out the radar sites. "Buster is extremely bright, and he had a great team," General Horner recalled. "It was Buster's idea about using the army helicopters."[18] Attack helicopters had almost everything required for the mission: flight, firepower, and, most important, the ability to hover near the target to ensure its total destruction. A review of the rotary-winged assets available in Saudi Arabia produced a hybrid solution that returned Special Operations to the table. This included

Photo: U.S. Air Force

The MH-53J Pave Low is a modified version of the HH-53 Super Jolly Green Giant heavy lift helicopter that became famous in the Vietnam War. The rugged Pave Low was the only helicopter in the military at the time of Operation Desert Shield/Desert Storm to possess the GPS (Global Positioning System) navigation device necessary for pinpoint accuracy in special operations missions.

U.S. Army Aviation, which was about to receive an important role in the air campaign.

Politics has been described as the art of making the impossible possible. Almost as soon as Glosson's revised plan was approved, comments were made over what was perceived as an ingratiating move to get acceptance for Operation Eager Anvil by including Army Aviation. The claim cannot be entirely dismissed, for later much was made of the army Apaches having the honor of firing the first shots in Operation Desert Storm. But the fact was that the radar sites needed to be destroyed at a precise moment in time, and that total destruction needed to be conclusively verified. With the ground SOF option eliminated, that meant helicopters. Coincidentally, what was arguably the best attack helicopter unit in the United States military was at that very moment pulling guard duty along the Saudi border. And as no single helicopter type could do everything demanded in the mission, the revised plan provided an opening to the personnel of Air Force Special Operations Command (AFSOC).

The Black Hole tapped the players. The MH-53J Pave Low III helicopters from the Air Force Special Operations' 20th Special Operations Squadron were the only ones in theater equipped with new Global Positioning System receivers, the only navigational aid that possessed the pinpoint accuracy required for the mission. The Pave Lows would act as pathfinders to guide a force of heavily armed army Apache attack helicopters from the 1st Battalion, 101st Aviation Regiment (Attack—1-101st) to the targets. Thus, the helicopters had complementary flaws, which was why the decision was made to pair them. The Pave Lows had the navigation system but not the necessary firepower. The Apaches had the firepower, built around their tank-destroying laser-guided Hellfire missiles, but not the navigation system. There were other factors that needed attention, including a limited communications suite, and the Apache's relatively short range and reputation as a high-maintenance machine. But unless Saddam Hussein launched a preemptive strike of his own, the 1-101st had time to fix those and other potential problems.

Updating his briefing, Glosson quickly presented the revised version of Eager Anvil to General Schwarzkopf. When he was told why the army Apaches had to be led by the Special Operations Pave Lows or the mission would have to be scrubbed, Schwarzkopf signed off on it. In return, however, Schwarzkopf told everyone involved he would keep close tabs on developments. Colonel Johnson was given the good news as well as the CINCCENT's ominous injunction, "Do not screw this up."[19]

Major General J. H. Binford Peay III, commander of the 101st Airborne Division, was on vacation with his family when the deployment order to Saudi Arabia was issued on August 10. An inspiring leader and efficient organizer who would be promoted to the rank of full general in 1993 and, in 1994, appointed commander in chief of CENTCOM, Peay had trained his staff so well that by the time he arrived at the division's home in Fort Campbell, Kentucky, two days later, the deployment was well under way. Not only had there been little warning to alert those in camp, units of the division were literally scattered throughout the country. All of them had to stop what they were doing and return to Fort Campbell to prepare for extended duty in Saudi Arabia.

Because of the fear that Iraq might at any moment follow up its invasion of Kuwait with one of Saudi Arabia, Peay's orders explicitly told him to expedite the deployment his AH-64A Apache "shooters" in advance of the rest of the division so they could provide a protective aerial shield along the northern Saudi border. All of the helicopter units in the division were well run. But there was one, with the motto "Expect No Mercy," that had established a truly outstanding reputation: the 1-101st led by Lieutenant Colonel Dick Cody. The Apaches and Cobras of the 1st Battalion, 101st Aviation Regiment (Attack) would be the first to go into harm's way.

Lieutenant Colonel Cody and his advance group arrived at the airfield at Dhahran, on the east coast of Saudi Arabia, on August 17, and immediately discovered their first challenge: the heat. The August daytime temperature on the tarmac of King Fahd International Airport was 142 degrees Fahrenheit. Later, Brigadier General Henry H. Shelton, the 101st's assistant division commander (and a future chairman of the Joint Chiefs of Staff), colorfully said, "Hell cannot compete with the heat in Saudi Arabia."[20] He described the experience as "standing in a scalding hot shower while holding a hair dryer" aimed at one's face.

Unloading the cargo from the air force transports and then getting the 1-101st helicopters assembled and operational would take three days. Initially, the aircrews did helicopter maintenance, which included nightly painting of the rotor blades to counter sand erosion, in nearby hangars set aside for military use. Later they would use portable clamshell shelters to protect the birds from the unrelentingly hostile desert environment.

Cody's men were not alone for long. Two days after they arrived, additional advance elements of the 101st Division appeared in Saudi Arabia. By the end of the month, an "aluminum air bridge" of air force C-141Bs and C-5Bs delivered 117 helicopters, 487 vehicles, 123 equipment pallets, and 2,742 troops. Later, the entire force would move to Camp Eagle II, a two-

Photo: U.S. Department of Defense

Airmen roll an AH-64A Apache helicopter off a C-5A Galaxy aircraft at an air base during Operation Desert Shield. The Apaches from Lt. Col. Dick Cody's unit, in the 1st Battalion, 101st Aviation Regiment, were among the first units deployed in Operation Desert Shield. In fact, Cody's unit was deployed so quickly his men barely had time to complete their POR (Preparation for Overseas Replacement), the contingency planning checklist required of everyone going into combat.

Photo: U.S. Department of Defense

Maintenance crewmen resurfacing a rotor blade inside a portable shelter known as a clamshell. Aircraft maintenance, particularly for helicopters, was a major effort during Operation Desert Shield/Desert Storm. The harsh desert conditions were particularly taxing on helicopter rotor blades because the fine sand would cut the surface as easily as a hot knife through butter. As a result, rotor blade maintenance was conducted daily.

mile-by-three-mile base near the airport that eventually contained five thousand tents, named in honor of Camp Eagle I, which had been the 101st's base camp during the Vietnam War.

When his division was fully deployed in early October, General Peay would field the most powerful attack helicopter force ever created. But well before then, part of Peay's force would be reassigned to a Special Operations top-secret mission: Operation Eager Anvil.

September 25, King Fahd International Airport

Lieutenant Colonel Dick Cody, together with his boss, Colonel Tom Garrett, commander of the 101st Aviation Brigade, entered Colonel Jesse Johnson's office in one of the terminal buildings at King Fahd International Airport. After informing his guests of the classified nature of the subject he was about to discuss, Johnson proceeded to brief them on the basics of Operation Eager Anvil. He showed them photos of three Iraqi radar sites spread across an area of almost seventy miles in the desert of western Iraq. In satellite photos of each ten-acre site, they recognized a well-dispersed assortment of military equipment, trucks, and vehicles. These included low-altitude Squat Eye, high-altitude Flat Face, and older Spoon Rest surveillance and acquisition radars, along with a troposcatter dish for secure communications, and what appeared to be power generator buildings, electronic warfare command-and-control vans, and a barracks. Protecting each site were three ZPU-4 AAA guns, their deadly 14.5 mm quad-mounted machine guns pointing menacingly at the sky.

Johnson told the two men of the original plan to use Special Operations ground troops to blow a hole in the Iraqi IADS in the initial minutes of Desert Storm, and that the ground raid option had been dropped. Nevertheless, the hole still needed to be blown. Johnson then delivered his punch line to Cody directly, saying that 1-101st had been selected by the planners to attack the sites.

Like any good commander, Cody, a second-generation American whose grandfather was born in Lebanon and had anglicized the family name of *Oude* to *Cody*,[21] believed in himself, in his men, and in his equipment. He had often said, "The Apache is the finest combat helicopter ever produced—bar none." In his case, he backed up that belief with performance. Cody himself had flown more than four thousand hours in helicopters, with more than five hundred in the Apache. His aircrews and maintenance teams were arguably the best in the army in 1990. The Apaches were notorious for being high-maintenance machines, with an average of three hours in the maintenance shed for every hour in the air, yet Cody's crew chiefs were able to sustain an astonishing operational helicopter average of 94 percent—and this included operations in the Saudi desert, where wear-and-tear attrition levels were more than double those in the States. And his aircrews were unexcelled in their flight and targeting ability. Johnson knew all this, of course. But he needed to hear it straight from Cody. The stakes were already high for the Special Operations community. But there was another reason for Johnson's insistence—one of a personal nature.

In 1980, Johnson had been an army major and security team commander during Operation Eagle Claw, the attempt to rescue American hostages in Tehran. That operation literally blew up in a tragic ball of fire in Iran when a navy Sea Stallion helicopter crashed into an air force Hercules transport on the refueling site code-named Desert One (see chapter 3). The memory of that failure had not dimmed with time, and Johnson was determined not to have that happen again. He immediately put the screws to Cody. Johnson wanted "100 percent" assurance that his Apaches could do the job.

Cody replied, "That's not a problem."

Johnson thanked the men and said that specific orders would follow.

Not long after he returned to his headquarters, Lieutenant Colonel Cody was informed he could begin training with Lieutenant Colonel Richard Comer and his MH-53J Pave Low IIIs from the 20th Special Operations Squadron for Operation Eager Anvil. Only after he was well into the planning details and the training, would Cody wonder if he had bitten off more than he could chew.

One of Cody's first decisions for the operation was to name the task force Normandy in honor of the 101st Airborne's troops in World War II who had parachuted into Normandy, France, on D-day. A far tougher decision was selecting ten crews for the mission out of the twenty-four available on his battle roster. Rather than cherry-pick experienced individuals and then create new two-man flight crews to train for Eager Anvil, Cody opted for experienced crews that already worked well together. This decision applied to the maintenance teams as well, as they would be an integral part of the task force and forward-deployed up until mission launch. This way the focus would remain on the mission, while simultaneously providing experience in how to function as a team. Cody later said that any of his 1-101st crews could have successfully conducted the mission, that there was no B-team in his unit. Inevitably, though, those who were selected came to be known as the A-team, and those not, the B-team.

Training commenced immediately. To maintain secrecy, Cody did not go on detached duty from the 1st Battalion as commander of the Eager Anvil task force. Instead, he continued with his regular duties and integrated his new responsibilities into his regular schedule. This was to provide cover and operational security against Iraqi operatives who were already closely watching coalition forces all over the Persian Gulf. Meanwhile, Task Force Normandy was getting busy.

Three Apache teams trained from September 26 until early December, first in Area of Operations Normandy and later in adjacent AO Carentan in northern Saudi Arabia. But intelligence determined that Team Blue's target was not linked to any of the five KARI operations centers. Cody incorporated Team Blue into Teams Red and White so that two stronger teams would take the fight to each of the enemy radar sites. It added redundancy to a plan that was part of an even larger construct to destroy the KARI system in the first hours of what was looking like the biggest war for America since Vietnam.

Part of General Horner's staff that had been feeding information and ideas to Buster Glosson throughout late 1990 had been a study group led by Brigadier General Larry "Poobah" Henry, a legendary Wild Weasel "Bear" (an electronics warfare officer who flew in the rear seats of F-100Fs and F-105F/Gs) from the Vietnam era. Perhaps the air force's top expert on IADS suppression, Henry had spent the summer and much of the fall developing a complete order-of-battle for the KARI system, including its function and likely degradation during combat. Then he developed a plan to kill KARI in just a few hours. Later known as Poobah's Party, the operation was a modern-day

Photo: U.S. Department of Defense

Two AH-64A Apache helicopters fly over the desert during Operation Desert Shield. The Apache is the army's primary attack helicopter. The cockpit for the two-man crew has the pilot sitting in the rear seat and the co-pilot/gunner in the forward seat. The Apache's main battery includes Hellfire missiles capable of destroying such high-value targets as tanks or other armored vehicles and smaller Hydra 70 rockets. A 30 mm M230 chain gun is located beneath the chin of the Apache.

siege that included every kind of deception possible, including Trojan horses inside the Iraqi defensive network itself.

The idea was that at the exact moment Task Force Normandy was destroying the two radar sites, ten F-117A stealth fighters would be penetrating Iraqi airspace to destroy the five KARI regional control centers, along with key KARI command, control, and communications facilities in Baghdad and other locations. With the "brain" of the KARI system cut off from the outer ring of radars, SAMs, and AAA guns, the Iraqi defenses would go to "local" control, light up their radars, and become the biggest target in the history of electronic warfare. But before any of that happened, Task Force Normandy would have to do their job or the entire plan would fall out of sync before it began. This was just one of many reasons that both Cody and Comer were driving their men so hard in training for the mission.

Throughout the fall and winter of 1990, training proceeded, though not without incident. One day, at King Fahd International Airport, a Hellfire missile spontaneously launched itself from an unmanned Apache that was not powered up, with all its systems "safed." The errant missile shot ballistically across the base, straight into an air force munitions dump, causing a massive string of explosions as the weapons cooked off. Amazingly, nobody was killed or injured, but the accident set off a string of investigations, both technical and personal, of the entire 1-101st.

Several technical problems also needed to be addressed. The biggest was the matter of extending the range of the Apaches, which would have to fly almost five hundred miles from their forward operating base (FOB) to the targets. Initially, plans called for the establishment of a forward fueling and arming point actually inside Iraq, where the task force would land and refuel. But after a near-disastrous trial showed many of the same problems with blowing dust that had wrecked Operation Eagle Claw a decade earlier, an alternative was sought.

One option was to add a pair of 230-gallon auxiliary fuel tanks on the inboard stores stations of the Apaches, but this would require additional Apaches to haul enough Hellfires to destroy the targets. The eventual solution, which has been used ever since on the AH-64, was an asymmetrical arrangement with two quad Hellfire launchers on the outer stores positions, with one fuel tank and a nineteen-round 2.75-inch rocket launcher on the two inboard spots. Never before tried, the configuration initially met with institutional opposition from the Army Aviation authorities back home, but eventually it was approved. The new arrangement now gave the Apaches up to twenty minutes at the targets, though they were planning on needing only five.

Making sure that the Apaches got to the targets on time was the responsibility of Lieutenant Colonel Comer and his AFSOC MH-53Js, though Eager Anvil would take them into the uncharted territory of GPS navigation under combat conditions. In 1990–1991, the NAVISTAR GPS satellite constellation was still incomplete, causing gaps in the times of day when the system could deliver an accurate navigational fix. This meant that the time of the Eager Anvil strike, and thus the start of Operation Desert Storm, was at the mercy of a handful of satellites controlled on the other side of the world in Colorado Springs. And Task Force Normandy was not the only part of Desert Storm that would ride on that particular GPS window. Seven B-52Gs of the 2nd Bombardment Wing, flying nonstop from Barksdale Air Force Base near Shreveport, Louisiana, would be launching thirty-five GPS-guided cruise missiles at targets in northern Iraq at the same time as Task Force Normandy's ingress to their targets.

The upside of the effort to make GPS work for this attack plan can be summarized in one word: precision. In 1990, GPS could deliver three-dimensional accuracy within thirteen meters (about forty-three feet) of ground truth. Since the GPS system also delivered highly accurate timing pulses, it meant that the Pave Lows could hit their navigation checkpoints literally to the second. The only trick was to let the Apaches know when a particular checkpoint had been reached without breaking radio silence, so they could update their AHRS's (attitude-heading reference systems). The solution, which proved to be surprisingly simple, was to drop infrared chem lights, which were visible only on FLIR sensors and night vision goggles, so the Apaches were able to minimize any drift from the prescribed route.

December 27–30, 1990, Riyadh

It was Christmastime in Saudi Arabia, where it is not a national holiday. In Riyadh, a small group of colonels and lieutenant colonels were facing a general who, though heavyset, would never be mistaken for Santa Claus and who was reviewing Operation Eager Anvil for the final time. They were Colonel Jesse Johnson, Colonel Gary Gray, commander of 20th SOS, and lieutenant colonels Cody and Comer. They were in the "war room," General Schwarzkopf's subbasement command center deep below the Saudi Arabian Ministry of Defense and Aviation building. Sitting beside General Schwarzkopf were General Colin Powell, chairman of the Joint Chiefs of Staff, and Secretary of Defense Dick Cheney. If any of the colonels wondered at the unusual presence of the secretary of defense and the Joint Chiefs chairman at the briefing, they never commented on it.

Roughly thirty feet wide and twenty feet long, the room was filled with long tables topped with telephones, stacks of paper, and other tools and accessories necessary for staff officers at the nerve center of a major military campaign. Intelligence maps, updated constantly, adorned the walls. A large projection screen television, usually tuned to CNN, hung from the ceiling. At each corner of the room was a television set that would display weather maps and other vital information about the region. The room normally was filled with the noise of ringing phones, conversations, the shuffling of paper, and the footfalls of people constantly going in and out. But moments earlier, all the staff aides had been dismissed. The television sets were off, and the room was something it had not been for a long time—quiet.

When Schwarzkopf finished going over the operation with the colonels, he stared at them and asked one final question, "Can you guarantee me 100 percent success?"

Over the past few weeks, General Schwarzkopf had put this question, or a variation of it, to high- and low-ranking officers responsible for different plans and operations within the Desert Storm campaign. In some cases he demanded that the individual sign his name right then and there to the documents or maps. While it's arguable that a written guarantee enhances a plan's success, it certainly made clear whose heads would roll should it fail; Schwarzkopf was obviously planning for personal retribution against these men in the event of failure. Now he was asking them to put their careers, and in some cases their lives, on the line. The query was not unexpected. That

Photo: U.S. Department of Defense

Senior American military commanders and civilian leaders in the war room. Seated from left to right are Under Secretary of Defense for Policy Paul D. Wolfowitz, Chairman of the Joint Chiefs of Staff General Colin Powell, Secretary of Defense Dick Cheney, CENTCOM Commander in Chief General H. Norman Schwarzkopf, CENTCOM Deputy Chief of Staff Lieutenant General Cal Waller, and Major General Robert Johnston. Standing immediately behind them are, from left to right, commander of the marine forces in Operation Desert Shield/Desert Storm Lieutenant General Walt Boomer, 9th Air Force Tactical Air Command commander Lieutenant General Charles "Chuck" Horner, 3rd Army commander Lieutenant General John Yeosock, 7th Fleet commander Admiral Stan Arthur, and Special Operations Forces commander Colonel Jesse Johnson. The two men in front of the wall in the left rear are unidentified.

question had been repeated often since Colonel Johnson had asked it in August. Cody's best response to those worried about the mission's feasibility was to show them the mission training videotapes. Everyone who saw them went away impressed. But that had been practice. Now it was the real thing.

The colonels stared back at the general. Could they guarantee success? "Yes, sir" came the replies.

General Schwarzkopf said, "Then you get to start the war."[22]

Operation Eager Anvil had its final approval. Task Force Normandy would have the honor of scoring the first hits in the war. The decision regarding the mission's ultimate execution was now in Saddam Hussein's hands. If he did not agree to a diplomatic solution within three weeks, at an unspecified date after January 15, 1991, Operation Desert Shield, the defense of Saudi Arabia, would become Operation Desert Storm, the liberation of Kuwait.

January 1991

> Americans are weak. They have no stomach for a fight.
>
> —Excerpt from a telephone call from Barzan al-Tikriti, Iraq's ambassador to the U.N., to his half-brother, Saddam Hussein, following an inconclusive marathon meeting in Geneva, Switzerland, between Secretary of State James Baker, Iraq foreign minister Tariq Aziz, and Barzan al-Tikriti, January 9, 1991

> As far as I am concerned, I have done what I have to do—I don't know whether others will do something, but it appears to me that it is perhaps a little late for embarking on any other [peace] efforts.
>
> —U.N. Secretary General Javier Pérez de Cuéllar, January 15, 1991

> Wolfpack Execute Mission.
>
> —Message issued at 12:30 P.M., January 16, 1991, by Lieutenant General Chuck Horner to all units participating in Operation Desert Storm

A growing concern about operational security caused General Schwarzkopf to take extraordinary measures to deceive Saddam Hussein and Iraqi troops guarding the border. For weeks, large numbers of coalition aircraft had conducted nighttime flights along the border. The result was that the Iraqi air defenders became lulled by the repetitive masses on their radar screens. Schwarzkopf also forbade any offensive preparations, particularly deployments to forward operating bases, until the last possible minute, and then they had to be under the strictest secrecy. Task Force Normandy was not cleared to fly to its FOB at Al Jouf, about 150 miles south of the Iraqi border, until January 14. When Task Force Normandy departed from Camp Eagle II, it did so at night, and not even the crew at the intermediate refueling site at King Khalid Military City were aware of the task force's true purpose.

On January 15, colonels Cody and Comer finally were free to tell their pilots the complete details of the mission. Maps and the latest satellite photos were distributed. These had annotations with truly amazing details, including the location and probable sex (male) of a pet dog at one site, which had been nicknamed Jammal. Coordinates, flight paths to and from the targets, intelligence updates, GPS navigation points, and the joint timing of the attack were discussed. The most important, and bedeviling, aspect of the mission was making sure that both targets, approximately sixty-nine miles apart, were knocked out at exactly the same time so that no warning could be raised. Thankfully, the new GPS receivers in the Pave Lows made this a mere

Photo: U.S. Department of Defense

A tent city in Saudi Arabia, one of many that were erected to house military units participating in Operation Desert Shield/Desert Storm. Note the wire fence topped with razor wire in the foreground.

test of flying skills, something Lieutenant Colonel Comer and his AFSOC crews were supremely confident in. There was an undercurrent of pride and confidence in the pilots. Lieutenant Tom Drew, leader of Team White, later said he'd felt no fear. Rather, he was more nervous about whether or not they would do well on the mission.

They were all aware of the ongoing diplomatic efforts, and even at this late date they weren't sure whether or not they'd be leading the fight. Then, at about 2:00 P.M., Task Force Normandy received the order, "Wolfpack Execute Mission." Brigadier General Buster Glosson had chosen the code name Wolfpack not for any reason stemming from military history; rather, it was in honor of his alma mater, North Carolina State University. But the message meant, "We go!"

That evening, after he had conducted some preliminary flight preparations on his Apache, Lieutenant Drew sat beside his helicopter and stared up at the stars. He later said, "A lot of things went through my mind. I wondered if I would live long enough to see the sun come up in the morning, what my wife and daughter were doing at home, and how would Iraq retaliate."[23] Moments later, it was time to put those thoughts aside and climb into the cockpit.

At 12:56 A.M., January 17, on a cold, moonless night, Task Force Normandy, composed of nine Apaches, four Pave Lows, and a Black Hawk helicopter assigned to tactical recovery of aircraft and personnel, began lifting off. Team White, which had to travel the farthest, was airborne first, followed by Team Red five minutes later. With all navigation lights off, only fifty feet off the ground and flying at 120 knots per hour, they headed for targets code-named California and Nevada.

Upon completion of the mission, the Apaches were to radio one of the following code words: "Charlie" meant minimal destruction; "Bravo" signaled that the target was partially destroyed; "Alpha" announced total destruction. In less than two hours, they would know whether or not the guarantee of 100 percent success was real or would come back to haunt them.

The teams took indirect routes to their targets, taking advantage of the dry gullies of the wadis and the larger sand dunes that allowed them to fly under the Iraqi radar. Just after 2:00 A.M., Team White, with pilot Warrant Officer Thomas R. "Tip" O'Neal in the lead Apache behind the Pave Lows, was twelve miles south of the Iraqi border. That was when his copilot, Warrant

UH-60 BLACK HAWK

The UH-60 Black Hawk is a medium-lift assault helicopter that can perform a wide variety of missions, including tactical transport of troops, electronic warfare, and aeromedical evacuation. It is the most advanced twin-turbine military helicopter in the world. The Black Hawk is equipped with armor protection, self-sealing fuel tanks, and advanced avionics and electronics for increased survivability and capability. Its rotor blades are able to survive impacts from 23 mm cannon fire. Variants are in use by all branches of the U.S. military. It is the army's front-line utility helicopter.

SPECIFICATIONS

Manufacturer: Sikorsky
Crew: Minimum 2 pilots
Power plant: Two General Electric T700-GE-701 free-turbine turboshafts producing 1,560 shaft horsepower each
Length: 64 feet 10 inches (19.76 meters)
Height: 16 feet 10 inches (5.13 meters)
Rotor diameter: 53 feet 8 inches (16.36 meters)
Maximum speed: 222 mph (193 knots; 357 kmh)
Combat radius: 368 miles (1,200 nautical miles; 2,220 kilometers)
Ceiling: 19,000 feet (5,790 meters)
Maximum takeoff weight: 24,500 pounds (11,113 kilograms)
Armament: Two 7.62 mm M60 machine guns, M240 machine guns, or M134 miniguns

Photo: U.S. Department of Defense

Officer David A. Jones, voiced a warning over the intercom. There had been a burst of light in front of and below them. It was followed quickly by what appeared in the night vision goggles to be shooting stars sparkling up from the desert. Momentarily confused, O'Neal pushed the goggles away from his eyes and peered ahead in the darkness. He then saw the Pave Lows fire a few quick machine gun bursts. "Don't worry about it, Dave," he said, relieved. He told his copilot that a Pave Low was just clearing its machine guns.

But Lieutenant Colonel Cody, flying "Tail-End Charlie," had a better angle and knew differently. Iraqi border guards or someone in a Bedouin camp had heard them flying just fifty feet overhead and blind-fired machine guns and an SA-7 Grail shoulder mounted SAM in their direction.[24] "Shit. People know we're coming," he said to himself. He'd learn soon enough if a warning had gone out.

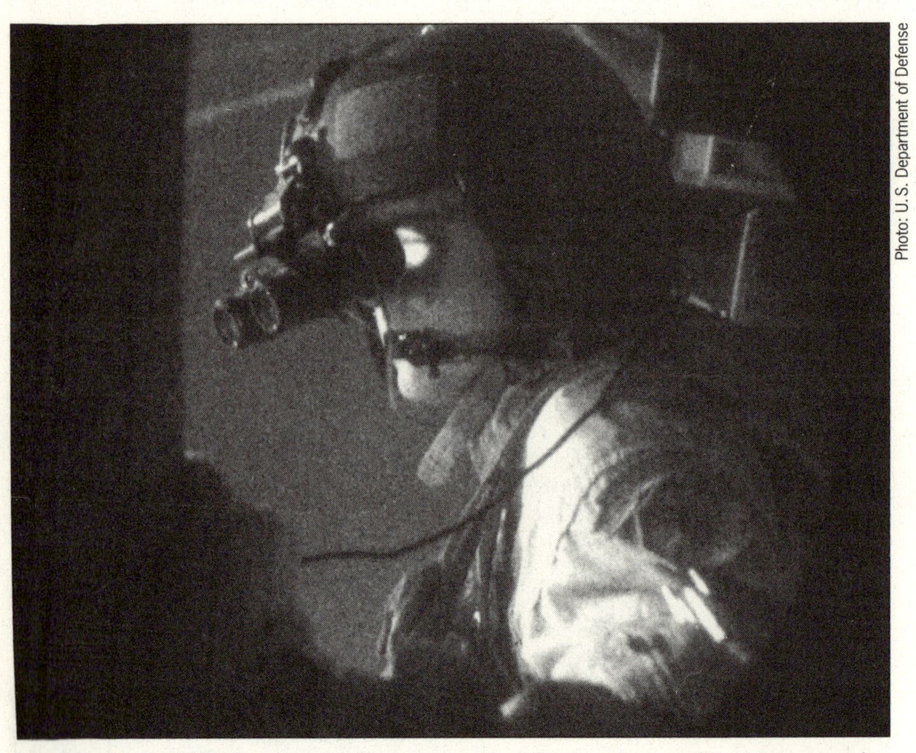

Photo: U.S. Department of Defense

A soldier in a helicopter scans the ground while wearing night vision goggles (NVGs). Nicknamed "nods," night vision goggles are one of a number of night vision devices (NVDs) used by the military that amplify available light from the moon and stars from 2,000 to 5,000 times. A person using NVGs does not look through them, as with binoculars. Instead, the wearer views an amplified electronic image on a phosphor screen. NVDs were first used in the 1950s, and advances in technology have allowed American special operations soldiers using NVDs to, in their phrase, "own the night."

They had been in the air approximately forty-five minutes when, twenty kilometers south of the target sites, the Pave Lows paused. They had reached the final GPS navigation reference point. Out of each was dropped a glowing bundle of chem lights. One by one, each Apache hovered over the bundle on the desert and updated its AHRS, and then set up for the final run to the target. The Pave Lows, along with the backup Apache and Blackhawk, then banked away to hover at the rendezvous site and await the return of the Apaches.

Even during the brief moment when they had been under fire, the helicopter pilots had not broken radio silence. Now, with tension mounting and having slowed to sixty kilometers per hour, they closed in on their targets. Just after 2:30 A.M., the pilots began to see lights in the distance. At 2:37 A.M., the two Apache groups, separated by sixty-nine miles, had simultaneously reached their objectives and were in position. Along the width of the targets and out of earshot, the Apaches aligned themselves four abreast. The targets had been divided down the middle. Each pair of Apaches was initially responsible for primary and secondary targets. Each Apache, fresh from its navigation fix, activated its laser, mounted its target acquisition designation system and fed into the onboard weapons computers the coordinates for the primary and secondary targets.

They suddenly saw movement at the sites and lights being extinguished in the trailers that housed the Iraqi troops. Someone or something had alerted the Iraqis. Finally, at 2:38 A.M., one minute before Operation Desert Storm's official start time, the team leaders issued an order to their teammates: "Party in ten." Simultaneously from the eight Apaches, sixteen Hellfires burst out of their racks with a deceptively soft whoosh and headed toward their targets at Mach 1. Ten seconds later, the Hellfires smashed into power generator buildings and other primary targets and exploded. Trailers, radar antennas, control buildings, antiaircraft artillery, and communications vans either vanished in a thunderous fireball or were shattered into pieces that were flung violently into the night air. Dozens of panicked figures ran madly back and forth.

At one site, a Hellfire exploded in a doorway just as an Iraqi technician ran into the doorframe. Another Iraqi had the horror of opening a door only to have the last thing he saw, the oncoming glow of a Hellfire missile, blow up in his face. The destruction was total, with every piece of equipment targeted in the original attack plan having been struck.

The Apaches then closed in to fire their secondary batteries. This time, it was an arpeggio of death. At just over a mile out, they loosed their volleys of Hydra 70 rockets. New explosions punctuated the night as vehicles disintegrated, their gas tanks adding to the fiery destruction. Red-hot flechettes tore through the air, slicing communications and power cables, the thin metal

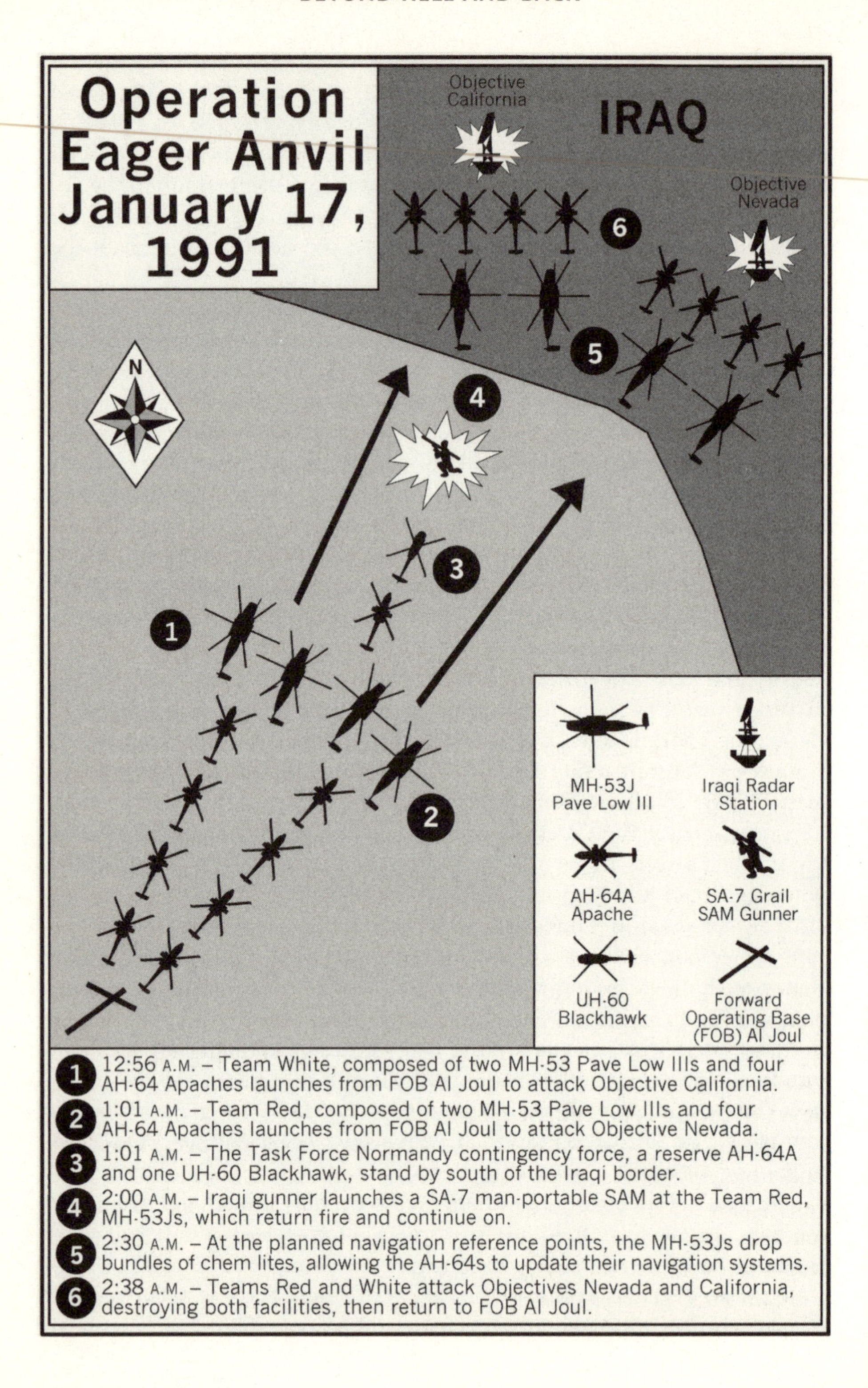
Operation
Eager Anvil
January 17,
1991
Objective
California
IRAQ
Objective
Nevada
N
6
5
4
3
1
2
MH-53J
Pave Low III
Iraqi Radar
Station
AH-64A
Apache
SA-7 Grail
SAM Gunner
UH-60
Blackhawk
Forward
Operating Base
(FOB) Al Joul
1 12:56 A.M. – Team White, composed of two MH-53 Pave Low IIIs and four AH-64 Apaches launches from FOB Al Joul to attack Objective California.
2 1:01 A.M. – Team Red, composed of two MH-53 Pave Low IIIs and four AH-64 Apaches launches from FOB Al Joul to attack Objective Nevada.
3 1:01 A.M. – The Task Force Normandy contingency force, a reserve AH-64A and one UH-60 Blackhawk, stand by south of the Iraqi border.
4 2:00 A.M. – Iraqi gunner launches a SA-7 man-portable SAM at the Team Red, MH-53Js, which return fire and continue on.
5 2:30 A.M. – At the planned navigation reference points, the MH-53Js drop bundles of chem lites, allowing the AH-64s to update their navigation systems.
6 2:38 A.M. – Teams Red and White attack Objectives Nevada and California, destroying both facilities, then return to FOB Al Joul.

F-15 EAGLE/STRIKE EAGLE

The Eagle's air superiority is achieved through a mixture of unprecedented maneuverability and acceleration, range, weapons, and avionics. It can penetrate enemy defense and outperform and outfight any current enemy aircraft. The F-15 has electronic systems and weaponry to detect, acquire, track, and attack enemy aircraft while operating in friendly or enemy-controlled airspace. The weapons and flight control systems are designed so one person can safely and effectively perform air-to-air combat. The F-15's superior maneuverability and acceleration are achieved through high engine-thrust-to-weight ratio and low wing loading. Low wing loading enables the aircraft to turn tightly without losing airspeed. It also has an internally mounted tactical electronic-warfare system, "identification friend or foe" system, electronic countermeasures set, and a central digital computer. The F-15E Strike Eagle variant is the all-weather long-range strike and ground-attack variant.

SPECIFICATIONS

Manufacturer: Boeing
Crew: Two
Power plant: Two Pratt & Whitney F100-229 turbofan engines with afterburners producing 19,000 pounds of thrust each
Length: 63 feet 9 inches (19.44 meters)
Height: 18 feet 6 inches (5.6 meters)
Wingspan: 42 feet 10 inches (13 meters)
Speed: Mach 2.51 plus 665 mph (2,698 kmh)
Range: 2,400 miles (3,900 kilometers)
Ceiling: 60,000 feet (18,300 meters)
Maximum takeoff weight: 81,000 pounds (36,450 kilograms)
Armament: One M-61A1 Vulcan 20 mm multibarrel internal gun and a combination of Sidewinder, Sparrow, Maverick, AMRAAM, and Slammer missiles and laser-guided bombs

Photo: U.S. Department of Defense

walls of the living and radar control trailers, and flesh with indiscriminate ease. And when the Apaches had closed to about a half mile, their 30 mm chain guns went to work, perforating the trailers and vehicles, and, as Pulitzer Prize–winning journalist Rick Atkinson wrote in *Crusade,* "rekilling the dead." Only Jammal, the pet dog identified at target California, survived. Video cameras on the White team Apaches recorded him escaping into the desert when the first Hellfire exploded.

Within four minutes, it was over. The Apaches hovered over the sites a final moment, their cameras recording the deadly results that the Pentagon would copy and provide to news services. Then they turned and proceeded south to the rendezvous point. It was time to radio the Pave Lows, who would forward their messages.

"California. Alpha, Alpha."

"Nevada. Alpha, Alpha."

As Task Force Normandy approached the Iraqi border, above them F-117s and other strike aircraft were already flying unopposed into Iraq. In fact, the first wave of F-15E Strike Eagles from the 4th Fighter Wing flew so low that the Apaches were heavily buffeted in their jet wash. "Poobah's Party" was fully under way, with the ten F-117As destroying the brains of the KARI system, just as planned. Within minutes, the outer ring of KARI radars saw what looked like a pair of aerial strike forces headed straight at downtown Baghdad. Immediately, the SAM batteries, reduced to local control, fired off a barrage of missiles, apparently killing forty-four of the radar-painted enemy aircraft.

Unfortunately for the Iraqi radar operators, what they had really seen was a fleet of modified target drones and tactical decoys, not strike aircraft. And

F-117A NIGHTHAWK

The F-117A Nighthawk is the world's first operational aircraft completely designed around stealth technology. It created a revolution in military warfare by incorporating low-observable technology into operational aircraft. It is equipped with sophisticated navigation and attack systems integrated into a digital avionics suite. It carries no radar, which lowers emissions and cross-section. It navigates primarily by GPS and high-accuracy inertial navigation. Missions are coordinated by an automated planning system that can perform all aspects of a strike mission, including weapons release. Targets are acquired by a thermal-imaging infrared system, slaved to a laser that determines the range and designates targets for laser-guided bombs.

Photo: U.S. Department of Defense

SPECIFICATIONS

Manufacturer: Lockheed
Crew: One
Power plant: Two General Electric F404-F1D2 turbofans producing 10,600 pounds of thrust each
Length: 63 feet 9 inches (20.08 meters)
Height: 12 feet 9.5 inches (3.78 meters)
Wing span: 43 feet 4 inches (13.2 meters)
Maximum speed: 700 mph (1,130 kmh)
Range: 535 miles (860 kilometers)
Ceiling: 33,000 feet (10,000 meters)
Loaded weight: 52,500 pounds (23,814 kilograms)
Armament: Two internal weapons bays with one hardpoint each capable of carrying Paveway and GBU laser-guided bombs or Maverick and HARM air-to-surface missiles

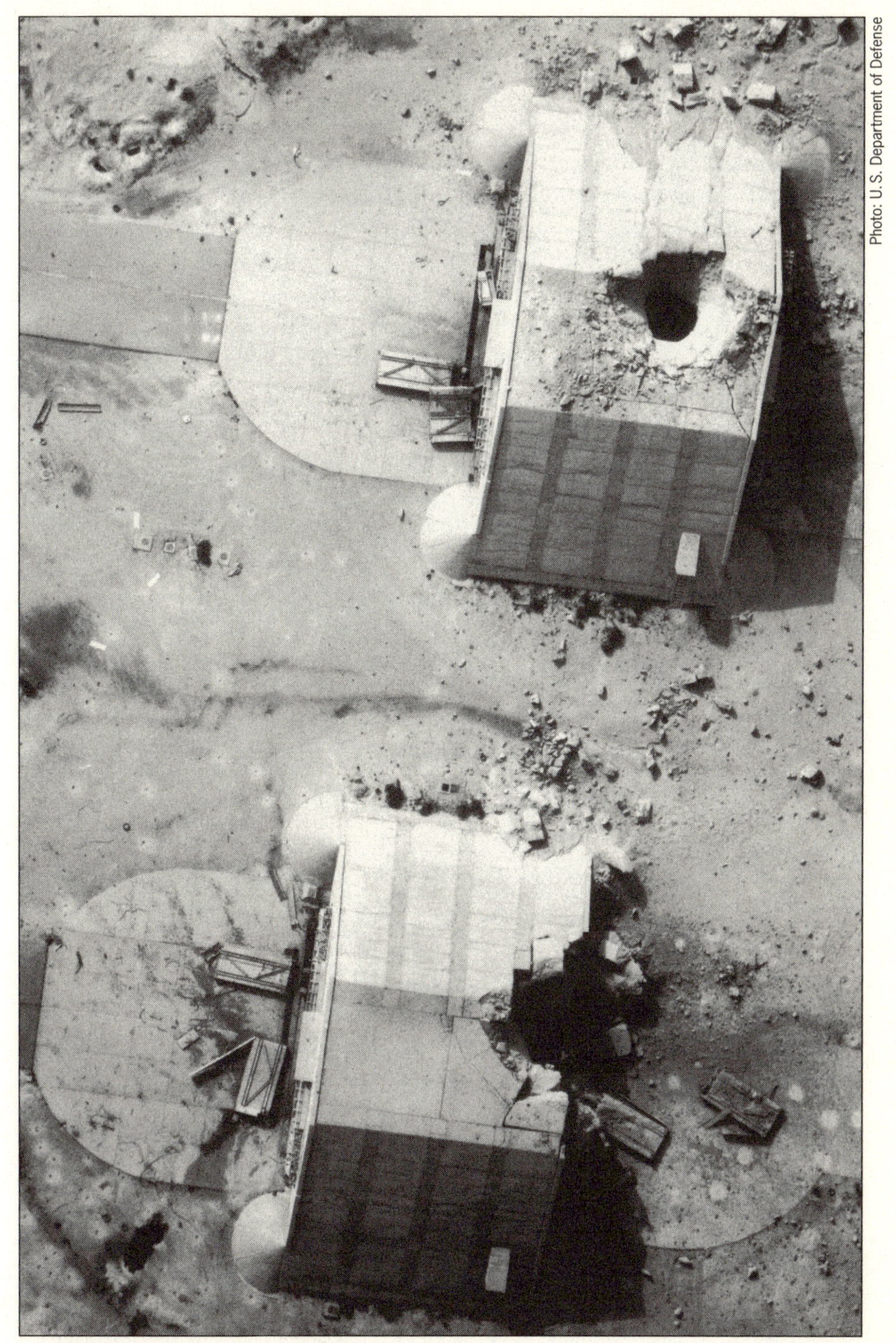

Photo: U.S. Department of Defense

The payoff: Two reinforced concrete aircraft hangars at the Ahmed Al Jaber Airfield destroyed during the air campaign of Operation Desert Storm.

at the same time the SAM gunners were killing dozens of worthless targets, dozens of F-4G Wild Weasels, F/A-18 Hornets, A-6E Intruders, and A-7E Corsairs rose from their low-level orbits and fired off between one hundred and two hundred (the actual number is still classified) AGM-88 HARMs (high-speed antiradiation missiles). Now lit up like a boulevard of car dealerships, the radar installations of the KARI system were decimated, along with most of their skilled operators. Combined with attacks by F-117s, Tomahawk cruise missiles, and other coalition aircraft, the KARI system was effectively dead before sunrise of January 17. (The only coalition casualty was a single F/A-18C, believed to have been shot down by an Iraqi MiG-25 Foxbat.)

The flight home for Task Force Normandy was uneventful, and the rapid pace of the war did not even allow the unit to celebrate together. Lieutenant Colonel Comer and his Pave Lows went immediately to a FOB where they would undertake search-and-rescue missions for the rest of the war. The Apaches made their way back to the rest of 1-101st and got ready to support the coming ground war, which would kick off the following month. For all involved, it was back to work with no time to consider what they had accomplished.

But as General Schwarzkopf later acknowledged, Task Force Normandy had "plucked out the eyes"[25] of Iraq's air defense in the west.

1. Flanagan, *Lightning*, 120.
2. Chuck Horner, Lt. Gen., USAF (Ret.), interview by Dwight Jon Zimmerman. August 11, 2006.
3. Putney, *Airpower Advantage*, 19.
4. Ibid.
5. Ibid., 21.
6. Ibid., 132.
7. Ibid., 126.
8. Ibid., 131.
9. Chuck Horner, interview by Dwight Jon Zimmerman, August 11, 2006.
10. Clancy, *Shadow Warriors*, 409.
11. U.S. Army Special Forces Command (Airborne) Fact Sheet, GlobalSecurity.org, 2005.
12. Clancy, *Shadow Warriors*, 407–408.
13. Putney, *Airpower Advantage*, 3.
14. Atkinson, *Crusade*, 21.
15. Ibid., 94–95.
16. Chuck Horner, interview by Dwight Jon Zimmerman, August 11, 2006.
17. Glosson, *War with Iraq*, 39.
18. Chuck Horner, interview by Dwight Jon Zimmerman, August 11, 2006.
19. Clancy, *Shadow Warriors*, 415.
20. Flanagan, *Lightning*, 59.
21. Taylor, *Lightning in the Storm*, 153.
22. Pushies, *U.S. Air Force Special Ops*, 35.
23. Flanagan, *Lightning*, 127–128.
24. Putney, *Airpower Advantage*, 455.
25. Mackenzie, "Apache Attack."

5

The Rescue of Captain Scott O'Grady

The post–cold war disintegration of Yugoslavia into the autonomous republics of Slovenia, Croatia, Bosnia-Herzegovina, Serbia, Montenegro, and Macedonia in 1991 was followed by a bitter civil war that began in April 1992. When the United Nations proved unable to stop the fighting, the United States led a NATO effort to enforce peace and facilitate reconstruction in the region. The aerial campaign of this effort, begun in 1993, was Operation Deny Flight, designed to keep the skies over the former Yugoslavia clear of combat aircraft from the warring republics. Heavily restricted by overbearing rules of engagement and a command structure that was normally incapable of reacting quickly enough to make military force a useful option, Deny Flight was only marginally successful. One of its few success stories was the rescue of Air Force Captain Scott O'Grady, who had been shot down by an enemy SAM days earlier. The instrument of his rescue was a unique force known as a Marine Expeditionary Unit (Special Operations Capable).

Thursday, June 8, 1995, 1:25 A.M.

"Clear to RTB."

The message was from Magic, the call sign for a NATO airborne early warning aircraft. Captain Thomas Oren "T. O." Hanford, code-named Basher One-One, and his wingman, Captain Clark Highstrete, Basher One-Two, of the 510th Fighter Squadron, were now free to return to base at Aviano, Italy. For the past two and a half hours, Hanford and Highstrete had conducted an uneventful combat air patrol (CAP) mission in their F-16C fighter jets off the Croatian coast, part of NATO's Operation Deny Flight. Their objective was to keep the skies clear of any combat aircraft from the warring republics. If any got into the air, they were authorized to shoot it down. Though things had been quiet, that did not mean their mission was a milk run, particularly after what had happened six days earlier.

Trained and armed by Russia, the Serbs had created a sophisticated anti-aircraft defense system that included the supersonic Russian-built SA-6 surface-to-air missiles (SAMs), formally designated the 9M9 Kvadrat ("square"), and known to the NATO nations by the code name Gainful. On June 2, an SA-6 launched from a mobile Serbian SAM battery had downed an F-16C piloted by U.S. Air Force Captain Scott O'Grady—code name Basher Five-Two. Since then, everyone was extra alert; no one on a Deny Flight mission wanted to be the next pilot to have his day ruined by one of the Serbs' supersonic SAM calling cards.

Normally, after being freed from patrol, Hanford would have banked north for Aviano and the hot meal and soft bed that awaited him. But this time he paused. Far below, in a countryside that reminded some Americans of West Virginia, was a fellow pilot who, depending on one's perspective, was

F-16 FIGHTING FALCON

The F-16 Fighting Falcon is a compact, highly maneuverable multirole fighter aircraft. The cockpit and its bubble canopy give the pilot unobstructed forward and upward vision, and greatly improved vision over the side and to the rear. The avionics systems include a highly accurate inertial navigation system in which a computer provides steering information to the pilot. The plane has UHF and VHF radios plus an instrument landing system. It also has a warning system and modular countermeasure pods to be used against airborne or surface electronic threats. The fuselage has space for additional avionics systems.

Photo: U.S. Department of Defense

SPECIFICATIONS

Manufacturer: Lockheed Martin
Crew: One
Power plant: One Pratt & Whitney F100-PW-200 (14,590 pounds of thrust; 23,770 pounds of thrust with afterburning) or one General Electric F110-GE-100 afterburning turbofan (17,155 pounds of thrust; 28,985 pounds of thrust with afterburning)
Length: 49 feet 5 inches (14.8 meters)
Height: 16 feet (4.8 meters)
Wingspan: 32 feet 8 inches (9.8 meters)
Speed: Mach 2-plus at altitude
Range: 2,000-plus miles (3,200 kilometers)
Ceiling: 55,000 feet (15,240 meters)
Maximum takeoff weight: 42,300 pounds (16,875 kilograms)
Armament: One M-61A1 20 mm Gatling gun; external pylons can carry up to six air-to-air missiles, conventional air-to-air and air-to-surface munitions, and electronic countermeasure pods

the quarry or the objective of an international manhunt; whose mattress was the cold, damp ground; whose blanket was a waterproof sheet of Tyvek paper imprinted with a topographical map of Bosnia and assorted pieces of survival information; whose physical condition was unknown; and whose "neighbors" had much fresh-spilled ethnic-cleansing blood on their hands. Captain O'Grady had already beaten the odds by staying out of the reach of the hostile ground patrols searching for him for six days. But at some point, his luck would run out.

Less than two years earlier, in October 1993, the American public was shocked by television images of the bodies of dead American soldiers being dragged by angry crowds down dusty streets in Mogadishu, Somalia. And in 1980, Americans had witnessed footage of Iranians spitting on the burned corpses of the aircrews that had been immolated when an RH-53D Sea Stallion helicopter crashed into a C-130 Hercules transport during Operation Eagle Claw, the failed attempt to rescue hostages held in the American embassy.

Would Scott O'Grady become a similar victim? Though his death was unlikely, it couldn't be entirely ruled out because the Serbs had already demonstrated by their actions in the civil war that was wracking the former Yugoslavia that they didn't care much about international agreements such as the Geneva Conventions. But the real point was that the Serb military wanted to capture O'Grady in the worst way. The propaganda value alone would have been immense. Then of course there was the almost certain chance that they'd use O'Grady to extract as many concessions as possible before setting him free. The American and NATO military assets in the region were determined to rescue him—but that could happen only if and when they got a fix on his location. The "if" part of that thought carried the rescuers' unspoken fear that O'Grady might be dead. No one had heard from him since the shootdown. Though hope remained, with each succeeding day of no contact, it became fainter.

Captain Hanford checked his fuel gauge. He had six thousand pounds of fuel left, giving him approximately forty minutes of flying time. His wingman was in slightly better shape. He radioed Magic, the NATO early warning aircraft: "We have twenty more minutes of play time. I'm going to stay out here and monitor SAR Alpha." SAR Alpha—Search and Rescue Alpha—was the radio channel O'Grady would be using to call for help.

"Roger," Magic responded. "You're clear to call on it if you want."

At about 1:30 A.M. local time and approximately eighty-five miles from the crash site of Scott O'Grady's F-16, T. O. Hanford embarked on a new mission. Hanford instructed his wingman to monitor signals from Magic while he did the searching. Hanford turned off his squelch filter control to better hear the weak signal that would come from a radio with low battery power, and dialed the UHF SAR Alpha frequency that was established for June 2. The frequency was changed daily for security reasons. With everything ready, Hanford then keyed his mike: "Basher One-One looking for Basher Five-Two." Then he listened.

This routine, while flying in a twenty-five-mile-long racetrack oval pattern over the area, went on for approximately fifteen minutes, with Hanford alternately calling and listening. Each time the only response was static. He was recording the track and replaying it, hoping to pick up a signal he might have missed the first time. But there was nothing.

The odds against Hanford hearing anything were daunting. O'Grady's radio was line-of-sight. That meant O'Grady could be transmitting, but if a hill stood between him and Hanford's fighter, Hanford couldn't pick up his signal. Also, in order to reduce the risk of Serb direction-finding equipment getting a lock on his transmissions, O'Grady would be sending out the shortest possible signals. There was no telling what, if any, strength was left in the batteries of O'Grady's radio, or if the radio was even serviceable. Ejection out of a disintegrating jet at high speed is, to oversimplify, extremely stressful. A lot of things have to go right, very quickly. Though surviving in-flight ejection had improved since the days of the Vietnam War, when the odds of death or maiming were almost a coin toss, injury or equipment damage during ejection was still possible. Finally, even though transmission range increased at night, Hanford was still close to the hundred-mile limit of O'Grady's PRC-112 survival radio, but that limit assumed a fully charged battery.

Twenty minutes passed. No response to Hanford's calls.

But Hanford was unwilling to call it quits. After telling Magic that he was staying for another twenty minutes, he made the risky decision to fly closer to the crash site region. He knew this would place him within the outer range limit of a known SAM defense ring, and possibly within range of a mobile SAM unit like the one that had downed O'Grady. The only way he'd know for sure was when his threat receiver warned him that an SA-6 was coming at him at Mach 2.8, almost three times the speed of sound.

Despite the risky move, minute after frustrating minute passed with no change. Once again Hanford checked his fuel status. Five minutes remained before he'd reach "bingo," the point where he'd have to break off and fly home. Then Hanford heard a blip—a surge in the static—but when he replayed it, it turned out to be a false read.

"Basher Five-Two, this is Basher One-One on Alpha." The time was 2:06 A.M.

Static.

Then, faintly, Hanford heard, ". . . Basher Five-Two . . ."

The snippet of a signal was weak. The voice sounded tired. Hanford wasn't sure if he had reached O'Grady or a search-and-rescue helicopter looking for O'Grady.

Using precise diction, Hanford carefully transmitted, "This is Basher One-One. I can barely hear you—say your call sign."

The response came: "Basher One-One . . . Basher Five-Two."

Hanford changed his flight pattern from an oval to a ten-mile circle in an attempt to increase his reception time. Again, he heard the tantalizing, weak signal from the ground.

"Basher Five-Two . . ."

And again, a cautious Hanford responded, "Understand you are Basher Five-Two. This is Basher One-One on Alpha."

"BINGO. BINGO."

It was the onboard computer. Though its digitized soprano voice was pleasant, its message was not. Hanford immediately had to make a hard choice. He could leave just when he had established contact with someone who *might* be Captain Scott O'Grady, or he could stay—knowing that the only way he could return to base would be after a nighttime in-flight refueling. His decision would also affect his wingman because no fighter was allowed to fly alone. Coming at the end of what was already a long night, that wasn't exactly a comfortable option.

Hanford knew what he had to do. He ignored the warning. And he waved off his wingman's warning as well.

If Scott O'Grady was down there, Hanford had to confirm it.

And *if* it were a trap . . . well, he'd find that out, too.

Hanford keyed his mike: "Basher Five-Two, this is Basher One-One, say again."

"This is Basher Five-Two, read you loud and clear."

Finally, Hanford got a distinct message. A wave of relief and joy swept through him as he answered, "Basher One-One has you loud and clear."

At that point, his flight path took him out of range. When he returned, Hanford again heard from the ground, "This is Basher Five-Two, how do you hear?"

"Basher Five-Two. This is Basher One-One," Hanford answered. Then Hanford's headset crackled with a message that, in four small words, symbolized the hopes of countless Americans who had been keeping vigil during the six-day drama.

"I'm alive! I'm alive!"

Hanford acknowledged. He now believed that the person he was talking to was Scott O'Grady. But he needed to absolutely certain. The last thing he wanted was to forward information that would result in a NATO SAR team flying into a trap. Fortunately, Hanford had served in Korea, and he knew O'Grady had as well. He then transmitted a question only the real Scott O'Grady would know how to answer.

"What was your squadron in Korea?"

"Juvats! Juvats!"

At Kunsan Air Base, South Korea, O'Grady had been a member of the 80th Fighter Squadron, nicknamed the Juvats, or headhunters, after their motto, *Audentes fortuna juvat*—"fortune favors the bold." Hanford was from the sister 35th Fighter Squadron, whose nickname was originally the Black Panthers but during the Vietnam War was changed to "the Pantons." Hanford had his confirmation.

"Copy that, you're *alive*! Glad to hear your voice," he radioed. Hanford's cheeks felt wet. Tears of joy streamed down as he circled high in a night sky that had just become a lot more friendly for one cold and hungry American pilot stranded in a dark and hostile land.[1] It also was the beginning of an epic special operations mission, executed under extremely difficult conditions and exacting time constraints.

The twenty-nine-year-old Brooklyn, New York, native whose fate was the focus of a multinational effort had dropped into a land that U.S. Secretary of State Warren Christopher called "the problem from hell."[2] It is an exaggeration, perhaps, but an apt analogy to say that upon the decline of the Greek gods' spiritual hegemony over the region, Ares, the god of war, and his sister Eris, the goddess of strife and discord, took refuge in the western Balkans, an area then known as Illyria.

Yugoslavia, originally named the Kingdom of Serbs, Croats, and Slovenes, was an independent Balkan state created out of the post–World War I chaos that followed the collapse of the Austro-Hungarian Empire. From 1945 to 1980, Yugoslavia had been ruled by Josip Brozevitch (or Broz), more famously known by his nom de guerre, Tito. A Communist, Tito forged his power base as a resistance leader fighting a guerrilla war against the Nazis in World War II. He was elected premier in 1945. At a time when most small nations allied themselves either with the free world led by the United States, or the communist world led by the Soviet Union, Tito successfully pursued a path of nonalignment, playing the Soviets off against the U.S. and its NATO allies. As a result, Yugoslavia was able to obtain millions of dollars of Russian military aid and training without suffering the heavy-handed, iron curtain consequences inflicted on the Soviet Union's Eastern European Warsaw Pact allies.

Yugoslavia was an imposed political creation that for less than one hundred years grouped under one national roof peoples whose religious and secular rivalries and hatreds had origins dating as far back as the first century. In 1908, the phrase "Balkan Powder Barrel" was a long-standing cliché.[3] Yet, despite such a past, many governments believed that the region had finally managed to put an end to its violent history.

In 1980 Tito died. In 1984, in "a spirit of friendship, solidarity, and fair play,"[4] Yugoslavia hosted the Winter Olympics in Sarajevo. In 1991, four republics, Slovenia, Croatia, Bosnia-Herzegovina, and Macedonia, separated from Yugoslavia.

Then the bloodletting began.

Friday, June 2, 1995

> I'm sorry that other events dictated that we started a little late today.
>
> —President Bill Clinton addressing the 1995 Men's and Women's NCAA Basketball Championship teams, 2:30 P.M. EDT[5]

On April 12, 1993, Operation Deny Flight—sometimes irreverently referred to as "Deny Life" by aircrews at Aviano, Italy, because the many back-to-back ten- to fourteen-hour days prevented them from taking advantage of their tourist paradise at the foothills of the Italian Alps[6]—was launched. Twelve NATO nations and almost 4,500 personnel participated in the operation that finally ended on December 20, 1995. Its mission was threefold:

1. To conduct aerial monitoring and enforce compliance with U.N. Security Council Resolution (UNSCR) 816, which banned flights by fixed-wing and rotary-wing aircraft in the airspace of Bosnia-Herzegovina, the "No-Fly Zone" or NFZ.
2. To provide close air support (CAS) to U.N. troops on the ground at the request of, and controlled by, United Nations forces under the provisions of UNSCRs 836, 958, and 981.
3. To conduct, after request by and in coordination with the U.N., approved air strikes against designated targets threatening the security of the U.N.-declared safe areas.[7]

Deny Flight was the aerial part of an international effort to end the brutal civil war raging in the former Yugoslavia. That effort began in September 1991 when the United Nations imposed an arms embargo on the warring republics. In April 1992, it dispatched the United Nations Protection Force (UNPROFOR), a ten-thousand-strong peacekeeping contingent, to establish safe zones for civilians and enforce a cease-fire. But not only was UNPROFOR too small and too lightly armed to impose its will on the combatants, it was incapable of providing adequate protection and security for itself. On May 25 and 26, NATO aircraft struck a Bosnian Serb ammunition depot in the city of Pale. The Serbs responded by taking more than 350 U.N. peacekeepers hostage, stepping up their attacks against U.N.-designated safe areas, and preventing relief convoys from reaching those areas. In addition, the Serbs warned that they were prepared to shoot down any NATO aircraft.

It was against this background that Captain Scott O'Grady suited up for his forty-seventh Deny Flight mission on the morning of June 2, 1995. O'Grady had been an F-16 pilot for four years and had logged approximately eight hundred hours in the jet also known as the Fighting Falcon. O'Grady was part of the famous 555th Squadron, the "Triple Nickel." The 555th was originally formed as a bomber squadron and flew B-26 Marauder medium bombers in the European theater of operations during World War II. The squadron was inactivated shortly after the war's end. It was reactivated in 1964, this time as a fighter squadron, and it achieved distinction in the Vietnam War as the leading air-to-air combat squadron with a tally of thirty-nine MiGs shot down. The only three air force aces of the war, pilots who had shot down a minimum of five enemy planes, had all served in the 555th, which was justifiably proud of its record and reputation.

Throughout Deny Flight, the 555th was stationed at Aviano, Italy, causing it to fall under U.S. Air Force or NATO rules of engagement, depending on the circumstances. The rules of engagement for Deny Flight missions called for patrols composed of two plane elements to be conducted south and thus theoretically well away from the known air defense centers near the towns of Bihać and Banja Luka, just below the 45th parallel. While U.S. and NATO forces would be flying at an altitude that would keep them out of range of the small, shoulder-mounted SA-7 surface-to-air missiles, they would still be exposed to missile attack.

The Russian-made SA-6 Gainful is a radar-guided, two-stage, solid fuel missile approximately sixteen feet long and twelve inches in diameter. Because it can fly at almost three times the speed of sound, a pilot has only a handful of seconds, if that much, to react once he discovers that the SA-6 radar used to guide the missile (NATO code name Straight Flush) has locked onto his aircraft. But what makes the SA-6 particularly dangerous is the mobility of the missile transporter-erector-launcher (TEL) and its tracking radar. Both are mounted onto tracked, self-propelled chassis, with each SA-6 TEL carrying three missiles. So, even though the Serbian air defenses were reported to be roughly along the 45th parallel, there was no guarantee that any of their SA-6 batteries hadn't secretly been moved south to set up an ambush.

For the fateful mission he flew on June 2, O'Grady would be the wingman for Captain Bob Wright, who thanks to his last name was christened with the nickname Wilbur. This would be the fifth Deny Flight mission O'Grady and Wright would fly together.

As O'Grady saw that morning, there was nothing special in their "frag" orders—so named because their instructions were a fragment of the overall operation scheduled for that day. The pre-mission briefing covered such essentials as duration of the mission, location and altitude, armament for their aircraft, communications frequencies of the day, location of the tankers, and any notable ground activity that might have an impact on the mission.

The briefing lasted about an hour. This was followed by a series of checks on equipment, gear, airplane—the thousand and one big and little things that must be done prior to each mission before a pilot climbs into the cockpit (even down to the removal of identifying unit patches in order to delay or prevent a captor from learning more than the minimum name, rank, and serial number of his captive).

Having completed these rituals, O'Grady strapped himself into his cockpit, proceeded through a final twenty-minute ground check, then got the "run-up" signal from the crew chief and began taxiing into takeoff position—behind and off to one side of Captain Wright. As leader, Wright would take off first. Sometimes, elements will take off simultaneously. The sight of two shining, sleek jet fighters going from a standing start to a near vertical accelerating leap into the sky in virtually the blink of an eye is nothing short of breathtaking. This time, though, it would be a sedate (though Webster's would challenge a fighter jock's definition of that word) two-stage departure. Twenty seconds after Wright's F-16 gracefully lifted off the runway, O'Grady released the brakes of his fighter, advanced the throttles first to full (or military) power, then quickly to afterburner level. The explosive surge of the afterburner hurled his $25 million high-performance aircraft down the runway and into the beautiful Italian sky.

The time was 1:15 P.M.

In short order, O'Grady and Wright reached their combat air patrol station twenty-seven thousand feet above the hills of Bosnia. Wright chose for the first leg of their watch a patrol flight path that ran from northwest to southeast. For the next four to six hours, they would fly a twenty-five-mile-long racetrack oval pattern, monitoring activity at the Serbian airfield at Udbina. Their position allowed them to be close enough to intercept any unauthorized air traffic in the no-fly zone, yet still keep them at a safe distance from the known SAM threats.

At 2:30 P.M., they left their station to take the first of two scheduled inflight refuelings from a tanker flying over the Adriatic Sea. They returned to station south of the town of Bihać for their second leg. This time Wright changed the direction so that their oval went from west to east. A few minutes after they had settled into their new routine, Wright's threat-warning system sounded an alert. Ground-based tracking radar, the kind used to guide SAM missiles, was "painting" his aircraft. Wright immediately called out over the Guard frequency monitored by all NATO planes and command stations, "Basher Five-One, mud six, bearing zero-nine-zero."

O'Grady, in position about a mile behind, added, "Basher Five-Two, naked." Decoded, Wright had said that a possible SAM-threat ground-based radar east of his position had made a "hit" on him. O'Grady's message was that his system hadn't detected anything. An E-3 Sentry code-named Magic, NATO's version of the U.S. Air Force's airborne warning and control system (AWACS) and responsible for monitoring electronic emissions in the area, replied to Wright, "Basher Five-One, your mud six is uncorrelated." Translation: the AWACS aircraft had detected nothing.

Wright and O'Grady shrugged. The intelligence briefing that morning had not raised any red flags about suspicious or increased military ground activity pertinent to Deny Flight operations. Their aircraft's defense system warning could have been of a real threat, or it could have been nothing more than

E3 SENTRY (AWACS)

The E-3 Sentry is an airborne warning and control system (AWACS) aircraft that provides all-weather surveillance, command, control, and communications needed by commanders of U.S. and NATO air defense forces. It is the premier air battle command and control aircraft in the world today. The E-3 Sentry is a modified Boeing 707/320 commercial airframe with a rotating radar dome. It contains the million-watt Doppler radar system, which permits surveillance from the earth's surface up into the stratosphere and over land or water. The radar (an AN/APY-1 or AN/APY-2) has a range of more than 200 miles (320 kilometers) for low-flying targets and farther for aerospace vehicles flying at medium to high altitudes. The radar combined with a friend-or-foe identification subsystem can look down to detect, identify, and track enemy and friendly low-flying aircraft by eliminating ground clutter returns that confuse other radar systems.

SPECIFICATIONS

Photo: U.S. Department of Defense

Manufacturer: Boeing
Crew: Flight crew: 4; AWACS specialists: 13–19
Power plant: Four Pratt & Whitney TF33-PW-100A turbofan engines, each producing 21,000 pounds of thrust
Length: 152 feet 11 inches (46.61 meters)
Height (to top of radome): 41 feet 4 inches (12.6 meters)
Wingspan: 145 feet 9 inches (44.42 meters)
Speed: 500 mph (800 kmh)
Range: 1,000 miles (1,610 kilometers)
Maximum takeoff weight: 347,000 pounds (156,000 kilograms)

the Serbian SAM batteries making an effort "full of sound and fury" but "signifying nothing." After a few minutes with no follow-up alerts, the two pilots settled back into their normal routine.

Then, while they were flying the eastbound leg of the racetrack, there was another warning. This time, O'Grady's threat alarm sounded. Somebody *was* tracking him.

The time was 3:03 P.M.

Now the airmen's roles were reversed. It was O'Grady who reported the "mud six, bearing zero-nine-zero," and Wright who responded that he was "naked" and did not detect the radar. Six seconds later, O'Grady heard the warning signal that no pilot wants to hear. A SAM target-tracking radar had locked onto his F-16. Though Magic did not confirm, O'Grady didn't need it. He knew he had to initiate countermeasures—now! The SAM could already be airborne. O'Grady promptly horsed his F-16 into a body-punishing series of maneuvers to try to break the radar lock.

"Counter. Counter." This was more bad news. The digitized female voice warning from his onboard computer told him the maneuvers weren't working. He ejected chaff—aluminum strips designed to confuse radar—bursting out of his fighter.

Suddenly an SA-6 shot into the space between Wright's and O'Grady's planes.

"Missiles in the air!" shouted Wright.

O'Grady never heard him. Just as those words were being spoken, a second missile gut-shot O'Grady's F-16 with a contact hit on the belly. The missile's high-explosive fragmentation warhead tore the fighter in two, and the wrecked and burning foresection containing Captain Scott O'Grady spiraled in a five-mile death plunge into and through the cloud layer below. O'Grady, battling the g-forces, grabbed the yellow handle of his ejection seat . . . and pulled.

In 1995, Admiral Leighton W. "Snuffy" Smith Jr. was commander in chief, U.S. Naval Forces Europe. Like other top American commanders, he had a corresponding senior command position in the NATO forces. He was in his office on the phone with General George Joulwan, the commanding general of the NATO ground forces in Europe, when his executive officer, Captain Rusty Petrea, walked in and passed him a note: "F-16 shot down near Bihać."

Admiral Smith passed the ominous news to General Joulwan and then ended the conversation. Everything he had been planning only minutes before now went by the boards. He had a rescue operation to oversee. As Admiral Smith began working out his options, a call came from Lieutenant General Michael E. "Mike" Ryan, commander of both the U.S. 16th Air Force and NATO Air Forces, South. Lieutenant General Ryan confirmed the bad news.

Photo: U.S. Department of Defense

U.S. Air Force Lieutenant General Mike Ryan speaks to the men who participated in the Captain Scott O'Grady rescue mission.

With that, Admiral Smith phoned his liaison to the U.N. forces in Bosnia, Air Commodore Michael C. Rudd of the Royal Air Force. Smith wanted Rudd to deliver a message to UNPROFOR commander General Bernard Janvier, with instructions for it to be passed on to General Ratko Mladic of the Bosnian Serb Army (a man who would later be brought up on war crimes charges for his role in the atrocities that occurred at Srebrenica, Sarajevo, and elsewhere). The message was: U.S. forces were going in to rescue the F-16 pilot. If any Bosnian Serbs tried to stop the effort, they would be killed. And because this would be a search-and-rescue operation, any SAM site that threatened the aircraft would be destroyed. Guaranteed.

Having issued that warning, Admiral Smith next turned to issuing the necessary orders for the rescue. He knew this was a formality. Many people were already very busy. Soon, more would join them.

Meanwhile, Scott O'Grady, dangling from his parachute, saw a military-type truck stop on the road thousands of feet below. What appeared to be uniformed men began to emerge from its back.

"Dear God, let me land in a safe place, without harm," he prayed.[8]

* * *

At 1:30 P.M. EDT, White House Press Secretary Mike McCurry was briefing the press corps. The subject: Bosnia. President Bill Clinton's policy was being hammered in the Republican-dominated Congress and the media, and thus was the day's top briefing item. Inevitably, questions comparing the situation in Bosnia to the Vietnam War were raised, and just as inevitably, deflected.

An hour earlier, the Pentagon had issued a brief press release stating that an air force F-16 had been shot down. This prompted an exchange that was revealing in its opacity:

> PRESS: Mike, does the White House have any word of the fate of the pilot?
>
> MCCURRY: The information available to us is the same information that's been made available by the Pentagon.
>
> PRESS: Mike, they didn't say, and this is an hour later. It's a pretty simple question.
>
> MCCURRY: The information we have is the same information they've already briefed on over there.

The questions then moved on to other subjects, and the briefing ended at 2:08 P.M.

At 2:20 P.M., President Clinton stood in the Rose Garden and made the following statement to the press pool:

> Good afternoon. I am very concerned about the loss of our F-16 over Bosnia and the fate of the American pilot. We are following that situation closely.
>
> I have spoken today with President Chirac about the situation in Bosnia and about the meetings that Secretary [of Defense] Perry and General Shalikashvili [chairman of the Joint Chiefs of Staff] will be attending. I've spoken with Secretary Perry and will meet with him and General "Shali" later today. We've also been in touch with the NATO commanders and with other governments.
>
> I want to reiterate and make absolutely clear that our policy on Bosnia remains firm. For reasons that I think are obvious, I will have no further comments on this situation today.

* * *

President Clinton then walked back into the White House. The time was 2:21 P.M. One obvious element was missing from the Pentagon press release, the press briefing, and President Clinton's statement: the F-16 pilot's name.

* * *

At the same time, the 24th Marine Expeditionary Unit, Special Operations Capable—MEU(SOC)—was embarked aboard the ships of the USS *Kearsarge* amphibious ready group as it steamed past the heel of the Italian peninsula and into the Adriatic Sea. A few days earlier, the amphibious assault ship *Kearsarge* had been participating in Operation Tridente, a NATO amphibious exercise off the coast of Sardinia. But when things began to go sour in Bosnia at the end of May, Vice Admiral Donald Pilling, commander of the U.S. Navy 6th Fleet and commander of NATO's Allied Naval Forces Southern Europe, ordered Tridente ended. He told the amphibious ready group (ARG) composed of the USS *Kearsarge*, the USS *Nashville*, and the USS *Pensacola*, and their support/escort ships, to expedite their transit to the Adriatic for possible operations in the former Yugoslavia.

The tradition of U.S. amphibious operations is a long one, reaching back to the Mexican-American War when General Winfield Scott's combined force of soldiers and marines landed at Veracruz in 1847. It reached its peak in

Photo: U.S. Department of Defense

The USS *Kearsarge*, undergoing sea trials in this 1993 photo, was one of a group of new amphibious assault ships designed to operate in littoral waters. The ships contain a complete assault package, ranging from troops and amphibious assault craft and transport helicopters to fixed- and rotary-winged aircraft capable of providing combat air support.

globe-spanning operations during World War II. But the concept of an assault-ready group composed of dedicated attack, escort, and support ships, a marine assault force, and aircraft, and specifically tasked to conduct operations in littoral zones, is a relatively recent creation. Grown from the World War II "tractor" groups used for amphibious invasions in the Pacific, ARGs, with their embarked marines, are the last remnants of a force that at one time had delivered divisions into battle.

ARGs are normally built around a helicopter assault ship with a flight deck that superficially resembles a World War II aircraft carrier. The *Kearsarge* (LHD-3) is the third vessel of the *Wasp*-class (LHD-1) amphibious assault ships. The *Kearsarge* is 844 feet long, displaces 40,500 tons at full combat load, and at the time of Operation Deny Flight, had a crew of approximately 1,300, berths for about 1,900 marines, and carried more than forty aircraft, including helicopters and AV-8B Harrier II vertical or short takeoff and landing (VSTOL) fighter-bombers.

But the most potent aspect of the *Kearsarge* is its versatility. On its own, it can simultaneously deploy landing craft, launch a helicopter assault, along with dedicated fighter-bomber and attack helicopter protection. This ability to "bite and hold" the enemy with alligator-like ferocity has earned these units the nickname 'Gator Navy.

The general rule for Special Operations Forces units is that they are highly specialized and trained, and composed of individuals (always volunteers) who have passed an extraordinarily rigorous mental and physical screening process. As with any generalization, there is an exception. In the special operations world of the 1990s, that exception was the MEU(SOC). As Tom Clancy described in his book *Marine*: "The MEU(SOC) is based upon the concept that given special training and equipment, regular units can be made capable of accomplishing both their normal duties and certain other extraordinary missions."[9]

The first MEU(SOC) unit was deployed in 1986. By 1995, the Marine Corps had seven such units, with two or three forward-deployed at any time around the world. Though MEU(SOC)s previously had handled everything from the evacuation of U.S. nationals in hot spots such as Liberia, Haiti, and Somalia, to combat in Operation Desert Storm, their accomplishments had gone largely unnoticed by the American public. That was now about to change.

The *Kearsarge* was approaching the northern Adriatic when it received the situation report from Admiral Pilling. The *Kearsarge*'s response was to go to a three-hour alert, which meant that within three hours of receiving mission launch orders, helicopters filled with marines would be lifting off the flight deck. Captain Jerome Schill, commander of the amphibious squadron, and then-Colonel Martin "Marty" Berndt (he was already a brigadier general selectee), commander of the 24th MEU(SOC), quickly called their staffs together to prepare a tactical recovery of aircraft and personnel, or TRAP, mission. The size and makeup of the TRAP force would be based on determination briefs that would identify the different team packages they would need, which depended on different estimates of rescue complexity and threat levels. Colonel Berndt's 24th MEU(SOC) had practiced TRAP missions back at home station in the United States with four different-size forces, labeled Alpha through Delta. For the proposed rescue of O'Grady, Berndt and his staff decided on a Delta, or D-TRAP, a platoon-size package and the largest such force they were prepared to launch.

Within an hour, the naval and marine staffs were satisfied that they had successful framework plans in place for the rescue of Captain O'Grady. Until the time they received the good-to-go order, they would war-game every rescue scenario they could imagine to ensure they were as prepared as possible.

All that was missing was a solid fix on Scott O'Grady's location—and knowledge of whether or not he was still alive.

O'Grady was alive. And, for the moment, free. He had landed in a grassy clearing about a mile or two away from the truck he had seen from the air, and approximately fifty feet away from the road. Quickly he shed his parachute and dashed into a nearby grove of trees. He had his survival kit, locator beacon to signal his position to search-and-rescue aircraft, and his radio. It was only after he had found fragile cover behind a large, exposed tree root that he discovered that he had left behind his auxiliary survival kit, which contained a backup radio and half his ration of water.

But it was too late to return to the clearing. The hunters had arrived.

Saturday, June 3, 1995

> I know all Americans join with me in sending their prayers to the family and loved ones of an American pilot who was shot down yesterday while doing his duty flying over Bosnia.
>
> —President Clinton in his radio address from the Oval Office

While the previous day had not gone poorly for Admiral Smith, neither had it gone particularly well. The key problem for him was that he and the rest of NATO didn't know if Captain O'Grady was dead or alive. O'Grady's F-16 was in Captain Wright's blind spot when it was hit, and Wright was initially too busy saving his own skin to devote any time to keeping an eye on O'Grady. When Wright was able to spare a glance O'Grady's way, he was able to get only a glimpse of the jet's burning foresection before it disappeared into the clouds below. During debriefing, Wright could not say for certain whether or not O'Grady had successfully ejected. He just did not know.

Further uncertainty was added by Serbian general Mladic, who claimed that his troops had already captured the pilot but refused to release any other information. Admiral Smith and his advisers chewed over this news like a dog with a bone. One early reason for hope that O'Grady had survived were Serbian video clips of the downed F-16's cockpit section: the ejection seat was missing. What exactly did this mean? Did the Serbs really have O'Grady, or were they simply confident they would capture him soon? Was O'Grady alive and being kept under wraps? If so, why? Was he hurt or dead, and were the Serbs keeping that information to themselves? Or were the Serbs bluffing? All attempts by NATO to draw out the truth were stonewalled.

Admiral Smith suspected that General Mladic was bluffing because he knew something that he was certain the general did not—the name of the pilot. One of the early decisions made by Admiral Smith was issuing an order not to release O'Grady's name to the public. So far, everyone, including the powers that be in Washington, were complying. Until he had solid intelligence otherwise, Admiral Smith would proceed under the assumption that O'Grady was alive and holed up somewhere, waiting for the cavalry to come and rescue him.

O'Grady had successfully eluded the searchers who were combing the immediate area. Once a pair had come within a few feet of his hiding place. They had moved away without seeing him. A combination of factors aided him in this "escape"—it was night, he had remained so still he had barely breathed, the underbrush was sufficiently thick to obscure the shape of his body, and O'Grady was convinced a certain amount of divine assistance helped as well. That thought caused him to touch the small silver cross on his neck, a gift from his sister, Stacy. He then checked the right breast pocket of his flight suit, where he kept for good luck the St. Christopher medallion given to him years ago by the mother of a high school friend. It wasn't there. His left breast pocket was empty as well. He had forgotten the medallion in his locker back at Aviano.

Sunday, June 4, 1995

Though the Serbs' claim of having captured an American pilot continued to be unconfirmed, they were in possession of the wreckage of O'Grady's F-16. CNN's *Headline News* and other media outlets ran stories with pictures of the wreckage. Admiral Smith and others involved in the rescue effort analyzed the images and reaching conflicting conclusions. Some said O'Grady couldn't have survived. Others thought he could. One thing they knew for sure: they didn't know.

Meanwhile, on the *Kearsarge,* officers continued to review different force-package options for the rescue; the marines assigned to the Delta TRAP package checked and cleaned yet again their equipment and weapons, and aircrews worked on maintaining the readiness of the helicopters and Harriers.

All were alert, waiting, and hoping.

Since his landing, Captain Scott O'Grady had periodically sent out short message bursts from his radio. He didn't dare broadcast for long for fear that the Serbs had radio-direction-finding vehicles in the area to track his transmissions. But the night had passed without any response.

Now it was day. The familiar noise caused Captain O'Grady to stare up through the treetops. It was the distinctive sound of a low-flying helicopter. For a second, O'Grady's hopes lifted. But as the sound neared, he became wary. The rotor beat didn't seem to be the same as an American search-and-rescue helicopter. Then he saw it—a silhouette that looked roughly like an American Huey: a French-built Gazelle. The Serbs had taken to the air in an effort to find him, and for some reason were able to get away with it despite the NATO "no-fly" patrols. O'Grady sought as much cover as possible and then stopped moving. For fifteen minutes the Gazelle searched the area; then its sound become more faint as it started to leave. O'Grady sighed. But he knew his relief was temporary. He had to find a safer place. But he'd have to wait until night before he dared move.

In the meantime, he decided to eat. Earlier he had searched the immediate area for any berries but had found nothing. "Dinner" was tree leaves washed down with one of his last remaining four-ounce water packs.

That afternoon the Gazelle returned. The Serbs weren't giving up.

Neither was Captain Scott O'Grady.

Monday, June 5, 1995

> LARRY KING: Anything you can tell us about the pilot?
>
> PRESIDENT CLINTON: No, except that we're working on it [the rescue] very hard.
>
> LARRY KING: Is he signaling? Is there a report of signals out of Bosnia?
>
> PRESIDENT CLINTON: Well, you know what the news reports are, but I can tell you that I have been keeping on top of this ever since the first report of the missing plane. And we're doing everything we can, but it's best to say as little as possible.
>
> —Excerpt from Larry King's interview of President Clinton on *Larry King Live*

Monday afternoon was a time of good news/bad news for Admiral Smith. The good news was a report of emergency beacon signals from the kind of device O'Grady would have. The bad news was multifold. Bad weather over Bosnia had been hampering the search efforts. In particular, low cloud cover and fog prevented helicopters and jets from making low-level flights over the search area. Also frustrating was that the signals were apparently coming from different locations, and there was no corroborating voice transmission. The tantalizing energy-beacon transmissions were maddeningly conflicting. They could mean that O'Grady was still on the run. Or they could mean that the Serbs had found the device and were playing deception games with the rescue effort, trying to bait the Americans into an ambush.

Despite such thin data, Air Force Chief of Staff General Ronald Fogelman went ahead and mentioned the beacon signals in a Pentagon press conference. Because this was the only piece of real information since the shootdown, the result was predictable. The news-hungry media's pot boiled over. According to some insiders, General Fogelman got into hot water with Defense Secretary William Perry over the disclosure. The disagreement would all blow over eventually, but until something definite happened one way or another, tempers in the chain of command would only get shorter. To those working on the rescue, it was amazing that there was no additional breach of security, official or otherwise. O'Grady's name was still unknown.

Meanwhile, General Mladic continued to make his claims of capture without backing them up with proof. With no evidence forthcoming, Admiral Smith remained convinced that Mladic did not have O'Grady, at least, not yet. That evening, the clouds again rolled in over Bosnia.

Their names were Alfred and Leroy. They were cows, and as such, Captain O'Grady should have given them female names. But he realized that only after he had christened his bovine companions, who contentedly chewed on meadow grass as close as four feet from his hiding place. While their grazing provided a welcome distraction, their presence was also a potential danger. The last thing O'Grady needed was to have the cattle herder discover him as he was rounding up his cows. Fortunately, after about an hour, the cows wandered away.

That evening it rained. The thunderstorm soaked O'Grady to the skin. But his discomfort was overridden by another survival consideration: he could replenish his water supply. Using a rubber sponge from his survival kit to soak up puddles of water gathering on his rucksack and survival tarp, he squeezed small streams of liquid into his water bags and additional self-sealing plastic bags. Hours later, he had added a new pint of water to his supply, and sponged some additional water down his dry throat.

Later that evening he decided to make an all-out effort to get in contact with a possible rescuer. First he turned on his locator beacon. Then he switched on his radio. Within a half hour of transmitting, he heard a faint message: "Basher Five-Two, this is Flashman . . . Can you hear me?"

O'Grady quickly keyed his microphone: "Flashman, this is Basher Five-Two."

The pilot in the aircraft above repeated, "Basher Five-Two, this is Flashman, if you hear me, on Guard [a search and rescue frequency]."

O'Grady replied again. Then waited a few minutes. There was no response. Disappointed, he turned off his beacon and radio.

Tuesday, June 6, 1995

> PRESS: What can you tell us about the downed American pilot—prospects or otherwise?
>
> KENNETH H. BACON: There's not much new to report. Unfortunately, the beacon signal has not been picked up today. We continue to look vigorously, but we do not have anything we can tell you on this.
>
> PRESS: The Serbs are now apparently claiming they do not have him. Is there any—
>
> KENNETH H. BACON: I understand they're claiming that. There have been a number of conflicting statements about this from the very beginning. My goal is to try to *not* make any conflicting statements about this, so we're going to just tell you that the search is continuing.
>
> —Press briefing by Kenneth H. Bacon
> of the Office of the Assistant Secretary
> of Defense, 1:45 P.M. EDT

When word of reception of O'Grady's emergency locator beacon signal was first relayed to the *Kearsarge*, the 24th MEU(SOC) increased its alert status from Alert-180 (three hours) to Alert-60 (one hour) so that the rescue force could take off within sixty minutes of a "go" signal. At the same time, other search-and-rescue assets tried to get a fix and a follow-up on the signal. But as the hours ticked by with no result, the alert status was reduced. Hope had faded, but it had not yet vanished. The marines assigned to the Delta TRAP force continued to wait and prepare in the event that the situation changed.

Captain O'Grady had found a supplement to his diet of bland leaves: ants. They tasted as sour as a lemon, but after trying one and not feeling any ill effects, the hunt was on, this time with him as the hunter.

Wednesday, June 7, 1995

> We've conducted thousands of sorties, more than 60,000 sorties in Deny Flight alone. These missions have not been risk-free. During these 60,000 sorties, there have been two aircraft shot down, one British, and just a few days ago, the American F-16. The risks will remain, but the value of Deny Flight is unquestionable in terms of the thousands of civilians saved from the shelling and bombing that would otherwise have occurred.
>
> —Secretary of Defense William Perry,
> excerpt from a prepared statement to the
> Senate Armed Services Committee and
> House National Security Committee

> PRESS: Anything on the pilot?
> CHRISTINE SHELLY: I have nothing on that.
>
> —Excerpt from U.S. Department
> of State daily press briefing
> conducted by Christine Shelly

It was evening when Captain T. O. Hanford and his wingman began their preflight routine. Since the shootdown, air operations over Bosnia had been greatly revised. The Deny Flight missions had been significantly scaled back, and approximately five hundred SAR sorties to find Scott O'Grady had been flown. As each day passed, more and more people involved in the rescue effort came to believe they knew why O'Grady had not yet been found, but none would speak of it. Until his body was brought forward, no one wanted to be the first to say he was dead. Still, after six days . . . It would have been different if O'Grady were a Special Operations officer trained in survival techniques—but an air force pilot roughing it for days? Not likely in the opinion of a number of "experts" interviewed by the press.

Captain Hanford was one of the skeptics regarding O'Grady's survivability. Even so, he knew he and everyone looking for O'Grady had to lend a hand, even if he did think it was a wild goose chase.

The moon was full, which Captain O'Grady didn't like as he stepped into the clearing he had just reached. But he weighed the possibility of being discovered that night against needing to get a fix on his location and sending out another signal, and he decided to take a chance. Once he reached the middle of the clearing, he set down his gear and took out his GPS receiver to get a fix on his location. Within a few minutes, he got the response he needed—his receiver had picked up signals from four satellites; three were the minimum needed to determine a position. So now he could relay his latitude and longitude to anyone he raised on his radio.

Munching on some meadow grass and protecting himself as best he could against the cold, Captain Scott O'Grady began his vigil transmitting.

Thursday, June 8, 1995

> Four words I thought I would never use in one sentence: Good news from Bosnia.
>
> —White House Press Secretary Mike McCurry

> To all my Viper buds and other Shit Hot Fighter Gods on the net—It was a good day at Aviano!
>
> —E-mail from Captain Scott Zobrist, 510th Fighter Squadron

The radio frequency of a PRC-112 survival radio is not secure. That means the radio's channel functions like an old-fashioned telephone party line. Anyone who knows the frequency and has powerful enough equipment can listen in—friend and enemy alike. So if the young pilot was to be rescued, things were going to have to happen fast. Early on the morning of June 8, Lieutenant Commander Reid Davis was mid-watch officer in the combat information center (CIC) on board the *Kearsarge.* Like other authorized eavesdroppers, he was monitoring the air operations network, which covered a variety of frequencies set aside for military use. And like the others, he was hearing nothing out of the ordinary. That began to change at about 2:00 A.M., when he started hearing talk containing the words "Basher Five-Two." A few minutes later, he picked up the ship's phone and woke up Captain Schill. Shortly after Davis hung up, he heard another message. This was from an aircraft code-named Ghost, an AC-130 gunship: "We got a positive authentication for Basher Five-Two."

The time was 2:17 A.M. At Aviano and Vicenza (approximately seventy miles southwest of Aviano along the foothills of the Alps), and aboard the *Kearsarge* in the Adriatic Sea, calls starting going out over secure lines and frequencies. NATO was coming alive to go in and get one of its own out of harm's way.

Colonel Berndt was in his stateroom when he got the word. Not only was he already awake, he was busy. Earlier, the combined air operations center in Vicenza had requested he produce a new plan, in which the 24th MEU(SOC) would provide assistance to a Basher Five-Two rescue attempt conducted by

Photo: U.S. Department of Defense

Part of the *Kearsarge*'s arsenal parked on its flight deck, including CH-46 Sea Knight, UH-1 Iroquois "Huey," AH-1W Super Cobra, and CH-53 Super Stallion helicopters.

other search-and-rescue forces. Admiral Smith had a variety of rescue assets available to him. The two most likely to be called on were the 24th MEU(SOC) and an AFSOC Special Operations detachment in Brindisi. Colonel Berndt understood that Admiral Smith wanted to have as many options as possible and was planning appropriately. His stateroom radio was tuned to the air operations net, and while he and a member of his staff worked up the plan, they half-listened to the transmissions.

They were nearing the end of their work when they started to hear the one-sided conversation from Hanford about Basher Five-Two. Berndt quickly guessed he was hearing the air half of an air-to-ground conversation, and that the ground half he could not hear was coming from Scott O'Grady.

At 2:35 A.M., Colonel Berndt's revised search-and-rescue support plan was ready.

It would never be used.

As luck would have it, Admiral Smith wasn't on board his flagship, the USS *La Salle* (AGF 3), when Captain Hanford made contact with Captain O'Grady. He wasn't even in the Mediterranean theater of operations. He was in London, having participated earlier in the day in a scheduled function hosted by the British army. Admiral Smith was asleep in his room at the U.S. Navy's headquarters when he got the call confirming contact with Scott O'Grady. Within minutes, Admiral Smith was in uniform and dashing down the three floors to the headquarters' command center. As he was getting updated with the latest intelligence, he mulled over his options. The 24th MEU(SOC) was alternating its alert status regarding the rescue with an AFSOC special operations unit, part of the joint special operations task force based in Brindisi, located on the heel of the Italian peninsula boot. The *Kearsarge* was off the Croatian coast and approximately a hundred miles from O'Grady's location.

Time was now the critical factor. No one could say with any certainty if the Serbs had been monitoring the recent transmissions and were attempting to get their own fix on O'Grady's location, or were planning stepped-up air defense measures. The air defense danger and the complexity of organizing the rescue operation caused some to think that it would be better to conduct the rescue at night. This would mean Captain O'Grady would have to spend another day on the ground. This information was passed to Captain Hanford, still orbiting over O'Grady's location, who dutifully gave O'Grady the news. Everyone in the room had heard O'Grady's response. He wanted out *now.* None could blame him. Admiral Smith got on the secure line to Captain Schill.

It was organized chaos aboard the *Kearsarge* when Captain Schill answered the phone. Admiral Smith asked him how long it would take for the TRAP team to deploy once he issued his order. Captain Schill answered that they were presently on Alert-60—within sixty minutes of his order, the TRAP team would be in the air. Admiral Smith told him to get everyone and everything in place and stand by for further orders.

Smith's next call was to General Mike Ryan, commander of the 16th Air Force. Smith was convinced that whomever he sent on the rescue mission was going into harm's way. Therefore, the admiral wanted that rescue team to have the strongest support possible. In military parlance, Admiral Smith needed a SEAD (suppression of enemy air defenses) package, along with a combat air patrol (CAP) unit, to augment the rescue force. General Ryan was working on the assets he could provide as part of a SEAD/CAP package when he got Admiral Smith's call. General Ryan assured him that when the team took off, it would have a lot of friends backing them up.

Meanwhile, aboard the *Kearsarge,* Captain Schill made a decision that caused the risk factor of the ARG to spike. He wanted to cut to the minimum the transit time for the TRAP team. He ordered the ARG and its escorts, cruising at about fifty miles off the Dalmatian coast, to cross the Croatian twelve-mile territorial water border and close to within six miles of the coast. There simply wasn't time to dot the diplomatic i and cross the diplomatic t—permission would likely have been refused anyway. If the ships were attacked, the locals could claim they were simply defending themselves from hostile action.

There was also all manner of danger lying below the warships' hulls. Conducting combat operations in littoral zones is, in a word, hazardous. The *Kearsarge* had a draft of twenty-seven feet. The *Nashville*'s was twenty-three feet and the *Pensacola*'s was twenty feet. The navigation charts claimed local sea depths varying from forty-five to sixty feet. The charts had been recently updated, but that was still no guarantee that the sea bottom would be at the depth noted. And an uncharted rock was only one of the worries. The possible threat of underwater mines, either recently laid or relics from World War II, also existed. The only positive knowledge would come with an explosion. And there was the chance of yet a third, passive threat. Sunken ships, going back to the time of the ancient Greeks, littered the seabed. The possibility of hitting one was remote but still there. While colliding with the wreckage of a Roman trireme or a German U-boat loaded with Nazi gold may have a more romantic cachet than contact with the rusted hull of a smuggler's trawler, the result could still stop the rescue effort cold. With no time to conduct vital intelligence, much faith had to be placed in the accuracy of the charts and the quick response abilities of crews manning sonar and radar screens.

At 3:00 A.M., the Delta TRAP team—the largest and most powerful of the 24th's preplanned TRAP packages—was ordered to report to the officers' wardroom. As the officers filed into the low-ceilinged room, other marines began gathering in the hangar deck. There, in the vast man-made cavern, the drone of the ventilation system and smell of jet fuel combined with sounds from the flight deck above where helicopter and Harrier engines were being started and warmed up. Words shouted over the din on the ship's public address system confirmed what the noise and activity suggested. The Special Operations team in Brindisi would not be used. The rescue mission was a go for the Marines of the Delta TRAP package.

At 4:00 A.M., the marines began breaking out the landing force operational readiness material—antitank rockets and heavy weapons. As planned by Colonel Berndt and his staff, the Delta TRAP package was anything but small or subtle. The platoon-size force would also contain a mortar team, which was unusual for a rescue operation. The marines were going in loaded for bear, ready to fight hard for O'Grady if they had to.

Another order came down: conduct live-fire weapons checks of personal weapons. In groups, the marines lined up in front of the large opening below the aft elevator deck. Soon explosive staccato barks of M-16 combat rifles and M9 pistols added to the noise, and the air filled with the scent of that most martial of colognes, spent gunpowder. For forty-eight marines, some still in their late teens, it was their first action. They lined up in assigned rows called sticks beside the hundred-pound packages of prepositioned gear and faced the long sloped ramp on the starboard side of the hull that connected the hangar deck to the flight deck. They were together and at the same time alone in the unique way that happens when men prepare for combat. If things went badly for them at the landing site, reinforcements in the form of two quick-reaction groups, code-named Sparrowhawk and Bald Eagle, would be ready. However, nobody needed to be reminded that this was the same kind of situation that had killed nineteen Americans in Mogadishu less than two years earlier. If there was a Serbian ambush waiting for them ashore, the rescue of Scott O'Grady could easily turn into a bloodbath.

At 4:50 A.M., the marines received the order: board the helicopters. What all but a few of the marines officers did not know was that they'd be going in under United Nations and not U.S. rules of engagement (ROE). The reasons were complex, the most important being possible retaliation against the approximately two hundred U.N. staff members still being held hostage by the Serbs ashore. U.S. ROE allowed for American forces to attack and destroy weapons systems if they were being targeted by tracking radars. But under U.N. ROE, forces had to wait until they were actually being shot at before engaging the enemy. This raised the risk level for the TRAP team because now

AV-8B HARRIER II

The AV-8B Harrier II is a single-seat, light-attack aircraft that provides offensive air support to a marine air-ground task force. By virtue of its vertical or short take-off and landing (VSTOL) capability, the AV-8B can operate from a variety of amphibious ships, rapidly constructed expeditionary airfields, forward sites (e.g., roads), and damaged conventional airfields. This makes the aircraft particularly well suited for providing dedicated close air support. The mission of the marine VMA VSTOL squadron is to attack and destroy surface and air targets, escort helicopters, and conduct other such air operations as may be directed. In 1991, Harrier IIs were the first U.S. Marine Corps tactical aircraft to arrive for Operation Desert Storm over the Persian Gulf. During the forty-two days of combat, eighty-six Harrier IIs flew 3,380 combat sorties (4,083 combat hours) and delivered more than six million pounds of ordnance.

SPECIFICATIONS

Photo: U.S. Department of Defense

Manufacturer: Boeing
Crew: One
Power plant: One Rolls-Royce Pegasus 105-vectored thrust turbofan engine producing 21,750 pounds of thrust
Length: 46 feet 4 inches (14.12 meters)
Height: 11 feet 8 inches (3.55 meters)
Wingspan: 30 feet 4 inches (9.25 meters)
Speed: 675 mph (1,085 kph) at sea level
Range: 1,200 nautical miles (1,100 kilometers)
Ceiling: 38,000 feet (11,582 meters)
Maximum takeoff weight: 31,000 pounds (14,060 kilograms)
Armament: One GAU-12/U Equalizer 25 mm five-barrel Gatling gun, plus a maximum of 13,200 pounds of bombs, rockets, missiles, or extra fuel tanks

their escorting AV-B Harriers and AH-1W Cobra attack helicopters did not have the option, if it became necessary, of clearing a path through a blocking SAM ring in order to reach O'Grady or return to the *Kearsarge*. They'd have to let the enemy shoot first and hope like hell that support aircraft radar jammers, chaff, flares, and other passive defenses would be sufficient protection to get them through trouble.

The marines grabbed their hundred-pound loads and began marching up the long, steep ramp that was barely wide enough for two fully loaded servicemen side by side. At the top they stopped to wait for the deck crewman who would guide them onto the flight deck and to one of two CH-53 Sea Stallion helicopters. The nonskid coating on the flight deck glistened with predawn condensation. All deck surfaces exposed to the elements had this coating. It was a faded gray and had the texture of freshly applied flashing compound. A stiff breeze, caused when the accelerating ship steered into the wind for takeoff operations, carried the predawn chill and stink of jet fuel to the nostrils of the marines. The whine of Harrier jet engines and the hollow pillow-against-mattress thwack of rotor blades beating the air made voice communication impossible. All instructions were now being issued through hand signals.

Originally, the TRAP mission had been intended as a night operation. But the late hour of confirmation of O'Grady's location and getting approval and themselves ready had pushed back the time when they could take off. The pale light of the false dawn warned them all—the rescue would be conducted in broad daylight.

Leaning into the wind and crouching to stay well below the spinning rotors, the marines, including Colonel Berndt, were led by the ship's combat cargo personnel onto the waiting Sea Stallion helicopters. Also ready in the flight line were their immediate escorts, two Cobra attack helicopters and four Harrier II fighters.

In the early morning light, the rescue craft began taking off in assault formation straight down the flight deck. Once aloft, they circled the *Kearsarge* in a holding pattern as they firmed up their formation. Then they received a message from the *Kearsarge*: the mission was on hold. The SEAD/CAP package, a combined air force, navy, and marines effort composed of F-15 Eagles and Strike Eagles, an E-3 Sentry AEW (airborne early warning), and F/A-18D Hornets carrying HARM antiradiation missiles designed to take out SAMs, was still getting organized.

Minute after minute passed. As the delay increased, so did concerns about the aircraft's fuel states. The Cobra helicopters had the smallest gas tanks and were the first to return for refueling. Later, some would claim the delay lasted thirty minutes, some said forty, and others claimed a forty-five-minute wait.

At 5:45 A.M., the TRAP team finally got the go order. Captain Hanford, in the air for almost six hours by now, radioed O'Grady, "The cavalry's coming."

Not long after he sent that transmission, Hanford received a message ordering him back to base. He didn't want to go, but he had been up far longer than anyone had anticipated. Now it was time for the pilots in the arriving CAP to take over. Reluctantly, Hanford radioed O'Grady the situation and said that until he was rescued by the marines, he would be talking to Captain Vaughn Littlejohn, one of the CAP pilots. Flying as Littlejohn's wingman in the CAP was Captain Scott Zobrist.

Four minutes after receipt of the go order, the TRAP team went "feet dry," which meant they were now flying over land. To reduce the SAM threat, the team was flying at high speed and under the radar at about two hundred feet above ground level. The terrain was flat; the visibility was good. As they got farther inland, Major William Tarbutton saw the mountains rising ahead, along with the weather condition that had hamstrung the search for Scott O'Grady: fog and low-level clouds. Major Tarbutton quickly realized the original flight plan was inoperable under these conditions. He needed a new

AH-1 COBRA

The AH-1 Cobra was the world's first rotary-winged aircraft to be designed specifically as an armed attack helicopter. The need for a dedicated attack helicopter became apparent during the early months of the Vietnam War, when many helicopters were lost to ground fire. The AH-1 was fast, heavily armed, and highly maneuverable. Its ability to cover unarmed helicopters made it a powerful combatant in Vietnam and other conflicts. Its precedent-setting design led to many variants, making it one of the most successful military helicopters. The Cobra was eventually replaced in the army by the AH-64 Apache. However, the U.S. Marine Corps has ordered upgraded versions, including the new AH-1Z Super Cobra.

SPECIFICATIONS

Manufacturer: Bell Helicopter Textron
Crew: Two
Power plant: Two General Electric T700-GE-401 engines producing 1,775 shaft horsepower each
Length: 58 feet (17.7 meters)
Height: 13 feet 9 inches (4.2 meters)
Rotor diameter: 48 feet (14.6 meters)
Speed: 169 mph (148 knots; 277 kmh)
Range: 294.4 miles (256 nautical miles; 485 kilometers)
Ceiling: 18,700 feet (5,703.5 meters)
Rate of climb: 1,620 feet per minute (8.2 meters per second)
Maximum takeoff weight: 10,000 pounds (4,500 kilograms)
Armament: M197 3-barreled 20 mm Gatling cannon, 2.75-inch rockets, TOW, Hellfire, Sidewinder, and Sidearm missiles.

Photo: U.S. Department of Defense

route to O'Grady, one that would keep them clear of the SAMs as they flew above the mountains. He keyed his mike and called the AWACS "traffic cop" keeping track of all the air activity, Magic.

The playwright George Bernard Shaw once said, "England and America are two countries separated by a common language." Something similar could be said of the different branches of the military. When Major Tarbutton contacted Magic, he requested new "steers" to the pickup point. Seconds ticked away in silence as the team got closer to the mountains. What Major Tarbutton didn't know was that his plain-language request was interpreted by Magic as a code-word request—and their code-word checklist did not contain the word *steers*. In air force parlance, what Major Tarbutton needed was a new vector. Major Tarbutton realized the confusion when he received a clarification query from Magic. Quickly, new vectors were issued, and the TRAP team banked away into its new route, in the open air layer between fog and clouds.

With reference points above and below obscured, the team was now flying on instruments, the most important of which was the relatively new Global Positioning System (GPS) recently installed on U.S. aircraft. GPS units were also standard issue in survival equipment packages like the one Captain O'Grady had. When O'Grady and Captain Hanford established contact, O'Grady, afraid that his radio's battery power would expire at any moment, promptly gave Hanford his GPS coordinates. This information was quickly passed up the line to the *Kearsarge*. Though the GPS unit on the CH-53 carrying Colonel Berndt malfunctioned, the units on the other helicopters were operational, and the team arrived at its navigational checkpoints on schedule.

By 6:30 A.M., the team reached the ridge that separated them from Scott O'Grady's last known location. Even though Colonel Berndt was flying with the team, the actual mission commander and thus the person directly responsible for running the operation was Major William Tarbutton, pilot of the lead Sea Stallion. He next ordered the Cobra attack helicopters to cross the ridge and establish contact while the rescue helicopters hovered. If there was a trap, the heavily armed and armored Cobras would deliver a very bloody nose to the ambushers. Cobra pilot Major Scott Mykleby led his wingman over the fog-shrouded ridge.

Less than ten minutes later, Mykleby authenticated contact with O'Grady. But there was still a problem with the fog. Unless a hole appeared in it, they couldn't land. In the meantime, Mykleby requested O'Grady to try to guide them to the location exactly over his position. O'Grady responded by telling him the helicopters were now north of where he was hiding. When O'Grady thought they were overhead, Mykleby told him to mark his position with smoke. A few seconds later Mykleby saw a smudge of orange appear in the fog. As soon as he saw the smoke, Mykleby ordered the CH-53s in.

A hole then opened in the fog, and if they were to take advantage of it before it closed, the team needed another smoke marker. But O'Grady didn't have any more. Acting quickly, Major Nick Hall in the second Cobra opened the canopy door and dropped a yellow smoke grenade just as the rescue choppers came into view. It was now the moment of truth for the entire operation.

Major Tarbutton, piloting the lead CH-53, saw that not only was the hole in the fog small, it was shrinking. They could see they were over a clearing on the ground, but they didn't know its size or much about its features. There had been no time to do any sort of visual reconnaissance of the area, and the era of Predator UAVs (unmanned aerial vehicles) was still some years in the future. With almost zero visibility, there could be no approach; none was possible. The only way to the pickup site was straight down. Major Tarbutton had more than six thousand flight hours in helicopters and had been a pilot for presidents Reagan and Bush. He didn't hesitate. He stood the huge chopper on its tail in what Captain Paul Fortunato, piloting the second Sea Stallion, later called "the big tail stand" and dropped the CH-53 like a stone into the fog hole. A moment later, Captain Fortunato copied the maneuver and followed him in.

The helicopters finally righted themselves at tree level. Only fifteen feet above the ground, Tarbutton saw the pickup point for the first time. The landing site was rocky, and a sturdy barbed wire fence intersected it. And it was *really* small. Making room for both of the big CH-53s would be tricky. With his crew chief guiding him over the fence, Tarbutton got his helicopter into position and landed. As soon as his Sea Stallion touched the ground, as they had been trained, the marines exited the helicopter like quicksilver and fanned out to secure the perimeter of the landing zone.

Captain Fortunato tried to land, but at his first touchdown point the rocky terrain blocked the aircraft's exit ramp. There wasn't much room for maneuver, but somehow he managed. The second landing was good. As soon as the ramp dropped, the marines began storming out . . . to be greeted by a scraggly-bearded, pistol-packing wild man wearing a tattered flight suit and a bright orange beanie hat, running toward them as if the hounds of hell were at his heels. It was Captain Scott O'Grady.

People have been known to be shot for running toward a marine helicopter with a weapon in hand. And O'Grady did wind up in at least one marine's gun sight. Fortunately for him, he was expected. Sergeant Scott Pfister had just emerged from Captain Fortunato's helicopter when he saw O'Grady. The marine ran up to O'Grady, knocked the pistol out of his hand, picked it up, and then hustled him over to Major Tarbutton's Sea Stallion, where, with Pfister pushing and Colonel Berndt pulling, Captain O'Grady was hauled into the helicopter.

The time was 6:41 A.M. The rescuers had been on the ground less than five

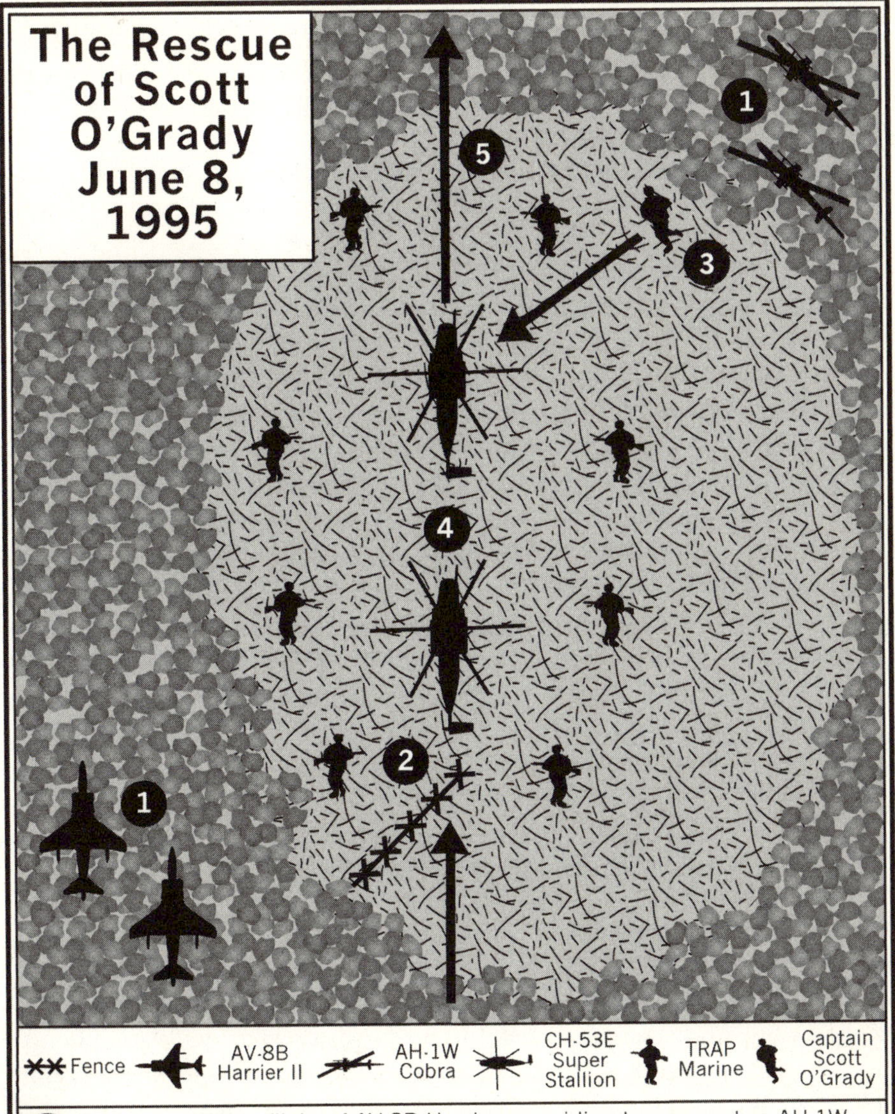

1. 6:27 A.M. – With a flight of AV-8B Harriers providing top cover, two AH-1W Cobra attack helicopters check the landing zone, contact Captain O'Grady to verify his identity, and lay smoke to mark his position.
2. 6:38 A.M. – Despite ground fog and one helicopter hitting a fence, two CH-53E Super Stallions land successfully in the landing zone, and deploy the embarked TRAP marines in a perimeter around the two aircraft.
3. 6:41 A.M. – Seeing the marines on the ground, the Cobra lead pilot orders Captain O'Grady to move towards the CH-53Es; O'Grady is met by a crew chief and taken aboard.
4. 6:43 A.M. – With O'Grady aboard, the mission commander recalls the marines of the ground force, who reboard the CH-53Es.
5. 6:48 A.M. – With all aboard, the CH-53Es lift off, form up with the Cobras, and head east for the Adriatic and USS *Kearsarge*.

minutes. As O'Grady was made comfortable and the marines were called back, Major Tarbutton gave everyone listening to the mission radio channel the heads-up: they had O'Grady.

In London, Admiral Smith and everyone in the communications center burst into loud cheers and applause.

But between the TRAP team and the *Kearsarge* lay eighty miles of hostile territory. The Bosnians were now aware the team was in-country, and their SAM tracking radars were up and running.

The instant the marines were all in and accounted for, Major Tarbutton and Captain Fortunato lifted off and headed for the *Kearsarge.*

Though it was still early morning, the sun's warmth was causing the fog to break up and the sky to clear. As soon as they had sufficient visibility, the TRAP team helicopters dropped back to the deck and began a high-speed run for the sea barely fifty feet above ground. Even so, a Bosnian radar site picked them up and began tracking the TRAP force, a fact that was confirmed by an EA-6B Prowler jamming aircraft. Immediately the request was made to take out the site. But because they were operating under the U.N rules of engagement, the request was denied.

The helicopters continued to barrel on at 150 mph at minimum altitude. Within a few minutes, the four helicopters cleared the mountains and reached the flat costal plain. They were almost home free.

Aviators identify the position of objects relative to themselves using an imaginary clock lying faceup in front of them. Twelve o'clock high is straight ahead and above, six o'clock low is directly behind and below, etc. It was not long after the four helicopters reached the plains that Major Tarbutton and the other pilots saw a distinctive spiral smoke trail pointing at them.

"SAM ten o'clock!" said Major Mykleby over the radio.

Almost immediately a second started rocketing toward them. They were being attacked by shoulder-fired surface-to-air missiles. The Cobras and Sea Stallions immediately did a SAM break maneuver, abruptly splitting out of formation while firing flares and chaff to confuse the missiles' guidance systems.

They had evaded one threat. But then, at their three o'clock, they came under small arms and 23 mm antiaircraft artillery (AAA) fire. The force had flown into a Serbian AAA trap.

But the rescue team, O'Grady in hand, had no intention of engaging the enemy. Dropping down to rooftop level to avoid enemy fire, they roared onto the most direct route to the sea and safety. As the CH-53 he was in maneuvered away from the antiaircraft threat, Sergeant Major Angel Castro Jr., sitting in the passenger compartment, his back against the hull, suddenly felt something hit his back. He turned around, trying to find what it was. Beside him, Corporal Anthony Parham showed him the Serbian bullet that had hit Castro's flak jacket. Castro told Parham to keep it as a souvenir.

Photo: U.S. Department of Defense

U.S. Air Force Captains T. O. Hanford, Scott F. O'Grady, and Bob Wright (from left to right) discuss the rescue of Captain O'Grady at a press conference following the rescue. Captain T. O. Hanford was the pilot who, six days after O'Grady's shoot-down over Bosnia, successfully intercepted his SOS.

Suddenly the blade inspection method (BIM) light on Major Tarbutton's instrument panel went on. To help monitor the degradation of integrity from stress fractures or other causes, helicopter rotors have a hollow core filled with pressurized nitrogen. Any drop in pressure activates the BIM light. A rotor blade was losing pressure, probably caused by an enemy round puncturing it. Standard operating procedure on helicopters with rotor blades potentially coming apart is to slow down, but that was not an option for Tarbutton.

Meanwhile, Captain Fortunato was having problems of his own. His transmission chip light had gone off, meaning that the gears in his CH-53 power plant were chipping off, sending slivers of steel through the helicopter's transmission. Worst-case scenario: the transmission would seize, the engine would stop, and down they'd go in an uncontrolled crash. Best-case scenario: the transmission would seize, the engine would stop—but only *after* they'd got to the *Kearsarge*. Captain Fortunato kept on flying.

The countryside abruptly gave way to a city—a port. They were almost in the clear. But directly in their path was an airport, with civilian air traffic. The helicopters didn't stop, not even when they saw a civilian jetliner making its landing approach. A collision appeared imminent. The marines saw the jetliner abruptly pull up and away just in time, and the TRAP force continued on to the sea.

Then they were "feet wet"—over water. They could start to relax.

By 7:22 A.M., the TRAP team had the *Kearsarge* in view, and the aircraft of the TRAP force began to land. When the CH-53 carrying O'Grady landed, he exited the chopper to a host of cheers and backslaps from the deck crew. He was quickly taken below to the ship's infirmary, while the members of the TRAP force began to egress the aircraft and "safe" their weapons. Safety and standard procedures dictated that they turn in all the ammunition and other ordnance they had been issued just hours earlier. That task completed, they headed below for a well-earned breakfast and some rest.

Meanwhile, the ship's doctors were examining Captain O'Grady, who was suffering from a mild case of hypothermia and dehydration. He also had a mild case of trench foot, some second-degree burns on his neck and cheeks from the attack, and he had lost about twenty-five pounds. But he was essentially fine and would recover quickly. As for the rest of the force, there had been no casualties, a small miracle given the AAA/SAM trap they had flown through just before going feet wet. By any standard, the TRAP mission was an unqualified success and would become a model for MEU(SOC) operations in the years ahead.

When word reached the White House of O'Grady's successful rescue, there were ecstatic celebrations throughout the building. In an administration with a poor record of military operations since taking office, this was a badly needed first success. So pleased was President Clinton, that he allowed himself an illicit cigar in celebration, in defiance of the newly enacted No Smoking rules of the White House.

Mission accomplished.

As a coda to the mission, the Pentagon subsequently released the following statement to the press:

> Captain Scott Francis O'Grady, U.S. Air Force, has been identified as the F-16 pilot who was shot down over Bosnia and has now successfully been rescued by NATO search and rescue forces. Captain O'Grady, whose home of record is Spokane, Washington, is assigned to the 555 Fighter Squadron, Aviano Air Base, Italy.

* * *

The Internet was still a new, young, and relatively unfamiliar means of communication in 1995, but not to Captain Scott Zobrist of the 555th Fighter Squadron, who had seen the value of having an e-mail account that would give him low-cost instant access to friends and family back home. After he had landed his F-16 at Aviano and completed his postmission duties, Zobrist returned to his quarters, turned on his computer, and logged onto his e-mail

Photo: U.S. Department of Defense

Well-wishers in Hangar 1 at Aviano Air Base greet Captain O'Grady following his rescue.

Photo: U.S. Department of Defense

Captain O'Grady's rescue was a worldwide media event as evidenced by the large group of international journalists and camera crews that attended his press conference at Aviano Air Base.

account. The ecstatic Zobrist couldn't wait to send a message detailing the great news of the Scott O'Grady rescue mission. A few minutes later, he had completed his blow-by-blow account of the pickup, including code words and other details. At 1:32 P.M., Aviano time, his message went out to his friends.

As Pentagon officials trying to control the information flow about the rescue discovered later that day, Captain Zobrist's e-mail had been forwarded to other sites and was one of the hottest topics on message boards on the World Wide Web—and then in newsrooms. The officials were among the first, though certainly not the last, to be trumped by the power of the Internet. It was an operational security lesson that would be remembered in the years ahead.[10]

1. O'Grady, *Return with Honor*, 135–38.
2. Phillips, *Bosnia-Herzegovina*, 7.
3. Taylor, *The Fall of the Dynasties*, 130.
4. International Olympic Games Web site. "Birth of the Olympic Movement."
5. White House press release, June 2, 1995.
6. Barela, "Calm Before the Storm."
7. NATO Regional Headquarters Allied Forces Southern Europe Fact Sheet: "Operation Deny Flight."
8. O'Grady, *Return with Honor*, 38.
9. Clancy, *Marine*, 213.
10. Much of the detail for this account came from a panel held at the annual meeting of the U.S. Naval Institute in April 1996 in Annapolis, Maryland, along with personal interviews with a number of 24th MEU(SOC) officers following their return stateside in the fall of 1995.

6

The Immaculate Mission: ODA 551 in the Karbala Gap

When Operation Iraqi Freedom was launched on March 20, 2003, it set into motion the greatest use of Special Operations Forces in the history of warfare. In the north of Iraq, Special Forces (SF) Operational Detachment-Alphas (ODAs)—A-Teams—would form the backbone of the offensive that utilized Kurdish militia. In the west, Special Operations actions would prove to be so successful that Saddam Hussein came to believe that the main thrust of the offensive would come from the west. In truth, the main effort was in the south, from V Corps and the 1st Marine Expeditionary Force operating out of bases in Kuwait. Intelligence about enemy positions along the Tigris and Euphrates river valleys was critical for the southern offensive. As one of V Corps' planners noted, "Information, not fires or effects, is the coin of the realm [because] you can only kill what you know is out there." The task of ODA 551 was to covertly set up an observation site in the strategically important Karbala Pass, south of Baghdad, and report its findings. The team's mission was supposed to last a few days. Eventually, ODA 551 would conduct operations without the enemy discovering them for ten days. This is the story of the men from the U.S. Army Special Forces—the Green Berets—whose achievement caused members of the Special Operations community to call what they did "the Immaculate Mission."

> The Karbala Gap is scary to me, because it's very near the Red Line that we expect will trip the use of chemical weapons. And if the Iraqis are ever going to use chemicals, that's where you'd expect them.
>
> —Colonel Stephen Hicks, Operations Chief, V Corps[1]

It was late afternoon on March 21, 2003, at a base in the Persian Gulf region. Operation Iraqi Freedom was just two days old. Earlier that morning, Captain Daniel L. Runyon, commander of Operational Detachment-Alpha 551, had received his "go" orders. The mission, the preparation for which had caused the team to go into "isolation" for almost a week in the fall of 2002 back at their base at Ali al Saleem Airbase in Kuwait, was on. Time was of the essence, and ODA 551 had to leave that evening.

In the army Special Forces, there is a half-century tradition that takes place once a mission is assigned—whether it's real, for training, or an exercise. Known simply as isolation, it's a period when the members of the ODA go into their team room or some other designated area within a deployment base, and build or finish a detailed mission plan. Isolation can last anywhere from a few hours to several days.

What goes on inside the room (and sometimes, rooms), technically called an isolation facility or ISOFAC, has an almost Zen-like quality for those inside. The isolation analysis process covers an extensive variety of mission-related tasks and is a testament to the extraordinary authority that ODA teams have regarding the mission itself, an authority impossible for a unit of similar size and command in a conventional army table of organization.

During isolation, the ODA team tears apart the mission and examines each of its stages from every angle: weapons and equipment (both standard and specialized), transportation to and from, duration, logistics, communications, combat air support, size and deployment of likely enemy forces, infiltration and exfiltration sites, discovery by enemy scenarios, whether or not additional training or rehearsals are needed, and more. Even mission acceptance is analyzed. In a conventional unit, when a superior officer gives a mission order to a subordinate, the subordinate must carry out the order even if its chance of success is slim. Not so with an ODA team. If their analysis concludes that the failure factor for the mission is too high, the team can and will reject the mission. It is not a question of whether or not the mission itself is high risk. These are highly trained men who are part of an elite brotherhood, and they know what they can and cannot do.

And what ODA 551, part of Bravo Company of the 2nd Battalion, 5th Special Forces Group (in military parlance 2/5th SFG), decided they could do was fulfill the mission they had just been given—one considered by many superior officers on the need-to-know list to be the most difficult and dangerous mission tasked to Special Operations Forces in Operation Iraqi Freedom. Simply put, Team 551's mission was to infiltrate and set up a covert observation post in the strategic Karbala Gap, 350 miles inside Iraq, just 50 miles south of Baghdad, and literally in the backyard of the Medina Division of the Republican Guard.

* * *

In military terms, the Karbala Gap is a choke point, and one of the most important pieces of terrain on the road to Baghdad. It is a narrow (about two miles at its widest), flat, almost featureless stretch of desert bordered on the east by the holy city of Karbala and the Euphrates River, and on the west by the lake named Bahr al Milh. The U.S. Army is heavily dependent on mechanized vehicles, and this was the only place west of the Euphrates River where its armored units could transit on their drive north. To the skilled eyes of military professionals, the Karbala Gap had the look of a killing ground, precisely the kind of choke point that one learns to look for in basic field operations training at military academies around the world. And Lieutenant General Raad Hamdani, commander of the Republican Guard II Corps, which was responsible for defending the area south of Baghdad that included the Karbala Gap, was one such military professional. Described as "one of the few truly competent officers"[2] in a senior command post in Saddam Hussein's army, General Hamdani began his military career as a platoon commander during the 1973 Yom Kippur War as part of the contingent Iraq sent in support of Syria. Since then, General Hamdani had managed to rise in rank and responsibility in the Iraqi military. This was no small feat—in the deadly paranoid and politically charged climate surrounding the Iraqi dictator—for someone who was neither Saddam Hussein's relative nor a tribal member.

When Operation Iraqi Freedom (OIF) was launched, reports that General Hamdani received about the offensive in the south was that a substantial portion of the coalition's forces was advancing along the west bank of the Euphrates River. He noted that "if the Coalition were going to strike up the west side of the Euphrates, the critical point or the 'neck of the bottle' was the gap between Karbala and [Bahr al Milh]." To cover this key terrain, he ordered the Medina Division, which was deployed on the east side of the Euphrates, to cross the river and "cover the road between Al-Musayyib and Karbala."[3] But when he informed his superior, General Ibrahim Abd Al Sattar Mohammad Al-Tikriti, the Republican Guard chief of staff, of his intentions, the general countermanded the order.

As General Hamdani later recalled, "Saddam had declared that no Republican Guard forces would deploy west of the Euphrates River. Apparently he was afraid that forces west of the river would become trapped if the bridges were destroyed and would not be available for defending Baghdad."[4] General Hamdani chose not to tell his superior that two of the Medina Division's three battalions were already on the east bank and were getting into position, relying for cover on the chaos of poor and contradictory communications going to and from headquarters in Baghdad.

Since the U.S. Army's V Corps in Kuwait had earmarked the Karbala Gap as part of its route to Baghdad, it needed to know everything possible about the

Medina Division and other enemy forces in and around the area well before it arrived. Part of the information the corps sought included something that made everyone's skin crawl: Iraq's chemical and biological weapons arsenal. Saddam Hussein had already shown the world his willingness to use these weapons when they were deployed in the Iran-Iraq War as well as against the Kurds in northern Iraq and Iraqi Shiites in the south. Another factor that made ODA 551's mission to the Karbala Gap so crucial was the relatively small number of American troops involved in the campaign.

When the planners at the Pentagon and CENTCOM at MacDill Air Force Base near Tampa began drawing up the details for what would become Operation Iraqi Freedom, the Bush administration made the strategic decision to use an "economy of force" of approximately 150,000 troops in the offensive. Operation Desert Storm, in comparison, deployed about 500,000 troops. The belief in the White House was that the technological advantage of American weapon systems would overcome the two-to-one numerical advantage in manpower possessed by Iraq's army, even though that army would have the additional advantage of fighting on the defensive.

Though the concerns about Saddam Hussein's weapons of mass destruction would ultimately prove to be false, at the time, every participant in Operation Iraqi Freedom fully expected to be "slimed"—attacked by chemical and/or biological weapons. If ever there were a place for Saddam Hussein to unleash his devil's brew, the Karbala Gap, with its choke-point topography and close proximity to Baghdad, was it.

When ODA 551 drew up its list of specialized items needed for the mission, in addition to stripped-down MRE (Meal, Ready to Eat) ration packs and a 1,000 mm Meade computerized refracting telescope, the team made sure it included the CBW (chemical and biological warfare) medical kits and uncomfortable, bulky MOPP (mission-oriented protective posture) IV outer clothing and gear. Not that anyone on the team had any illusions about surviving such an event. They would have little if any warning of a chemical attack if it came, and chances of donning the bulky MOPP IV suits, driving out of the "slime" zone, and decontaminating themselves successfully were low at best.

As the team went about the final details of its mission preparation, the members half-listened to a television running the satellite feed from MSNBC, stealing an occasional glance at the screen. Two retired army four-star generals, Wayne Downing and Montgomery Meigs, were providing commentary about the early developments in the offensive. Downing was a former commander of U.S. Special Operations Command, and Meigs was a former commanding general of the U.S. Army Forces, Europe.

The much-anticipated Shock and Awe air campaign was scheduled to

Photo: U.S. Department of Defense

Two Marines wear MOPP (mission-oriented protection posture) gear during a weapons-of-mass-destruction scare in the early stages of Operation Iraqi Freedom. The fear that Saddam Hussein would use his nuclear, biological, and chemical arsenal against the coalition forces was ever present with the troops during the offensive. Note that the marines have used duct tape to secure the gas mask filter canisters.

strike Baghdad that evening. As the retired generals talked about what had been reported and speculated about what would happen next, B-2A Spirit stealth bombers from Whiteman Air Force Base in Missouri were in the air on their globe-spanning flight path to southwest Asia. In addition, coalition aircraft stationed on bases and aircraft carriers in the region were getting ready to make their own bombing runs in what would be the single most precise and concentrated air attack in history.

The main focus in the television program was the ground campaign. For the past eighteen months, there had been a quiet agreement among retired and former Special Operations Forces (SOF) professionals, including those who had taken jobs with the press and other media outlets, not to discuss potential or ongoing SOF operations. And when the commentator asked Downing about Special Operations' role in the campaign, he dodged the questions, speaking at length but ultimately revealing little.

The commentator then turned to General Meigs and asked him what he would do if he were in charge of Operation Iraqi Freedom. Meigs exploded ebulliently, punching a map of the region with his finger at a spot that caused the blood to run cold of those members of Team 551 who were watching the TV. And then Meigs said, "The first thing I would do is take some of those great Special Forces soldiers and put them right here, in the Karbala Gap, to keep an eye on things!"

The team members were stunned. They stopped their packing and listened to Meigs continue his explanation. Though they knew that Meigs had just paid the Special Forces a great compliment, he was also outing them—down to calling which side of the gap they were planning to work. Outside were the MH-47 Chinook SOF helicopters tasked to fly them to their landing zone in Iraq, about one hundred kilometers south of the Karbala Gap. Their ground mobility vehicles (GMVs), Hummers customized for special operations use, were about to be loaded, and they were almost finished packing.

At the eleventh hour and on national television, a retired four-star general wholly out of the loop had unwittingly blown the operational security for their mission. With the Iraqi embassy in Washington, D.C., and the Iraqi consulate at the U.N. in New York City, as well as other diplomatic allies in the country, there was no way Saddam Hussein would *not* be informed about the general's remarks. It was even possible that Saddam himself was watching MSNBC in one of his bunkers, since for years it had been public knowledge that he was in the habit of watching international cable and satellite news programs.

Clearly, the general's televised prediction was a shock to every member of the team, though nobody was under any illusions about the mission now being scrapped. And clearly, Meigs's comment was the speculation of an experienced professional, not someone intimately involved with the planning of the ground campaign, which had kicked off just a day earlier. The thing to do was to try to put the gaffe out of their minds and get back to being the SOF professionals they all were. Still, it was something that would stay with them for the next two weeks through what would become one of the most amazing odysseys in SOF history.

ODA 551's mission had originated more than a year earlier, during the initial planning for Operation Iraqi Freedom at CENTCOM headquarters at MacDill AFB. There the staff of General Tommy Franks, the CENTCOM commanding general, was looking over the standing plans for invasion options for Iraq, trying to fit them into the requirements being laid down by Secretary of Defense Donald Rumsfeld.

Fresh from its victory against the Taliban and Al-Qaeda in Afghanistan in Operation Enduring Freedom, CENTCOM was flush with political capital and possibilities. Yet, even with a mandate from the White House to proceed, Iraq was turning into a problem for the planners.

There were three key limitations facing Franks and the CENTCOM planning staff when considering their Iraqi invasion plans:

- **Force size**—Secretary Rumsfeld, working to transform the American military at the time, wanted to minimize the size of the U.S. forces needed to defeat the Iraqis. Emboldened by the extremely economical victory in Afghanistan in 2001, he pressured Franks and his planners to use only the forces necessary for the job, and minimize reserves and logistical and support units.
- **Geopolitics**—The political landscape of the Persian Gulf had changed significantly since Operation Desert Storm in 1991, and the Allied coalition was badly eroded. Only the United Kingdom and a handful of other nations in what was called the "Coalition of the Willing" were likely partners in any invasion of Iraq. Furthermore, basing options in the region were severely limited.
- **Visibility**—While not many nations in the Persian Gulf were willing to openly support an invasion of Iraq, if the United States chose to go ahead and do it, more than a few wanted the job done quickly and without large-scale fanfare. In other words, as long as the campaign, or the parts of it that directly involved them, could be done without significant media coverage, some of Iraq's neighbors[5] were willing to act as friendly host nations for small forces with the ability to operate without attracting attention.

Given the troop level and diplomatic restrictions that would eventually be placed on War Plan 1003V, the official designation for Operation Iraqi Freedom, one real option for focusing CENTCOM's limited combat power would be the widespread use of SOF units throughout Iraq. The unquestioned success of SOF units in Afghanistan during Operation Enduring Freedom–Afghanistan (OEF-A) had given them an immense boost in the mind of CENTCOM planners and leaders. Now, for the first time, SOF forces would go to battle as full partners and peers with their conventional warfare counterparts.

The role of Special Operations Forces in Operation Iraqi Freedom eventually became known as Cobra II. It was the largest use of special operations in history. Larger even than Operation Overlord, the invasion of Normandy in 1944 (even when the Jedburgh teams stationed throughout occupied France are included), Cobra II would become what one senior coalition military leader later called "a snake-eaters' ball"—a reference to the nickname given special operations troops in the Vietnam War.

Key among the tasks given to SOF forces was a series of deep-penetration missions, including special reconnaissance (SR) and direct action (DA). SF ODAs would be tasked to secure bridges, seize airfields, search for weapons of mass destruction (WMDs), and provide liaison services for the conventional forces headed for Baghdad. U.S. Navy SEALs, along with Polish commandos and British Royal Marines, would take critical oil assets including platforms, islands, and the strategic Al-Faw Peninsula at the tip of the Persian Gulf.

Of all of these jobs, however, none was more critical to the troopers of the U.S. Army's V Corps than keeping an eye on the Karbala Gap. In 2003, there was absolutely no doubt in the minds of planners and everyone else involved in Operation Iraqi Freedom that the Iraqis would use chemical weapons on any large force invading their territory. The obvious place to use them would be choke points, like the Karbala Gap. The Iraqis had also stationed their most powerful combat unit, the Medina Division of the Republican Guard, near Karbala, a city holy to the Shiites. A counterattack by the Medina Division—either conventional or with WMDs—against advancing U.S. forces bunched up in the gap was a deadly possibility.

When the CENTCOM staff put together its wish list of missions and tasks for the SOF units assigned for Operation Iraqi Freedom, the Karbala Gap special reconnaissance was at the top of the list. Though the mission contained what seemed to many outside the SOF community (as well as a few within it) to be an almost impossible set of challenges to overcome, the 2/5th SFG and ODA 551 would prove to be up to the task.

Special Forces, 2002

The U.S. Army Special Forces Command (SFC) is composed of five active-duty and two National Guard Special Forces Groups (SFGs), each assigned to cover a major part of the world as their primary area of responsibility (AOR). Normally, these are assigned to one of the various unified commands, such as European Command (EUCOM) or CENTCOM. Generally, 5th SFG was the unit allotted to CENTCOM, but the requirements of Operation Iraqi Freedom meant that portions of two other Special Forces Groups, the 3rd and the 10th, would also be needed for the planned invasion.

The 5th SFG, based out of Fort Campbell, Kentucky, had for decades been the busiest of the Special Forces Groups. It was assigned to Southeast Asia during the 1960s and 1970s, and then the Middle East and southwest Asia in the 1980s. This meant that duty with the 5th SFG was hard and tedious, especially because of the long travel times during deployment.

The terrorist attacks on 9/11 found 5th SFG, and all the other groups within the Special Forces Command, short on personnel and resources—a result of overuse and budget cuts in the late 1990s. The Clinton administration had heavily relied on them to help build goodwill and influence at various hot spots around the world at the same time that the Republican Congress was limiting funding for foreign aid and assistance. As a result, Special Forces soldiers whose skills made them particularly valuable to security-conscious multinational corporations left the service in droves to reap the benefits of the high-paying private sector jobs that awaited them. This forced then-SFC commanding general Jerry Boykin to reduce the number of ODA teams per company from six to five, so that the quality of the individual soldiers and their equipment would not be diluted in order to satisfy the requirements of an administrative organization table.

When 5th SFG was alerted in the fall of 2001 that it would soon be conducting operations against the Taliban and Al-Qaeda in Afghanistan, the ODAs of the 2/5th SFG and 3/5th SFG were still short of personnel. Ideally, SF Operational Detachment-Alphas are carefully balanced twelve-man teams composed of a mix of specialists who are able to conduct missions across the full spectrum of military operations with little or no outside support. Typically, an ODA is one or two men under strength due to transfers, rotations, and schoolhouse training. But when then Colonel John Mulholland, the commander of 5th SFG, went to select his initial ODAs for insertion into northern Afghanistan as part of OEF-A in the fall of 2001, even the best of his teams were significantly under strength.

One of these was ODA 555, known as the Triple Nickel. They were scheduled to be the very first team into Afghanistan. The core team itself was well stocked with the NCO specialists in weapons, communications, and medicine that were needed for the mission. What it lacked was command personnel, particularly a team commander, normally a first lieutenant or junior (recently promoted) captain. This led Colonel Mulholland and the 2/5th SFG commander, Lieutenant Colonel Chris Conner, to take an experienced team captain from ODA 551 and place him in command of Team 555 when it deployed to Bagram, north of Kabul, on October 19. So when the ramp of an SOF helicopter dropped that dark and dangerous night, the first American Special Forces soldier to step into the hostile land of Afghanistan was the new commander of ODA 555, Captain Daniel L. Runyon.

The basic mission for the Triple Nickel and other ODA teams deployed in Afghanistan was to work with Afghan warlords who had banded together in the anti-Taliban Northern Alliance to help them defeat the government that was providing sanctuary to Al-Qaeda as well as to destroy Al-Qaeda strongholds. After the team linked up with its CIA contacts, it was delivered to Mohammed Fahim Khan, one of the Afghan warlords of the Northern Alliance. Khan then had General Baba Jan, one of his deputies, lead the team to Bagram Air Base, where the group climbed to the top of the wrecked control tower. From there, Baba Jan pointed out Taliban and Al-Qaeda targets for miles around. With that intelligence in hand, Team 555 went to work.

Attached to Team 555 was a U.S. Air Force combat controller, Sergeant

William Calvin Markham. A specialist in the delivery of precision weapons from aircraft, Markham set up his array of radios, as well as his laser rangefinder and designator called a SOFLAM (Special Operations Forces laser marker). His "shopping list" in hand, Markham began calling in everything from navy F/A-18 Hornets launched from carriers in the Arabian Sea, to heavy bombers taking off from air bases in the United States, on the other side of the world. On just the first day, Markham destroyed more Taliban and Al-Qaeda positions, vehicles, guns, and armor around Bagram than General Baba Jan's insurgent forces had been able to in more than a year.

For the next three weeks, Captain Dan Runyon, Sergeant Cal Markham, and Team 555 raised their own version of hell against the Taliban and Al-Qaeda forces in the Panjshir Valley. At the same time, other Special Forces teams were delivering similar precision strikes throughout Afghanistan. At Mazar-e-Sharif to the west, SF teams, some on horseback, joined with the forces of Northern Alliance warlord General Abdul Rashid Dostum to break the back of the enemy and force them into headlong retreat through Bagram, where they were attacked by bombs targeted by Markham and Team 555.

As the operation in Afghanistan continued, the relationship between the Americans and Northern Alliance troops became so strong that the Afghans started taking extreme measures to protect and sustain the U.S. soldiers. For example, whenever a mixed group of Afghan and Special Forces troops were targeted by enemy fire, the Afghans would cover the Americans with their own bodies rather than chance the loss of even one of the Special Operations Forces warriors.

When he later asked General Baba Jan why he and his men had shielded them with their own bodies, Markham recalled the general saying, "Well, if something happened to him or one of his commanders, someone else would take over. But if something happens to you or your teammates, the Taliban will go back on the offensive, raping and killing all the way to Uzbekistan."

This was perhaps the ultimate example of the Special Forces' definition of the term *rapport*, and was one of the many reasons why the transition to a democratic Afghan government initially went so smoothly compared with what happened in Iraq eighteen months later. For Captain Dan Runyon, however, it was how he and every other Green Beret liked to do business.

Unconventional warfare, or UW, is the core mission of SF soldiers and teams, and Operation Iraqi Freedom–Afghanistan was like a field-test laboratory for the trade in the fall of 2001. Just twenty-five days after their arrival, Captain Runyon and Team 555 had the honor of being the first Special Forces team into Kabul, where they reoccupied the U.S. embassy compound. Once inside the compound, they swept the facility for unexploded munitions and booby traps before letting the marines and State Department personnel take over. After that, Runyon and Team 555 conducted what the Special Operations community calls support and sustainment operations (SASOs) before returning to Fort Campbell in spring 2003.

When the Triple Nickel returned to the States, most of 5th SFG was already back from Afghanistan, having been relieved of their SASO duties by SF soldiers from other groups, including the National Guardsmen of the 20th SFG. The 5th SFG was told it was being reserved for possible action in Iraq. Upon receiving those orders it promptly went into training to get ready. One of the first and most welcome tasks was the assimilation of new SF soldiers, freshly minted from the John F. Kennedy Special Warfare Center and School, located at Fort Bragg, North Carolina.

These fresh graduates of the famous Qualification, or Q, Course would provide enough manpower to flesh out the thin ranks of the 5th SFG ODAs. Thankfully, casualties in Afghanistan had been limited. Only three 5th Group Green Berets had been killed and a handful more wounded. The result was that each of the three battalions of the group would be able to field fifteen full-strength A-teams for the coming invasion of Iraq. All would be needed.

Another of the teams' immediate needs was across-the-board refresher training, especially with firearms and heavy weapons. While some of the ODAs had been in some nasty firefights, the majority had managed to make it through their Afghan adventures without firing their weapons at all. Since the Special Forces prides itself on having the best riflemen in the U.S. Army, marksmanship skills had to be restored and sustained in the run-up before the men would go into combat in Iraq. Coupled with this was training on new equipment and weapons, including radio and medical equipment, and the state-of-the-art Javelin antitank missile.

Perhaps the most important new and enhanced capability was in an area where American Special Operations Forces warriors had always been weak: mobility. Traditionally, U.S. SOF personnel had been lavishly fitted out with all manner of transport, from helicopters to fixed-wing aircraft and even miniature submarines, to get them where they needed to go. But once they arrived where they were to conduct operations, "mobility" wound up being defined as how fast two good feet in boots could travel. This situation got several ugly reality checks during the 1990s, which caused U.S. Special Operations Command (SOCOM) and SFC to review what teams needed once they were on the ground in hostile territory.

During Operation Desert Storm in 1991, a number of ODAs were so limited in their mobility that when they were dropped into SR sites behind enemy lines, they often had to be extracted by helicopter when under fire from enemy troops. One of these teams, led by a young Chris Conner, would have been wiped out but for a helicopter pilot who went to extremes to recover them. That mobility lesson, or rather that *lack* of mobility, was engraved indelibly on the future battalion commander's mind. Fortunately, 5th SFG had been at the cutting edge of ground mobility development since the 1990s.

Initially, like the rest of the U.S. military, 5th SFG used high-mobility multipurpose wheeled vehicles (HMMWVs) for deployed operations "downrange" (SOF for *overseas*). By the late 1990s, however, 5th SFG had gotten its own heavily modified version of the HMMWV, the ground mobility vehicle, or GMV. Equipped with a more powerful turbocharged diesel engine, beefed-up suspension and tires, mounts for either an M2 .50 caliber machine gun or Mk. 19 40 mm automatic grenade launcher, and others for M240 7.62 mm medium machine guns or M249 SAW (squad automatic weapon) 5.56 light machine guns, the beefed-up GMV was, in effect, "an HMMWV on steroids."

All these modifications allow the GMV to carry enough weapons, radios, ammunition, fuel, supplies, food, and water to keep a four-man crew in the field for a week. The extra power, new tires, and suspension make it perhaps the most mobile military ground vehicle in the world today. In fact, about the only thing that the GMV cannot do is fit inside the MH-53M Pave Low

GROUND MOBILITY VEHICLE (GMV)

The ground mobility vehicle is a HMMWV (high-mobility multipurpose wheeled vehicle) manufactured by AM General and customized for Special Operations by Letterkenny Army Depot. Production of the HMMWV began in 1985, and presently there are eleven variants, excluding the models built for Special Operations. Actual specifications for GMVs are classified, but it can be stated that the vehicles feature protective armor; heavy duty and reinforced chassis, suspension, engine, transmission, tires; and are augmented by a weapons system package that includes either an M2 .50 caliber machine gun or Mk. 19 40 mm grenade launcher and an M240B 7.62 mm machine gun; rated payloads are as much as 5,100 pounds. Special Operations GMVs are designed to carry sufficient fuel, supplies, communications equipment, and munitions to allow them to independently operate in hostile environments for extended periods of time.

SPECIFICATIONS

Photo: U.S. Army

Manufacturer: AM General
Engine: 6.5 liter OHV V8 turbo or naturally aspirated diesel
Horsepower: 205 @ 3,200 rpm (turbo); 160 @ 3,200 rpm (diesel)
Length: 196.5 inches (5 meters)
Height: 76 inches (1.93 meters)
Payload: 2,300 pounds (1,043 kilograms)
Gross vehicle weight: 12,100 pounds (5,489 kilograms)
Cruising range: 275 miles (443 kilometers)
Acceleration (0–30 mph): 9.4 seconds
Acceleration (0–50 mph): 26.1 seconds

IV SOF helicopter. Its large size means that the only helicopter the GMV fits into (barely!) is the MH-47 Chinook, operated by the 160th Special Operations Aviation Regiment (SOAR). However, the GMV can be air-dropped by parachute, and can easily roll on/roll off C-130 Hercules, C-5 Galaxy, or C-17 Globemaster transports.

The GMV was not the only ground mobility option 5th SFG ODAs would have for Operation Iraqi Freedom. All the virtues that make the GMV a great military vehicle undercut its utility in covert operations—it just does not blend into the indigenous vehicle pools of the Middle East or southwest Asia. This became an important consideration in Afghanistan in late 2001, and the search for a solution turned up a pair of intriguing choices. These included Polaris four-wheeled all-terrain vehicles (ATVs), which were quite agile and useful in the rugged mountain terrain. Also, the ATVs were relatively small and lightweight, which meant they could be flown into an area even in an MH-60 Black Hawk.

A more utilitarian solution was the Toyota Tacoma four-wheel-drive pickup truck. Such trucks are as common as AK-47s in southwest Asia and would allow the Special Forces soldiers to hide in plain sight while conducting their missions. Shortly after 9/11, when it became clear that 5th SFG was headed to Afghanistan, the group procurement office bought every one of the trucks it could find at dealerships in and around nearby Clarksville, Tennessee. These Tacomas were then customized with roll bars, racks for fuel and ammunition cans, and additional electrical wiring for radios. Once they were ready, they were shipped to teams in Afghanistan.

The Toyotas proved extremely popular, and were so heavily used that they were considered expended and not returned stateside when 5th SFG came home in spring 2002. One pleasant surprise was that the trucks not only fit into the MH-47 Chinooks and cargo aircraft, if loaded carefully they even fit into the air force MH-53M Pave Low IVs. This opened up all kinds of possibilities for 5th SFG planners in Operation Iraqi Freedom.

Already it was clear to the planners that one of the most limiting constraints they would face in the upcoming campaign in Iraq was a shortage of SOF helicopters. The need to continue the support of anti-insurgency operations in Afghanistan, the Philippines, the Horn of Africa, and elsewhere in the world meant that the 160th SOAR and Air Force Special Operations Command (AFSOC) would be stretched to the limit. Any additional options for deploying SF teams and their ground mobility assets would become a critical consideration for the coming campaign.

All these new tools and capabilities would be needed for Operation Iraqi Freedom. The CENTCOM planners decided to use SOF teams as stand-ins for some jobs that normally would have been given to conventional force battalions or brigades with hundreds or thousands of personnel.

ODA 551: The Team

When Captain Daniel Runyon returned to Fort Campbell and his old team, ODA 551, he found some pleasant developments. The good news was that the team's members who had been seconded to other ODAs and the 5th SFG staff for Afghanistan had also returned. And Runyon had received enough transfers and new SF soldiers from the Q Course at Fort Bragg to form a nearly complete ODA.

The ODA structure, which had been set back in the 1960s by Lieutenant General William Yarborough, one of the founders of U.S. Army Special Forces and a legend in the Special Operations community, was a marvel of balance and flexibility. The team commander is a senior first lieutenant or a captain. His executive officer (XO) is a chief warrant officer (CWO), and the senior enlisted adviser is the team sergeant. The core of the teams consists of pairs of weapons, communications, medical, and engineer sergeants, along with another sergeant who specializes in intelligence and mission planning. The group can easily divide into two teams of six, called "split teams," one headed by the team captain and the other by the XO.

The ODA represents an almost perfect blend of talents added to a solid base of experience and maturity, with the additional benefits of regional language skills and cultural training. While the training of each Special Forces soldier probably represents an investment of more than $1 million by the U.S. government by the time he becomes a member of a team, the result is a soldier as comfortable taking tea with the new president of Afghanistan as he is going on a hazardous reconnaissance mission 350 miles behind enemy lines.

When he returned to the command of ODA 551, Captain Runyon was at the top of his profession. The near-legendary performance of Team 555 in Afghanistan was already public knowledge, though Runyon had managed to avoid the publicity that had resulted from an overzealous media relations policy out of the Department of the Army in the Pentagon. With little regard for their future personal security on downrange operations, the army had arranged for team members from ODA 555, 574, and 595 to appear on the PBS news magazine series *Frontline*, as well as to be interviewed by a reporter for the *Washington Post*. Since Runyon had only been seconded to Team 555, he managed to dodge the media request and went back to work with ODA 551.

And he had plenty of talent to work with. In Team 551 (whose members for security reasons are identified here with only their first names), Runyon had excellent leadership thanks to CWO2 Clay, a solid XO, and Team Sergeant Chris, also a seasoned SF veteran. The core team positions broke down this way:

- **Communications sergeants:** Andy, senior communications sergeant backed up by Shane, his assistant.

- **Engineering sergeants:** Joey was senior, while "Stinky" was the junior engineering sergeant.
- **Weapons sergeants:** Alex was the senior weapons sergeant, while Jim acted as his assistant.

Rounding out the team was the medical sergeant, Tracy, along with Chris, the intelligence and planning sergeant. Also assigned to Team 551 was an air force tactical air control party (TACP) named Mike, to assist with communications and precision weapons guidance when needed. So what Runyon had to work with was an almost-complete ODA with a TACP, heavy on communications talent, which the planned SR mission would need while in the Karbala Gap. In fact, every member of the team was highly qualified and experienced. The only hole was that the team had only one medical sergeant, whose absence was made up for by the skills cross-training that is standard in Special Forces.

In fact, the teams of Bravo Company, 2/5th SFG were among the best ever fielded by the Special Forces, something that did not escape Lieutenant Colonel Conner's notice when he began making assignments to the teams of his battalion. Conner's assignment in OIF was commander of Task Force 52. Scheduled to operate out of the Ali al Salem Air Base in Kuwait, Task Force 52 was assigned to provide SOF services for the coalition forces south of Baghdad during the invasion. This meant that Conner's battalion would have a number of teams making deep penetration SR and DA missions prior to the planned initiation of hostilities.

The toughest of these were a pair of SR missions: one to the Karbala Gap in support of V Corps, and another in support of the I Marine Expeditionary Force (MEF) along the Tigris River southeast of Baghdad. The Karbala Gap SR, along with several other deep-penetration missions, went to Bravo Company, while the I MEF SR and other marine support missions went to Charlie Company. When the time came to give out the Karbala Gap mission, Conner handed it to Captain Dan Runyon and Team 551.

The Mission Plan

ODA 551's assigned mission was actually simplicity itself: set up a covert observation position inside the Karbala Gap, west of the city of Karbala, and maintain surveillance on troop and vehicle traffic in the area. However, finding that site and getting there safely and covertly was extremely challenging. Thus, the first job for the team was a feasibility study, to examine the practicality of the mission. So the men went to their team room in one of the old buildings that the 5th SFG calls home at Fort Campbell, and went to work. Team rooms are the inner sanctums for ODAs, combining the functions of an armory and a clubhouse. Here the members are free to speak, regardless of rank, and to put forth ideas designed to allow the team to accomplish its missions. Once there, ODA 551 broke the study down into tasks, and went to work on the members' particular specialties. The job of finding a hide site where they could set up their observation post fell to the intelligence sergeant, Chris, with assistance from Runyon and Clay. Initially, the prospects were not promising.

The basic problem was that the few miles of open ground between the town and Bahr al Milh was as flat as a billiard table, with little in the way of ground cover, and unless the view was obscured by dust or fog, the entire area could be seen by anyone on the west side of Karbala and along the east-west road just to the south. In addition, the packed and eroded earth was just slightly less hard than reinforced concrete, so there would be no chance to dig and build a hide site.

As if the topography were not enough of a problem, the area was also on the far right flank of the armored Medina Division of the Republican Guard and the entire area was heavily trafficked. Once again, it seemed obvious that if ever there were a place where Iraqis would use chemical weapons, the Karbala Gap was it. In fall 2002, there was absolutely no doubt that Saddam Hussein would order their use if any Allied force got within a hundred kilometers (a little over sixty miles) of downtown Baghdad. So getting "slimed" (being exposed to chemical weapons) by blister agents (like mustard gas) or nerve gas (VX or other similar agents) was all but certain if the team spent too much time in the area.

Another worrisome problem was the matter of getting there. Despite years of bomb strikes during Operation Southern Watch, the Joint Task Force–Southwest Asia mission of monitoring and controlling the airspace south of the 33rd parallel in Iraq, the Karbala area was still heavily defended by surface-to-air missiles (SAMs) and antiaircraft guns (AAA). This meant that even the MH-47 Chinooks and MH-53M Pave Low IVs with their terrain-following radar and advanced electronic countermeasures (ECM) suites could not be expected to survive close to the target area. Therefore, ODA 551 would have to be delivered to a covert landing zone some distance from their planned hide site. That meant that they would have to use vehicles of some kind to get to their target area inside the Karbala Gap.

Chris, like the other intelligence sergeants of 2/5th SFG, spent days going over the latest maps from the intelligence community. He also made use of a new resource: one-meter resolution reconnaissance photos, taken by commercial imaging satellites like the *Ikonos-1* operated by Space Imaging, a division of Lockheed Martin. The bad news was that the photos and maps showed no obvious hiding places, and ODA 551 would need to hide for a long time in "Indian country." And the site had to accommodate not just two men and a couple of man-portable radios, but a dozen men with three or four vehicles, a pile of radio and observation gear, and enough supplies to last the two to four days that V Corps' commander, Lieutenant General William S. "Scott" Wallace, expected the "Victory Corps," as it is sometimes called, to take to get from Kuwait to the Karbala Gap.

Already, the ODA team from Charlie Company assigned to conduct a similar covert deep penetration observation mission for the I Marine Expeditionary Force SR had thrown in the towel. Their feasibility study showed no probable hide sites along the banks of the Tigris River, and they had turned the mission down, causing the mission to be canceled. Now ODA 551 faced the same terrain problem, and it appeared likely that they might need to make the same negative choice. Then someone got an inspired idea, one that would save the mission and help ODA 551 make Special Operations history.

Chris and others in the team began to examine the area on the eastern edge of Bahr al Milh, with an eye to how powerful the combination of water and time might be. While the ground around the Karbala Gap had the consistency of cement, even cement can be eroded by the flow of water from heavy annual rains over a few hundred years. It was therefore possible, even likely, that water running downhill from Karbala to the lake might have carved channels, or wadis, in the packed earth.

Over time, these channels might have become fairly deep—perhaps twenty to thirty feet, and look much like a miniature Grand Canyon. The largest of these channels would probably be right against or near the lake shore, and, coupled with the mostly monochromatic featureless terrain, would be difficult to see on even the one-meter resolution overhead photos the team had been supplied with. The real intelligence breakthrough came when further studies of the maps found a disused artillery and bombing range along the southeastern edge of the lake. The impact and explosions from the ordnance would have torn up the ground, enhancing the chances for erosion. If there was going to be a wadi big enough to set up an SR site in the Karbala Gap, this was the place it would likely be found.

But therein lay the ultimate problem. Finding the wadi, if it even existed, meant sneaking into the former artillery range in darkness, not tripping over any unexploded ordnance and getting maimed or killed, and then searching with night vision goggles (NVGs) to find the wadi. If ODA 551 found it, they would have to conceal and camouflage their vehicles before dawn, and then maintain total stealth until V Corps arrived.

However, if they could not find the wadi, the team would need to leave the area with enough time to reach a dayover site (SOF for "hiding place") before daybreak. That meant there would be a window of only a few hours to find the presumed wadi. Even though the wadi's existence was little more than a calculated risk, that the members of the team were able to make such an educated guess caused ODA 551 to accept the mission and proceed with their planning, equipping, and training.

The decision having been made, the team broke into small groups to work on the individual problems of fleshing out the plan. Andy, Shane, and Mike worked to put together a communications, or "commo," package of satellite links, radio sets, and crypto gear to get the collected information back to Task Force 52 at Ali al Salem, V Corps' headquarters, and the Allied Combined Air Operations Center at Prince Sultan Air Base in Saudi Arabia. Joey and Stinky worked out the transportation problem, along with logistics requirements. Finally, Alex and Jim worked on the team's weapons mix, as well as the spotting and sensor equipment they would need to sight targets in the gap.

When they were ready, the team presented their plan to Lieutenant Colonel Conner and the 2/5th SFG battalion staff. Comments were made, suggestions offered, and alternatives explored. When it was all done, Runyon and Team 551 got the green light to assemble what they needed to make the mission work, finish their stateside training, and get ready for deployment to Kuwait.

Now things began to pick up speed.

The feasibility study clearly showed that given the distance and terrain that ODA 551 would have to travel into the Karbala Gap, along with the number of personnel and the load that needed to be carried, the best transportation option would be a trio of the new GMVs. This created another problem: transport of the ground transport. The only way to deliver the GMVs to the planned landing zone south of the Karbala Gap would be in the MH-47 Chinooks of the 160th SOAR. The difficulty was that the SOF aviation component supporting Task Force 52 at Ali al Salem was composed of only AFSOC aircraft, including MH-53M Pave Low IVs. The only MH-47s in the region were committed to SOF operations in western Iraq, such as hunting SCUDs (surface-to-surface missiles), WMDs, and high-value leadership targets.

Despite the limited supply of the big SOF transport helicopters, Colonel John Mulholland, who was coordinating all special operations in southern Iraq, made the commitment to supply the MH-47 sorties when they were needed. The team would need to stage from Ali al Salem in Kuwait, then fly to another SOF in a friendly host nation adjacent to Iraq. From there they would meet up with the Chinooks and insert into Iraq when the time came.

Movement to Contact

Shortly after New Year's Day 2003, ODA 551 quietly moved to Ali al Salem Air Base in Kuwait to get ready for the start of OIF. The base had a violent history, having been overrun by the Iraqis in August 1990, then nearly bombed to rubble during Operation Desert Storm in 1991. Since that time, the complex had been completely rebuilt, including a number of new buildings specifically to support OIF.

There, in a nondescript numbered hangar, ODA 551 and over three dozen other 5th SFG teams were making final preparations for their assigned missions. For two months, the desert around the bases hummed with activity as teams learned how to pilot their GMVs, Toyota trucks, and ATVs in the talcum-powder-fine sand. Rifle ranges were busy around the clock, as were repair shops for aircraft, helicopters, vehicles, radios, weapons, and all other manner of gear.

At the same time, each team's plan was updated daily as new intelligence data arrived and to account for any shifts in the regional political situation. This took place rapidly, as Saddam Hussein and George W. Bush sparred for position in the court of world opinion. Then things came badly unhinged. On March 1, the Turkish parliament voted to deny the Allied coalition access to their airspace and territory to invade Iraq from the north. Suddenly, the Allied war plan was a one-dimensional attack coming up from Kuwait, and ODA 551's mission to the Karbala Gap now became critically important.

As laid out, ODA 551 was part of a much larger Special Operations Group master plan that would flood Iraq with SOF teams covering every part of the country. From Navy SEALs and Polish GROM ("thunder") commandos taking oil terminals in the northern Gulf, to 10th SFG teams working with peshmerga militia soldiers from the Kurdistan Workers Party, or PKK, in the Kurdish north, SOF would be the spearhead of the coalition's invasion. In particular, the teams of Task Force 52 would fan out across southern Iraq, helping secure bridges and other key targets, along with providing liaison support for conventional forces when they arrived. Their entry plan, however, depended upon a number of things going right in an environment of continually shifting events.

The final version of 1003V, code-named Cobra II at CENTAF headquarters, was to roll out as follows:

- **Phase I:** Expected to run about ten days, Phase I would see Task Force 52 and other SOF units begin the clandestine insertion of teams into Iraq.
- **Phase II:** Phase II was planned to be a short three- to five-day air campaign, known as Shock and Awe, designed to attack leadership targets around Iraq, along with preparing the battlefield for the invasion forces.
- **Phase III:** Conventional ground forces, including the U.S. Army's V Corps, the marines of the I Marine Expeditionary Force

and Task Force Tarawa, along with the British 1st Division, would invade, beginning an expected four-month campaign to liberate Kuwait.

- **Phase IV:** Following the end of major combat, all Allied forces would transition to support and sustainment operations (SASOs) and begin reconstruction of the country.

The expectation was that phase I would commence on or about March 19, which was codenamed C-day. As scheduled, ODA 551 would go in shortly before the start of phase III, to maximize the value of their time on station in the Karbala Gap, assuming that they made it there. It did not work out that way, however.

March 19 arrived, and just as the first of the deep-penetration missions from Task Force 52 were launching into Iraq, intelligence came into the CIA indicating that Saddam Hussein and his sons would be vulnerable to an airstrike for a few hours. Taking the chance, President Bush ordered an air and missile strike (which missed), and suddenly, the last shreds of Cobra II came apart, and things suddenly became more complicated for ODA 551.

For Operation Iraqi Freedom commander General Tommy Franks, everything his staff had planned in the past eighteen months was now worthless, and operational surprise against the Iraqis was completely lost. With Saddam Hussein and his forces fully alerted, all Franks could do was the unexpected, which he promptly did. Unlike every American military campaign since 1991, in which the ground attack was preceded by an air campaign, Franks decided to reverse the sequence and send his ground forces in first, and then follow with the Shock and Awe air campaign. It was an inspired improvisation, given all that had gone wrong with the diplomacy and planning to date. The ground forces would be turned loose to run full speed for Basra, Baghdad, and their other objectives. Unfortunately, that change completely ruined the intricate and detailed plans of the SOF units.

With only a few of his ODAs already on the ground in Iraq, Lieutenant Colonel Conner had to make a number of quick decisions to get his part of the SOF campaign under way. Most of his ODAs would have to be infiltrated either by their own vehicles or flown into an airfield being seized in the desert south of Karbala. All around the region, other SOF commanders were making similar decisions. For ODA 551, it meant getting ready to insert into Iraq days ahead of schedule.

Meanwhile, late on the afternoon of March 20, the ground forces crossed into Iraq from Kuwait, covered live by Ted Koppel on ABC News, among others. Later that evening, the U.S. Navy SEALs and their GROM teammates seized the two oil platforms, with the Royal Marine Commandos taking the Al-Faw Peninsula. By morning, the channel to the port of Um Qasr had been

MRE: MEAL, READY TO EAT

Meal, Ready to Eat (MRE) is a self-contained full-course meal of approximately 1,200 calories contained in lightweight packaging designed for use by the U.S. military where formal kitchen services are unavailable. The contents include a main course of starch; crackers; a cheese, peanut butter, or jelly spread; a dessert or snack; powdered beverage mix; an accessory packet; a plastic spoon; and a flameless ration heater. The packaging for an MRE must be capable of withstanding parachute drops from 1,250 feet and nonparachute drops from 100 feet. Minimum shelf life is three and a half years at 80 degrees Fahrenheit (27 degrees Celsius) or nine months at 100 degrees F (38 degrees C). It must also be able to withstand short-term temperature extremes of minus 60 degrees F (minus 51 degrees C) to 120 degrees F (49 degrees C). Depending on contents, each package weighs 13 to 18 ounces.

Photo: U.S. Department of Defense

seized. The only real problem was the air campaign, since many of the bomber aircraft, such as B-2s, had to fly all the way from the continental United States. Shock and Awe would have to wait until the following evening, March 21. So, too, would ODA 551's entry into Iraq.

Working quickly, the team loaded all their equipment, supplies, and vehicles into a Hercules transport aircraft and moved to another SOF base located in a friendly host nation adjacent to Iraq. They then jammed a week of last-minute loading, packing, and preparation into less than twenty-four hours before their new liftoff time—just after the fall of darkness on the night of March 21. The tasks that had to be accomplished ranged from the high-tech, such as loading crypto codes, satellite photos, maps, and other data into computers, to more mundane tasks, like compressing their food load. This meant taking conventional Meals, Ready to Eat (MREs), stripping off the excess packaging, and then stuffing three meals into the tough plastic bag normally meant for only one. It was just one of the ways that the SF teams managed to pack enough of what they would need into the three GMVs.

They were taking more with them than their own mission plan stated.

Runyon, along with Clay and Chris, had looked at the two- to four-day estimate for elements of V Corps to reach them and immediately realized that whoever had laid out the movement plan had probably never read Cornelius Ryan's classic book *A Bridge Too Far*. The story of a 1944 Allied airborne assault that failed due to overly optimistic planning, underestimating the enemy, and poor use of intelligence, *A Bridge Too Far* was a bible and a cautionary tale for those going deep behind enemy lines. With that and other historic military precedents in mind, Runyon ordered his men to pack as much extra food and other consumables into the GMVs as possible, in case something happened to slow down V Corps on its way to Karbala. It was an insightful decision.

Just before dark, the team helped the crew chiefs of the MH-47 Chinooks from the 160th SOAR—the "Night Stalkers"—carefully load the GMVs. This had to be done delicately, as there was little or no clearance between the vehicles and the interiors of the helicopter cabins. In fact, the springs of the GMVs had to be compressed slightly with ratcheted web straps to make the vehicles fit just right. Then, with everything loaded, the eleven men of the team mounted the helicopters and launched into the night sky.

Into Battle: Infiltration

The crews of the three MH-47s concentrated on their difficult task of flying in formation, never more than five hundred feet above ground level. Flying with the assistance of NVGs and the advanced avionics of the M-47s, the Night Stalker crews made the difficult task look easy. In fact, at about two hours to the landing zone, it was a relatively short hop for the helicopter crews that evening, not even requiring an in-flight refueling from one of the AFSOC MC-130 Combat Talon tanker-transports. There were, however, a few moments of excitement along the way.

Coincidently, at precisely the same time that ODA 551 was flying to their insertion point south of Bahr al Milh, the CENTCOM Air Forces (CENTAF) launched the long-awaited Shock and Awe air campaign. In addition to helicopters from the 160th SOAR, the skies over Iraq were filled with hundreds of strike and support aircraft, along with hundreds of cruise missiles on the way to their targets. This made the airspace south of Baghdad *very* crowded, so the CENTAF planners had carefully laid out a plan to "deconflict" the skies that busy night. In theory, as long as the MH-47s stayed at their prescribed flight level, no harm would come to them. Nevertheless, several members of ODA 551 when looking out the windows of the choppers noticed what looked like "lit cigars" flying above them. What they had seen was a stream of navy Tomahawk cruise missiles coming in from the Red Sea, just a few hundred feet over their heads.

Exactly on schedule, 2:00 A.M. local time on March 22, the helicopters arrived at their planned landing zone, approximately one hundred kilometers from their target area in the Karbala Gap. It took only a few minutes to offload the GMVs, and then the helicopters departed, leaving ODA 551 on its own. Quickly, the men mounted their GMVs and drove about four hours to their planned dayover site in the Wadi al-Salem. Digging in, they spent the day sleeping, checking gear, and getting updates on their target area from Task Force 52 back in Kuwait. Then, as darkness fell, they again loaded onto the GMVs and headed north into the Karbala Gap for the most dangerous part of their mission: to find a secure "hole in the ground."

ODA 551 had a fixed amount of time to transit to the Karbala Gap, find a hide site, and dig in before dawn. If they could not find a hide site by a certain time, they would abort, exit the Karbala area, and move back to the dayover site and request an extraction from the 160th helicopters. That, however, was not on Captain Runyon's mind. He was in his element: 350 miles behind enemy lines with no way of quick extraction and surrounded by enemies. Nevertheless, Runyon and Team 551 moved carefully through the desert,

Photo: U.S. Army

Because of a fear that their transport aircraft would be hit by antiaircraft fire in the heavily defended Karbala Gap, ODA 551 had to be dropped off in a location south of the gap. Here the team is in position in its "dayover" site, a deep wadi. Two of the team's three GMV's are hidden beneath camouflage cover (middle left and center foreground). A third GMV (center) is partially covered.

Photo: U.S. Army

The wadi that ODA 551 used during its mission turned out to be ideal. It was perfectly situated to monitor traffic and other activity in Karbala Gap and at the same time wide and deep enough to provide sufficient cover from search parties. The team benefited from another advantage as well: the wadi was located in the middle of an artillery range. Iraqi search parties refused to enter it for fear of encountering unexploded munitions.

doing their best not to draw attention to themselves. Despite the mobility of the GMVs, they kept their speed down, working to reduce dust and other signs of movement along the desert floor.

The transit to the Karbala area took several hours, and when the team arrived they found their hunch had been dead-on. Almost immediately, they found exactly what they were looking for. Just yards from the edge of the lake, Bahr al Milh, ODA 551 found an eroded wadi fifteen to twenty feet deep and wide enough to actually drive their GMVs into. The sides were steep and solid, and nothing in it could be seen unless someone was either directly overhead or on the edge of the wadi itself.

And as they scanned the area, they realized that they had also found the perfect spot for reconnaissance. Their location had clear lines of sight to Karbala in the east and both of the main highways that ran north-south and east-west. Using specialized sensors and optics, including a large 1,000 mm Meade telescope, they could survey the entire area for miles. They quickly used camouflage nets to hide their vehicles and equipment, finishing the job just as dawn broke. The first part of their mission had been a success. Now they got down to the work they had been sent to do.

In the Gap

After the three GMVs were driven into the wadi, shut down, and covered with camouflage nets, the team members obscured as much of the tire tracks, footprints, and other indicators of their search as possible and descended into the wadi. Once setup at the hide site was completed, the team established communications with their headquarters and began to call in activity reports of what was happening in the Karbala Gap.

A round-the-clock observation schedule was set, and the team dug in for their planned stay. This normally meant one of the communications sergeants or the TACP would man the radios, while two or three other Green Berets manned the optics and sensors. The rest would sleep when possible and police the area to make sure nothing blew out of the wadi that could draw attention to them. Movement was limited, done slowly and carefully. Like their submarine counterparts who "run silent and run deep," Team 551 was staying silent and keeping deep in their wadi.

From the very beginning, the ODA 551 SF soldiers worked hard not to be seen. At no time during their stay did they run the engines on their GMVs or even boil water for coffee for fear of the noise being heard or thermal signature detected. The satellite communications links were set up at the bottom of the wadi to reduce the chances of sidelobe detection by Iraqi security

Photo: U.S. Army

ODA 551's hide site in a wadi in the Karbala Gap. The wadis were virtually invisible in high-resolution satellite photographs. The team made an educated guess about their existence and their suitability for hiding in what was otherwise a flat and featureless landscape as seen in the horizon. One of ODA 551's ground mobility vehicles is completely hidden beneath a camouflage cover (lower right). Another GMV is in the process of being covered (center).

troops. Team members chewed tobacco rather than risk detection from an errant match or cigarette showing up on a pair of Iraqi NVGs. Even their communications with CENTAF aircraft were limited to minimize any chance of radio direction-finding gear locating their position. Ironically, it seemed that everyone on the Allied side knew exactly where they were, though few actually believed at first that they were there.

On the morning of March 23, a small blue symbol appeared on Blue Force Tracking (BFT) system screens around the world. It showed that an Allied unit had been inserted into the Karbala Gap. The automatic satellite-tracking BFT would make ODA 551 a legend among those who saw the system screens during the next ten days. The team intentionally left on one GMV's BFT transponder, mainly to make sure that Allied aircraft, artillery, rockets, and guided missiles did not attack them! However, the reality of what that little blue BFT symbol meant was whispered about in awe and wonder at headquarters, control centers, and even the Pentagon and White House.

For all the respect and awe of their peers in the American military, however, there was little doubt that Team 551 fully understood the realities of their situation. Always in the back of the team's mind was the very real possibility of chemical attack, if and when V Corps arrived. Because of the sudden rise of aerial attacks on units in, near, and transiting the Karbala Gap, the Iraqis soon began to suspect that a recon team of some sort was in the area, and search parties were sent out, though none of them entered the area of ODA 551's hide site. ODA 551 continued to lie low, sharing their wadi hide site with a 110-pound female hyena, which howled in indignation at having her den requisitioned. Such was life in the most valuable piece of Allied real estate in Iraq.

The team's first several days on watch in the gap were busy ones, as they called in a number of close air support (CAS) strikes on tanks and artillery positions near Karbala. Battle damage assessment (BDA) showed that these strikes destroyed nine tanks and an artillery tube, along with a number of other armored vehicles in revetments. These were all likely assigned to the right flank of the Medina Division of the Republican Guard.

But Team 551's real contribution was more long-term, as they watched the major supply routes (MSRs) running through the Karbala Gap. Everything from Iraqi fuel tankers to troop reinforcements came through the area, and were noted and reported by the team for later attack by Allied strike aircraft. They were careful, however, not to have too many of the targets they sighted attacked right in the gap. Dan Runyon and his team lived by the old hunter's rule that one does not kill where one lives and wanted to avoid drawing too much attention. It was a good policy because as it turned out they were staying much longer than anticipated.

Almost as soon as ODA 551 got settled, outside events began to make their

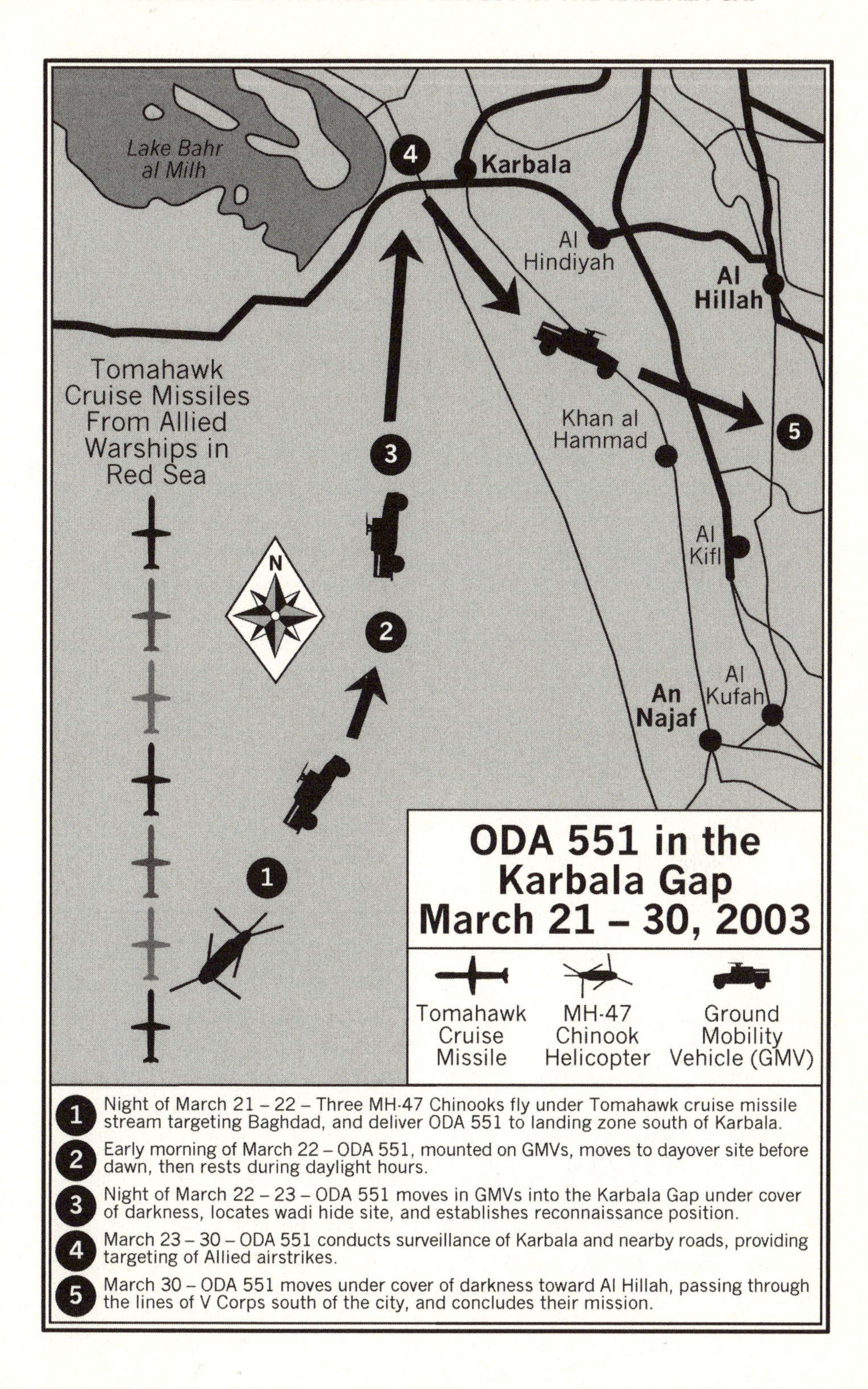
Lake Bahr al Milh
Karbala
Al Hindiyah
Al Hillah
Khan al Hammad
Al Kifl
Al Kufah
An Najaf
Tomahawk Cruise Missiles From Allied Warships in Red Sea
N
1
2
3
4
5
ODA 551 in the Karbala Gap March 21 – 30, 2003
Tomahawk Cruise Missile
MH-47 Chinook Helicopter
Ground Mobility Vehicle (GMV)
1 Night of March 21 – 22 – Three MH-47 Chinooks fly under Tomahawk cruise missile stream targeting Baghdad, and deliver ODA 551 to landing zone south of Karbala.
2 Early morning of March 22 – ODA 551, mounted on GMVs, moves to dayover site before dawn, then rests during daylight hours.
3 Night of March 22 – 23 – ODA 551 moves in GMVs into the Karbala Gap under cover of darkness, locates wadi hide site, and establishes reconnaissance position.
4 March 23 – 30 – ODA 551 conducts surveillance of Karbala and nearby roads, providing targeting of Allied airstrikes.
5 March 30 – ODA 551 moves under cover of darkness toward Al Hillah, passing through the lines of V Corps south of the city, and concludes their mission.

lives more interesting. V Corps made a fast run up from Kuwait to the town of Hillah, though not without incident. Almost as soon as a unit of the Iraqi military made contact with elements of V Corps, normally the armored brigades of the 3rd Infantry Division (Mechanized) (3rd MID), they would dissolve into the countryside. All that would be left by the side of the road were piles of uniforms and boots, usually neatly folded as if they would be picked up shortly by their former owners. What then followed was a bizarre orgy of firefights and killing, as many uniformed Iraq soldiers, assisted by foreign volunteers, became Fedayeen Saddam paramilitary fighters.

These suicidal fighters attacked armored vehicles including M1A1 Abrams tanks and M2 and M3 Bradley fighting vehicles with little more than AK-47 combat rifles and RPG-7 rocket-propelled grenades; they died by the thousands, though taking a toll on American soldiers and vehicles along the way. They also had the effect of keeping the Americans awake 24/7 on the drive up from Kuwait and exhausting their supplies of fuel and ammunition. By the time that the lead elements of 3rd MID got to Hillah, they were literally out of gas, bullets, and energy, and had to stop. In fact, all of the American units were strung out along hundreds of miles of roads from Kuwait, trying to untangle massive traffic jams while fighting off attacks from the Fedayeen Saddam.

Apache attack helicopters of the 11th Aviation Brigade staged a major deep attack against the Medina Division on the other side of Karbala from

Photo: U.S. Department of Defense

A Marine Corps Abrams tank prepares to leave a tactical assembly area near Karbala. Though the Republican Guard's Medina Division was stationed around Karbala, it did not counterattack V Corps' advance through the Karbala Gap.

Photo: U.S. Army

The *shamal,* a massive dust storm that struck Iraq on March 24, 2003, effectively shut down the coalition's advance in Operation Iraqi Freedom. In the upper middle of this photograph (in the circle), two ODA 551 members are sitting in their hide site in the Karbala Gap. The team later commented that the dust storm made the area look like a landscape from Mars.

Team 551's position. But poor operational security meant that the Iraqis were alerted when the Apaches overflew the city of Karbala, which erupted in AAA fire. The flak trap damaged most of the Apaches, and one went down with both its crewmen captured. The Apache went down in a field east of the city, and thankfully nobody back at V Corps headquarters got any wild ideas about sending Team 551 to the rescue. More than once during their stay, non-SOF staff officers got "inspired ideas" about things for the team to do, which Lieutenant Colonel Conner back at TF-52 headquarters at Ali Al Salem managed to quash.

Then, a massive dust storm called a *shamal*, the worst in decades, fell over the region late on March 24. For two days, a dense red dust haze, as thick as pea-soup fog, shrouded the battlefields of Iraq, bringing the offensive to a temporary halt. Though the Iraqis benefited from the pause in ground operations, it allowed soldiers and marines to catch some badly needed rest and for the logistics trains to catch up with the frontline units and get them resupplied. Air operations also nearly came to a halt, the exception being aircraft equipped with GPS-guided weapons, which could bomb through the

U.S. Marine Corps 3rd Infantry Division vehicles drive through the *shamal* during Operation Iraqi Freedom. Shortly after ODA 551 got into position in the Karbala Gap, a major sandstorm swept across Iraq, effectively shutting down the offensive until it passed.

haze. And for Team 551, their duties were limited to staying hidden and waiting for the *shamal* to clear.

When conditions did clear on March 26, the team took up its reconnaissance duties again with a bit of concern. Though rested and resupplied during what was now being called an operational halt by General Wallace, V Corps was now sitting in front of Hillah, having lost its momentum. With it looking like V Corps would be there for some time, the planned relief of ODA 551 was pushed back.

Getting Out: Exfiltration

Even before the start of their mission, the members of ODA 551 suspected that the planned three- to five-day wait for V Corps to get to Karbala might be optimistic. Food, water, and most importantly, battery power were carefully rationed to maximize the team's time on station. However, when the originally scheduled time doubled and looked as if it might triple, concern turned to outright worry.

With V Corps stuck in front of Hillah, Task Force 52 began to consider alternative ways of extracting ODA 551 from the Karbala Gap. Unfortunately,

Photo: U.S. Army

Iraqi military traffic on the highway near ODA 551's covert observation post in the Karbala Gap.

Photo: U.S. Army

An Iraqi cement complex near ODA 551's observation post. Despite being this close, ODA 551 managed to stay in their location undetected for ten days and return to friendly lines without incident.

the air-defense situation in the gap had proved most hostile, thanks to the Iraq AAA guns and SAMs. This meant that an extraction by the MH-47s of the 160th SOAR was out. V Corps was pleased with the work the team was doing, but even the conventional-force officers began to worry that ODA 551 was pushing its luck.

Finally, on March 29, Captain Runyon and ODA 551 got the news they had been waiting for. The good news was that they could leave the wadi and the Karbala Gap. The bad news was that they would get absolutely no help doing so. After examining a very short list of options, TF-52 and V Corps decided since only about fifty miles separated ODA 551 from V Corps' northernmost line of advance, the best way to get Team 551 home was to let them drive out on their own.

On the tenth day of a mission that was supposed to last half that long at the most, ODA 551 packed up its gear, policed the wadi one last time, and prepared to leave their "hole away from home." They were short of food and getting rather rank, not having bathed in over a week. None had wanted to risk a dip in the nearby lake for fear of being spotted. Also, the brackish water of Bahr al Milh well reflected its name, "Sea of Salt."

Then, with the team ready to leave, disaster stared them in the face. When the GMV drivers turned the ignition switches to start the engines, nothing happened. Not one of the GMVs could be started, and suddenly every member of the team felt his blood run cold. The problem was that the decision not to run the motors of the GMVs meant that the vehicles' batteries had not been charged since their arrival. Tasked with powering radios and other gear for a period that exceeded the original estimation, the batteries had simply run down to the point that none of the vehicles could crank up.

At this moment, however, the decidedly low-tech training from their Q Course days came back to Andy and Shane. The two communications sergeants collected every battery the team had and removed two of the batteries from the GMVs. They then spent several hours building an ad hoc battery network, wiring all the cells together to try to give the battery remaining in the third GMV enough juice to crank and start. If that worked, they hoped to then reinstall the batteries in the other two GMVs and jump-start those from the one running vehicle. If this didn't work, they faced a long walk through hostile territory.

When Andy and Shane were finished, the other team members crossed their fingers as the driver hit the GMV's starter. It worked. Quickly they reinstalled the other vehicles' batteries and jumped those from the running one. Then, after allowing the batteries of all three vehicles a chance to charge, Team 551 carefully exited the wadi and slowly headed south.

As the team exited the Karbala Gap they had a chance to look around—and discovered that their infiltration route had taken them through a live

Photo: U.S. Department of Defense

A U.S. Army Special Operations Forces Humvee drives along a stretch of highway in West Baghdad. As a result of accurate reconnaissance from ODA 551, V Corps was able to use the Karbala Gap as its main route to Iraq's capital.

minefield! With no choice but to retrace their original path, the team cautiously transited the dangerous ground, finally breaking into the clear. They then headed toward the forward lines of the 3rd MID. However, they were not yet home free. In fact, all the team members felt the most hazardous part of their mission was just ahead: passing though the lines of their conventional counterparts.

Historically, two friendly units meeting up and moving through each other is a dangerous evolution due to the opportunities for friendly fire casualties as the two wary forces approach. "Pass through the lines" movements are particularly risky for SOF units, given their unusual vehicles, clothing, and other unconventional appearances. To avoid "blue-on-blue" exchanges, every conventional unit in CENTCOM had been seeded with SOF liaison teams, most drawn from 19th SFG. These would then move to the front lines and coach each side during the ODA's approach.

This day, the procedure worked as planned, and ODA 551 passed through the 3rd Mechanized Infantry Division front lines near Najaf without incident. They then reported to the V Corps SOF coordination element and finally stood down. After a decent meal and some well-deserved rest, the team turned in their load of ammunition, which included *every round* they had been issued back in Kuwait! Only then did the reality of their achievement begin to take hold.

ODA 551 had executed their mission without firing a shot in anger. In SOF terms, they had run a near-perfect mission, having never been found by the Iraqis. Despite the blown entry schedule at the beginning of OIF, being sandwiched between the ground and a stream of cruise missiles on entry, and the battery and minefield crises on the way home, what Captain Dan Runyon and ODA 551 had done at the Karbala Gap was rapidly becoming the stuff of legend. But their role in OIF was far from over.

After a bit of rest and new orders, ODA 551 moved into unconventional warfare and support and sustainment operations. Much of their efforts were directed toward securing the two mosques in Karbala, among the most holy in the Shiite branch of Islam. They also got to help with the annual pilgrimage to the shrines, the first freely open to the world since 1979, when Saddam took power. The team was finally relieved on April 29, 2003, and returned to Fort Campbell shortly after.

Meanwhile, V Corps had resumed the offensive, with 3rd MID rolling though the Karbala Gap as if it were a parade ground. It took the division just a day to move to the international airport just outside Baghdad. They then conducted their famous "Thunder Runs," which broke the back of the Iraqi defenders. Within days, the Iraqi capital fell to the combined pincers of V Corps and I MEF, and phase III came to an end less than four weeks after the start of OIF.

For ODA 551, the Karbala Gap mission was the first of many deployments to Iraq, which continue to this day. Dan Runyon was promoted to major and took command of Bravo Company of 2/5th SFG in the fall of 2003. Several years later, Runyon retired from the army, taking a job as a baseball coach in the town just outside the gates of Fort Campbell. It's a quiet life for a man who gave so much amazing service to his country, which is perhaps as it should be. After all, having commanded the "Immaculate Mission" to the Karbala Gap, what more could a grateful nation have asked of him and his SOF warriors?[6]

1. James Kitfield, "March on Baghdad Brings Mix of Power, Flexibility," *National Journal*, April 4, 2003.

2. Woods, et al., *Iraqi Perspectives Project*, 123.

3. Ibid., 137.

4. Ibid., 137.

5. Gordon and Trainor, *Cobra II*, 110–111.

6. Much of the information for this chapter was gathered by John D. Gresham and Tony Koltz in a series of interviews conducted at Fort Campbell, Kentucky in the summer and fall of 2003, and the winter of 2004.

7

Twenty-first-Century Alamo: Task Force Viking at Debecka Pass

Operation Iraqi Freedom, the campaign that resulted in the ouster of the Saddam Hussein regime, was launched by an international coalition of forty-nine nations led by the United States on March 20, 2006. The plan called for a three-prong ground offensive: in the southeast from Kuwait up the Tigris and Euphrates river valleys, in the west from Jordan, and in northern Iraq from the Kurdish-controlled territory above the U.N.-established Green Line boundary. Originally, the main effort in the north was to be led by the U.S. 4th Infantry Division (Mechanized—MID). But the Turkish parliament at the last moment rejected the American request for permission to use Turkish territory and airspace to transport the 4th MID and other American units. The plan was quickly amended to make the attack in the north into a Special Operations–based offensive. Using a new, more circuitous aerial route that bypassed Turkish airspace, Joint Special Operations Task Force (JSOTF)–North, composed of the 173rd Airborne Brigade, two battalions and the headquarters of the 10th Special Forces Group, and the 3rd Battalion of the 3rd Special Forces Group, deployed to northern Iraq and became the primary American military units for the northern offensive.

On April 6, 2003, thirty-one Special Forces soldiers—Green Berets—and Air Force Special Operations combat controllers in teams ODA 391 (nicknamed "the Roughnecks") and ODA 392 and ODA 044 were supporting a group of peshmerga militia as part of Task Force Viking. Its purpose was to reach and establish a roadblock on an important highway junction in northern Iraq. Within hours of setting up the roadblocks, the group came under counterattack by a superior Iraqi combined force of tanks, towed and self-propelled artillery, and mechanized infantry. The group hastily took up defensive positions on a piece of high ground near the village of Debecka that they named "the Alamo."

This is the story of what happened at that twenty-first-century Alamo and how the teams' actions radically changed the military's view of Special Operations Forces and their doctrine.

Nine-One Don't Run.
—Unofficial motto of Operational
Detachment-Alpha 391

The sun had been up for a little less than two hours. The green fields of unripe winter wheat glistened with the early morning dew. Farther south, beyond the fields and hidden behind the haze that limited sight to about a mile and a half, the horizon rose dramatically in a long, rugged mountainous ridge.

A road bisected the fields and intersected a major route known as Highway 2, which paralleled a long ridgeline. A three-hundred-foot-wide traffic circle, or roundabout, with a monument containing a likeness of Saddam Hussein in the middle, formed the highway junction. About a hundred feet north up Highway 2, a white Toyota pickup truck was parked on the shoulder of the road. If this were the farmland of rural America or Western Europe, the presence of the Toyota on the road's shoulder would have caused a passerby to think that a farmer was doing an early-morning inspection of his fields.

But this was northern Iraq, and Operation Iraqi Freedom was less than three weeks old. The Toyota was a wreck—shattered by the devastating impact of .50-caliber machine gun bullets and 40 mm grenades fired by Special Forces soldiers from Operational Detachment-Alpha 392 and half of ODA 391, who were stationed at the roundabout with their allies, a band of Kurdish militia known as peshmerga—"those that face death."[1]

As sometimes happens in the ways of war making, this otherwise anonymous traffic circle near the village of Debecka, the objective of this part of Task Force Viking, and the high ground and mountain pass just northeast of it was about to become a "meeting place" in the same manner that befell a once-unknown small town in south-central Pennsylvania called Gettysburg.

But Sergeant First Class Frank Antenori, the team sergeant of ODA 391, wasn't thinking of Gettysburg in 1863 as he stared into the haze to his south. He knew that mechanized infantry from the Iraqi 34th Infantry Division, at least a battalion of Iraqi armor including twelve tanks and fifteen armored

Photo: U.S. Army

Three Roughnecks and their GMV near Debecka Pass. Mounted on the passenger side is an M240B machine gun. Strapped on the back of the GMV, above the five-gallon fuel cans, are two Javelin missile launch tubes. This GMV is equipped with an Mk. 19 grenade launcher on the top of the cab. Attached to the Mk. 19 is a laser rangefinder sight.

personnel carriers, was in the area, and probably the Iraqis knew where he and his fellow Special Forces (SF) soldiers were. Their orders were to deny the enemy use of Highway 2. Earlier, in addition to the Toyota, he and his men had blown up a truck, shot up an SUV and a motorcycle messenger, and fired on a busload of Iraqi troops, who quickly retreated.

Sergeant Antenori was wondering, "What will the enemy do next?"

The answer was not long in coming.

Chief Warrant Officer (CW2) Martin "Marty" McKenna, the executive officer of ODA 391, was standing lookout behind the M2 .50-caliber machine gun in one of the detachment's two ground mobility vehicles at the roundabout. He called out a warning and pointed. Everyone turned to look south down the road that bisected the fields. Some large Iraqi vehicles, possibly troop trucks, slowly emerged from the thick haze, heading toward them. The lead truck's lights were flashing, the established signal for surrender.

Staff Sergeant Andrew Pezzella, 391's senior communications specialist, asked, "Marty, what do you want to do?"

The trucks were out of effective range of the long-reaching M2, and they were too far away for the Special Forces troops to tell positively if they were civilian or military. "Let's watch them," McKenna told the group.

For the next few minutes, the trucks continued their slow drive toward the roundabout, the headlights of the lead vehicle continuously flashing. Suddenly, a little more than two hundred feet to their left, thick clods of dirt and wheat stalks erupted from the field, followed by the sound of an explosion.

"What the hell was that?" one of the soldiers shouted.

Almost immediately a second geyser of dirt and wheat, right next to the first, was flung into the air.

"*Mortars!*" shouted Sergeant Antenori, in sudden realization.

Four more rounds soon slammed in the field near the location of the first two.

Sergeant Todd Gannon of ODA 392 was standing watch in one of his detachment's two GMVs that were stationed as sentries on a small hill about three hundred feet from the roundabout. He had his binoculars up and was scanning the area, searching for the Iraqi mortar crew that was shooting at them. He paused when his scanning came to Debecka. "I see them. I see them," he said. Near the village, he spotted two Iraqi mortar teams.

The presence of mortar crews meant that infantry was in the area, getting ready to attack. If that attack could be coordinated with accurate mortar fire, which would happen as soon as the mortar crews adjusted their aim, the Green Berets and their peshmerga allies, standing in the open without any cover whatsoever, would be in serious trouble.

Captain Matt Saunders, commander of ODA 392, ordered his men at the roundabout and on the hill to mount up in their GMVs. With 391 holding the intersection, Captain Saunders announced he was going to take 392 and knock out the mortars. GMVs, described as "Humvees on steroids," are M1025 HMMWVs customized and heavily armed for Special Operations Forces (SOF) missions. Each GMV mounted an M2 .50-caliber machine gun or an Mk. 19 40 mm grenade launcher as well as the smaller 7.62 mm M240B machine gun, to say nothing of the other weapons stored throughout the vehicles. The four GMVs of ODA 392 had more than enough firepower to take out the mortar crews and any likely defense hiding near it.

Saunders and the GMVs had just started down the road when 57 mm proximity fused rounds began exploding in the air about nine hundred feet away from the roundabout. What was later discovered to be a ZSU-57-2 mounting two 57 mm cannons, an Iraqi self-propelled vehicle usually used for antiaircraft defense, had just joined in the attack. Though this incoming fire was ineffective, it was potentially more of a threat than the mortars. Proximity rounds contain sensors in their tips and are designed to explode at predetermined distances above the ground or near a metallic object like an aircraft, nullifying protection from foxholes or aboveground shelter.

When the Iraqi trucks were about a mile away from the roundabout, Staff Sergeant Andrew Pezzella claimed he saw muzzle flashes coming from the trucks. Sergeant Antenori, sitting in the front passenger seat of his GMV, trained his binoculars on the trucks, as did McKenna, but the thick haze still obscured the trucks too much for them to get a clear view. A brief argument ensued, with Pezzella, his upstate New York accent contrasting with the drawls of those from the South and West, insisting that soldiers in the trucks were shooting AK-47s at the group, and the others insisting that it was just flashing truck lights. The discussion died down when all but Pezzella decided, as if they were spectators at a football match, to watch what would happen when the GMVs from 392 got within range of the Iraqi mortar crew.

As a result, only Sergeant Pezzella saw a large cloud of smoke suddenly appear in front of the trucks and spread across the field. While the others' attention continued to be focused on the drama about to unfold on their left, Pezzella strained to see through the combination of smoke and haze about a mile in front of them. Large, low-profile dark, shadowy vehicles in the fields flanking the road slowly began to emerge from the gloom.

"Tanks! Tanks! Tanks!" Pezzella shouted at the top of his lungs. The cry was picked up by Staff Sergeant Robert Farmer, 391's junior engineer, a hard-charging spark plug of a man from the hills of West Virginia. He was standing in the gunner's position in Sergeant Antenori's GMV and began banging on the roof over Antenori's head to get his attention. A baffled Antenori got out of his GMV and stared down the road straight ahead.

The vehicles weren't tanks. But they were something almost as bad—MTLB armored personnel carriers. The Russian-built tracked transport had a crew of two and (barely) room for eleven passengers, and roughly looked like a self-propelled flatbed of a tractor-trailer wrapped in armor. Its low profile—it was slightly less than six feet high—meant that approximately just the top half of the highly maneuverable transport cleared the bearded wheat stalks that were being methodically ground under its tracks. Each mounted a 7.62 mm machine gun in its turret, and the personnel carrier's half-inch armor was strong enough to shrug off fire from the GMVs' machine guns.

Though one of the peshmerga vehicles mounted a 106 mm recoilless rifle, the Kurds were not trained to slug it out with Iraqi armor. The peshmerga militia dashed into their vehicles and started driving back up the mountain pass road, their trophies forgotten.

Meanwhile, the Americans stood thunderstruck at the sight before them. Eight armored personnel carriers and four trucks with troops—at least 120 soldiers, probably more—a serious Iraqi battle group had been assembled and in coordination with artillery support was heading their way.

"We're being attacked?" Sergeant Antenori thought. "The Iraqis don't attack; they surrender or run. This can't be."

Antenori and a few others in the group had fought in Operation Desert Storm twelve years earlier, where demoralized Iraqi troops surrendering without a shot were more common than those who put up a fight. The Roughnecks' complacency had been further enforced by an incident earlier that morning when they had taken the ridges behind them. At one ridge an Iraqi infantry unit had surrendered after skirmishing with the peshmerga and then receiving a couple of short warning bursts from one of the Roughnecks' M2s.

Sergeant Antenori was still struggling over how well the Iraqi commander of the counter-attack had snookered him when the MTLBs began throwing out camouflage smoke. As the billowing clouds began to spread, one of the soldiers at the roundabout shouted, "*Shoot!* Start shooting!" The stupefying spell that had held them was broken. Immediately, those manning the .50-caliber M2 machine guns and the Mk. 19 automatic grenade launchers responded. The rounds couldn't penetrate the armor of the MTLBs, especially at the extreme range they were firing, but they would cause the Iraqi vehicle commanders in the MTLBs to close their hatches, thus restricting visibility and possibly slowing their advance. It would also keep the Iraqi infantry inside the MTLBs.

As this was going on, CW2 Marty McKenna got on the radio, raised Master Sergeant Ken Thompson in one of the GMVs of ODA 392, and told him to return to the roundabout fast because they were under attack. From his angle, Thompson could see only one MTLB, but he didn't argue and passed the warning on to Captain Saunders. A moment later, the four GMVs were roaring back to the roundabout, without having attacked the mortar crew.

About the same time ODA 392 returned, the MTLBs stopped. Initially Sergeant Antenori thought the Special Forces had successfully halted the enemy advance. Then he discovered how wrong he was. As big and dangerous as the eight MTLBs and troops in the trucks were, they were merely the undercard of what was coming up from the south. Out of the thick smoke and haze clanked and rumbled the headliner: four T-55 main battle tanks. The Green Berets were not only outnumbered, they were now also seriously outgunned.

A Russian-built export as well, the T-55's main gun was a high-velocity 100 mm cannon. The kinetic energy punch from one of the tank's roughly four-inch-diameter, high-explosive shells was so great that a near miss was virtually as destructive as a direct hit.

The shock of seeing the MTLBs and the T-55s operating together momentarily caused everyone to forget that they did have a weapon designed for this occasion: the new FGM-148 Javelin antitank missile. Earlier, ODA 391's expert on the weapon, Staff Sergeant Jason Brown, had used one to destroy a troop transport truck. If ever there was a time to break out the man-portable, fire-and-forget, infrared-guided antitank missiles, that time was now. While the gunners kept up their covering fire, Sergeant Brown was frantically rummaging through the back of his GMV for a Javelin command launch unit (CLU), the reusable targeting device attached to the disposable missile launch tube. His relief in quickly finding it just as quickly turned into dismay. The CLU has a forward-looking infrared (FLIR) sensor that has to be activated before the Javelin can be fired. Brown had turned off his CLU after he had shot the truck, and once it was attached to a new launch tube, it would take thirty seconds for the CLU to "cool down" sufficiently for use.

One of the T-55s, now about a half mile from the roundabout, fired its main gun. The 100 mm round flew over their position and exploded in the ground almost two hundred feet behind them.

Sgt. Jeffrey Adamec and Sgt. Ken Thompson from 392 also tried to set up Javelins as the other three T-55s fired their shots; all the rounds hit high and wide. A gunner and loader in a T-55 can fire five rounds a minute; a good team can get off seven. The Roughnecks might have had ten seconds to spare, but they definitely didn't have thirty seconds to set up their shot.

"Let's go, let's go!" Sergeant Antenori shouted. Sergeant Brown was standing in the middle of the road, eye glued to the CLU sight, oblivious to the activity around him.

"Come on! *Let's go!*" Sergeant Antenori shouted again. Marty McKenna needed no further urging. He yelled at Brown, "Take the shot! Take the shot!"

But the CLU still hadn't sufficiently cooled down. Calmly, as if he were kneeling at the firing range at Fort Pickett, Brown replied in his slow Oklahoma drawl, "Just give me a couple seconds, I almost got it."

But the Pennsylvania-born team sergeant of ODA 391 was having none of that. Antenori ran up, grabbed Brown, and screamed for him to get into a GMV.

Sergeant Brown didn't have time to do so. Nor did Sergeant Adamec. Another volley started screaming toward them. With CW2 McKenna's GMV in the lead, the GMV drivers floored the accelerators and raced up the road back toward the ridge from where they had come, with Brown draped over the hood of one GMV and Adamec holding onto the rear tire mount of another. Amazingly, neither lost his Javelin or CLU in the wild ride back to the ridge.

As they neared the high ground that formed the foothills of the first ridge, they found themselves stuck behind the retreating Kurdish caravan of slow-moving trucks. The old and overloaded trucks, with peshmerga hanging off the sides, could barely do ten miles an hour up the narrow road. The GMV gunners continued to fire their heavy weapons at the enemy. The extreme range coupled with the tank crews safely buttoned up inside their turrets made the effort more symbolic than practical. The Iraqis calmly returned fire. It was a shooting gallery situation, but despite tank rounds falling all around the GMVs and Kurdish trucks, no one had been hit.

The GMVs reached the summit of the first piece of high ground. Earlier the ODAs and the peshmerga had used the same spot to stage their first ambush. As the Kurds continued retreating up the road, McKenna quickly and expertly surveyed the familiar ground, pulled off the road, and stopped. Though it lacked terrain that could be used for cover, the location had a good command of the valley below and was large enough for them to spread out to form a proper defense. "We'll circle the wagons and 'Alamo' here," he thought.

The next few minutes was a swirl of organized chaos as the ODA teams set up defensive positions in the middle of combat. ODA gunners in the GMVs continued to lay down defensive fire with their heavy weapons, shooting such a rapid series of bursts that the recoil from their M2s and Mk. 19s caused the heavy-duty suspension in the GMVs to sway. Iraqi tank and artillery rounds tore up dirt and rocks around the ridge. Normally, each team had two men from Air Force Special Operations Command (AFSOC) trained as one of two types of forward air controllers capable of calling in combat air support—special tactics squadron (STS) combat controllers or tactical air control party (TACP) controllers. Due to a shortage of such personnel, each team had only one. While the others worked on defense, the three forward combat controllers in the group, Sgt. Jake Chandler of 391, Sgt. Saleem Ali of 044, and Sgt. Todd Gannon of 392, broke out their UHF radios and, each using a different frequency, began hailing any friendly strike aircraft in the area. At the same time, Sergeant Antenori was on the team radio, frantically trying to contact his commanding officer, Captain Eric Wright, who was with the other half of ODA 391 farther up the ridge behind them, clearing a path through the defensive berm and minefield they had encountered earlier. But the team radio was line-of-sight, and a very large hill blocked Antenori from the rest of 391.

Sgt. Jake Chandler was the first to make contact with an airborne warning and control system (AWACS) aircraft that was controlling strike aircraft in the region. Weeks earlier, when Chandler first joined ODA 391, he went to great lengths to tell Sergeant Antenori what a forward air controller "find" 391 had in getting in him. He was not a mere TACP controller; he was an STS and a highly skilled one, at that. The details that made an STS superior to a TACP controller might be of major concern if one were in the business, but Antenori cut to the chase, and bluntly asked, "All I want to know is, can you drop bombs on bad guys?" Chandler replied confidently, "I can drop any bomb, from any plane, on any target you want."

If ever there was a time to put that skill to good use, it was now. With the sounds of battle adding emphasis to his words, Chandler shouted into the microphone, "We're taking fire from a bunch of tanks just a couple hundred meters to our front. We were almost overrun but have managed to Alamo up on some high ground. What's the ETA [estimated time of arrival] for the fighters?"

"Roger, we copy all—ETA thirty minutes," the voice of the AWACS controller replied.

The answer left Chandler dumbfounded. What he had forgotten in the excitement brought on by the combat was the operational problem presented by the Turkish government's decision the previous month. Because it had refused to allow American combat aircraft to operate out of bases in Turkey, and initially refused permission to use Turkish airspace, any and all support aircraft had to go "the long way around the barn" to get to combat areas. The closest aircraft dedicated to supporting offensive operations in the north were on an American aircraft carrier stationed in the eastern Mediterranean. Its air wing possessed approximately ninety aircraft of all types from F-14 Tomcat strike fighters to EA-6B Prowler electronic jammers and SH-60 Sea Hawk helicopters. Unfortunately, all were either already busy or far away.

Just a few minutes earlier, the Roughnecks didn't have thirty seconds to spare in their own defense. Now, somehow, the Roughnecks had to find a way to survive on their own for at least thirty minutes.

Meanwhile, Sergeant Antenori had given up trying to raise Captain Wright. Together with driver Staff Sergeant Steven Brunk, he started breaking ammo boxes out of their storage racks and hauling them to the machine gunners, who were firing the last rounds from their ready canisters. At the same time, others were breaking out more Javelin missiles from the GMVs.

As this was happening, Sgt. Jason Brown was getting ready for his second Javelin shot of the day. Somehow he had managed to hold onto both the GMV and his Javelin CLU during the wild ride up to point Alamo. The CLU on his Javelin was now fully chilled. But that was probably the only good news of the moment because his engagement situation was not just adversely optimal, it flat-out sucked.

Special Operations teams such as the Green Berets are trained to sneak in, launch a surprise attack, and sneak out before the enemy knows who hit them, with what, and from where. Here the enemy knew their numbers, knew where they were, and knew their position was both isolated and exposed. The only thing the Iraqis didn't know was that for the next thirty minutes the ODA teams were on their own without air support—but that secret was more harm than help. The Iraqi commander, undoubtedly believing that American aircraft would arrive soon, had the incentive to strike fast and hard before the airplanes arrived.

The Javelin weapon system had a preferred target range of 2,000 meters (about a mile and a quarter) and a maximum official range of 2,500 meters (roughly a mile and a half). Those distances were established under controlled test firings in perfect weather conditions with stationary targets on level terrain and with no one shooting at the tester. Looking through his computerized sight, Brown estimated that his targets were at least 2,700 meters away (roughly a mile and two-thirds). With the tactical situation worsening by the second, he didn't have the luxury of waiting for the armored vehicles to get closer.

But Sergeant Brown had studied the manuals and practiced on the Javelin simulators back at Fort Pickett, Virginia, and Fort Bragg, North Carolina, until he was a "virtual" expert. He had even instructed the others in the team, having each take the Javelin training course twice. As he became more familiar and proficient with the system, he began to think that instead of overstating the specs the manufacturer had actually understated the Javelin's effective range.

Taking all this into account, he activated the missile's battery coolant unit (BCU) that turned on the Javelin's seeker and subsystems, centered one of

Photo: U. S. Department of Defense

The engine in a Javelin antitank missile has just ignited in this live-fire exercise in Kuwait. The operator (seated) is holding the Javelin's command launch unit (CLU), which is a reusable triggering system. Once the missile has been fired, the launch tube is discarded. The flared base of the launch tube is designed to further reduce the small back blast of the small charge that ejects the missile out of the tube. The enlisted man kneeling beside the operator has night vision goggles strapped to his helmet.

the Iraqi armored personnel carriers in his sights, got a lock signal from the CLU, and squeezed the trigger.

With a loud, hollow pop the primary launcher propelled the Javelin out of its tube. About a second later and before the Javelin had traveled thirty feet, the main thruster ignited with a louder *shoosh*. Sergeant Brown's life and the lives of his buddies were now riding on the success or failure of a $78,000, 1.76-meter antitank missile traveling at approximately Mach 1.

Granting some individual differences, for the most part the ground forces of the U.S. Army and Marine Corps all share the same basic table of organization of their units from squad (lowest) to corps (highest). But the U.S. Army Special Forces Command (SFC) units are administratively broken down into Special Forces Groups (SFGs), each with three types of teams providing the building blocks for SF field operations.

As mentioned in the previous chapter, SF ODA teams are, in theory, composed of twelve Green Berets: a captain (the team commander), a warrant officer (the team executive officer, or XO), and ten noncommissioned officers (sergeants of various ranks and specialties). Though all are cross-trained in one another's skills, each team has senior and junior specialists in weapons, engineering, medicine, and communications. The ODA, also called an A-team, can be broken into two parts for split-team operations, which makes them quite versatile.

When more than one ODA is used in the field, usually an Operational Detachment-Bravo (ODB) controls them. ODBs are the fourteen-man SF teams acting as company headquarters units. ODB teams are led by a major, and in 2004 they normally controlled four or five ODAs.

Usually controlling three ODBs and their subordinate ODAs are Operational Detachment-Charlie (ODC) teams, commanded by a lieutenant colonel. ODCs are battalion command teams, and they also provide logistic support for ODA and ODB teams under their command.

Three ODCs and a command group make up a Special Forces Group; five active-duty and two Army National Guard SFGs make up SFC based at Fort Bragg, North Carolina. Each active-duty SFG has a regional orientation, focusing on operations for individual unified commands worldwide. For example, 5th SFG normally is assigned to U.S. Central Command, which operates in the Middle East and southwest Asia. European Command (EUCOM), which covers Europe, the Mediterranean, and most of Africa, is assigned 3rd and 10th SFGs. It was these two units that would be most active in northern Iraq in the spring of 2003.

Of all the problems faced by CENTCOM commander General Tommy Franks in the spring of 2003, none was more frustrating and potentially dangerous than the situation in northern Iraq. Originally, the Allied war plan had a specific plan for northern Iraq. Code-named Cobra II by the CENTCOM staff, the plan had projected the army's 4th Infantry Division (Mechanized) entering northern Iraq through Turkey, then fighting south through Mosul, Tikrit, and down into Baghdad.

The 4th MID was a fully digitized formation with all of the vehicles linked via digital data links to share information. This meant that every member of the division could access information from any other vehicle in the unit, from how much fuel and ammo they had on hand to the threats they were in contact with and were engaging. There can be little doubt that the 4th MID would have sliced through the Iraqi divisions deployed between the Turkish border and Baghdad like a hot knife through butter but for one small problem.

They could not get to Iraq through Turkey.

On March 1, 2003, the newly elected Turkish parliament narrowly voted to deny the United States ground access for American forces to transit to Iraq. Botched American diplomacy and a parliament trying to show its independence to other nations in the region meant that the only way into Iraq for conventional ground forces would be from Kuwait. If the 4th MID were ever to get to Iraq, they would have to do so the long way around through the Suez Canal and Persian Gulf. And that was the easy part of the problem for General Franks.

The real problem was up to twenty Iraqi divisions north of Baghdad that were now free to be moved at Saddam Hussein's discretion. One possibility was that they might be sent south of the Iraqi capital to help defend the city against the Allied invasion coming up from Kuwait. More likely, however, was a final chance to settle an old score with Saddam's most despised ethnic minority: the Kurds. Although they had survived attacks with chemical weapons and twenty-five years of genocidal oppression, the Kurds now had little more than their own militia, the peshmerga fighters of the PKK—the Partiya Karkerên Kurdistan, or Kurdistan Workers' Party—to defend them.

It was this "little more" that was about to make the difference.

For years since Operation Desert Storm in 1991, the 10th SFG had been discreetly working with the PKK to help keep the Kurdish north safe until Saddam could be overthrown. But light militia armed with little more than AK-47s combat rifles and RPG-7 rocket-propelled grenades was not going to be able to do much against the tanks and artillery of the Iraqi army. Unless of course something extraordinary was added to the equation that was about to play out in northern Iraq. That something would have to be Colonel Charles Cleveland, the 10th SFG, and whatever else could be flown into northern Iraq.

Charlie Cleveland was one of the most talented officers ever to command an SFG—extraordinarily high praise, considering that one of his peers at the time was Colonel John Mulholland. Mulholland, the legendary 5th SFG commander who had liberated Afghanistan in just forty-nine days in 2001, was in charge of all SOF units south and west of Baghdad. But Cleveland was about to get a major change in his job description: commander of Joint Special Operations Task Force–North (JSOTF-N).

Originally, JSOTF-N's mission was to act as advisers to the PKK, which would have formed a vanguard for the 4th MID on their drive south. As such, JSOTF-N had been last in line for getting resources and support for their operations in northern Iraq. The Turkish parliament's vote on March 1, however, made short work of that situation. Suddenly, as the days to the start of OIF began to run out, Charlie Cleveland began to move to the front of the line for units and assistance. He also began to consider a war plan that would not just have the PKK defending the Kurdish people along the Green Line that separated the Kurds from the rest of Iraq.

Taking inventory, Cleveland could count on the 2nd and 3rd Battalions of his own 10th SFG (in military parlance, 2/10th SFG and 3/10th SFG). Mounted in armed Land Rovers, they had been primarily involved in peacekeeping operations in the Balkans over the past decade. In fact, 1st Battalion/10th SFG (1/10th SFG) was still committed to NATO peacekeeping operations in the Balkans, leaving Cleveland with only two-thirds of a full group. Fortunately, SFC had prepared a worthy replacement for the 1/10th SFG: 3rd Battalion/3rd SFG (3/3rd SFG), based out of Fort Bragg, North Carolina.

Normally assigned to duties in Africa, 3/3rd SFG had originally trained to work down in the western desert of Iraq with 5th SFG, along with the British and Australian Special Air Services (SAS). To give them the capability to work in the trackless deserts of the area, 3/3rd SFG had recently been reequipped with the new GMVs so that they would have the mobility and firepower to deal with the expected Iraqi opposition. However, as the situation in northern Iraq had deteriorated over the winter of 2002–2003, the decision was made to give 3/3rd SFG to Colonel Cleveland to help flesh out the rest of 10th SFG.

The move proved to be a godsend for Cleveland and the situation in northern Iraq, where his 10th SFG troopers were underarmed by comparison. In addition, the 3/3rd SFG brought some real muscle to the situation in the form of a battalion headquarters (ODC 033), three company headquarters (ODBs 370, 380, and 390), and no fewer than fifteen ODAs. It more than doubled the firepower of 10th SFG and provided Cleveland options that had not been available in the original plan.

The 3/3rd SFG had spent the previous winter learning how to make best use of their new GMVs, along with all the new weaponry that came with them. This meant learning the Javelin and Stinger missile systems, along with new radios, sensors, and how to tie them all together. So by the time they deployed overseas in late winter 2003, the 3/3rd SFG was one of the sharpest and most dangerous combat units in all of Special Forces Command.

Shortly before the 3rd Battalion/3rd Special Forces Group (3/3rd SFG) landed in Romania in late February 2003, all their SFG ODAs received mission assignments and were told to conduct feasibility analyses. Operational Detachment-Alpha 391 had been given an airfield seizure mission and concluded in their analysis that trying to infiltrate an Iraqi air base would almost certainly end in failure with heavy casualties. They presented their findings to their battalion commander, Lieutenant Colonel Rand Binford, who was running ODC 033.

After seeing all the different scenarios they presented, Binford agreed with their assessment. But even though the decision to cancel the mission was made "without prejudice," the result was still the same: ODA 391 was now without a job. So while Captain Eric Wright and his men were ferried to Romania along with the rest of the battalion, they were forced to stand on the sidelines and watch all the other teams get ready for war. The ribbing they took from the members of the other teams didn't help their morale one bit.

Then things got brighter.

Colonel Cleveland was by this time a very busy gent. Along with commanding the 10th SFG, he also wore the hat of commander, JSOTF-N. By this time, JSOTF-N's mission, framed in the broad terms of an operation order, was to conduct "unconventional warfare and other Special Operations in Joint Special Operations Area North to disrupt Iraqi combat power in order to prevent effective military operations against Combined Forces Land Component Command forces."

In plain terms, Captain D. Jones, assistant operations officer for the 3/10th, later said the 10th SFG's "mission in the north was to hold"[2] thirteen of the Iraqi divisions stationed along the Green Line—the U.N.-established border in the north that established a "safe zone" for the Kurds. It also included neutralizing sites suspected of containing biological or chemical weapons of mass destruction. Because of the Turkish parliament's vote on March 1, those roles were about to be enlarged.

One problem, however, was that while Colonel Cleveland was a commander of a large SOF unit, most of his experience had been with the typically lightly armed and equipped troops of 10th SFG in the European theater. The 3/3rd SFG, in comparison, was both highly mobile and packed a higher-than-average punch.

Lieutenant Colonel Binford suspected that Colonel Cleveland's lack of familiarity with the battalion was causing him to underestimate its potential for offensive operations in the north, and he wanted to alert him to the kind

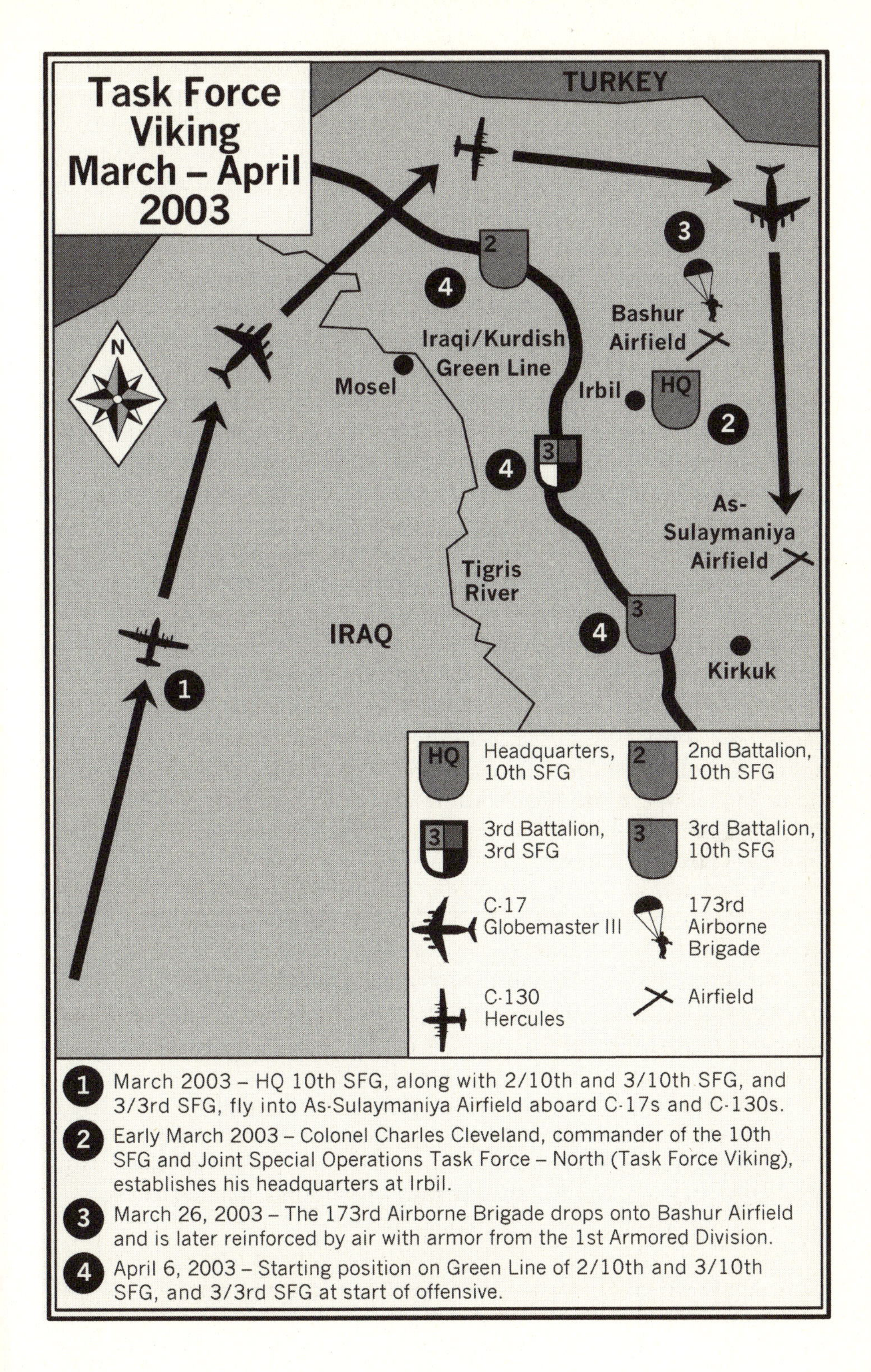

1. March 2003 – HQ 10th SFG, along with 2/10th and 3/10th SFG, and 3/3rd SFG, fly into As-Sulaymaniya Airfield aboard C-17s and C-130s.
2. Early March 2003 – Colonel Charles Cleveland, commander of the 10th SFG and Joint Special Operations Task Force – North (Task Force Viking), establishes his headquarters at Irbil.
3. March 26, 2003 – The 173rd Airborne Brigade drops onto Bashur Airfield and is later reinforced by air with armor from the 1st Armored Division.
4. April 6, 2003 – Starting position on Green Line of 2/10th and 3/10th SFG, and 3/3rd SFG at start of offensive.

of firepower he really had at his disposal. To do that, Binford needed a team to display its inventory. Since all the other units in the battalion were busy, he sent down word to ODA 391 to prepare a modular demonstration, or mod demo, for the "Old Man." The instructions were not to make it an elaborate show; just line up the GMVs and get ready to do a walk-around with the colonel.

But Captain Eric Wright, the commanding officer of 391, was having none of the "keep it simple" directive. As he saw it, this wasn't just a show of firepower; it was a last-chance audition to go from being an understudy waiting in the wings to a player in the "big show." His men all agreed, and they drove their GMVs to an empty hangar and lined them up. Then everything from each GMV was taken out and displayed on the concrete hangar floor.

The result was as if Costco or Ikea had created a military-themed showroom. It was quite an inventory. A partial listing of what each GMV carried included:

- One .50-caliber M2 heavy machine gun and 3,000 rounds of ammunition *or* one Mk. 19 40 mm automatic grenade launcher with 1,000 40 mm grenades
- One M240B 7.62 mm machine gun with 2,000 rounds
- One M24 7.62 mm sniper rifle with 100 match rounds or one SPR 5.56 mm sniper rifle with 200 rounds *or* one Barrett .50-caliber sniper rifle with 100 rounds
- One 12-gauge Mossberg sawed-off shotgun with 50 rounds *or* one M249 5.56 mm Squad Automatic Rifle (a light machine gun) with 1,000 rounds
- Eight AT-4 disposable lightweight antitank rockets
- Two FIM-92 Stinger man-portable surface-to-air missiles
- Eighty pounds of C4 and TNT demolitions, detonators, triggers, fuses, and detonation cord
- One SOFLAM laser rangefinder/target marker
- One MIC LIC minefield-clearing ordnance unit
- One SATCOM radio along with various UHF, VHF, and other radios
- Surveillance telescope
- Thermal imaging gear
- Combat medical kit
- Food, water, and fuel sufficient for operations lasting ten days and over a distance of eight hundred miles

The only thing missing in the inventory, aside from the proverbial "partridge in a pear tree" (the "kitchen sink" was in the form of a heavy-duty coffeemaker), was the team's allotment of eight Javelin antitank missiles and two CLUs. They had not arrived in time for deployment but were expected any day.

Fully loaded, the gross weight for each GMV was 12,200 pounds—more than one ton over its maximum rated capacity. By comparison, a 2006 Lincoln Navigator SUV has a gross weight of 7,449 pounds, and that includes a maximum payload of 1,607 pounds. The reason for the overload was simple. In World War II, paratroopers from the 101st and 82nd Airborne divisions landed in Normandy on D-day with supply loads of weapons and ammunition that exceeded their own body weight because no one knew when they would be resupplied. Though weapons and equipment had changed and improved since 1944, the principle was still the same for their Special Operations progeny: take as much as possible on a mission—and then take some more.

The result was an overstuffed "gun truck." The wonder was that the vehicle's suspension, even though it was heavy duty, didn't collapse under the added weight. Yet somehow, the made-in-America customized product from the Letterkenny Army Depot of Chambersburg, Pennsylvania, held up without any problem.

When Colonel Cleveland and his staff arrived at the hangar later that day, his reaction could not have pleased the men of ODA 391 more. He was impressed, and as he was given the guided tour, Colonel Cleveland's mind was racing in high gear, thinking how he could put such firepower and mobility to use. When the demonstration concluded, he told the team that they would be going to Iraq.

The colonel was as good as his word. Before the week was out and even though they still didn't have a mission, ODA 391 and its GMVs, complete with full loads of Javelins that arrived soon after the mod demo, were loaded into air force transports and flying to 10th SFG's forward operating base (FOB) at an airfield near the capital city of a Kurdish province in Iraq called As Sulaymaniyah, located about fifty miles west of the Iranian border.

Following behind the 3/3rd SFG, as transport aircraft became available, would be an amazing array of combat units drawn from American EUCOM. The most impressive would be the famous 173rd Airborne Brigade out of Italy, which parachuted onto the As Sulaymaniyah airfield from C-17 Globemasters. These were followed by a small force of M1A1 tanks and other armored vehicles drawn from the 1st Armored Division ("Old Ironsides") in Germany, also airlifted by Globemasters. Perhaps most interesting, however, was one simple fact: all of these conventional assets were falling under the command of JSOTF-N, an SOF task force commanded by an SF professional. Just two years earlier, such a situation would not have happened. Now, with Special Operations Command on an equal level administratively as the conventional U.S. Army, Navy, and Marine Corps branches as a result of the Goldwater-Nichols Department of Defense Reorganization Act and the Nunn-Cohen Amendment, it was becoming part of the landscape of twenty-first-century American military operations.

Slowly but surely, Colonel Cleveland was acquiring the necessary resources to ensure that the Kurds could be defended from Saddam's forces in northern Iraq. And with the arrival of 3/3rd SFG, he now could begin to go on the offensive. His overall operation named Task Force Viking would be going into action once a few details were worked out. One of these was a task assigned to ODA 391 to the east.

Captain Wright's team initially found itself escorting a chemical-biological inspection squad (CBIS) that was checking a ruined Ansar al-Islam WMD facility near the town of Surgot, just off the Iranian border. Ansar al-Islam was a radical fundamentalist Kurdish Sunni Islamist group believed to be linked to Al-Qaeda. ODA 391 was not the only team that chafed under an unexpected ancillary role during the opening days of the offensive. All of the teams in the 3/3rd SFG were in the same situation. The problem was essentially one of command and control administration. Lieutenant Colonel Binford was in the process of setting up ODC 033's own forward operating base (FOB) at Irbil, a city roughly a hundred miles northwest of As Sulaymaniyah. Until that happened, the teams all found themselves marking time while the war swept around them along the Jordan-Iraq border in the southwest and the Kuwait-Iraq border to the southeast.

But within a few days, Captain Wright and his men got the call to head up to Irbil. The "head" of ODC 033 was up and running and ready to send its "body" ODBs and ODAs off to war. Its opponent: the Iraqi 34th Infantry Division. Battalions don't normally take the fight to an enemy division, and certainly not a Special Forces unit. The army's textbook formula for offensive operations calls for a minimum of three-to-one superiority for the attacker. In this case, Colonel Cleveland and JSOTF-N were reversing the formula.

Major Larry Dewey, one of the planners of the operation, later said, "Basically the mission was to fix and attrit the Iraqi forces that were located along the Green Line, the line separating the Kurdish area from the rest of Iraq. . . . We wanted to prevent them from withdrawing from that line to help defend Baghdad against the main conventional attack coming from the south."[3] The area north of the Green Line was divided into three combat areas of operations. The 3/10th SFG (ODC 102) was responsible for the southeastern eastern sector, while the 2/10th SFG (ODC 102) was responsible for the northwestern half.[4] In the middle, where their extra firepower and mobility could be focused on the Iraqi threat, would be ODC 033 and the teams of the 3/3rd SFG, including ODA 391, whose nickname, the Roughnecks, was taken from Robert Heinlein's book *Starship Troopers*.

The Iraqi 34th Infantry Division, which was located in the 3/3rd SFG's area of operations, contained three brigades. One was composed of truck-mounted infantry (the 90th with 2,500 men), one of armored (the 12th with 1,900 men), and the last of mechanized infantry (the 8th with 2,000 men). This was a formidable force by any standard, made more so by the fact that the 34th had good leadership and good personnel, a rarity in the Iraqi army of 2003. This made the 34th as dangerous as any Iraqi unit in the country and was the reason why 3/3rd SFG was matched up against it.

What Colonel Cleveland wanted Lieutenant Colonel Binford to do was to take his battalion of fewer than nine hundred SF soldiers, along with a larger, though variable, number of peshmerga militia, cross the Green Line, attack the superior force hunkered into well-constructed defensive fortifications, and knock it out of the war. If the offensive worked as planned, then the SOF would take a hard left turn to the southeast and continue the advance to Kirkuk to secure the oil facilities there and prevent their destruction by Iraqi forces. It was an audacious plan; when the men in 3rd Battalion saw the details, they loved it. It was fresh and would be totally unexpected—the kind of plan that would have been expected of a George Patton, not an SF colonel from Colorado Springs.

Lieutenant Colonel Binford deployed his three SF companies along the Green Line running from northwest to southeast, with ODB 370 in the north, ODB 380 in the middle, and ODB 390 in the south with four ODAs. ODB 390 was further broken down into two pairs of ODAs, with ODAs 391 and 392 to the south, and ODAs 394 and 395 a few thousand meters north. The plan was to have 394 and 395 try to flank the Iraqi positions along the ridge where the Green Line ran, and then link up with 391 and 392 and their peshmerga for the drive on Kirkuk.

One unique feature of the operations by ODB 390, drawn from Charlie Company of the 3/3rd SFG, was that they were not just riding behind the ODAs in GMVs. Instead, 390 was mounted in two unique vehicles converted from medium-size trucks back at Fort Bragg. Called "War Pigs" by their crews, these were a cut-down family of medium tactical vehicles (FMTV) flatbed trucks, with racks and cranes for everything a mounted SF company might need for resupply. Ammunition, fuel, food, medical supplies, and other necessities could now follow directly behind the ODAs. That way, if the ODAs and peshmerga got into a long firefight, they could be resupplied right on the battlefield, rather than having to withdraw to restock.

In addition, the two War Pigs functioned as mobile command posts and firebases. Each was armed with an assortment of M240 and M249 machine guns, and even had a 60 mm mortar mounted at the rear of the vehicle. Combined with an impressive communications suite of satellite links and radios, the War Pigs were among the most important innovations in SOF

Photo: John D. Gresham

The customized supply vehicle nicknamed "War Pig."

operations in a generation when they were introduced to combat in 2003. Unlike Desert Storm in 1991 and Mogadishu in 1993, U.S. SOF personnel were not going to be outgunned or outrun in northern Iraq in 2003.

On April 4, 2003, ODA 391 paired up with ODA 392 and met up with their insurgent force of peshmerga militia. This was composed of a four-man SF element from ODA 044 in a Land Rover and about eighty peshmerga militia out of a promised two hundred. While the peshmerga were lightly armed and mounted compared to the SF soldiers in their gun trucks, they were first-class soldiers. Some had years of combat experience in brushes with Saddam's military along the Green Line, and their force of ancient jeeps, SUVs, and pickup trucks belied their combat potential.

Eighteen months earlier in Afghanistan, the SF soldiers of the 5th SFG had delivered a practical lesson about the military power of insurgent militia forces when trained and advised by SF soldiers and backed by American airpower. Under the inspired leadership of men like Colonel John Mulholland and Lieutenant Colonel Chris Conner, the militia fighters of the Afghan Northern Alliance had defeated their Taliban and Al-Qaeda opponents in roughly seven weeks. It had been a military achievement to rival those of Genghis Khan and Hannibal, and something a fifty-thousand-man Soviet army had failed to do in a decade.

Military analysts and professionals around the world had been taken aback by what happened in Afghanistan in the fall of 2001, though not the SOF professionals of SOCOM. For them, Operation Enduring Freedom–Afghanistan (OEF-A) had been the validation of a half-century-long battle to make Special Operations a full peer with other service communities. Now, for the second time in just eighteen months, SOF warriors were going on the offensive with insurgents in their core specialty: unconventional warfare (UW).

With a large American flag mounted on the side of one of the GMVs, thirty-one Americans and their allies started their vehicles and headed down their attack route southwest into harm's way. Confident of their own skills, the Americans had little doubt of their eventual victory. What they could not imagine was that just a few miles down the road lay an opportunity for glory and legend.

So far it had been a good war for Task Force Viking. The attack on April 6 had tuned into a stutter-step affair, with a 6:00 A.M. bombing attack conducted by a three-plane cell of B-52 bombers from the 5th Bomb Wing stationed in Minot Air Force Base in North Dakota, which was operating from RAF Fairford in England.

Photo: U.S. Army

The Roughneck and peshmerga convoy on the road in northern Iraq to Debecka Pass.

Photo: U.S. Army

Some of the peshmerga who rode with the Roughnecks at Debecka Pass. A recoilless rifle is mounted on the vehicle in the center foreground. Another vehicle has a twin-barreled antiaircraft gun mounted in its rear.

The ground attack did not start as scheduled when the bombing stopped because the peshmerga militia who were supposed to lead the attack had not yet arrived. When they did, about a half hour later in their white Land Rovers and trucks, they looked more like a tough, rowdy gang than a dangerous military force. The Kurds' uniforms were a motley assortment of pants, shirts, and jackets—some military, many not. None wore helmets; more than a few had no boots, some only sandals. Some carried AK-47s. Others had different makes. Some of the SUVs were modified to transport recoilless rifles or Russian built DShK twin-mount 12.7 mm heavy machine guns.

But their informal approach to uniforms, weaponry, and vehicles was not reflected in their attitude about the upcoming battle. These were hard men whose people had suffered for generations from oppressors who had taken away their nation and at times outlawed their language and culture. Even attempts at genocide were woven into the tragic tapestry of Kurdish history. They would fight and kill Iraqis, no quarter asked or given.

Fortunately, the delay in launching the ground attack proved to have little consequence. With the peshmerga in the lead, 391 covering the right flank, 392 the left, and 044 coordinating command and control with the nearby peshmerga units, the group discovered that the predawn air strike had been so effective it had caused the surviving, panic-stricken Iraqi armor to evacuate its well-constructed defensive positions. Their only active opposition was scattered defensive fire against the peshmerga militia, who responded with their heavy machine guns and recoilless rifles.

Forty-five minutes after the B-52s' bombs stopped falling, the group reached its first objective, a piece of ground code-named Rock. Because it was in a depression dominated by a ridgeline from which an Iraqi counterattack could be expected, the group decided to continue on and find a site that could be better defended before stopping.

As they approached the second ridge, the peshmerga engaged in a brief firefight with Iraqi defenders. One lone Iraqi infantry unit, demoralized by the bombing and deserted by their tanks, surrendered to the Kurds after a couple of warning shots from an M2 from ODA 392 were fired over their heads. Upon interrogation, the major commanding the unit revealed that the tanks had retreated to their headquarters in Makhmur, a town almost ten miles down the road.

Part of the Kurdish militia escorted the Iraqi POWs back across the Green Line. The rest of the group continued the advance and soon encountered a T-55 tank parked awkwardly on the side of the road. Closer inspection revealed that the tank was in perfect shape. Apparently abandoned by the panicked crew, the driver had accidentally "high-centered" the T-55 by driving it over some boulders large enough to lift the tracks off the ground.

Sergeant Frank Antenori loved deer hunting. And since ODA 391 had a reputation as the black sheep ODA of the 3/3rd SFG, the opportunity to tag a trophy like this T-55 and validate ODA 391's success to anyone coming by later was irresistible. He reached over and broke out a can of black spray paint from a storage compartment, ran over to the tank, and to the amusement of the rest of the group, began spraying "Roughneck 91" and "STS" on its turret. As Air Force Sergeant Jake Chandler pointed out, since the B-52s had "knocked out" the tank, it was important to acknowledge its role in the operation. The tagging done, and souvenir photos taken, Antenori and Chandler climbed back into their GMVs, and the group continued down the road.

At about 10:00 A.M., the teams were more than a mile deep into enemy territory, the farthest advance of all the 3rd Battalion teams in action that day. Though the Roughnecks didn't know it at the time, the initial air strikes for the flanking groups had not been as effective as the one in front of the Roughnecks' position. As a result, the other combined forces encountered an entrenched enemy determined to stop them. As they reached each forward progress phase line in their offensive plan, the Roughnecks transmitted the news to Lieutenant Colonel Binford at ODC 033 headquarters at Irbil (or Arbil), approximately thirty to forty miles north.

When Wajih Barzani, the leader of Kurdistan Democratic Party special operations, heard the news, he announced he was going to that part of the front. The KDP was a rival to the PKK, and the two political groups' jockeying for power in the Kurdish-controlled territory was an element that complicated American operations in northern Iraq. A convoy was organized with two Green Beret GMVs as escort. Reporters embedded with the ODC 033 also heard the news and decided since that was where the action was, that was where they wanted to be. Soon, a long line of vehicles was heading down the road toward Debecka.

The biggest opposition for the Roughnecks turned out to be a passive one in the valley between the two ridgelines. Iraqi army engineers had graded a twelve-foot-high dirt berm across the road they were using and had planted a minefield around it. After the peshmerga partially cleared the minefield, the teams split. Captain Wright took half of 391 and would finish clearing a path in the minefield and blow a hole in the berm to open the way for an unimpeded advance by supporting troops or, if necessary, a retreat. The rest of 391, 392, 044, and the peshmerga would continue to "exploit the initiative" and continue the advance.

When the advancing group reached the final ridge before entering the valley, they pulled up at the crest of a dominating height that would come to be called Press Hill. Sergeant Frank Antenori, CW2 Marty McKenna, and Captain Matt Saunders, commanding officer of 392, got out of their vehicles and carefully walked to the top to do a personal reconnaissance before they continued forward. In an age where remote-controlled unmanned aerial vehicles with thermal imagers have become standard, it's often forgotten how effective trained eyes with a map and pair of binoculars can be on a battlefield.

Though overall visibility was restricted to just under two miles due to ground haze, the men had a good view of the immediate area. About a mile away, running parallel to the base of the ridge, was Highway 2. Intelligence had stated that this road was the main artery between Mosul to the north and Kirkuk to the south. As expected, there was some civilian traffic, but the three were surprised to see a heavy volume of military trucks and SUVs on the road. It was obvious the Iraqi army was using the highway to deploy reinforcements back and forth along the Green Line.

With a growing sense of excitement at the opportunity before them, the Green Berets returned to their vehicles, and the mixed convoy resumed their movement south toward the valley. Ten minutes later they reached the last piece of high ground before the valley south of the Green Line. Though their location on the ridge was less than ideal because of the distance from the road junction, the relatively flat, treeless valley offered no place for concealment to set up an ambush. Initially, they'd see what they could accomplish from the ridge. The Special Forces teams spread out, charged their machine guns, and sat down to wait for any counterattack from the Iraqis. Soon a troop transport truck came into view. A few well-placed bursts from an M2 knocked it out.

Suddenly, a number of peshmerga in the group leaped into one of their trucks and roared south down the highway. When the peshmerga truck reached the vehicle, the militia leaped out and, in the harsh standards of the region, delivered summary sentences of death to surviving Iraqi soldiers. A few minutes later, the peshmerga returned, dragging their wrecked trophy behind.

Not long after that, the Roughnecks saw coming from the south up Highway 2 an Iraqi SUV of a type commonly used by officers—and destroyed it with machine gun fire as well. Then one of the Green Berets saw a truck containing troops leaving Debecka and heading south. A number of men in the teams began swearing. The range was too far for their machine guns. And as the truck was driving away from their position, toward Kirkuk, it appeared they'd have to let it go.m

That's when Sgt. Jason Brown said that he could knock it out with a Javelin.

Sergeant Antenori was skeptical. By the time Brown could get the Javelin assembled and ready to fire, the truck would probably be well out of range, if not out of sight. But Brown insisted, saying, "I hauled that damn thing around in the 82nd Airborne for three damn years and never got a chance to shoot it." Brown had attended one of the training courses for Javelin gunners at Ft. Benning, Georgia. He'd seen the fielding teams conduct their live-fire tests but never fired one himself.

With coalition troops at the moment fighting in Baghdad, word that this second Gulf War was over could come at any day, if not hour. And Jason Brown wanted to fire at least one Javelin in anger before the war ended. When CW2 Marty McKenna added his own request to let Brown take the shot, Antenori relented. Sergeant Brown was as proud as a kid with a new bike on Christmas morning as he got out the Javelin missile launch container and began attaching it to a CLU. The others got into the act as well, and the next thing Sergeant Antenori knew, it seemed that everyone had pulled out a digital or video camera of one type or another to record the moment for posterity.

By the time Sergeant Brown was ready to fire, Sergeant Antenori, who could see the truck clearly only through his binoculars, said skeptically, "Jason, that truck has to be at least two miles away now. You are never going to hit that thing."

But Brown replied in his Oklahoma drawl, "No, Frank. I got it. Can I shoot?"

Sergeant Antenori gave his okay. Sergeant Brown pulled the trigger. The group watched, fascinated, as the Javelin performed its two-stage launch. Instead of a flat trajectory like the wire-guided Dragon antitank missile it had

FGM-148 JAVELIN

The Javelin is a fire-and-forget missile with lock-on before launch and automatic self-guidance. It is capable of taking either a top-attack flight profile against armored vehicles, impacting the generally thinner top layer, or a direct-attack mode against fortifications. The warhead is fitted with two shaped charges, a precursor warhead to detonate any explosive reactive armor, and a primary warhead designed to penetrate base armor. The missile is ejected in a "soft launch arrangement" reaching a safe distance away from the operator before the main rocket motors ignite. The disposable Javelin launch tube is attached to a reusable command launch unit (CLU), which aims and launches the Javelin.

SPECIFICATIONS

Manufacturer: Raytheon/Lockheed Martin
Power plant: Solid fuel rocket
Length: 43 inches (1.1 meter) missile, 47.25 inches (1.2 meter) launch tube
Diameter: 5 inches (127 millimeters) missile, 5.6 inches (142 millimeters) launch tube
Weight: 26 pounds (11.8 kilograms) missile, 14.1 pounds (6.4 kilograms) CLU
Warhead: 18.5 pounds (8.4 kilograms) tandem-shaped charge high-explosive antitank (HEAT)
Range: 8,200 feet (2,500 meters)
Guidance system: Imaging infrared guidance, fire and forget
Command launch unit: Passive target acquisition/fire control with integrated day/thermal sight. Magnification 4x day and 4x or 9x thermal.

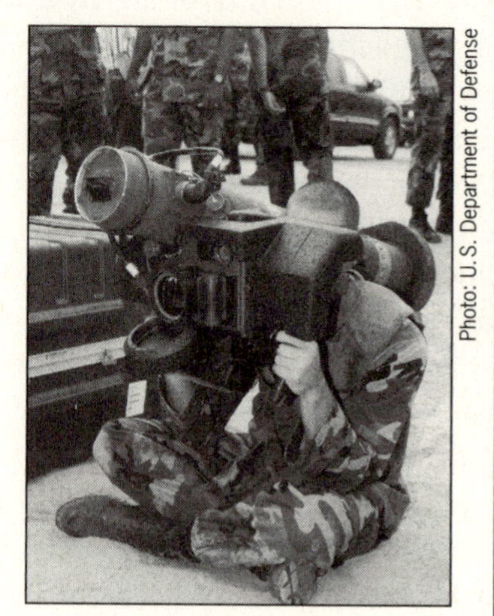
Photo: U.S. Department of Defense

replaced, the fire-and-forget Javelin suddenly shot straight up like a bottle rocket and disappeared into the low clouds.

The group waited. And waited.

Sergeant Antenori turned away, convinced that the shot was a $78,000 dud.

Suddenly some of the men in the group began whooping and hollering, their cheers punctuated by the sound of a high-explosive detonation coming from long distance. Sgt. Jason Brown had scored the Javelin's first "kill" in northern Iraq. More important, he had done so at a range well beyond the manufacturer's spec sheet limit: almost 3,000 meters (about 1.8 miles).

Sergeant Antenori was impressed, but he quickly got the group back to the business at hand. After a short conference, the group decided that their vantage point was still too far away for them to effectively shut down military traffic on Highway 2. Despite the lack of cover, they decided to set up a roadblock at the traffic circle ahead.

A few short minutes later, they arrived at the roundabout and began to deploy. M2 heavy machine guns and Mk. 19 grenade launchers were rechecked and charged. The plan was to stop and turn around any Iraqi civilian vehicle and destroy military transports for as long as the ammunition held out or until a superior enemy force arrived.

Not long after they were set up, an Iraqi soldier on a motorcycle appeared on the road and was summarily killed. The motorcycle quickly became another peshmerga trophy. Then, coming down Highway 2 from the north, a white Toyota pickup emerged from the haze. The problem was that both civilians and the military used the popular vehicle, and not all Iraqi Toyotas were painted military tan. As the pickup approached, the group started waving, signaling it to stop. Instead, as it got nearer, the Toyota began to speed up dangerously.

Sergeant Antenori ordered Sgt. Robert Farmer, holding a Mossberg 500 shotgun, to fire a warning shot. His blast turned into a fusillade as the rest of the group misinterpreted the shot as the signal to open fire on a possible suicide car bomber. The driver was killed instantly and the Toyota almost obliterated. When they tried to check if the driver was military or civilian, the Americans discovered the body was mutilated beyond recognition. The peshmerga leader dismissed their misgivings with a blunt, "He's Iraqi." Nonetheless, the incident reminded the Americans about the rules of engagement regarding civilians. They'd have to be more cautious next time.

The next approaching vehicle was clearly military: a tan bus loaded with armed soldiers. Any lingering doubt evaporated when some of the soldiers leaned out the bus's windows and began shooting with their AK-47 automatic rifles. They opened fire too soon, far beyond the AK-47's range. But the truck was well within the range of the team's M2 .50-caliber heavy machine guns. As soon as the M2s opened fire, the Iraqi truck driver slammed on the brakes and wheeled the truck around and raced away with an unknown number of casualties.

Later, the small convoy of four Iraqi troop trucks arrived, just after 10:00 A.M. This was followed by the Iraqi counterattack, totaling over 150 troops, eight MTLBs, four T-55s, and artillery support including a ZSU-57-2 mobile flak gun, truck-mounted BM-21 122 mm rocket launchers, and towed D-20 152 mm howitzers. This was an impressive force, and it was being led by an experienced and competent Iraqi commander.

When a nation purchases major weapon systems from another nation, it also buys into its war-making philosophy. Because Iraq purchased most of its weapons from what used to be the Soviet Union, Soviet advisers had taught the Iraqi army how to use and organize those weapons. SOF units were extremely familiar with Soviet-era, now Russian, military doctrine. According to that doctrine, as soon as the infantry exited the MTLB armored personnel carriers, the T-55 tanks were to seek protected defilade positions to provide artillery support for the infantry advance. At the moment, the Iraqi task force was executing the tactic with textbook precision.

As dangerous as the tanks were, the real threat was the Iraqi infantry. If the Roughnecks could get the infantry to prematurely deploy, once the soldiers were out in the open, they would be vulnerable to containment by the Roughnecks' machine gun and automatic grenade fire. If that happened, despite shelling from the tanks and artillery, the Roughnecks stood a better chance of surviving. Best of all, every minute that the Iraqis stayed deployed in the open was one minute closer to the ultimate battle-winner for the Americans: airpower, in deadly and unlimited quantities.

Sergeant Jason Brown's Javelin roared into the sky in a steep ballistic arc, plummeted through the thinner top armor covering the MTLB's engine compartment, and exploded. But Brown didn't see that "kill," his second of the day, or the surviving Iraqi troops staggering out of the wrecked armor personnel carrier's rear. He was too busy setting up another Javelin and firing at another MTLB. Elsewhere on the height, Sergeant Jeff Adamec, who had also arrived at point Alamo with Javelin and CLU in hand, took his missile shot. A third Iraqi armored personnel carrier erupted in smoke and flame, with dead, wounded, and dying soldiers blown out the rear by the concussion.

The destruction of the third MTLB caused an abrupt change in the other armored personnel carriers' movements. Quickly the infantry in the surviving MTLBs exited the rear doors and joined the survivors from the other transports in fanning out. Then, as if a bunch of teenagers had suddenly been given the keys to the twelve-ton monsters, the MTLBs on both sides of the highway began "cutting cookies," fishtailing, and performing other joyride-style stunts, otherwise known as evasive maneuvers. Within moments, crisscross tracks of churned up crops and clods of dirt were added to the battlefield among the wrecked and burning vehicles, patches of burning grain, thick smoke, and dead and wounded bodies.

Meanwhile, the death and destruction continued. Down on the highway a troop truck disintegrated like a plastic child's toy under the impact of two Javelins. Sergeant Eugene "Gino" Zawojski of 392 knocked out two MTLBs and Sgt. Eric Strigotte of ODA 044 fired a Javelin that destroyed another troop truck. Seven enemy targets had been destroyed and all at ranges that were greater than what the manufacturer advised. Only one missile failed to hit its target, disappearing into the sky never to be seen again. It was an amazing performance for a new weapons system that none of the Green Berets had ever fired before!

As the Roughnecks had hoped, moments after the Iraqi infantry exited their vehicles, the tanks had spread out to assume defilade position along the

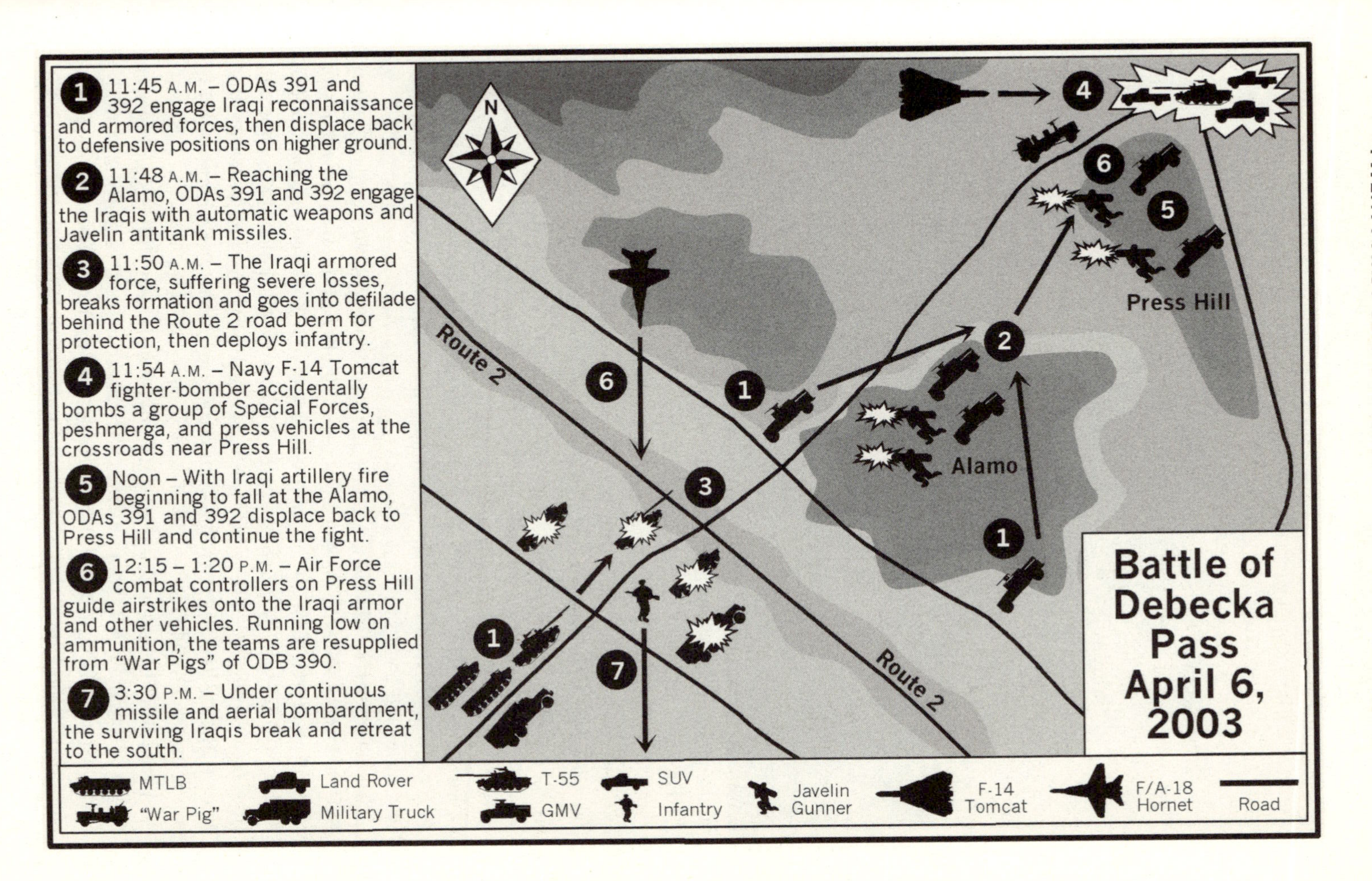
1 11:45 A.M. – ODAs 391 and 392 engage Iraqi reconnaissance and armored forces, then displace back to defensive positions on higher ground.
2 11:48 A.M. – Reaching the Alamo, ODAs 391 and 392 engage the Iraqis with automatic weapons and Javelin antitank missiles.
3 11:50 A.M. – The Iraqi armored force, suffering severe losses, breaks formation and goes into defilade behind the Route 2 road berm for protection, then deploys infantry.
4 11:54 A.M. – Navy F-14 Tomcat fighter-bomber accidentally bombs a group of Special Forces, peshmerga, and press vehicles at the crossroads near Press Hill.
5 Noon – With Iraqi artillery fire beginning to fall at the Alamo, ODAs 391 and 392 displace back to Press Hill and continue the fight.
6 12:15 – 1:20 P.M. – Air Force combat controllers on Press Hill guide airstrikes onto the Iraqi armor and other vehicles. Running low on ammunition, the teams are resupplied from "War Pigs" of ODB 390.
7 3:30 P.M. – Under continuous missile and aerial bombardment, the surviving Iraqis break and retreat to the south.
N
Route 2
Press Hill
Alamo
Route 2
Battle of Debecka Pass April 6, 2003
MTLB
"War Pig"
Land Rover
Military Truck
T-55
GMV
SUV
Infantry
Javelin Gunner
F-14 Tomcat
F/A-18 Hornet
Road

Photo: U.S. Army

A Roughneck is launching a Javelin at an Iraqi target during the battle at Debecka Pass.

only feature in the valley that could provide such protection: the earthen berm along Highway 2. The civil engineer who designed this stretch of road could not have created a better defilade fortification had he been in uniform. The berm that provided the base for the highway was about six feet high, and because the slopes were steeply angled, the T-55s were able to hug the sides of the berm so that only the tops of the turrets were visible. The tanks had just enough clearance to fire their main guns, while the rest of the vehicle was protected from fire and observation.

The Roughnecks tried to get a lock on the tanks' turrets with their Javelins, but the targets' infrared signatures were too small, and the heat from the late-morning sun radiating off the highway macadam further confused the CLUs and missile seekers. Worse, because the highway ran parallel to the ridge, the Iraqi tanks could move back and forth and lay down fire from different positions without exposing themselves to missile fire. At that moment, the issue was severely in doubt.

At the same time, the disorganized Iraqi infantry survivors began running to the berm, seeking its protection as well. Some made it successfully—dodging, weaving, and using the drifting clouds of smoke as cover. Others were cut down by machine gun and grenade fire from the Roughnecks. As this was happening, two Iraqi command vehicles arrived and were immediately taken under fire by the Roughnecks. Bullets and grenades smashed into both vehicles as the surviving occupants dashed for cover. Almost everything that moved south of the ridge was taken under accurate and deadly fire.

Sergeant Antenori, meanwhile, had ducked back into his GMV and was once again on the team radio trying to raise Captain Wright back at the defensive berm and minefield. As enemy near-misses pounded the ground around their position, spraying men and vehicles with rocks and dirt, Antenori finally managed to reach Wright and update him on their situation. Though the ODAs hadn't suffered any casualties, they were getting desperately low on ammunition for the M2s and Mk. 19s. They were also now critically low on Javelins. Captain Wright said he'd call up more ammo from their War Pigs in the rear, and he'd be up there with his GMVs as fast as possible.

The situation was desperate, but amazingly the Roughnecks had accomplished their two primary goals: they had stopped the Iraqi counterattack

Photo: U.S. Army

The Roughnecks' observation post at Alamo in Debecka Pass. Lying on the ground in middle of the photo is a Javelin launch tube; to its right, on a tripod, is a Special Operations Force laser marker (SOFLAM), a compact, lightweight, man-portable targeting system. In the distance, in the middle of the photograph, are two columns of smoke from destroyed Iraqi military vehicles.

dead in its tracks *and* they had managed to stay alive—miraculously without suffering any casualties—for the thirty minutes specified by the faceless airborne controller. All they needed was a resupply of ammo and for the friendly aircraft flying in above the layer of clouds—and hopefully over their position—to come down and help.

With their thirty-minute wait elapsed, the Roughnecks' combat controllers returned to their radios and renewed their calls for air support. This time 392's TACP Tech Sgt. Todd Gannon obtained a contact, and it was a big one: the lead pilot of a two-plane element of navy F-14 Tomcats from one of the American carriers supporting the offensive. Sergeant Gannon quickly informed the pilot about what was happening and the location of friendly and enemy forces. He ended with a request to take out the T-55s in defilade along Highway 2. The Tomcat leader acknowledged and informed him that they'd fly down for a confirming visual pass before making their first attack run.

The Northrop Grumman F-14 Tomcat, made famous by actor Tom Cruise in the movie *Top Gun*, became operational in 1972 and since about 1980 was known as "the king of American carrier flight decks."[5] Originally designed as the navy's premier air-to-air combat fighter, in 1991 modifications were made in the swing-wing twin engine aircraft so that it could also conduct air-to-ground operations. The Tomcats were considered especially good at close air support (CAS) due to their highly accurate LANTIRN targeting pods and dedicated weapons officer in the rear cockpit. In this capacity the Tomcat could carry a maximum bomb load of thirteen thousand pounds, just one ton less than the maximum bomb load of a WWII-era B-17 Flying Fortress. In 2003, the Tomcat was at the end of its operational lifespan and was gradually being phased out by the new F/A-18E/F Super Hornet. Operation Iraqi Freedom would be the last time it would see combat action.

Todd Gannon relayed the good word about the F-14s to the rest of the Roughnecks. Moments later, they saw two Tomcats break through the clouds and at low level, just a few hundred feet above the ground, cross the highway, and fly over their position in a comforting high-pitched roar before soaring back into the clouds. The cavalry had arrived.

Meanwhile, just to the rear of the battle, the peshmerga and press convoys from Irbil had already passed through the path cleared by Captain Wright and his men. By the time Captain Wright and the rest of 391 began their trip to point Alamo, a group of between twenty to thirty vehicles had gathered on the road beside the abandoned T-55 that Sergeant Antenori had tagged. Captain Wright stopped briefly to confer with Major Eric Howard, commander of ODB 040, who had been escorting one of the convoys before resuming his advance. Based on Sergeant Antenori's report, once he left the cluster of vehicles, he took the GMVs off road and was driving southeast in an attempt to get into a position to deliver a flanking Javelin attack on the T-55s.

Captain Wright's group was almost in position for his flanking maneuver when he saw the two Tomcats emerge from the clouds for their bombing run. The lead F-14 pilot reported to Sergeant Gannon at point Alamo that he had the targets in sight. "Cleared hot," Gannon replied, giving him permission to drop his bombs.

At the same time, one of the reporters by the abandoned T-55, John Simpson of the BBC, was gathering information for a television report he was going to file. He noticed out of the corner of his eye the Tomcats flying in their direction. As he looked up at the F-14s, he suddenly saw a "white and red painted" object detach from the underside of the lead Tomcat and fall toward him.

At the same moment, Captain Wright and his men, sergeants Gerry Kirk, Ken Wilson, Lihn Nguyen, Rich Turner, and Mike Ray, watched in horror as the bomb from the Tomcat arced through the air and exploded in the middle of the peshmerga and press by the T-55. Knowing that they had just suffered a devastating "blue-on-blue" attack, he called out to his men to head back to the crossroads to try to save as many of the wounded as possible.

Photo: U.S. Army

The immediate aftermath of the friendly fire incident near Debecka Pass. A navy F-15 Tomcat mistakenly dropped a bomb on the group of Kurds, American Special Forces soldiers, and journalists that had gathered near an abandoned Iraqi T-55 tank.

The next thing John Simpson knew, he was lying on the ground, eardrums perforated, blood pouring from shrapnel wounds in his legs, and surrounded by smoke, dust, and the screams of wounded and dying men. The white-and-red-painted 750-pound bomb had exploded about thirty feet from where he was standing. Men were dead and dying, and most of the vehicles around him were on fire and exploding.

As the F-14s had flown above the clouds to prepare for their bomb run, the pilots had lost their sense of cardinal direction and spatial orientation—they had drifted north of their attack position. When the Tomcats reemerged from the clouds, they mistook the cluster of peshmerga and reporters' vehicles beside the abandoned T-55 for Iraqi troops and vehicles, and attacked. It was the worst single friendly-fire incident of the entire war in Iraq.

Suddenly the radio net was alive with frantic calls to the Tomcats from Sergeant Gannon and the other forward air controllers, all on the same frequency.

"Cease fire! Cease fire!"

"Abort! Abort! Abort!"

"Blue on blue! Blue on blue!"—the signal for friendly fire.

The Tomcats immediately broke off and flew back above the clouds, where they circled and waited for further instructions.

As the Tomcats withdrew, Captain Wright's GMVs pulled to a stop about three hundred feet away from the carnage at the crossroads. Smoke was pouring from burning vehicles. Dead and wounded lay scattered about. Other victims of the bombing staggered around aimlessly. Sgt. Mike Ray was 391's trained medic, but all Green Berets receive combat lifesaver training so that they can provide basic triage assistance. The key skill here is the setting of tourniquets, which can save lives and extend the "golden hour" a badly wounded casualty has to reach medical care.

Munitions in the burning peshmerga vehicles began cooking off. The Green Berets ignored the sounds of exploding bullets as they ran to the wounded. But then a Kurd RPG flew just above the ground between Sergeants Wilson and Ray, missing them by less than twelve inches. Seeing the near miss, Captain Wright immediately ordered two men to drive the GMVs another hundred yards farther away to reduce the chance of a round hitting and exploding in the heavily armed vehicles.

Meanwhile, Sergeant Ray established a casualty collection point (CCP) in a nearby large depression that was low enough to protect the wounded from exploding ammunition. He then ordered the other Green Berets to bring all the wounded to the spot for emergency care. Then he began his own search for wounded.

He discovered in a nearby ditch three wounded men, one of them a Kurd who was severely injured. Of the other two men, one was speaking English into a satellite telephone. It was John Simpson, and he was delivering a live report about what had just happened to anchor Maxine Mawhinney, broadcasting live in the BBC News 24 studio back in Great Britain.

As Sergeant Ray approached to help, Simpson was saying into the receiver, "Well, it's a bit of a disaster . . . I was in a convoy of eight or ten cars in northern Iraq coming up to a place that has just recently been captured. American special forces in a truck, two trucks, I think, beside them, plus a very senior figure—"

At that point, Sergeant Ray, seeing the shrapnel wounds in Simpson's leg, knelt down to give first aid and began asking about his wounds. Simpson, obviously in shock and still trying to be a professional combat journalist, glared at him and said, "Shut up. I'm broadcasting! Oh, yes, I'm fine—am I bleeding?"

"Yes," replied Sergeant Ray. "You've got a cut."

"I thought you were going to stop me," said Simpson, who then went back to giving his report to Maxine Mawhinney on the other end of the satellite phone. Sergeant Ray quickly bandaged him and then moved on.[6] As he did, John Simpson described it as "a scene from hell here. All the vehicles on fire. There are bodies burning around me, there are bodies lying around, there are bits of bodies on the ground." He went on to describe the burning vehicles and exploding ammunition.

Simpson then added he thought that "A very senior member of the Kurdish Republic's government" was injured.[7] The "senior member" was Wajih Barzani, who was not only the Kurdish special operations military commander, he was also the brother of Massoud Barzani, the Kurdistan Democratic Party leader. Wajih Barzani, one of the most powerful political figures in Kurdistan, was now lying unconscious in the CCP, with a serious wound to the head and shrapnel wounds all over his body.

Captain Wright was at the CCP when Barzani was brought in. When he discovered who the Kurd was, Wright said to Sergeant Ray, "Mike, this guy better not die—he's Barzani's brother." As soon as the triage was finished, the Kurdish leader's followers picked him up and carried him to one of the undamaged vehicles, which then raced back to a hospital in Irbil, some distance away. From Irbil, Wajih Barzani was flown to a military hospital in Germany. Other wounded began leaving at about the same time, as did a number of the journalists. Within hours, global and regional news organizations of all types, from television and radio to Web sites, including the official Kurdistan Regional Government site, were carrying reports of the friendly fire incident.

Meanwhile, as Sgt. Mike Ray was making life-and-death decisions about the wounded, Captain Wright was rushing among the vehicles, helping carry or directing people to the CCP, among them a slightly wounded Major

Howard and two other Green Berets from ODB 040 who were performing triage of their own. He helped them get to the CCP, and just as he did so, an overheated spare gas can from one of the nearby burning vehicles erupted and splashed burning fuel down the road.

Captain Wright immediately grabbed Sergeants Nguyen and Turner and told them to get all the spare gas cans off the vehicles, particularly those nearest the wounded. It was nerve-wracking work. Many of the vehicles were still burning, and a number of the gas cans were so hot the men had to wear heat-resistant gloves. Though the cans could have exploded at any moment, no one hesitated. The three managed to get all the dangerous gas cans out of their racks and to a place well away from the wounded at the CCP.

As Captain Wright was dealing with the emergency at Objective Rock, the situation at the Alamo had just taken its own turn for the worse. The Roughnecks were beginning to feel confident about their standoff situation when suddenly a heavy artillery shell exploded a thousand yards below their position. A nearby battery of Iraqi D-20 152 mm howitzers had just joined the counterattack. Within minutes, a second round landed, this time about 650 feet away. Someone, probably from one of the tanks, was acting as a forward observer and corrected the artillery fire. These initial rounds were targeting shots. As soon as the Iraqis had the range, the Alamo would come under a deadly volley of fire.

When a third shell landed just over 150 feet away, the Roughnecks made a dash for their GMVs. They had been granted an unexpected bit of good luck, and they were not about to waste it. The loader of the Iraqi howitzer had made a crucial mistake with the third shot. Instead of a high-explosive shell, which even as a near miss would have undoubtedly inflicted casualties, the D-20 had fired a smoke shell. Hidden by the expanding clouds of smoke, the SF soldiers leaped into their vehicles, raced up the road, and took up new defensive positions at the top of the ridge along Press Hill. As they spread out, the men had a clear view of the Iraqi forces in the valley on one side, and of the carnage at Objective Rock on the other.

Although Sergeant Antenori knew what had happened back at Objective Rock, he didn't realize how serious the situation was until he was able to see it from his vantage point on Press Hill, about a thousand feet from Objective Rock. It didn't take an expert to tell that there were a large number of critical casualties that needed help. As the only other trained medic in ODA 391, he knew he had to go down and assist.

Antenori immediately ran over to Marty McKenna to tell him what he wanted to do. He found McKenna with Sgt. Jacob Chandler and Sgt. Saleem Ali of ODA 040. Chandler and Ali had set up a combat air support observation post off to one side of their position at Press Hill and were assembling a twelve-pound SOFLAM laser rangefinder and designator. This would allow them to spot individual targets for the incoming fighter-bombers and hopefully avoid additional friendly fire incidents. Shortly after they had arrived at Press Hill, they reestablished contact with the Tomcats. The Tomcat jockeys, particularly the pilot who had dropped the bomb, was in a world of psychological hurt. He had just killed "friendlies" on the ground, whom he had been sent to protect and support. This was the kind of mental trauma that can last a lifetime but right now needed to be put aside so that he could get back into the fight.

Sergeant Chandler managed to calm the Tomcat crews enough to get them refocused on the mission. Another bomb run was set up. This time there was no friendly-fire accident, but the bomb missed, exploding harmlessly in a field nearby. With fuel now running low, the F-14s had to return to their carrier. Chandler was then told by the AWACS controller that they were being replaced by an incoming pair of F/A-18 Hornets carrying Paveway-series laser-guided bombs (LGBs). Once they got the SOFLAM up and running, the Roughnecks would have the capability of laser pinpoint bombing accuracy on the T-55s—just what the Americans needed.

As this was going on, Antenori was telling McKenna about his intent to move back to the bombing site to help with the wounded. McKenna agreed, assuring him that the situation on Press Hill was under control. As Antenori reached his GMV, Sgt. Robert Farmer joined him and, after being told what was happening, volunteered to help. He also suggested that they get 392's medic, Sgt. Gino Zawojski.

For that, they'd need approval from 392's team sergeant, Ken Thompson. When they made their request to Thompson, not only did he agree, he said he'd come as well. Sgt. Jeffrey Adamec was also with the group, and he too volunteered. As it turned out, he had been trained as an infantry medic prior to his entry into the Green Berets. Within moments, all had grabbed their emergency medical kits, along with any spares they could find, and had run down to Objective Rock and the CCP.

When the group arrived, about a half hour had passed since the explosion. The sight was a shock even to those who had been through combat. Body parts were scattered all over the crossroads, a bootless foot here, a hand there, and a human brain shockingly intact and lying on the road. Everywhere, there was blood. They found Sergeant Ray working on the most severely wounded at the CCP, and they swung into action. Sergeant Zawojski immediately got down to business beside his fellow medic.

With the others working on the wounded, Sergeant Antenori began looking in and around the vehicles for any survivors. He found Major Howard, who had refused treatment for his wounds, coordinating the evacuation of casualties and helping the Kurds who weren't hurt. A final count among the Kurds revealed that sixteen had been killed and forty-five wounded, a number of them severely. The severely wounded translator for BBC reporter Simpson would later die at the hospital in Irbil. The other journalists and Special Forces troops in the group suffered either minor wounds or survived unscathed.

Before long, the last of the wounded were put on vehicles for the trip back to Irbil. The Roughnecks then headed back up to Press Hill to rejoin the fight. There they discovered a lot of the battle was still left to be fought. From their combat air support observation post, Sergeant Ali working the SOFLAM, and Sergeant Chandler communicating via radio to the navy Hornets had attempted to succeed with the F/A-18 Hornets where the F-14 Tomcats had failed.

But no matter how hard he tried, Sergeant Ali discovered he could not get the SOFLAM's laser designation system to establish a solid "spot" on the tanks for the LGBs to home in on. Every time he set the reticule on the tank, the laser for some reason aimed "high." The result was that the bombs fell harmlessly in the field behind the tanks. When he tried to compensate for the anomaly by setting the reticule low, the bombs would fall ineffectively on the wrong side of the berm.

After the last bombing attempt by the Hornets, Sergeant Chandler called them off and notified the AWACS controller to send strike aircraft loaded with cluster munitions—bombs containing bomblets that would scatter on release. That way, even a near miss, provided it occurred on the right side of the highway, would be as good as a direct hit.

Meanwhile, Iraqi artillery and tank fire continued to fall around the Roughnecks' position on Press Hill. Their ammunition situation was approaching the critical stage. ODA 391 was down to four Javelins as Sergeant Antenori passed a CLU to the team's junior weapons technician, Sgt. Lihn Nguyen. Their new position on Press Hill was high enough so that the T-55s in defilade presented more of a target profile.

Pointing out one Iraqi tank just to the left of the roundabout that appeared more exposed than the others, Frank Antenori told Sergeant Nguyen to take it out. As Antenori trained his binoculars on the target, Nguyen took aim and then took his shot. A few seconds later, the sound of a loud explosion rippled up the ridge, but from what or where, Sergeant Antenori, looking through his binoculars, couldn't see. The target T-55 hadn't been touched. But something else nearby had.

Where once had stood a large concrete monument with Saddam Hussein's likeness in the middle of the roundabout, there was now a concrete object surrounded by rubble. Antenori stared hard at Nguyen and cursed. Trying to ignore the sarcastic catcalls from the other Roughnecks, Nguyen protested that he *had* aimed and fired at the tank.

Sergeant Antenori angrily grabbed another Javelin and mated it with the

CLU. This time he'd take the shot himself. He set the sights of the CLU on the T-55 by the roundabout and half-pressed the trigger to activate the infrared sensor, but it refused to lock on the tank. He repeated the procedure a couple of times, but the target's infrared signature was still too small, and the heat from the pavement was still adding to the aiming problem.

Because of the design of the Javelin's guidance mechanism, once it was activated the missile had to be used within two minutes or its power source would render it useless. "Fire and forget" was "now or never." Then Sgt. Antenori saw an MTLB driving evasively in one of the fields. He quickly set the CLU sights on it and pulled the trigger. A few seconds later, the Javelin smashed into the top of the armored personnel carrier, blowing the hatches off and stunned Iraqi soldiers out its rear.

Sgt. Jason Brown had the group's last two Javelins, and he also tried to get a lock on the tanks. But the team's most experienced Javelin user, with four confirmed "kills" already to his credit, found he had no better luck. Quickly, he started looking for any target of opportunity, and found one in the form of an MTLB that had managed to get in defilade along Highway 2. It was attempting a high-speed, twenty-mile-an-hour dash across the field, trying to escape the deadly rain of missiles. Brown calmly took aim, tracked the armored personnel carrier, and fired.

As he discarded his empty missile tube, the MTLB exploded, and Sergeant Brown mounted his CLU on the team's last Javelin and centered its sights on an Iraqi truck filled with reinforcements racing up the road toward the roundabout. He pulled the trigger. Moments later, that target erupted in a ball of flame. The men of ODA 391 cheered wildly because with his fifth kill, Sgt. Jason Brown, one of their own, had become the first-ever "Javelin ace."

The Roughnecks had been in action since 6:00 A.M. Even though they had been driven back from their forward position at the roundabout, they had managed to hold off a superior enemy force for approximately two hours, since about 11:00 A.M. The Roughnecks had dodged mortar, tank, and artillery fire, and the Iraqis had been pounded by machine guns and grenades, Javelin missiles, and bombs. The F/A-18 Hornets were now in the area, waiting for new orders. At one point, something had to give.

At 1:10 P.M., the Iraqis did.

Suddenly, a burst of blue-white exhaust smoke erupted out the back of one of the T-55s. The Iraqi tank quickly drove up the side of the berm and onto Highway 2. The stalemate was over; it appeared the order to renew the Iraqi counterattack had begun.

Sergeant Eric Strigotte, the junior weapons expert of ODA 044, had one of the team's few remaining Javelins. As soon as he saw the tank clear the berm sufficiently to give him a clear shot, Strigotte took aim at the T-55. The Javelin had proved itself against the unarmored trucks and the thinly

An Iraqi T-55 main battle tank destroyed by a Javelin missile. Scattered around the tank is the extra ammunition for its main cannon which were blown off the external storage racks.

armored MTLBs. The manufacturer said it could penetrate the heavier armor of the T-55 or any other main battle tank for that matter. Now everyone on the ridge hoped the manufacturer's claim was accurate. The distance between Sergeant Strigotte and the tank was about a mile, a perfect "heart of the envelope" shot. In a few seconds, both sides would know, one way or the other. Sergeant Strigotte saw the crosshairs in the CLU go solid, indicating it had a lock on the T-55, and he pulled the trigger.

A few seconds later, the missile's warhead slammed through the barrel of the tank's main gun, detonating a chambered 100 mm round. The explosion flung the locked hatches of the T-55 wide open. Everyone on both sides watched the blazing Iraqi tank roll to a stop. A moment later the tank's stowed 100 mm cannon rounds began cooking off, causing the tank to shudder as each shell exploded, sending huge, volcanic gouts of flame through the open hatches.

A few minutes later, the Roughnecks saw about a dozen, perhaps fifteen, Iraqi infantry soldiers emerging from behind the berm of Highway 2, weaponless and waving white cloths or pieces of paper in surrender. Immediately the word went down the line to all the Roughnecks: cease fire—the enemy is surrendering.

As the group of Iraqi soldiers began to slowly walk up the road, the Green Berets began to discuss how they would handle the surrender. As they were doing so, several noticed a pair of white Toyota Land Cruisers emerge from the still-lingering haze on the road leading to Makhmur, where the counterattack had originated. The SUVs pulled to a stop beside the surrendering soldiers, and a number of men in white robes and armed with either pistols or AK-47s got out of the vehicles and rushed over to the soldiers. The next thing the shocked Roughnecks saw was a man who appeared to be the leader of the group from the SUVs pull out a pistol and shoot one of the soldiers in the head. The other men in white robes then began firing their automatic weapons into the group of unarmed troops.

The Roughnecks had just been given their first introduction to the Fedayeen Saddam—paramilitary fighters who had made V Corps' drive up from Kuwait so bloody.

While the men in white robes stood around as if checking to see if any of the soldiers were still alive and deciding what to do next, Sgt. Jake Chandler was back on the combat air support radio network, calling for a quick F/A-18 strike. Marty McKenna got behind the SOFLAM laser designator and aimed the laser spot on one of the SUVs and called out the coordinates to Sergeant Chandler, who passed them to the strike aircraft above. A moment later a thousand-pound LGB exploded in the middle of the group of white-robed men. When the smoke cleared, there was nothing left of either the executioners or their vehicles, only a bomb crater.

The Roughnecks took a quick inventory of their remaining Javelins and discovered that a grand total of three out of the nineteen they had brought with them that morning were left. That was reduced to two when Sgt. Jeff Adamec of 392 took a shot at a T-55 he thought was sufficiently exposed, and missed. Quickly the word was passed around, the last two Javelins were to be used only if there was a clear shot on a T-55 like the one Sergeant Strigotte had had.

In the meantime, the forward air controllers discovered they suddenly had many friends in the sky. The AWACS controllers had rounded up all the spare bomber and strike fighters available and were stacking them over the Debecka Pass battlefield. For the next two hours, the controllers directed air strikes using laser-guided and GPS-guided JDAM bombs ranging from five hundred to two thousand pounds onto the Iraqi positions. Then, just when they were needed most, the War Pigs of ODB 390 arrived on the scene.

The two vehicles had just returned from resupplying ODAs 394 and 395, which had been embroiled in their own fight a few thousand yards to the north while trying to flank the ridgeline. Caught in a mortar and artillery barrage, and under fire from Iraqi pillboxes on the ridge, only their exception mobility and liberal use of M2 machine guns and Mk. 19 grenade launchers had allowed them to exit the impact zone unscathed. Low on ammunition and needing to regroup, they had called to the War Pigs for a battlefield resupply of ammunition.

That task completed, the two War Pigs had responded to Captain Wright's call for ammunition and missiles, and now proceeded to quickly resupply the teams right on the ridgeline. Cans of .50-caliber machine-gun ammo and 40 mm grenades were quickly hefted from the War Pigs back to the gun trucks, along with eight badly needed Javelins in their launch tubes. Though nobody knew it at the time, the Roughnecks had just won the battle of Debecka Pass.

Within two hours, the surviving Iraqis had taken enough punishment. Late that afternoon, the Roughnecks saw the Iraqi troops abandoning their tanks and vehicles and running south from the battlefield back to Makhmur. The good news didn't stop there. Elsewhere along the front it appeared that the Iraqis were being steadily pushed back. ODAs 394 and 395 went back after the flank of the ridgeline and managed to successfully take the vital ground. Almost unbelievably, Colonel Charles Cleveland's visionary idea of going on the offensive with an SOF/insurgent UW strike was paying off.

The action at Debecka Pass would continue for another two days. But the real danger had passed when the demoralized Iraqi infantry retreated the afternoon of the first day. As Sgt. Frank Antenori stated in his book, *Roughneck Nine-One*: "When the time and the challenge came, Nine-One, Nine-Two, and Four-Four were the right guys in the right place with the right skills and the right weapons. We piled them up, and we didn't run."

It's sometimes easy to discount the importance of an action in wartime because it is fought by relatively few men or is small in its scope. Not so with the battle of Debecka Pass. Within days of their victory, the Roughnecks of 3/3rd SFG and their peshmerga counterparts were riding through the streets of the liberated city of Kirkuk, having seized over half of Iraq's critical oil infrastructure without any damage whatsoever. All along the Green Line, JSOTF-N and peshmerga fighters drove the Iraqis back, eventually linking up with the conventional forces coming up from Baghdad. And perhaps most amazingly, not one Green Beret had died in action during the operation.

Within weeks of the battle, 3/3rd SFG returned to Fort Bragg, immediately going into training for their next overseas deployment. But before they did, the teams from the Debecka Pass fight got something unusual in the SOF: recognition. The heavy media coverage of the battle, including John Simpson's live report from the battlefield, opened the opportunity for SOCOM and SFC to give the world a look at some of their finest warriors, and give those soldiers and airmen some well-deserved recognition.

Within weeks of their return, the Roughnecks were featured in a front-page *New York Times* article, which was followed by appearance in magazines and on documentary television. There were also a number of well-deserved decorations for the action at Debecka Pass, including Silver and Bronze Stars and coveted Army-Navy Medals. These are awarded for lifesaving, which was in abundance following the mistaken bombing by the F-14 at the crossroads.

More important, however, were the lessons that were quickly derived from what happened that busy day in northern Iraq. The destruction of the Iraqi battalion-size task force by just a handful of Green Berets and combat controllers caught the attention of military academics and leaders around the world, and for good reason. The amazing deadliness of the combination of new fire-and-forget battlefield missiles and precision airstrikes, along with integration of SOF personnel with irregular militia forces, had helped win two major wars in just eighteen months; it is a lesson still being analyzed today.

But perhaps the most important lesson of Debecka Pass was the value of carefully selected, well-trained, individual professional troops. The performance of those thirty-one men on the ridge showed the world exactly what American troops are capable of, despite the horror of the blue-on-blue incident to their rear. The numbers of American personnel committed to the campaign were minuscule, likely never exceeding three thousand sets of boots on the ground of northern Iraq. Within weeks of the victory, most were gone, allowing for the fastest and most effective reconstruction in all of postwar Iraq. Add to that the absence of American casualties, and it today stands as one of the greatest unconventional warfare campaigns in history.[8]

1. Combined Arms Research Library Digital Library, interview with Major D. Jones, 4.
2. Ibid.
3. Combined Arms Research Library Digital Library, interview with Major Larry Dewey, 5.
4. Ibid., 5.
5. Tom Clancy, *Carrier* (New York; Berkley Books, 1999), 145.
6. BBC News transcript, June 4, 2003.
7. Ibid.
8. Much of the information for this chapter was gathered by John D. Gresham in a series of interviews conducted at Fort Bragg, North Carolina, in summer and fall, 2003.

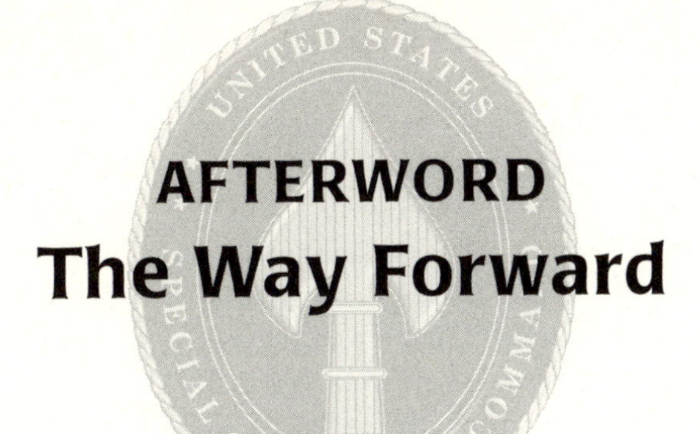

AFTERWORD
The Way Forward

Today, U.S. Special Operations Command—SOCOM—has approximately twenty-six thousand troops, and in 2007 it will celebrate its twenty-fifth anniversary. Of the five de facto branches of the military, SOCOM is both the youngest and the smallest. But it is a mistake to think that its youth and size make it a junior partner in the world of arms. Never before has the need for the men and women of SOCOM been greater. With the dissolution of America's cold war superpower adversary, the Soviet Union, the global landscape of armed combat now and for the foreseeable future is one filled with what in the past were called small wars, low-intensity conflicts, or military operations other than war. In the acronym-filled jargon of the military, these are LICs and MOOTWs, and they are the bane of conventional, large forces with their masses of troops, planes and armored vehicles.

The earliest days of Operation Enduring Freedom–Afghanistan demonstrated how effective Special Operations could be in an LIC. American SOF's stunning and unorthodox short campaign to drive the Taliban and Al-Qaeda out of Afghanistan seduced a national leadership eager to move on to more ambitious military efforts in Iraq and other places. Operation Iraqi Freedom was an even greater test for Special Operations and, for SOCOM, an even greater success. The SOF community's achievements in those two recent conflicts have burnished its reputation to a point where it is tempting to believe that these troops, who truly are the "pointed tip of the spear," can achieve the impossible.

The reality is that SOF units and personnel don't attempt the impossible; they simply have a different interpretation of what *is* possible. That difference in viewpoint comes from looking beyond the mere kinetics of combat and weaponry and knowing that physical power can be trumped by mental preparation and planning. Take the case of army Green Berets. With their extensive language and cultural training, these SOF units can often go where conventional forces cannot, blend in, and conduct their mission while essentially hiding in plain sight. Then, if the mission calls for it, they can strike out with seemingly unlimited force and mass to accomplish mission goals that often do seem beyond the realm of possibility.

SOF operators are men. They bleed when wounded, and they die in battle like their conventional-force brethren. But as their opponents in battle would tell if they could, they die hard. For those who remain, after their duty in uniform is over, they come to live among us as our relatives, friends, and neighbors, and some even become public personalities in civilian life. Former surgeon general Richard Carmona was an SF medic in the 1960s, and the late Earl Woods, father of golfer Tiger Woods, was himself a Green Beret.

When someone from the SOF community falls in battle, he is not forgotten, because as diverse as the Special Operations community is, it is still small. SOF is a tight-knit family created by the bonds of shared experience and risk, collective joy and mutual grief, and the sense of being part of the best of the world's finest military. Home for U.S. Special Operations Command—SOCOM—is MacDill Air Force Base, located on the south side of Tampa, on Florida's west coast. Near its main entrance is the United States Special Operations Memorial, which pays tribute to all Special Operations personnel from all service branches, men and women and civilians. As this book is being written, it is composed of three stone panels and a statue. On the panels are the names of more than eight hundred Special Operations professionals who gave their lives in service to the country. There are additional memorials and plaques at Fort Bragg, Camp Lejeune, and other large bases, but it's down at the unit level that the really special memorials exist.

A visit to an SOF base like Fort Campbell, Kentucky, reveals how long and deeply their losses are felt. Fort Campbell is the home of two premier American SOF units: the 5th Special Forces Group and the 160th Special Operations Aviation Regiment. Both have done long and difficult service for America, before and after 9/11. They have won at places such as Mazar-e-Sharif and Bagram, and suffered at others, including Mogadishu and the southern Philippines.

It is at Fort Campbell that in addition to memorials of stone and steel the Special Operations community adds a third: one of live wood. For 5th SFG at Fort Campbell, it's a small but thriving grove of trees behind the headquarters building.

Begun in 1989, the trees still display the gangly stature of arboreal youth and adolescence, and the plaques stand out a bit more now than they should. But this is typical of memorials that commemorate the passing of one life through the nurturing of another living thing. In one case, it is a new magnolia tree and plaque honoring the life of Sergeant First Class Daniel H. Petithory, a 5th SFG Green Beret.

Dan was the team sergeant of ODA 571, commanded by Captain Jason Amerine, which was charged with taking a popular Pashto insurgent leader to Kandahar, the center of the Taliban's power. Over just a few weeks, they fought a number of battles, raised a Pashto rebel militia, and were in the final stages of marching on Kandahar when the team was accidentally struck by an errant two-thousand-pound JDAM guided bomb dropped by a U.S. Air Force B-52 bomber. Dan and two other ODA 571 team members were killed, along with many of their Afghan militia. Almost killed, too, was that Pashto leader. Fortunately, Hamid Karzai, the present-day president of Afghanistan, survived. The friendly-fire incident was the worst loss of the early campaign in Afghanistan and one that still hurts today.

Dan's plaque and tree are there in the grove at Fort Campbell, along with those for the others from 5th SFG who have given their last full measure. It's a small reminder, but for those who are SOF professionals, it's something they can all see and use to remember that nothing is accomplished without cost—and that in their business "cost" often translates to the death of a brother-in-arms.

U.S. Special Operations Command will celebrate its twenty-fifth anniversary with all the high-profile public commendations that such a milestone deserves. But the enduring legacy of what those from the past accomplished is how those who come after them plan for the future. And SOCOM has lots of plans for the next few years, if the Congress and the country will permit them.

It took less than five years of denying funding and personnel to the SOF community in the 1970s to ensure the failure of Operation Eagle Claw and the disaster at Desert One. The price of that disaster was relatively cheap by present-day standards: eight military personnel dead, eight aircraft lost, and national humiliation in full view of the world. Today, the stakes are far greater. As Congressman Jim Saxton of New Jersey, the former chairman of the House Armed Services Committee's Terrorism, Unconventional Threats and Capabilities Subcommittee, said in March 2006, "I cannot think of a higher priority for funding anywhere in the federal government than the SOCOM budget. It represents a direct investment in keeping America and Americans safe here at home."[1]

As this is being written, SOCOM's component commands are in the midst of their most significant growth since the command stood up in 1987. The

Photo: John D. Gresham

Photo: John D. Gresham

active-duty Green Beret SFGs each are being given a fourth battalion, a 33 percent personnel increase. Air Force Special Operations Command is finally, after three decades of work, about to replace their aging MH-53M Pave Low IV helicopters with new, state-of-the-art CV-22 Osprey tilt-rotor aircraft. And the 160th SOAR is also being expanded with new-production MH-47G helicopters so that the Night Stalkers can replace their well-worn Chinooks.

Five years of continuous operations in the global war on terrorism have worn hard on men and equipment, and unless the international political situation drastically improves, the burden on these individuals and their tools will continue. America must continue to build its SOF community to a size large enough to sustain the fight. The current planned expansion is due to be completed by 2013. That it took more than five years of planning and expanding the SOF training pipelines just to get the new manpower pool in place to grow the command is a measure of how hard it is to make new warriors for this difficult trade.

America's SOF units are the sharp end of the spear in fighting terrorism worldwide, and one needs only to remember 9/11 to recall how bad things can get when a government fails to keep watch. The good news is that American SOF professionals' dedication to the Constitution and country are not grounded in superficial displays of patriotic bumper stickers, baseball caps, and waving of the flag. It's personal.

This is because nobody asked them to become SOF professionals; every one of them volunteered, more than once. These men asked for the privilege to serve in some of the finest combat units on the planet, filled with its finest warriors. They've pledged their lives. They will fulfill their commitment with whatever level of support they receive, financial and otherwise. Let us hope as citizens that we will be wise and worthy enough of such dedication and commitment from these amazing warriors. For as a Bible passage favored by SOF forces states:

> Also I heard the voice of the Lord, saying,
> Whom shall I send, and who will go for
> us? Then said I, Here am I; send me.
>
> —Isaiah 6:8

1. Opening statement to the House Armed Services Committee, Subcommittee on Terrorism, Unconventional Threats and Capabilities, Hearing on the Fiscal Year 2007 Budget Request for the U.S. Special Operations Command. *Special Operations Technology* online edition, www.special-operations-technology.com/print_article.cfm?DocID=1366 (accessed December 4, 2006).

BIBLIOGRAPHY

1. OPERATION KINGPIN: THE SON TAY RAID

BOOKS

Ballard, Jack S. *Development and Employment of Fixed-Wing Gunships 1962–1972.* Washington, DC: Air Force History and Museums Program, 1982.

Davidson, Phillip B. *Vietnam at War: The History 1946–1975.* New York: Oxford University Press, 1988.

Day, Dwayne A., John M. Logsdon, and Brian Latell, eds. *Eye in the Sky: The Story of the Corona Spy Satellites.* Washington, D.C.: Smithsonian Institution Press, 1998.

Francillon, René, J. *Tonkin Gulf Yacht Club: U.S. Carrier Operations off Vietnam.* Annapolis, MD: Naval Institute Press, 1988.

Guenon, William A., Jr. *Secret and Dangerous: Night of the Son Tay POW Raid.* East Lowell, MA: WagonWings Press, 2005.

Haas, Michael E. *Apollo's Warriors: United States Air Force Special Operations During the Cold War.* Montgomery, AL: Air University Press, 1997

Hobson, Chris. *Vietnam Air Losses: United States Air Force, Navy and Marine Fixed-Wing Aircraft Losses in Southeast Asia 1961–1973.* Hinckley, England: Midland Publishing, 2001.

Isby, David C. *Weapons and Tactics of the Soviet Army.* London, England: Jane's Publishing Company Limited, 1981.

Kelly, Orr. *From a Dark Sky: The Story of U.S. Air Force Special Operations.* Novato, CA: Presidio Press, 1996.

McDonald, Robert A. *Corona Between the Sun and the Earth: The First NRO Reconnaissance Eye in Space.* Bethesda, MD: American Society for Photogrammetry and Remote Sensing, 1997.

McRaven, William H. *Spec Ops: Case Studies in Special Operations Warfare.* Novato, CA: Presidio Press, 1995.

Peacock, Lindsay. *Mighty Hercules: The First Four Decades.* RAF Fairford, England: Royal Air Force, 1994.

Peebles, Curtis. *Guardians: Strategic Reconnaissance Satellites.* Novato, CA: Presidio Press, 1987.

———. *The Corona Project: America's First Spy Satellites.* Annapolis, MD: Naval Institute Press, 1997.

Polmar, Norman, and Floyd D. Kennedy Jr. *Military Helicopters of the World: Military Rotary Wing Aircraft Since 1917.* Annapolis, MD: Naval Institute Press, 1981.

Polmar, Norman, and Allen B. Thomas. *Spy Book: The Encyclopedia of Espionage.* New York: Random House, 2004.

Schemmer, Benjamin F. *The Raid.* New York: Harper & Row, 1976.

Southworth, Samuel A., ed. *Great Raids in History: From Drake to Desert One.* Edison, NJ: Castle Books, 2002.

Special Forces and Missions. Alexandria, VA: Time-Life Books, 1991.

Stockdale, Jim, and Sybil Stockdale. *In Love and War: The Story of a Family's Ordeal During the Vietnam Years.* Annapolis, MD: Naval Institute Press, 1990.

Summers, Harry G., Jr. *The Vietnam War Almanac.* Novato, CA: Presidio Press, 1999.

Toperczer, István. *MiG-17 and MiG-19 Units of the Vietnam War.* Oxford, England: Osprey Publishing Limited, 2001.

———. *MiG-21 Units of the Vietnam War.* Oxford, England: Osprey Publishing Limited, 2001.

Tucker, Spencer C., ed. *The Encyclopedia of the Vietnam War: A Political, Social, and Military History*. New York: Oxford University Press, 1998.

Veith, George J. *Code-Name Bright Light: The Untold Story of U.S. POW Rescue Efforts During the Vietnam War*. New York: Free Press, 1998.

Wagner, William. *Lightning Bugs and Other Reconnaissance Drones: The Can-Do Story of Ryan's Unmanned Spy Planes*. Fallbrook, CA: Armed Forces Journal and Aero Publishers, Inc., 1982.

Wagner and Sloan. *Fireflies and Other UAVs (Unmanned Aerial Vehicles)*. Fallbrook, CA: Armed Forces Journal and Aero Publishers, Inc., 1982.

Zaloga, Steven J. *Soviet Air Defence Missiles*. Coulsdon, England: Jane's Information Group, 1989.

MONOGRAPHS

Lane, John J., Jr. *Command and Control and Communications Structures in Southeast Asia*. Air War in Indochina, Volume I, Monograph I. Maxwell Air Force Base, AL: Air University, 1981.

ARTICLES

Glines, C. V. "The Son Tay Raid." *Air Force Magazine*, November 1995.

Kamps, Charles Tustin. "Operation Kingpin: The Son Tay Raid." *Air & Space Power Journal*, Spring 2005.

Thomas, William C. "Operation Kingpin—Success or Failure?" *Joint Force Quarterly*, Spring 1997.

INTERNET

Amidon, Mark. "Groupthink, Politics, and the Decision to Attempt the Son Tay Rescue." *Parameters*, Autumn 2005. www.carlisle.army.mil/usawc/parameters/05autumn/amidon.htm (accessed August 21, 2006).

Encyclopedia Aeronautica (www.astronautix.com/).

———. *"Zenit-4."* www.astronautix.com/craft/zenit4.htm (accessed October 11, 2006).

———. *"Zenit-4M."* www.astronautix.com/craft/zenit4.htm (accessed October 11, 2006).

———. *"Zenit-4MK."* www.astronautix.com/craft/zenit4mk.htm (accessed October 11, 2006).

———. *"Zenit-4MKM,"* www.astronautix.com/craft/zenit4mkm.htm (accessed October 11, 2006).

Manor, LeRoy J. "The Son Tay Raid November 21, 1970." Air Commando Association. home.earthlink.net/~aircommando1/SONTAYRA1.htm (accessed August 12, 2006).

Mitchell, John. "The Son Tay Raid: A Study in Presidential Policy." GlobalSecurity.org, 1997. www.globalsecurity.org/military/library/report/1997/Mitchell.htm (accessed August 21, 2006).

Son Tay Raider Association, Web site. www.sontayraider.com/ (accessed October 11, 2006).

2. THE RESCUE OF BAT 21

BOOKS

Anderson, William C. *Bat-21*. Englewood Cliffs, NJ: Prentice Hall, 1980.

Ballard, Jack S. *Development and Employment of Fixed-Wing Gunships 1962–1972*. Washington, DC: Air Force History and Museums Program, 1982.

Davidson, Phillip B. *Vietnam at War: The History 1946–1975*. New York: Oxford University Press, 1988.

Eschmann, Karl J. *Linebacker: The Untold Story of the Air Raids over North Vietnam.* New York: Ivy Books, 1989.
Falzone, Joseph J. *Combat Search and Rescue: CSEL Enhancements for Winning Air Campaigns.* Maxwell Air Force Base, AL: Air University Press, 1994.
Haas, Michael E. *Apollo's Warriors: United States Air Force Special Operations During the Cold War.* Montgomery, AL: Air University Press, 1997
Hobson, Chris. *Vietnam Air Losses: United States Air Force, Navy and Marine Fixed-Wing Aircraft Losses in Southeast Asia 1961–1973.* Hinckley, England: Midland Publishing, 2001.
Isby, David. *Weapons and Tactics of the Soviet Army.* London, England: Jane's Publishing Company Limited, 1981.
Polmar, Norman, and Floyd D. Kennedy Jr. *Military Helicopters of the World: Military Rotary Wing Aircraft Since 1917.* Annapolis, MD: Naval Institute Press, 1981.
Turley, G. H. *The Easter Offensive.* New York: Warner Books, 1985.
Veith, George J. *Code-Name Bright Light.* New York: Free Press, 1998.
Whitcomb, Darrel D. *The Rescue of Bat 21.* New York: Dell, 1998.
Zaloga, Steven J. *Soviet Air Defence Missiles.* Coulsdon, England: Jane's Information Group, 1989.

MONOGRAPHS

Blumentritt, John W. *Playing Defense and Offense: Employing Rescue Resources as Offensive Weapons.* Maxwell Air Force Base, AL: Air University, 1999.
Brown, Francis M. *JV 2010: How the Precision Engagement of Offensive Airpower Applies to Military Operations Other Than War (MOOTW).* Maxwell Air Force Base, AL: Air University, 1998.
Colburn, Tracy W. *Running on Empty: The Development of Helicopter Aerial Refueling and Implications for Future USAF Combat Rescue Capabilities.* Maxwell Air Force Base, AL: Air University, 1997.
Combat Search and Rescue. Air Force Doctrine Document 2-1.6. Washington, DC, 2000.
Hallion, Richard P. *Control of the Air: The Enduring Requirement.* Washington, DC: Air Force History and Museums Program, 1999.
Lavalle, A. J. C., ed. *Airpower and the 1972 Spring Invasion.* USAF Southeast Asia Monograph Series, Volume II, Monograph 3. Washington, DC.: Office of Air Force History, 1985.
Lane, John J., Jr. *Command and Control and Communications Structures in Southeast Asia.* Air War in Indochina Volume I, Monograph I. Maxwell Air Force Base, AL: Air University, 1981.
Tilford, Earl H., Jr. *USAF in Southeast Asia: Search and Rescue in Southeast Asia.* Washington, DC: Center for Air Force History, 1992.
Van Nederveen, Gilles. *Sparks over Vietnam: The EB-66 and the Early Struggle of Tactical Electronic Warfare.* Maxwell Air Force Base, AL: Airpower Research Institute, 2000.

3. FOR WANT OF A NAIL . . . OPERATION EAGLE CLAW

BOOKS

Adams, James. *Secret Armies: Inside the American, Soviet, and European Special Forces.* New York: Atlantic Monthly Press, 1987.
Beckwith, Charlie A., with Donald Knox. *Delta Force.* New York: Avon Books, 2000.
Bowden, Mark. *Guests of the Ayatollah.* New York: Atlantic Monthly Press, 2006.
Clancy, Tom, with John Gresham. *Special Forces.* New York: Berkley Books, 2001.
Dobson, Christopher, and Ronald Payne. *Counterattack: The West's Battle Against the*

Terrorists. New York: Facts on File, 1982.
———. *The Terrorists*. New York: Facts on File, 1979.
Griswold, Terry, and D. M. Giangreco. *Delta: America's Elite Counterterrorist Force*. Osceola, WI: Motorbooks, 1992.
Haney, Eric L. *Inside Delta Force*. New York: Delta Trade Paperbacks, 2005.
Kelly, Orr. *From a Dark Sky: The Story of U.S. Air Force Special Operations*. Novato, CA: Presidio Press, 1996.
Kyle, James H., with John Robert Eidson. *The Guts to Try*. New York: Ballantine Books, 1995.
McKinney, Mike, and Mike Ryan. *Chariots of the Damned*. New York: St. Martin's Paperbacks, 1995.
Peacock, Lindsay. *Mighty Hercules: The First Four Decades*. RAF Fairford, England: Royal Air Force, 1994.
Peebles, Curtis. *Guardians: Strategic Reconnaissance Satellites*. Novato, CA: Presidio Press, 1987.
Polmar, Norman, and Floyd D. Kennedy Jr. *Military Helicopters of the World: Military Rotary Wing Aircraft Since 1917*. Annapolis, MD: Naval Institute Press, 1981
Southworth, Samuel A., ed. *Great Raids in History: From Drake to Desert One*. Edison, NJ: Castle Books, 2002.
Special Forces and Missions. Alexandria, VA: Time-Life Books, 1991.
Thompson, Leroy. *The Rescuers: The World's Top Anti-Terrorist Units*. Boulder, CO: Paladin Press, 1986.
Waller, Douglas C. *Commandos: The Inside Story of America's Secret Soldiers*. New York: Simon & Schuster, 1994.

INTERNET

Bowden, Mark. "The Desert One Debacle." *The Atlantic Online*, May 2006. iran.theatlantic.com/interactive_article_printable.html (accessed September 28, 2006).
Greely, Jim. "Desert One." *Airman*, April 2001. www.af.mil/news/airman/0401/hostage.html (accessed September 28, 2006).
———. "A Night to Remember." *Airman*, May 2001. www.af.mil/news/airman/0501/carney.html (accessed September 28, 2006).
Holzworth, C. E. "Operation Eagle Claw: A Catalyst for Change in the American Military." GlobalSecurity.org. www.globalsecurity.org/military/library/report/1997/Holzworth.htm (accessed October 11, 2006).
Koskinas, Gianni. "Desert One and Air Force Special Operations Command: A 25-Year Retrospective." *Air & Space Power Journal*. Spring 2005. www.airpower.maxwell.af.mil/airchronicles/apj/apj05/spr05/vignette4.html (accessed September 28, 2006).
Kreisher, Otto. "Desert One." *Air Force Magazine* Online, January 1999. www.afa.org/magazine/jan1999/0199desertone.asp (accessed September 28, 2006).
Skelton, Ike. *"Military Lessons from Desert One to the Balkans."* Strategic Forum, October 2000. www.au.af.mil/au/awcgate/ndu/sf174.htm (accessed September 28, 2006).

4. THE 100 PERCENT SOLUTION: TASK FORCE NORMANDY

BOOKS

Atkinson, Rick. *Crusade: The Untold Story of the Persian Gulf War*. Boston: Houghton Mifflin, 1993.
Bradin, James W. *From Hot Air to Hellfire: The History of Army Attack Aviation*.

Novato, CA: Presidio Press, 1994.

Clancy, Tom. *Armored Cav: A Guided Tour of an Armored Cavalry Regiment.* New York: Berkley Books, 1994.

Clancy, Tom, with John Gresham. *Special Forces: A Guided Tour of U.S. Army Special Forces.* New York: Berkley Books, 2001.

Clancy, Tom, with Chuck Horner. *Every Man a Tiger: The Gulf War Air Campaign.* New York: Berkley Books, 1999.

Clancy, Tom, with Carl Stiner and Tony Koltz. *Shadow Warriors: Inside the Special Forces.* New York: Berkley Books, 2003.

Davis, Richard G. *On Target: Organizing and Executing the Strategic Air Campaign Against Iraq.* Washington, DC: Air Force History and Museums Program, 2002.

Department of Defense. *Conduct of the Persian Gulf War.* Washington, DC: U.S. Government Printing Office, 1991.

Flanagan, E. M., Jr. *Lightning: The 101st in the Gulf War.* Washington, DC: Brassey's, 1994.

Giangreco, D. M. *Stealth Fighter Pilot.* Osceola, WI: Motorbooks, 1993.

Glosson, Buster. *War with Iraq: Critical Lessons.* Charlotte, NC: Glosson Family Foundation, 2003.

Hallion, Richard P. *Storm Over Iraq: Air Power and the Gulf War.* Washington, DC: Smithsonian Institution Press, 1992.

Isby, David. *Weapons and Tactics of the Soviet Army.* London, England: Jane's Publishing Company Limited, 1981.

Keaney, Thomas A., and Eliot A. Cohen. *Revolution in Warfare? Air Power in the Persian Gulf.* Annapolis, MD: Naval Institute Press, 1995.

Kelly, Orr. *From a Dark Sky: The Story of U.S. Air Force Special Operations.* Novato, CA: Presidio Press, 1996.

Mann, Edward C., III. *Thunder and Lightning: Desert Storm and the Airpower Debates.* Maxwell Air Force Base, AL: Air University Press, 1995.

McKinney, Mike. *Chariots of the Damned: Helicopter Special Operations from Vietnam to Kosovo.* New York: St. Martin's Paperbacks, 2001.

Morse, Stan, ed. *Gulf Air War Debrief, Described by the Pilots That Fought.* London, England: Aerospace Publishing Ltd., 1991.

Polmar, Norman, and Floyd D. Kennedy Jr. *Military Helicopters of the World: Military Rotary Wing Aircraft Since 1917.* Annapolis, MD: Naval Institute Press, 1981.

Pushies, Fred J. *U.S. Air Force Special Ops.* Osceola, WI: MBI Publishing, 2000.

Putney, Diane T. *Airpower Advantage: Planning the Gulf War Air Campaign 1989–1991.* Washington, DC: Air Force History and Museums Program, 2004.

Reynolds, Richard T. *Heart of the Storm: The Genesis of the Air Campaign Against Iraq.* Maxwell Air Force Base, AL: Air University Press, 1995.

Schwarzkopf, H. Norman, with Peter Petre. *It Doesn't Take a Hero.* New York: Bantam Books, 1992.

Smallwood, William L. *Strike Eagle: Flying the F-15E in the Gulf War.* Washington, D.C.: Brassey's Inc., 1994.

Taylor, Thomas. *Lightning in the Storm: The 101st Air Assault Division in the Gulf War.* New York: Hippocrene Books, 1994.

Thompson, Warren E. *Bandits over Baghdad: Personal Stories of Flying the F-117 over Iraq.* North Branch, MN: Specialty Press, 2000.

U.S. News & World Report. Triumph Without Victory: The Unreported History of the Persian Gulf War. New York: Times Books, 1992.

Waller, Douglas C. *Commandos: The Inside Story of America's Secret Soldiers.* New York: Simon & Schuster, 1994.

Warden, John A., III. *The Air Campaign: Planning for Combat.* Lincoln, NE: toExcel Press, 2000.
Zaloga, Steven J. *Soviet Air Defence Missiles*. Coulsdon, England: Jane's Information Group, 1989.

INTERNET

Aitar, Judy. "Perez de Cuellar Mission 'Unsuccessful.'" FAS.org, January 14, 1991. www.fas.org/news/iraq/1991/910114-168472.htm (accessed July 2, 2006).
Dabrowski, John. "15th Anniversary: 'Through the Eyes of a Command' Encompasses Task Force Normandy." Hurlburt Field Web site, January 20, 2006. www2.hurlburt.af.mil/news/story.asp?storyID=123014600 (accessed July 1, 2006).
Dollar, Rob. "North to the Euphrates." Fort Campbell Web site, February 28, 1996. www.campbell.army.mil/Euph5.htm (accessed April 1, 2006).
Fairhall, David, Larry Elliot, and Martin Walker. "Allied Planes Bomb Iraq: Kuwait's Liberation Begun, says US." *Guardian Unlimited*, January 17, 1991. www.guardian.co.uk/Iraq/Story/0,,877000,00.html (accessed July 2, 2006).
GlobalSecurity.org. "U.S. Army Special Forces Command (Airborne)," May 23, 2005. www.globalsecurity.org/military/agency/army/arsfc.htm (accessed July 18, 2006).
Gonzales, Amy. "Task Force Normandy: Iraq Veteran Recounts Desert Storm." Hurlburt Field Web site, February 3, 2006. www2.hurlburt.af.mil/news/story.asp?storyID=123016067 (accessed July 1, 2006).
Gordon, Michael R. "Raids, on a Huge Scale, Seek to Destroy Iraqi Missiles." *New York Times*, January 17, 1991. www.nytimes.com/library/world/011791iraq-raids.html (accessed July 2, 2006).
Gottlieb, Aryea. "The Role of SOF Across the Range of Military Operations." *Chronicles Online Journal*, undated 1995–1998. www.airpower.maxwell.af.mil/airchronicles/cc/sofpaper.html (accessed April 5, 2006).
Kopp, Carlo. "Desert Storm: The Electronic Battle." *Australian Aviation*, June/July/August 1993. Posted April 2006. www.saunalahti.fi/fta/storm-01.htm (accessed July 31, 2006).
Mackenzie, Richard. "Apache Attack." *Air Force: Journal of the Air Force Association*, October 1991. www.afa.org/magazine/perspectives/desert_storm/1091apache.html (accessed April 1, 2006).
Rosenthal, Andrew. "U.S. and Allies Open Air War on Iraq." *New York Times*, January 17, 1991. www.nytimes.com/library/world/011791allies-invade.html (accessed July 2, 2006).
U.S. Army Center of Military History. Air Assault in the Gulf: An Interview with Maj. Gen. J. H. Binford Peay III, interview conducted June 5, 1991. www.army.mil/cmh-pg/documents/SWA/DSIT/Peay.htm (accessed April 1, 2006).
———. Operations Desert Shield and Desert Storm Oral History Interviews: Col. Roy E. Beauchamp, interview conducted June 5,1991. www.army.mil/cmh-pg/documents/SWA/DSIT/DSIT103.htm (accessed July 4, 2006).
———. Operations Desert Shield and Desert Storm Oral History Interviews: Maj. Stephen B. Finch, interview conducted February 2, 1991. www.army.mil/cmh-pg/documents/SWA/DSIT/DSIT009.htm (accessed July 4, 2006).
———. Operations Desert Shield and Desert Storm Oral History Interviews: Col. Julian A. Sullivan Jr., interview conducted February 18, 1991. www.army.mil/cmh-pg/documents/SWA/DSIT/DSIT019.htm (accessed July 4, 2006).
———. Operations Desert Shield and Desert Storm Oral History Interviews: Dr. Robert K. Wright Jr., interview conducted December 13, 1991.

www.army.mil/cmh-pg/documents/SWA/DSIT/DSITC082.htm (accessed July 4, 2006).

WGBH Educational Foundation. *Frontline*: "The Gulf War," aired January 9, 1996. Oral History transcripts: Lt. Gen. Sir Peter de la Billiere. www.pbs.org/wgbh/pages/frontline/gulf/oral/billiere/1.html (accessed July 15, 2006).

———. *Frontline*: "The Gulf War," aired January 9, 1996. Oral History transcripts: Lt. Gen. Walt Boomer, USMC. www.pbs.org/wgbh/pages/frontline/gulf/oral/boomer/1.html (accessed July 15, 2006).

———. *Frontline*: "The Gulf War," aired January 9, 1996. Oral History transcripts: Gen. Fred Franks. www.pbs.org/wgbh/pages/frontline/gulf/oral/franks/1.html (accessed July 15, 2006).

———. *Frontline*: "The Gulf War," aired January 9, 1996. Oral History transcripts: Lt. Gen. Buster Glosson. www.pbs.org/wgbh/pages/frontline/gulf/oral/glosson/1.html (accessed July 15, 2006).

———. *Frontline*: "The Gulf War," aired January 9, 1996. Oral History transcripts: Gen. Norman Schwarzkopf. www.pbs.org/wgbh/pages/frontline/gulf/oral/schwarzkopf/1.html (accessed July 15, 2006).

———. *Frontline*: "The Gulf War," aired January 9, 1996. Oral History transcripts: Lt. Gen. Calvin Waller. www.pbs.org/wgbh/pages/frontline/gulf/oral/waller/1.html (accessed July 15, 2006).

5. THE RESCUE OF CAPTAIN SCOTT O'GRADY

BOOKS

Clancy, Tom. *Marine: A Guided Tour of a Marine Expeditionary Unit*. New York: Berkley Books, 1996.

Faulkner, Keith. *Jane's Warship Recognition Guide*. Glasgow: HarperCollins, 1996.

Isby, David. *Weapons and Tactics of the Soviet Army*. London, England: Jane's Publishing Company Limited, 1981.

Jane's Fighting Ships of World War II. London, England: Studio Press, 1989.

Kelly, Mary Pat. *Good to Go*. Annapolis, MD: Naval Institute Press, 1996.

O'Grady, Scott, with Jeff Coplon. *Return with Honor*. New York: Harper Paperbacks, 1996.

Polmar, Norman, and Floyd D. Kennedy Jr. *Military Helicopters of the World: Military Rotary Wing-Aircraft Since 1917*. Annapolis, MD: Naval Institute Press, 1981

Taylor, Edmond. *The Fall of the Dynasties*. Garden City, NY: Doubleday, 1963.

Zaloga, Steven J. *Soviet Air Defence Missiles*. Coulsdon, England: Jane's Information Group, 1989.

PERIODICALS

Auster, Bryce B. "One Amazing Kid—Capt. Scott O'Grady Escapes from Bosnia-Herzegovina." *U.S. News & World Report*, June 19, 1995.

INTERNET

Aisner, James E. "Flying High: Ian Walsh." *Harvard Business School Bulletin Online*. June 1999. www.alumni.hbs.edu/bulletin/1999/june/mbas/walsh.html (accessed March 30, 2006).

Barela, Timothy P. "Calm Before the Storm." AirForceLink, October 1995. www.af.mil/news/airman/1095/calm.htm (accessed April 19, 2006).

Broadstone, Herman C. *Rules of Engagement in Military Operations Other Than War, from Beirut to Bosnia. Small Wars Journal,* 1996. www.smallwarsjournal.com/documents/broadstone.pdf (accessed March 24, 2006).

Central Intelligence Agency. *Bosnia and Herzegovina*. The World Factbook. 2006.

www.cia.gov/cia/publications/factbook/geos/bk.html (accessed April 15, 2006).

———. *Croatia*. The World Factbook. 2006. www.cia.gov/cia/publications/factbook/geos/hr.html (accessed April 15, 2006).

Constance, Paul. "Pilot's Tale of Bosnia Rescue Lands on Net." *Government Computer News*, August 28, 1995. www.gcn.com/print/14_24/31516-1.html (accessed May 8, 2006).

FAS Military Analysis Network. "ZRK-SD Kub 3M9/SA-6 Gainful." April 20, 1999. www.fas.org/man/dod-101/sys/missile/row/sa-6.htm (accessed April 13, 2006).

510th Fighter Squadron. "Rescuing Captain Scott O'Grady." June 8, 1995. www.510fs.org/index.php?option=com_content&task=view&id=131&Itemid=76 (accessed March 30, 2006).

GlobalSecurity.org. "Aviano Air Base, Pordenone, Italy," April 26, 2005. www.globalsecurity.org/military/facility/aviano.htm (accessed April 14, 2006).

Hellenic Resources Network. U.S. Department of State daily press briefing, June 6, 1995. www.hri.org/usa/std/1995/95-06-06.std.html.

———. U.S. Department of State daily press briefing June 7, 1995. www.hri.org/news/usa/std/1995/95-06-07.std.html.

International Olympic Committee. "Olympic Movement." 2006. www.olympic.org/uk/organisation/movement/index_uk.asp.

NATO Regional Headquarters Allied Forces Southern Europe. AFSouth Fact Sheets: "Operation Deny Flight," updated July 18, 2003. www.afsouth.nato.int /operations/denyflight/DenyFlightFactSheet.htm (accessed April 19, 2006).

Phillips, R. Cody. *Bosnia-Herzegovina: The U.S. Army's Role in Peace Enforcement Operations, 1995–2004*. U.S. Army Center of Military History. 2005. www.army.mil/cmh-pg/brochures/Bosnia-Herzegovina/Bosnia-Herzegovina .htm#Strat (accessed March 23, 2006).

U.S. Department of Defense. News briefing, Admiral William Owens, Vice Chairman, Joint Chiefs of Staff. June 8,1995. www.defenselink.mil/transcripts /1995/t060995_t0608rsc.html.

———. News briefing, Brigadier General Terry Murray, USMC, et al. June 8, 1995. www.defenselink.mil/transcripts/1995/t060995_t0608-f1.html.

———. News briefing, Kenneth H. Bacon, Office of the Assistant Secretary of Defense (Public Affairs) June 6, 1995. www.defenselink.mil/transcripts/1995 /t060695_t0606asd.html.

———. "Rescued Pilot Identified." June 8, 1995. www.defenselink.mil/releases /1995/b060895_bt317-95.html.

———. "Secretary of Defense Statement on Rescued Pilot." June 8, 1995. www.defenselink.mil/releases/1995/b060895_bt318-95.html.

———. "U.S. Policy on Bosnia Remains Consistent." Prepared statement by Secretary of Defense William J. Perry, the Senate Armed Services Committee and House National Security Committee, June 7, 1995. www/pentagon.gov/speeches/1995/t19950607-perry.html.

The White House. Press briefing by Mike McCurry. June 2, 1995. clinton6.nara.gov/1995/06/1995-06-02-press-briefing-by-mike-mccurry.html.

———. Press briefing by Mike McCurry, June 5, 1995. clinton6.nara.gov/1995/06/1995-06-05-press-briefing-by-mike-mccurry.html.

———. Press briefing by Mike McCurry, June 8, 1995. clinton6.nara.gov/1995/06 /1995-06-08-mccurry-briefing-on-rescue-of-captain-o-grady.html.

———. Interview of the President and the Vice President on *Larry King Live*, June 5, 1995. clinton6.nara.gov/1995/06/1995-06-05-president-and-vp-in-interview-on-larry-king-live.html.

———. Message of the President to General George Joulwan, Commander-in-Chief U.S. European Command, June 6, 1995. clinton6.nara.gov/1995/06/1995-06-08-president-message-to-gen-joulwan-on-o-grady-rescue.html.

———. Radio Address by the President to the Nation, June 3, 1995. clinton6.nara.gov/1995/06/1995-06-03-president-radio-address-to-nation.html.

———. Remarks by the President Thanking the Armed Forces for the Rescue of Captain Scott O'Grady, June 12, 1995. clinton6.nara.gov/1995/06 /1995-06-12-president-thanking-armed-forces-for-o-grady-rescue.html.

———. Remarks by the President to the NCAA Basketball Championship Teams, June 2, 1995. clinton6.nara.gov/1995/06/1995-06-02-president-to-ncaa-basketball-championship-teams.html.

6. THE IMMACULATE MISSION: ODA 551 IN THE KARBALA GAP

BOOKS

Clancy, Tom. *Airborne: A Guided Tour of an Airborne Task Force.* New York: Berkley Books, 1997.

———. *Armored Cav: A Guided Tour of an Armored Cavalry Regiment.* New York: Berkley Books, 1994.

———. *Marine: A Guided Tour of a Marine Expeditionary Unit.* New York: Berkley Books, 1996.

Gordon, Michael R., and Bernard E. Trainor. *Cobra II.* New York: Pantheon Books: 2006.

Isby, David C. *Weapons and Tactics of the Soviet Army.* London, England: Jane's Publishing Company Limited, 1981.

Murray, Williamson, and Robert H. Scales Jr. *The Iraq War: A Military History.* Cambridge, MA: Belknap Press, 2005.

Polmar, Norman, and Floyd D. Kennedy Jr. *Military Helicopters of the World: Military Rotary-Wing Aircraft Since 1917.* Annapolis, MD: Naval Institute Press, 1981

Walker, Martin, ed. *The Iraq War.* Washington, DC: Brassey's, 2004.

Woods, Kevin M., with Michael R. Pease, Mark E. Stout, Williamson Murray, and James G. Lacey. *Iraqi Perspectives Project: A View of Operation Iraqi Freedom from Saddam's Senior Leadership.* Washington, DC: U.S. Joint Forces Command, 2006.

Zaloga, Steven J. *Soviet Air Defence Missiles.* Coulsdon, England: Jane's Information Group, 1989.

Zucchino, David. *Thunder Run.* New York: Grove Press, 2004.

PERIODICALS

Gresham, John D. "Special Forces Mounted Operations." *The Year in Special Operations 2004.* Tampa, FL: Faircount Publications, 2004.

———. "Special Operations Forces in Operation Iraqi Freedom." *The Year in Special Operations 2004.* Tampa, FL: Faircount Publications, 2004.

INTERNET

Boyer, Peter J. "The New War Machine." *The New Yorker,* June 30, 2003, posted June 23, 2003. www.newyorker.com/fact/content/articles/030630fa_fact3 (accessed October 29, 2006).

Brown, Drew, S. Thorne Harper, and Steven Thomma. "Battle Through, Around Karbala Gap Likely to be 'Hell of a Fight.'" Knight Ridder News Service, April 1, 2003. Accessed from *Stars and Stripes* Web site October 29, 2006. stripes.com/article.asp?section=104&article=13572&archive=true.

Dao, James. "War Plan Drew U.S. Commandos from Shadows." *New York Times,* April 28, 2003. Accessed from cnn.com/world October 29, 2006.

www.cnn.com/2003/WORLD/meast/04/28/nyt.dao/.
Gordon, John, IV, and Jerry Sollinger. "The Army's Dilemma." *Parameters*, Summer 2004. www.carlisle.army.mil/usawc/Parameters/04summer/gor&soll.htm (accessed October 29, 2006).
Kirkpatrick, Charles E. "Joint Fires as They Were Meant to Be: V Corps and the 4th Air Support Operations Group During Operation Iraqi Freedom." U.S. Army Headquarters, Europe & 7th Army Web site, posted June 8, 2004. www.history.hqusareur.army.mil/CASArticle.doc (accessed October 29, 2006).
Knight Ridder News Service. "Troops Prepare for 1st Major Ground Battle at Key Gap," April 1, 2003. www.jsonline.com/story/index.aspx?id=130158 (accessed October 29, 2006).
U.S. Congress. House Committee on International Relations, Subcommittee on Oversight and Investigations. Statement of Mr. Kevin M. Woods. April 6, 2006. www.internationalrelations.house.gov/archives/109/woo040606.pdf (accessed October 29, 2006).
U.S. Department of Defense. "Operation Iraqi Freedom." Defend America. www.defendamerica.mil/iraq/mission042203.html (accessed October 29, 2006).
WGBH Educational Foundation. *Frontline*: "Campaign Against Terror," aired September 11, 2002. Interview transcript of Colonel John Mulholland, U.S. Special Forces ODA 555 and ODA 595. www.pbs.org/wgbh/pages/frontline/shows/campaign/interviews (accessed October 28, 2006).

7. TWENTY-FIRST-CENTURY ALAMO: TASK FORCE VIKING AT DEBECKA PASS

BOOKS

Antenori, Frank, and Hans Halberstadt. *Roughneck Nine-One*. New York: St. Martin's, 2006.
Clancy, Tom. *Airborne: A Guided Tour of an Airborne Task Force*. New York: Berkley Books, 1997.
———. *Armored Cav: A Guided Tour of an Armored Cavalry Regiment*. New York: Berkley Books, 1994.
———. *Fighter Wing: A Guided Tour of an Air Force Combat Wing*. New York: Berkley Books, 1995.
———. *Marine: A Guided Tour of a Marine Expeditionary Unit*. New York: Berkley Books, 1996.
Department of the Army. *Weapons Systems 2003*. Washington, DC: U.S. Government Printing Office, 2002.
Franks, Tommy, with Malcolm McConnell. *American Soldier*. New York: Regan Books/HarperCollins, 2004.
Isby, David C. *Weapons and Tactics of the Soviet Army*. London, England: Jane's Publishing Company Limited, 1981.
Robinson, Linda. *Masters of Chaos*. New York: PublicAffairs, 2004.
Zaloga, Steven J. *Soviet Air Defence Missiles*. Coulsdon, England: Jane's Information Group, 1989.

PERIODICALS

Gourley, Scott R. "Soldier Armed." *Army Magazine*, June 2006.
Grant, Rebecca. *The War of 9/11*. Air Force Association Special Report. Arlington, VA: Aerospace Education Foundation, 2005. Downloadable at www.afa.org/media/reports/.
Gresham, John D. "Roughnecks at War: The Battle of Debecka Pass." *The Year in Special Operations 2004*. Tampa, FL: Faircount Publications, 2004

Oldham, Charles, ed. *Operation Iraqi Freedom*. Tampa, FL. Faircount Publications, 2003.

MONOGRAPHS

Thompson, Steve. *Joint Air Doctrine in the Global War on Terror*. Newport, RI: Naval War College, 2004.

INTERNET

Badkhen, Anna. "Blasts Rock Oil-Rich Northern Cities: Air Strikes Hit Mosul, Kirkuk While Kurds Watch, Wait." *San Francisco Chronicle*, March 22, 2003. www.sfgate.com/cgi-bin/article.cgi?file=/chronicle/archive/2003/03/22 /MN284719.DTL (accessed September 28, 2006).

BBC News. "This Is Just a Scene from Hell" transcript, posted June 4, 2003. news/bbc.co.uk/2/hi/middle_east/2921807.stm (accessed August 16, 2006).

Combined Arms Research Library Digital Library. "Operational Leadership Experiences: Interview with Major Andrew Morgado," February 11, 2005. cgsc.cdmhost.com/cgi-bin/showfile.exe?CISOROOT=/p4013coll13&CISOPTR=10 (accessed August 20, 2006).

———. "Operational Leadership Experiences: Interview with Major D. Jones," November 9, 2005. cgsc.cdmhost.com/cgi-bin/showfile.exe?CISOROOT= /p4013coll13&CISOPTR=116 (accessed August 20, 2006).

———. "Operational Leadership Experiences: Interview with Major Dennis Levesque," March 14, 2006. cgsc.cdmhost.com/cgi-bin/showfile .exe?CISOROOT=/p4013coll13&CISOPTR=194 (accessed August 20, 2006).

Dawn Syndicate, Internet Edition. "Friendly Fire Kills 18 Kurds, Injures 45 in Northern Iraq," April 7, 2003. www.dawn.com/2003/04/07top2.htm (accessed August 17, 2006).

Dyhouse, Tim. "'Black Ops' Shine in Iraq War." *VFW Magazine*. www.vfw.org /index.cfm?fa=news.magDtl&dtl=3&mid=1581 (accessed July 1, 2006).

FAS Military Analysis Network. "Javelin Antitank Missile," 1999. www.fas.org/man/dod-101/sys/land/javelin.htm (accessed July 2, 2006).

Gilmore, Gerry J. "Special Operations Troops Recount Iraq Missions." DefenseLINK News. February 5, 2004. www.defenselink.mil/news/Feb2004 /n02052004_200402057.html (accessed July 1, 2006).

GlobalSecurity.org. "On Point: The United States Army in Operation Iraqi Freedom. Chapter 5: Isolation of the Regime," 2004. www.globalsecurity.org /military/library/report/2004/onpoint/ch-5.htm (accessed July 1, 2006).

Harding, Luke, and Michael Howard. "18 Die as US Plane Bombs Kurdish Convoy in Worst 'Friendly Fire' Incident." *Guardian Unlimited*, April 7, 2003. www.guardian.co.uk/international/story/0,3604,931201,00.html (accessed August 17, 2006).

IslamOnline.net. "U.S. Aircraft Kills 4 U.S. Special Forces, 12 Kurdish Fighters," April 6, 2003. www.islamonline.net/english/news/2003-04/06/article07 .shtml (accessed August 17, 2006).

Kurdistan Regional Government. "18 Kurds Said Killed, 45 Injured in US Friendly Fire Incident." Agence France-Presses, posted April 6, 2003. old.krg.org/docs /articles/afp-wajeeh-injured-apr03.asp (accessed August 17, 2006).

Naylor, Sean D. "Nightmare at Debecka." ArmyTimes.com, September 22, 2003. www.armytimes.com.print.php?f=0-ARMYPAPER-2203854.php (accessed September 16, 2006).

News24. "'Scene from Hell' as US Bombs Own Troops," posted April 8, 2003. www.smh.com.au/articles/2003/04/06/1049567564574.html (accessed August 17, 2006).

Raytheon Company. "Warfighters Praise Javelin," posted October 1, 2003, updated July 20, 2005. www.raytheon.com/feature/javelin_warfighters/battle/index.html (accessed August 29, 2006).

Shanker, Thom. "How Green Berets Overcame the Odds at an Iraq Alamo." *New York Times*, September 22, 2003. www.nytimes.com/2003/09/22/international /middleeast (accessed August 29, 2006).

ShiaNews.com. "American Pilot Drops Bomb on Kurdish Convoy," posted April 6, 2003. www.shianews.com/hi/Europe/news_id/0000426.php (accessed August 17, 2006).

Tyson, Ann Scott. "Crunch Time for Special Ops Forces." *Christian Science Monitor*, April 6, 2004. www.csmonitor.com/2004/0406/p02s01-usmi.html (accessed August 29, 2006).

MILITARY ABBREVIATIONS AND ACRONYMS

AAA: antiaircraft artillery
AEW: airborne early warning
AFSOC: Air Force Special Operations Command
AFSOF: Air Force Special Operations Forces
AHRS: attitude-heading reference system
AO: area of operations
ARG: amphibious ready group
ARRS: Aerospace Rescue and Recovery Service
ARS: Air Rescue Service
ARVN: Army of the Republic of Vietnam (South Vietnam)
ATO: air tasking order
AWACS: airborne warning and control system
BIM: blade inspection method
CAOC: combined air operations center
CAP: combat air patrol
CAS: combat/close air support
CBIS: chemical biological inspection squad
CCP: casualty collection point
CENTAF: Central Command Air Force
CENTCOM: Central Command
C4: plastic explosive
CINCCENT: Commander in Chief Central Command
CLU: command launch unit for a Javelin
COMUSMACV: Commander of U.S. Military Assistance Command Vietnam
CSAR: combat search and rescue
CW2: chief warrant officer 2
DMZ: demilitarized zone
ELINT: electronic intelligence
EUCOM: European Command
FAC: forward air controller
FFARP: forward fueling and rearming point
FMTV: family of medium tactical vehicles
FOB: forward operating base
GMV: ground mobility vehicle
GPS: Global Positioning System
HARM: high-speed antiradiation missile
HMMWV: high-mobility multipurpose wheeled vehicle (Humvee, or Hummer)
HUMINT: human intelligence
IADS: integrated air defense system
ID: Infantry Division
JCS: Joint Chiefs of Staff
JPRC: joint personnel receiving center
JSOTF: Joint Special Operations Task Force

JSOTF-N: Joint Special Operations Task Force-North
JSRC: joint search and rescue center
LANTIRN: low-altitude navigation and targeting infrared for night
LAW: light antitank weapon
LGB: laser-guided bomb
LORAN: long range navigation system
LZ: landing zone
MACV: Military Assistance Command Vietnam
MEU(SOC): Marine Expeditionary Unit (Special Operations Capable)
MIA: missing in action
MIC LIC: medium-intensity conflict low-intensity conflict
MID: mechanized infantry division
MTLB: Soviet/Russian-made armored personnel carrier
NAEW: NATO Airborne Early Warning
NATO: North Atlantic Treaty Organization
ODA: Operational Detachment-Alpha
ODB: Operational Detachment-Bravo
ODC: Operational Detachment-Charlie
OEF-A: Operation Enduring Freedom–Afghanistan
OIF: Operation Iraqi Freedom
PAVN: People's Army of Vietnam (North Vietnam)
POW: prisoner of war
RAF: Royal Air Force
ROE: rules of engagement
RPG: rocket powered grenade
SACSA: Special Assistant for Counterinsurgency and Special Activities
SAM: surface-to-air missile
SAR: search and rescue
SAS: Special Air Service (British or Australian)
SATCOM: Satellite communications
SEAD: suppression of enemy air defenses
SEAL: Sea-Air-Land team; the special operations unit of the U.S. Navy
SF: Special Forces
SFC: Special Forces Command
SFG: Special Forces Group
SFOD-D: Special Forces Operation Detachment-Delta
SOCOM: Special Operations Command
SOFLAM: special operations force laser marker
SOG: studies and observations group
STS: special tactics squadron, a forward air controller
TACP: tactical air control party, a forward air controller
TEL: transporter erector launcher
TEWS: tactical electronic warfare squadron
TRAP: tactical recovery of aircraft and personnel
UAV: unmanned aerial vehicle
UDT: underwater demolition team
UNPROFOR: United Nations Protection Force
WMD: weapons of mass destruction
XO: executive officer

INDEX

NOTE: The abbreviation "U.S." and the words "American" and "United States," which appear at the beginnings of the names of many groups and organizations in this book, have in most instances been omitted to save space. Thus, seek "U.S. Air Force" under "Air Force" and so forth.

INDEX

DWIGHT JON ZIMMERMAN is author of the critically acclaimed young-adult military history, *First Command: Paths to Leadership*. Zimmerman also contributed substantially to a series of successful young-adult military history books. This includes a book on World War II, *The Good Fight* by Stephen E. Ambrose (2001); a Civil War volume, *Fields of Fury* by James M. McPherson (2002); a volume on the American Revolution, *Fight for Freedom* by Benson Bobrick (2003); a volume on the Vietnam War, *10,000 Days of Thunder* by Philip Caputo (2004); and a volume on Reconstruction, *Into the West: From Reconstruction to the End of the Frontier* by James M. McPherson (2005). He has written on military-history subjects for *American Heritage*, the Naval Institute Press, *Vietnam* magazine, and numerous military-themed publications for Faircount International. In 2006, his essay on challenges faced by the Coast Guard was selected by the Naval War College for use in its curriculum. Zimmerman was the co-executive producer of the Military Channel's miniseries, *First Command,* based on his book. The miniseries won the 2005 Aurora Platinum Best of Show Award for Historical Programming. He lives in Brooklyn, New York.

JOHN D. GRESHAM is an author, researcher, game designer, photographer, and military commentator. He is the primary researcher and partner to Tom Clancy on his best-selling series of nonfiction "guided tour" books about military units. These include *Submarine* (1993), *Armored Cav* (1994), *Fighter Wing* (1995), *Marine* (1996), *Airborne* (1997), *Carrier* (1999) and *Special Forces* (2001). He also is the award-winning co-designer of *Supermarina I* and *Supermarina II* (Clash of Arms Games, 1996 and 1997), a naval war game based upon Larry Bond's award-winning "Command at Sea" game system. He has also provided interviews, commentary, and production assistance for various documentary series produced for the History, Learning, and Discovery channels. Gresham began his writing career full time with work on *Desert Storm* (1991), and then moved into his current role as researcher and partner to Tom Clancy. His latest book, *Defcon-2* (with Norman Polmar, 2006), is a single-volume history of the Cuban Missile Crisis. He currently resides in Virginia.